A CULTURAL HISTORY OF WOMEN

VOLUME 4

D1606621

A Cultural History of Women

General Editor: Linda Kalof

Volume 1
A Cultural History of Women in Antiquity
Edited by Janet H. Tulloch

Volume 2
A Cultural History of Women in the Middle Ages
Edited by Kim M. Phillips

Volume 3
A Cultural History of Women in the Renaissance
Edited by Karen Raber

Volume 4
A Cultural History of Women in the Age of Enlightenment
Edited by Ellen Pollak

Volume 5
A Cultural History of Women in the Age of Empire
Edited by Teresa Mangum

Volume 6
A Cultural History of Women in the Modern Age
Edited by Liz Conor

A CULTURAL HISTORY

OF WOMEN

IN THE AGE OF ENLIGHTENMENT

Edited by Ellen Pollak

Bloomsbury Academic
An imprint of Bloomsbury Publishing Plc

B L O O M S B U R Y

LONDON · OXFORD · NEW YORK · NEW DELHI · SYDNEY

Bloomsbury Academic

An imprint of Bloomsbury Publishing Plc

50 Bedford Square   1385 Broadway
London   New York
WC1B 3DP   NY 10018
UK   USA

www.bloomsbury.com

BLOOMSBURY and the Diana logo are trademarks of Bloomsbury Publishing Plc

Hardback edition first published in 2013 by Bloomsbury Academic
Paperback edition first published in 2016 by Bloomsbury Academic

British Library Cataloguing-in-Publication Data
A catalogue record for this book is available from the British Library.

ISBN: 978-08578-5100-0 (HB)
978-1-8478-8475-6 (HB set)
978-1-3500-0980-6 (PB)
978-1-3500-0984-4 (PB set)

Library of Congress Cataloging-in-Publication Data
A catalog record for this book is available from the Library of Congress.

Series: The Cultural Histories Series

Typeset by Apex CoVantage, LLC, Madison, WI, USA
Printed and bound in Great Britain

CONTENTS

SERIES PREFACE

A Cultural History of Women is a six-volume series reviewing the changing cultural construction of women and women's historical experiences throughout history. Each volume follows the same basic structure and begins with an outline account of the major ideas about women in the historical period under consideration. Next, specialists examine aspects of women's history under eight key headings: the life cycle, bodies/sexuality, religion/popular beliefs, medicine/disease, public/private, education/work, power, and artistic representation. Thus, readers can choose a synchronic or a diachronic approach to the material—a single volume can be read to obtain a thorough knowledge of women's history in a given period, or one of the eight themes can be followed through time by reading the relevant chapters of all six volumes, thus providing a thematic understanding of changes and developments over the long term. The six volumes divide the history of women as follows:

Volume 1: A Cultural History of Women in Antiquity (500 B.C.E.–1000 C.E.)
Volume 2: A Cultural History of Women in the Middle Ages (1000–1500)
Volume 3: A Cultural History of Women in the Renaissance (1400–1650)
Volume 4: A Cultural History of Women in the Age of Enlightenment (1650–1800)
Volume 5: A Cultural History of Women in the Age of Empire (1800–1920)
Volume 6: A Cultural History of Women in the Modern Age (1920–2000+)

Linda Kalof, General Editor

LIST OF ILLUSTRATIONS

INTRODUCTION

CHAPTER 2

CHAPTER 6

CHAPTER 7

CHAPTER 8

Introduction: Women Daring to Know in the Age of Enlightenment

ELLEN POLLAK

Nearly fifty years ago, the influential historian Peter Gay defined the Enlightenment as a "family" of male philosophers "united on a vastly ambitious program . . . of secularism, humanity, cosmopolitanism, and . . . above all, freedom . . . —freedom from arbitrary power, freedom of speech, freedom of trade, freedom to realize one's talents, freedom of aesthetic response, freedom, in a word, of moral man to make his own way in the world."[1] Today, this picture of the Enlightenment as the exclusive and essentially coherent project of a group of male European intellectuals of whom "the French philosophe . . . was the purest specimen" has changed dramatically.[2] Historians are now more attentive to local contexts and to differences in Enlightenment ideas and values across national boundaries and among social groups within discrete national contexts; they tend to view the Enlightenment as a multiple rather than a singular phenomenon, as a field of competing histories or a series of debates rather than a stable and unified system of ideas. More important, they have enriched accounts of Enlightenment culture by demonstrating the significant extent to which that culture was in fact shaped by the participation, contributions, and challenges of individuals and groups who were marginalized or excluded by dominant

Enlightenment philosophies and whose *freedoms* were in fact either nonexistent or seriously curtailed.[3] These individuals and groups included members of the poor and working classes, people of non-European descent, slaves and former slaves, and women of all classes, races, and national backgrounds.

Historians have also challenged the notion that it is possible to talk about the history of women as a singular or homogeneous entity. Even the meaning of the category "women," they point out, is historically contingent and often shifts depending on class, racial, and national context. Indeed, as we shall see in the following pages, the term *woman* in the eighteenth century often implied only women of the upper and middle classes and almost never included female slave laborers. In fact, however, the cultural history of women during the age of Enlightenment is not just the story of famous aristocratic women like Marie Antoinette, the controversial queen of France who became a lightning rod for public hostilities during the French Revolution, or of famous intellectual women like the learned English aristocrat Lady Mary Wortley Montagu and the noble French mathematician, physicist, and translator of the works of Sir Isaac Newton, the Marquise Émilie du Châtelet (1706–49). It is also the story of the many literate women of the middle and working classes who, with the advent of a burgeoning European and North American market for print, entered the public sphere by publishing in a variety of genres, including the novel, poetry, drama, the political pamphlet, periodical literature, and the philosophical treatise. It is the story as well of many anonymous women, some literate and some not, who worked in a range of roles in rural and domestic settings or who, as Linda Colley has observed of the English context, "formed the majority of urban populations, as servants, as workers in shops and taverns, as vagrants and as prostitutes at one end of the social spectrum; and, at the other, as residents and visitors drawn to amenities that the countryside could not offer: theatres, assembly rooms, lending libraries, concert halls, elegant squares and enticing bow-windowed shops."[4] Many of these women acquired political influence and agency through their status as consumers (through the boycott of tea and sugar in British consumer protests against colonial slavery, for example) or as workers (in bread riots and other forms of popular protest, such as the famous march on Versailles by Parisian market women during the early stages of French Revolution).[5]

The chapters in this volume seek to capture the variousness of women's cultural history in Europe and the Americas during the dynamic period known as the Enlightenment. This period of over a century, extending approximately from 1650 through the end of the eighteenth century, was marked by a series of watershed political events with momentous local as well as global consequences.

FIGURE 0.1: *Market Women's March on Versailles* (October 5–6, 1789). Anonymous engraving, 1789; Cabinet des Estampes; Bibliothèque nationale de France.

Among the most salient of these were England's Glorious Revolution, the republican challenge to divine-right monarchy that established that nation's first constitutional government in 1689; the American War of Independence in 1776; and the cataclysmic upheavals occasioned by the French Revolution in the 1790s. Each of these important revolutionary events was inspired and shaped by philosophical principles grounded in a belief in the salutary powers of human reason and, in particular, in the ability of rational beings to govern themselves. The scientific revolution of the seventeenth century, usually associated with the natural philosophies of such figures as Copernicus, Bacon, Galileo, and Newton, had privileged rational inquiry over religion and tradition as the basis for improvements in theoretical and practical knowledge of the natural world. Additionally influenced by shifts in socioeconomic structure and the increased global contact and communication made possible by the growth of mercantile capitalism, Enlightenment thinkers extended the implications of emergent scientific thought into the realms of politics and morality, arguing that the independent exercise of reason could lead as well to the betterment of society through public debate, the establishment of liberal democratic principles, and a cosmopolitan openness to other nations and other cultures.

As salutary as Enlightenment liberal and cosmopolitan principles might have been in theory, however, the global reach of the European Enlightenment was not wholly benign in either its practices or its effects. The same expansion of trade and travel that led to European prosperity also led to the prominence of European nations, most notably England and France, in the atrocities of the Atlantic slave trade, which reached its peak during the eighteenth century. That the same period also saw the beginnings of the abolition movement and of the tradition of Black Atlantic writers marks it as a time of tremendous importance in the history of modernity and of deep and disturbing contradictions whose legacy both thinkers and the general public continue to grapple with today.[6]

The Enlightenment represents an extraordinarily complex and heterogeneous moment for women in Europe and its colonies. A period of intense sociocultural transformation, it witnessed the shifts in class and kinship structures that produced the modern nuclear family, and it saw the consolidation of modern gender ideologies. Occurring within the broader geopolitical context of burgeoning commercial and imperial expansion, these developments had effects on women that were profound and varied across class, national, and racial divides. The rise of print culture and the emergence of a literary marketplace brought economic and cultural opportunities to educated women, despite the ostracism that attended women's entry into the public sphere, and women played a significant role in the early development of the novel, which would become the dominant literary genre of modernity. But while the flourishing of European culture afforded many women intellectual, artistic, and economic opportunities, those opportunities were also delimited by pernicious gender, class, and racial hierarchies. Within the colonial power relations sustained by the institution of slavery, women occupied uneven and sometimes contradictory positions as both victims and oppressors in metropolitan centers and their colonial peripheries. Modern liberal feminism grew up in this environment, as did the abolition movement, early racial science, and, incipiently, the science of sexuality.

This introduction examines European women's challenges to dominant Enlightenment philosophies that justified their exclusion from full participation in political and intellectual life—assertions of resistance vital to women's historic struggle for social justice. As we shall see, however, these challenges were also sometimes delimited by problematic assumptions and omissions of their own. For example, they often borrowed the conventional rhetorical habit, common generally in Enlightenment discourses of liberty, of using the concept of slavery to signify a range of social oppressions (in this case women's condition of legal and political dependency on men) without acknowledging the contemporary realities of chattel slavery or the material differences between conditions in Europe and the circumstances endured in (and en route to) the colonies by enslaved Africans of both sexes, whose forced labor provided so many of the comforts Europe enjoyed. (There was at the time little available critique of the systemic links between racial and gender oppressions.) With these tensions and contradictions in mind, we linger on the case of Phillis Wheatley—an African American, a slave, a distinguished poet, and a notable woman who played a critically important role in advancing the cause of enslaved people and who managed against extraordinary odds to defy both dominant ideologies and circumstances to bring her distinctive wisdom to the public. From Wheatley, we move on to consider the many other women—some known, many anonymous—who helped to usher in modernity.

WOMEN AND POLITICAL LIBERTY

"If all Men are born free, how is it that all Women are born Slaves?" Thus asks the early feminist philosopher and British Tory conservative Mary Astell in the preface to the third edition of *Some Reflections Upon Marriage* (1706).[7] Astell's largely rhetorical query aims to lay bare one of the central contradictions of liberal Enlightenment political thought: its promotion on the one hand of a doctrine of universal liberty and natural rights based on a belief in the rational capacity of human beings for self-governance, and its patent denial on the other hand of political and economic rights to women. In the passage in question, Astell is responding to John Locke, whose *Two Treatises of Government*, published in 1689, defended the rights of rational subjects to resist political tyranny. Repudiating Robert Filmer's patriarchalist theory of government, which defended the divinely ordained right of kings to absolute rule, Locke pronounced all men free and equal and argued that government was legitimate only when entered into by the consent of its citizens. But while Locke denied men the same exercise of arbitrary "political power" over their wives that he denied them over each other, he nevertheless granted them legitimate "Conjugal Power." This power he defined—in terms consistent with contemporary laws and practices that denied women citizenship and accorded married women no independent legal or economic rights—as "the Power that every Husband hath to order the things of private Concernment in his Family, as Proprietor of the Goods and Land there, and to have his Will take place before that of his wife in all things of their common Concernment; but not a Political Power of Life and Death over her, much less over any body else."[8] With considerable irony, Astell—herself a devout Anglican and believer in the divine right of monarchs to absolute rule—critiques the logic whereby Locke rejects absolute sovereignty in the state but defends it in the family:

Is it not . . . partial in Men . . . to contend for, and practice that Arbitrary Dominion in their Families, which they abhor and exclaim against in the State? For if Arbitrary Power is evil in it self, and an improper Method of Governing Rational and Free Agents, it ought not to be Practis'd any where; Nor is it less, but rather more mischievous in Families than in Kingdoms, by how much 100000 Tyrants are worse than one. What tho' a Husband can't deprive a Wife of Life without being responsible to the Law, he may however do what is much more grievous to a generous Mind: render Life miserable, for which she has no redress, scarce Pity which is afforded to every other Complainant. It being thought a Wife's Duty to suffer everything without Complaint.[9]

Astell's stinging sarcasm highlights the illogic whereby Locke privileges empirical and rational inquiry over adherence to customary practices and blind faith in traditional authority and yet sees fit to justify traditional gender hierarchies. In the following passage, her hyperbolic praise of liberal theory's justification of male prerogative on the grounds that men already make all the laws and own all the property and weapons is saturated with disdainful irony, as is the mock humility with which she refuses to challenge the "unanswerable" argument that women are inferior because men say so. As ready as she is to defend the rights of women, Astell wryly demurs, such specious reasoning is not worthy of a reply:

Men are possess'd of all Places of Power, Trust and Profit, they make Laws and exercise the Magistracy, not only the sharpest Sword, but even all the Swords and Blunderbusses are theirs, which by the strongest Logic in the World, gives them the best Title to everything they please to claim as their Prerogative; who shall contend with them? Immemorial Prescription is on their side in these parts of the World, Ancient Tradition and Modern Usage! Our Fathers have all along both Taught and Practis'd Superiority over the weaker Sex, and consequently Women are by Nature inferior to Men, as was to be Demonstrated. An Argument which must be acknowledg'd unanswerable, for as well as I love my Sex, I will not pretend a Reply to *such* Demonstration![10]

Not only does Astell here expose the logical fallacies whereby women are denied the status of rational subjects; under a mask of feminine modesty, she also demonstrates empirically the injustice of that denial in a display of her own superior rational abilities.

Astell's satiric rebuttals notwithstanding, Locke's *Two Treatises* constitutes one of the most important works of Enlightenment political philosophy, and Locke himself continues to hold a preeminent place as a philosopher of political liberty. During the Enlightenment, his work was held in high esteem, most notably in Scotland, France, and North America, where his ideas had a powerful influence on thinkers including Adam Smith, Denis Diderot, Voltaire, Jean-Jacques Rousseau, Thomas Paine, Benjamin Franklin, and Thomas Jefferson, as well as on the developing discourses of liberty that culminated in the last quarter of the eighteenth century in the American and French revolutions. But Astell too had direct and indirect disciples who continued to decry those who defended masculine privilege under the banner of liberty, even as republican doctrines of gender inequality were reconfigured and refined.

In 1791, in response to the French Revolution's founding document, *Déclaration des droits de l'homme et du citoyen* (*Declaration of the Rights of Man and of the Citizen*), for example, the prolific French playwright Olympe de Gouges published *Déclaration des droits de la femme et de la citoyenne* (*Declaration of the Rights of Woman and the Female Citizen*), in which she made the case for truly universal human rights, declaring women free and equal to men in their inalienable rights to liberty, property, security, and freedom from oppression and advancing, in a postscript, a model for a marriage agreement based on gender equality and the communal ownership of property. In a brief prefatory note to her *Declaration of the Rights of Woman*, de Gouges boldly questions man's right to assume "sovereign empire to oppress [her] sex." Observing that in the animal kingdom, male and female everywhere "cooperate in harmonious togetherness," she bitterly remarks that only enlightened man "has raised his exceptional circumstances to a principle":

> Bizarre, blind, bloated with science and degenerated—in a century of enlightenment and wisdom—into the crassest ignorance, he wants to command as a despot a sex which is in full possession of its intellectual faculties; he pretends to enjoy the Revolution and to claim his rights to equality in order to say nothing more about it.[11]

At the same time, she exhorts her own sex to claim the blessings of Enlightenment: "Woman, wake up; the tocsin of reason is being heard throughout the whole universe; discover your rights."[12] In an audacious move, de Gouges dedicated her *Declaration* to the imprisoned French queen, Marie Antoinette, a gesture motivated more by her feminism than by her opposition to republican ideals. Because of her outspoken criticism of the National Convention and of its excesses under the leadership of Maximilien de Robespierre, however, de Gouges was denounced as a counterrevolutionary and sent to the guillotine in 1793, less than a month after the execution of the queen.[13]

In the following year, England's most famous early advocate of liberal feminism, Mary Wollstonecraft, also defended civic equality for women in *A Vindication of the Rights of Woman* (1792). A radical thinker and political novelist inspired by events as they were unfolding in France in the 1790s but, like de Gouges, disturbed by the opposition to women's rights among the framers of the new French Constitution, Wollstonecraft dedicated her *Vindication* to the French politician Charles Maurice de Talleyrand-Périgord, one of the architects of the *Declaration of the Rights of Man*, who, in a report to the French National Assembly on education, had defended educating women differently from men on the grounds that women's happiness "requires that they do not aspire to exercise rights and political functions."[14] To make her case for serious consideration of women's political rights and against arguments for women's oppression based on arbitrary authority rather than logic or reason, Wollstonecraft reminds Talleyrand in her dedication of words he himself had used in the French constitutional debates:

> Consider, Sir, dispassionately, these observations—for a glimpse of this truth seemed to open before you when you observed, "that to see one half of the human race excluded by the other from all participation of government, was a political phaenomenon that, according to abstract principles, it was impossible to explain." If so, on what does your constitution rest? If the abstract rights of man will bear discussion and explanation, those of woman, by a parity of reasoning, will not shrink from the same test: though a different opinion prevails in this country, built on the very arguments which you use to justify the oppression of woman—prescription.[15]

Like Astell, Wollstonecraft seeks both to extend the empire of reason to women and to portray those who would justify women's exclusion from public life as themselves having abandoned rational argument. In the *Vindication*, she inveighs heavily against society's failure to educate women to be rational citizens. By "considering females rather as women than human creatures" and by encouraging them to develop exclusively feminine virtues, she maintains, men cultivate a "slavish dependence" in women, "cramping their understandings and sharpening their senses." It is her ambition to extend to women the opinion of the French philosopher Jean-Jacques Rousseau respecting men that "it is a farce to call any being virtuous whose virtues do not result from the exercise of its own reason," and since "Liberty is the mother of virtue," she contends, "as sound politics diffuse liberty, mankind, including woman, will become more wise and virtuous."[16]

DOMESTIC IDEOLOGY AND WOMEN'S BODIES

To circumvent the charges of illogic and hypocrisy leveled at them by advocates of women's equal access to civil rights and education, philosophers of political liberty who promoted doctrines of sexual difference often appealed to nature as a justification for women's exclusion from public life. Against the arguments of educational theorists like Astell and Wollstonecraft, who insisted that with equal education women were capable of the same level of intellectual achievement as men,[17] many Enlightenment philosophers maintained that women possessed an innate intellectual inferiority, and they often managed to rest their assertions on evidence marshaled from the research of contemporary anatomists seeking to locate sex differences in the size of women's skulls or in the characteristics of the female skeleton.[18]

Among the most influential of such thinkers was Rousseau, who in *Émile; or, On Education* (1762) laid out a model of educational reform for the ideal male citizen of civil society as he himself had conceived such society in his important work of political philosophy, *The Social Contract*, published that same year. In chapter 5 of *Émile*, Rousseau famously sets forth his theory that innate differences between the sexes demand differences in how men and women should be educated. He argues that "when woman complains . . . about unjust man-made inequality, she is wrong. This inequality," he maintains, "is not a human institution—or . . . the work . . . of prejudice but of reason." "Woman is made specially to please man," he writes; "it is [the law] of nature." Accordingly, her education "ought to relate to men. To please men, to be useful to them, to make herself loved and honored by them, to raise them when young, to care for them when grown, to counsel them, to console them, to make their lives agreeable and sweet—these are the duties of women at all times, and they ought to be taught from childhood."[19]

Rousseau argues further that a woman's "proper purpose" is to produce children,[20] and he advocates the reform of traditional childrearing practices, passionately promoting maternal breast-feeding over the custom, widely prevalent at the time across a wide spectrum of classes, of hiring wet nurses. Rousseau's enthusiasm for breast-feeding and his idealization of the maternal role for women placed him at the center of a growing cultural campaign to encourage women to suckle their own infants; this campaign extended throughout Europe in the second half of the eighteenth century.[21] For Rousseau, maternal breast-feeding was central to the realization of the idyll of domestic happiness that he located at the moral heart of civil society. "Let mothers deign to nurse their children," he declares with a certain utopian zeal, and "morals will reform themselves, nature's sentiments will be awakened in every heart, the state will be repeopled."[22]

Popular images of this bourgeois ideal of domesticity—with the self-sacrificing maternal woman at its core—proliferated after midcentury in a variety of visual and print media, ranging from paintings and conduct books to medical treatises and novels. In England, for example, the often licentious female protagonists featured in the popular fiction of the Restoration and the first half of the eighteenth century (in novels of amorous intrigue by Aphra Behn, Delarivier Manley, and Eliza Haywood and in Daniel Defoe's fictional autobiographies *Moll Flanders* and *Roxana*, which are narrated by a former thief and a former courtesan respectively) are displaced after 1740 by the chaste heroines of the domestic novels of Samuel Richardson and his successors.[23] The morally pure maternal figure is in turn eroticized, in part as a goad to women to abandon nonreproductive sexual pleasures and embrace the joys of motherhood. Thus, in his *Letters to Married Women* (1767), the English physician Hugh Smith reassures women that maternity and breast-feeding will not mar their sexual appeal: "though a beautiful virgin must ever kindle emotions in a man of sensibility; a chaste, and tender wife, with a little one at her breast, is certainly, to her husband, the most exquisitely enchanting object on earth."[24] And in his *Advice to Mothers* (1769), the Scottish physician William Buchan, a specialist in "domestic medicine," credits the act of nursing with erotic pleasures of its own: "The thrilling sensations . . . that accompany the act of giving suck, can be conceived only by those who have felt them, while the mental raptures of a fond mother at such moments are far beyond the powers of description or fancy."[25]

This sentimentalized, mother-centered model of domestic bliss and fecund sexuality is richly figured in a work by the French painter Jean-Baptiste Greuze, *La Mère bien-aimée* (*The Well-Beloved Mother*, ca. 1770, shown in Figure 0.2), in which a young mother, rendered physically helpless by her brood of adoring children,[26] lies back—one breast exposed—in a posture that could as easily be identified as exhaustion and resignation as beatific ecstasy, while her virile young husband, just entered with his hunting dogs and his gun, assumes a wide-legged posture of satisfaction with the scene. Interestingly, as Mary D. Sheriff points out, it is the husband who "becomes the main interest, and his point of view [that] dominates" in the painting, as if to signal that the woman's voluptuousness, even her own self-sacrificing pleasure, is reserved for the male viewer and for the fulfillment of his needs and his desires.[27]

The campaign to establish a scientific basis for essential sex differences was not only a way for political philosophers to stave off women's demands for equality in a revolutionary setting dedicated to the leveling of social differences; it was also, as Ruth Perry has argued in the case of England, a way of responding to the "new political and economic imperatives of an expanding . . . empire" by constituting women as a natural resource for the state (recall Rousseau's insistence that the state would be "repeopled" by maternal nursing).[28] The "enlightened" discourse of sentimental motherhood, largely invented and promulgated by men, became a strategy for policing women's bodies, "a new arena of male expertise, control, and instruction."[29] And like other developments affecting women's reproductive lives during the Enlightenment, most notably the appropriation by men of the formerly female occupation of

FIGURE 0.2: Jean Massard after Jean-Baptiste Greuze, *La Mère bien-aimée* (*The Well-Beloved Mother*) (1775). Art Gallery of New South Wales.

midwifery as the practice of medicine became increasingly professionalized, domestic ideology had social and economic repercussions for women across social classes. The crusade to promote maternal breast-feeding meant that the paid labor of working-class wet nurses was displaced over the course of the eighteenth century by the unpaid (voluntary) reproductive labor of middle-class women, who were "remunerated ideologically (with adoration)."[30] In this and other ways, domestic ideology enlisted the services of middle-class women in the consolidation of specific class interests.[31] By identifying virtuous femininity with full-time motherhood and "empowering" middle-class mothers as sexual objects, breeders, and guardians of the nursery (as, in effect, the "creator[s] of new citizens"[32] though unqualified to be citizens themselves), it implicitly relegated women who were either unmoved to perform the duties or unable to afford the luxuries of full-time motherhood to the status of wanton women and unnatural mothers. Toni Bowers has aptly dubbed breast-feeding in the eighteenth century "the class act *par excellence*." If, as Bowers rightly observes, maternal nursing distinguished "the selfless, virtuous, and affectionate domestic mother from the idle, selfish aristocrat" on the one hand,[33] it also set her apart from the "neglectful and callous" working-class woman on the other.

ENLIGHTENMENT AND WOMEN'S MINDS

Enlightenment beliefs in women's intellectual inferiority manifested themselves not only in debates about women's education but also in widespread disapproval of learned women. As illogical as it may seem that those without reason should be discouraged from using it, the Enlightenment designation of reason as an essentially male faculty meant that intellectual women were often seen as freakishly "unfeminine" or sexually ambiguous. The German philosopher Immanuel Kant, whose famous essay "An Answer to the Question: What Is Enlightenment?" (1784) adopted the Horatian dictum "Sapere aude!" (variously translated as "Dare to know!" and "Have the courage to use your own understanding!") as the "motto of enlightenment," nevertheless followed Rousseau when he addressed the question of women in 1764: "The content of woman's great science . . . is humankind, and among humanity, men. Her philosophy is not to reason, but to sense."[34]

But the disparagement of learning in women began long before Rousseau imagined Émile's idealized female counterpart, Sophie, or declared that "a brilliant wife is a plague to her husband, her children, her friends, her valets, everyone."[35] In England, women were not (and had not ever been) permitted to attend institutions of higher learning; if they acquired an education, they did so at home, usually with the assistance of male tutors or relatives. Nevertheless, before the Enlightenment, learning in women seems (perhaps paradoxically) to have had more cachet than it did in the eighteenth century. As early as 1694, Mary Astell, whose *Serious Proposal to the Ladies for the Advancement of Their True and Greatest Interest* (1694) had called for the establishment of a women's academy, observed the "unfashionable" status of learning in women as compared to 150 years earlier when, as William Wotton had testified, "it was so very modish . . . that the fair Sex seem'd to believe that *Greek* and *Latin* added to their Charms."[36] Twelve years later, she lamented that in contrast to boys, who have "all imaginable encouragement" to educate themselves, girls "are restrain'd, frown'd upon, and beat, not *for* but *from* the Muses; Laughter and Ridicule that never-failing Scare-Crow is [sic] set up to drive them from the Tree of Knowledge." Girls who excel in learning despite such deterrents, she further observed, "are star'd upon as Monsters, Censur'd, Envy'd, and every way Discourag'd."[37] Astell's words were echoed by her intellectual disciple Lady Mary Wortley Montagu, who wrote in her youth that "there is hardly a character in the World more Despicable or more liable to universal ridicule than that of a Learned Woman"[38] and, some fifty years later, sent her daughter, Lady Bute, the following advice for her granddaughter: "Caution . . . her . . . to conceal whatever Learning she attains, with as much solicitude as she would hide crookedness or lameness. The parade of it can only serve to draw on her the envy, and consequently the most inveterate Hatred, of all he and she Fools, which will certainly be at least three parts in four of all her Acquaintance."[39]

One is not surprised to find intellectual women characterizing female intellect as an active and extant faculty, however ridiculed, condemned, and hidden it may be. Less anticipated perhaps is the begrudging acknowledgment that a woman may "greatly succeed" in learning by one who finds intellectual activity in women distastefully defeminizing. Yet the following passage by Kant, alluding to two of France's most distinguished learned women, the scholar and translator Anne Le Fèvre Dacier and the mathematician and physicist Émilie du Châtelet, betrays just such an acknowledgment; notice that, like Montagu, Kant denies not that a woman is capable of reason but that her rationality "should show":

Deep meditation and a long-sustained reflection are noble but difficult, and do not well befit a person in whom unconstrained charms *should show nothing else* than a beautiful nature. Laborious learning or painful pondering, even if a woman should greatly succeed in it, destroy the merits that are proper to her sex, and because of their rarity they can make of her an object of cold admiration; but at the same time they will weaken the charms with which she exercises her great power over the other sex. A woman who has a head full of Greek, like Mme Dacier, or carries on fundamental controversies about mechanics, like the Marquise de [sic] Châtelet, might as well even have a beard.[40] (emphasis added)

The heterosexual trade-off here is clear. Women's "power" to make men love them depended on *appearing* not to think. In simultaneously admitting and denying female capacity, Kant in fact inadvertently exposes the arbitrary and fundamentally disciplinary character of the Enlightenment appeal to nature as a guarantee of female essence.

If Kant defined Enlightenment as "mankind's exit from its self-incurred immaturity" through the independent use of reason,[41] then the proper relation to knowledge he imagined for women located them somewhere outside the domain of enlightened intellectual inquiry—in a primitive or "immature" state of intellectual dependency. (As we shall see, individuals of non-European descent were often similarly situated.) Whether Kant would have agreed with his English contemporary Lord Chesterfield that women "are only children of a larger growth"[42] we cannot determine with certainty. But surely, as feminist philosopher Michelle Le Doeuff observes, the relation to knowledge that Kant reserved for women—not as inquiring subjects engaged in the quest for new knowledge but as guardians of wisdom produced by men—was precisely the dependent intellectual stance that "enlightened" men were in the process of casting off.[43] Nevertheless, as we shall see in the following pages, views like Kant's did not preclude women from taking an active part in the production of knowledge during the age of Enlightenment.

WOMEN AND THE PROBLEM OF SLAVERY

Dorinda Outram has written that "the way the Enlightenment thought about gender contradicted, undermined, and challenged its claims to legitimacy as a universally applicable project";[44] the same could be said for its assumptions about race. On this score, the arguments of Locke and Astell on liberty reveal as much about the age by what they leave out as by what they include. Although Locke denounces slavery in his *Two Treatises*, he makes no reference to the Atlantic trade or to colonial slavery, which were both already well under way by the time his work was published and about which he was certainly knowledgeable, having invested before 1680 in at least two transatlantic slaving concerns, the Royal Africa Company and the Bahama Adventurers. He also helped to draw up the *Fundamental Constitutions of Carolina* (1669), which provided "every freeman of Carolina . . . absolute power and authority over his negro slaves."[45] Both Locke's affirmation that all men are born free and Astell's assertion that redress against oppression is afforded to every other complainant than a wife bracket the contemporary realities under which hundreds of thousands of African slaves of both sexes were suffering brutal and dehumanizing treatment in European colonies and on the overcrowded slave ships that brought them there. If, as C. B. Macpherson pointed out long ago, Lockean political theory implicitly naturalized many existing social hierarchies by deploying a "differential" concept of rationality whereby those without property (i.e., women, paupers, and servants or other dependents) were excluded from the category of "the rational" and therefore from the privileges of freedom, it certainly did not include as rational beings those who were considered property themselves.[46] For Locke, such distinctions of race, class, and gender went without saying; they could be presupposed.

It is difficult to grasp the logic whereby Enlightenment theorists of political liberty could insist on their aversion to slavery even as the triangular trade and colonial slavery were becoming mainstays of the Western economy; nevertheless, slavery functioned as a standard metaphor for political tyranny in Enlightenment discourses of liberty and was fundamental to the self-understanding of many Europeans.[47] Locke's *First Treatise* announced itself by calling slavery "so vile and miserable an Estate of Man, and so directly opposite to the generous Temper and Courage of our Nation; that 'tis hardly to be conceived, that an *Englishman* . . . should plead for't"; and James Thompson's ode "Rule, Britannia!", a popular anthem first performed in 1740 to music by Thomas Arne and still able to inspire nationalist fervor in British subjects, is resolute and imperative in its famous refrain insisting that the condition of slavery is antithetical to English identity: "Rule Britannia! Britannia Rules the Waves / Britons never, never, never shall be slaves."[48] In France, Rousseau declared that "Man is born free; and everywhere he is in chains," but never addressed the realities of French colonialism or the Code Noir of Louis XIV then regulating policies in the French Caribbean, restricting the freedoms of Jews and Protestants and protecting the rights of slaveholders.[49]

As Astell's remarks and those of other early feminist writers attest, European women frequently used slavery as a figure for their condition of economic and legal dependency. The figure of slavery was often pointedly adapted to censure women's deplorable lack of political rights, their commodification as sexual objects, and their circulation in the affluent classes as property in a

FIGURE 0.3: William Hogarth's *Marriage à la Mode*, plate 1 ("The Marriage Settle-ment"), 1745. The Earl of Squanderfield and a wealthy merchant sign a marriage con-tract uniting their children, whose indifference to one another is mirrored in the two dogs chained together in the right foreground of the image. The lawyer Silvertongue "consoles" the bride-to-be. Credit: Alexander Turnbull Library, National Library of New Zealand.

marriage market whose commerce was conducted chiefly among men—a form of commerce famously satirized in William Hogarth's engraving "The Mar-riage Settlement," shown in Figure 0.3.

But the use of slavery as a figure also begged the question of the differ-ences that existed among women across racial groups in colonial contexts. That Astell does not acknowledge the condition of the enslaved women whose productive and reproductive labor was being forcibly exploited in the West Indies and the Americas, and over whom male slave owners *did* have what Locke called the "political power of life and death," may render her use of the slave metaphor problematic in the minds of some readers.[50] Colonial policies protected the rights of slave owners to appropriate the children born to slaves and even to increase their labor force by raping their female slaves. While European women of any class were potentially subject to abuse by their husbands or fathers with little or no legal recourse to protect them, their status as the wives and children of men who *did* have civil rights indirectly afforded them a measure of legal protection from encroachment and appropriation by other men. One might call this one of the questionable colonial "advantages" of European women's objectification within the proprietary structures of heteropatriarchal kinship. As Felicity A. Nussbaum has demonstrated and as Susanne Kord makes clear in her contribution to this volume, moreover, the very definition of the term *woman* was contingent in the period on distinctions of class, race, and nationality, so that some women (e.g., female slave laborers) were not even included in the category.[51] It is crucial to bear in mind this unstable and historically shifting character of the category "woman" as we consider the "cultural history of women" in any age.[52]

As Jane Austen's novel *Mansfield Park* (1814) demonstrates, moreover, many women of the property-owning classes (and sometimes their poorer relatives) enjoyed the economic comforts made possible by the exploitation of slave labor. Austen's novel is set in England in the period following the abolition of the slave trade in 1807, and although the subject of slavery remains largely on the peripheries of its plot, Austen makes clear through several allusions that the ease and security of Sir Thomas Bertram's English country estate depend on the profits of his Antiguan sugar plantation and that he travels to Antigua during the action of the novel to tend to his declining interests there.[53] Edward Said finds a troubling complicity with colonialism in what he considers Austen's "casual" but "unreflective" references to slavery in the novel. For Susan Fraiman, however, Said's assessment of *Mansfield Park* is belied by Austen's incisive critique of the "moral blight" that underlies the comforts of the Mansfield estate and that calls into question "the ethical basis for its authority both at home and, by implication, overseas."[54] According to Fraiman, the politics of gender situate Austen "off-center in relation to the dominant culture," complicating her relationship to its discourses and to the power relations they underwrite.[55] Other feminist critics have also addressed Austen's relation to the question of slavery and examined how *Mansfield Park* complicates the idea of English liberty precisely by exposing the ways in which racial and gender oppressions were intricately and significantly linked within the cultural logic of emergent modernity.[56]

Feminist approaches focusing on how ideologies of race intersected with and helped to constitute ideologies of gender and class have been brought to bear on women's writing from the early Enlightenment on. *Oroonoko, or The*

Royal Slave (1688/9), a short novel by the popular poet, playwright, and novelist Aphra Behn (1640–89) in which a white female narrator of the planter class details her encounter with New World slavery, has especially attracted attention in this regard. Frequently reprinted, translated, and adapted for the stage during the eighteenth century, Behn's narrative became a favorite reference point in the growing antislavery movement that began in the latter part of the eighteenth century. The story of an enslaved African prince who incites a failed slave rebellion in the British West Indian colony of Surinam, eventually murdering his pregnant wife, Imoinda, to prevent the appropriation of her body and their unborn child by unscrupulous white planters, *Oroonoko* has become a fertile site for examining the unstable identifications of its narrator across race, class, and gender divides and for exploring women's complex and often contradictory subject positions as both victims and oppressors in colonial contexts.[57]

While many European women writing in fictional as well as polemical contexts mobilized dominant discourses of liberty in order to complicate and critique them with varying degrees of subtlety, others were perfectly direct in their assaults on colonial slavery. In England, the author, educator, and evangelical reformer Hannah More became an active and influential member of the Society for Effecting the Abolition of the African Slave Trade (est. 1787), working closely with Thomas Clarkson, John Newton, and William Wilberforce, among other important religious and political figures, to influence public opinion against slavery and slave trading and to campaign for the passage of a parliamentary bill to abolish the trade. As part of her efforts, More published two popular and frequently reprinted poems denouncing slavery: *Slavery: A Poem* (1788) and *The Sorrows of Yamba; or, The Negro Woman's Lamentation* (1795; co-authored with Eaglesfield Smith). A member of the Bluestockings, a group of intellectual women in England organized and led by Elizabeth Montagu (1718–1800), More was also one of the earliest subscribers to the *Interesting Narrative of Olaudah Equiano, or Gustavus Vassa, the African*, an autobiographical narrative and antislavery polemic published in 1789 and promoted widely in support of abolition by its author and More's political associate, Olaudah Equiano.

In France during the same decade, Olympe de Gouges wrote two antislavery plays. The first, *Zamore et Mirza* (Zamore and Mirza), written and submitted to the Comédie Française (France's national theater and the official arbiter of which plays would be performed) in 1784, initially nearly landed her in jail and then was held up by the Comédie for four years, until de Gouges finally sidestepped official protocol and took it upon herself to have the work published and produced. When it was at last performed in 1788, with some revisions and under a new title, *L'Esclavage des Noirs* (Negro Slavery), it was quickly suppressed because it incited so much protest and disturbance in contemporary audiences, especially among colonial planters. De Gouges's other abolitionist play, *Le Marché des Noirs* (The Slave Market; 1790), was considered and refused by the Comédie Française and later burned by revolutionaries after her death in 1793. De Gouges also engaged in outspoken opposition to slavery in *Réflexions sur les hommes nègres* (Reflections on Black People), which was appended to the 1788 edition of *Zamore et Mirza*, and in her *Declaration of the Rights of Woman* (1791), which concludes with a resounding denunciation of colonial practices in the French Caribbean: "There is where nature shudders with horror; there is where reason and humanity have still not touched callous souls."[58] Like feminist philosophers before her, de Gouges drew an analogy between the condition of European (in this case, French) women and the condition of African slaves. Invoking the "commerce in women" that prevailed under the Old Regime and that, she warned, would corrupt the Revolution's call for universal liberty if reason were deceived into believing that there were no other options to be imagined, she likens "the woman whom a man buys" to "the slave on the African coasts," but she is quick to add this critical qualification: "The difference is great; that is known."[59] De Gouges's unreserved denunciation of the material realities of the slave economy and her bold acknowledgment of the specificities of the suffering of the enslaved have led one scholar to credit her with going "beyond the blindness of her times" to "think through and alter the analogy between slavery and the oppression of European women."[60] As de Gouges's experience at the guillotine clearly testifies, such activism did not come without a cost.

Not only European women publicly opposed slavery, however. In the next section, we move from Europe to North America, from the French to the American Revolution, and from the work of "free" women in Europe to the work and career of a woman of African descent writing under the conditions of American slavery.

PHILLIS WHEATLEY AND THE AFRICAN AMERICAN LITERARY TRADITION

When in 1772 the young poet Phillis Wheatley was required to appear before a committee of eighteen of Boston's most prominent male citizens (political leaders, poets, and clergymen among them) so they could satisfy themselves and the public that she had actually written the book of poems for which she was seeking a publisher, she was not being interrogated because she was a woman but because she was an African and a slave. That a young slave from Africa should have been able to master the English language and English literature and produce outstanding poetry was so astonishing to a public steeped in the popular belief that people of African descent were intellectually inferior and culturally backward that it was thought necessary to enlist the collective judgment of a governor, a lieutenant governor, and sixteen other highly educated white men to affirm that such a phenomenon had actually taken place.

Born in West Africa, probably around 1753, Phillis (named after the slave ship, the *Phillis*, on which she was transported across the Atlantic) arrived in Boston, where she was purchased by John Wheatley as a domestic slave for his wife, Susanna, in 1761. She was approximately seven years old at the time. Learning English quickly, she acquired an impressive education, mostly under the guidance of the Wheatleys' daughter, Mary, gaining mastery in history, geography, the Bible, and English and classical literature (including some Latin) and publishing her first poem in 1767, at about age fourteen. She went on to earn considerable admiration over the next few years for several individually published occasional poems, a number of them honoring or addressed to publicly prestigious individuals. One of her most celebrated works, her 1770 elegy "On the Death of the Rev. Mr. George Whitefield," was published in London as well as Boston and garnered her an international reputation.[61]

Nevertheless, despite such early acclaim, when Wheatley attempted with the help of her mistress, Susanna, to put out a small volume of her poems, it was not possible to obtain the subscriptions needed to support a Boston publication. Through her efforts and influence, Susanna was able to find a publisher in London who agreed to take on the volume, but only if a document attesting to the authenticity of the poems were provided to reassure a British readership that the work was not a fraud. In 1773 Wheatley's *Poems on Various Subjects, Religious and Moral* appeared, authorized by the requisite document from "the most respectable Characters in *Boston*," assuring "the World, that the POEMS . . . were (as we verily believe) written by PHILLIS, a young Negro Girl, who was but a few Years since, brought an uncultivated Barbarian from *Africa*, and . . . is . . . a Slave in a Family in this Town," and testifying that the author had "been examined . . . and [was] thought qualified to write them."[62] Shortly after the publication of her book, Wheatley was granted her freedom. Although she enjoyed celebrity for a time, meeting George Washington, among other eminent figures in England and North America, she eventually fell on difficult circumstances; after a failed marriage and two miscarriages, she died in poverty in 1778, at about the age of thirty-one.

FIGURE 0.4: Portrait of Phillis Wheatley by Scipio Moorhead. Frontispiece to her book *Poems on Various Subjects*. Rare Books and Special Collections Division of the Library of Congress.

Poems on Various Subjects, the first book published by an English-speaking black poet and the first book by an African American woman, turned Wheatley into something of an international sensation. Her youth and personal history, her exceptional mastery of the Western classical tradition and elite poetic forms, and her polite yet daring readiness to address individuals of enormous public stature all helped to foster her reputation as a prodigy. But as Henry Louis Gates observes, the trials and achievements of Phillis Wheatley had a significance that reached far beyond her personal or literary destiny. For Gates, Wheatley's encounter with the founding fathers in 1772 constituted "the primal scene of African-American letters," one in which not only Wheatley but her race was on trial.[63] Set up to determine whether her poems were authentic, whether her book would be published, and whether she would obtain her freedom, the interview was designed "to answer a much larger question: was a Negro capable of producing literature?"[64] As such, writes Gates, it helped to determine "the subsequent direction of the antislavery movement, as well as the birth of what a later commentator would call 'a new species of literature,' the literature written by slaves."[65]

Wheatley's writing was a pioneering achievement not only for its inaugural status and for the ordeal surrounding its publication but also for its bold engagement with the central issues of its time. Like de Gouges's work, Wheatley's poems take up the metaphor of slavery in discourses of political liberty, and, like Astell's, they address Enlightenment doctrines of intellectual incapacity, but they do so from a distinct vantage point: that of a slave. In her poem "To the Right Honourable William, Earl of Dartmouth, His Majesty's Principal Secretary of State for North America, &c.," for example, Wheatley uses the fact of her own enslavement to turn republican discourse against itself even as she mobilizes the metaphor of slavery to champion the cause of American emancipation from British colonial rule. Hailing the happy day when America shall "no more . . . in mournful strain / Of wrongs, and grievance unredress'd complain" and "no longer . . . dread the iron chain / [Of] wanton *Tyranny*," she explains that her "love of *Freedom*" and "wishes for the common good" spring from her own cruel experience of "tyrannic sway":

> I, young in life, by seeming cruel fate
> Was snatch'd from *Afric's* fancy'd happy seat:
> . . .
>
> Steel'd was that soul and by no misery mov'd,
> That from a father seiz'd his babe belov'd:
> Such, such my case. And can I then but pray
> Others may never feel tyrannic sway?[66]

The juxtaposition here of the realities of the Middle Passage as Wheatley herself experienced them and colonial America's dread of the metaphorical "iron chain" is at once jarring and unifying. The conventional rhetoric of colonial grievance against England typically effaced the difference between the reality and the figure of colonial slavery, but when Wheatley conjoins the two in these lines, she calls attention to the disturbing contradiction between American ideals of independence and the institution of chattel slavery. At the same time, however, her empathic endorsement of American emancipation and indeed her embrace of its metaphors paradoxically assert an unassailable moral logic that aligns, as by necessity, national independence and the end of slavery. A tribute to the Earl of Dartmouth and a prayer for the nation that points toward a time when tyranny of every kind will be no more, her poem thus becomes as well a critique of slavery and an exhortation for change.

Wheatley also powerfully addresses the tension between the idea of Enlightenment and the doctrine of African intellectual incapacity in her famous short poem "On Being Brought from Africa to America." So persuasive and unwavering is the voice of humility with which she narrates this pithy, eight-line work that she has often been criticized for overidentifying in it with the racist point of view of her oppressors in a simple expression of gratitude for the captivity that brought her from a "benighted" paganism to an enlightened Christianity:

> 'Twas mercy brought me from my *Pagan* land,
> Taught my benighted soul to understand
> That there's a God, that there's a *Saviour* too:
> Once I redemption neither sought nor knew.
> Some view our sable race with scornful eye,
> "Their colour is a diabolic die."
> Remember, *Christians*, *Negros*, black as *Cain*,
> May be refin'd and join th'angelic train.[67]

Such readings, however, overlook Wheatley's mordant ironies. Scholars routinely note that Wheatley was a great admirer of the eighteenth-century English poet Alexander Pope, whose neoclassical couplets she imitated, but few have mined the significance for her poetry of the fact that Pope was also one of England's great masters of poetic irony.[68] Like Pope, Wheatley exploits the compression of the closed heroic couplet to produce a brilliant sort of poetic double talk, one that here accommodates what W.E.B. Du Bois has referred to as a distinctly African-American "double-consciousness" rooted, in her case, in the contradictions surrounding her dual identity as an American and a slave.[69]

In this reading, the progress Wheatley describes from ignorance to enlightenment and from darkness to light is also a fall from innocence to experience, a journey of terrible illumination in which her blissfully benighted soul is awakened not just to the beauties of Christianity but also to the horrible truth of slavery. With the dawning of this cruel knowledge, she comes to understand both the universal human need for spiritual redemption from the condition of original sin and her own personal need for physical salvation from the condition of slavery. In the line, "Once I redemption neither sought nor knew," Wheatley alludes at once to a time before her conversion to the Christian faith and to a time before she was a slave, when she was free both from the knowledge of original sin and from the need to be ransomed, or materially "redeemed."

Wheatley's measured and well-behaved couplets deftly mask the indignation aroused in her by initiation into this bitter truth. The acerbic irony of the lines is not so different from that of Astell when, in a similarly conciliatory and indeed grateful voice, the latter recalls a time before she was initiated into the knowledge of her own inferiority, when, as she writes, "thro' Want of Learning, and of that Superior Genius which Men as Men lay claim to, she was ignorant of the *Natural Inferiority* of our Sex, which our Masters lay down as a Self-Evident and Fundamental Truth."[70] Both Astell and Wheatley signify their alienated relation to an Enlightenment that excludes them by using the pretense of an understanding and acceptance of its official wisdom, but they both also demonstrate another, higher and more authoritative, wisdom in the process in their canny knowledge of the arbitrary relations of power in which such "knowledge" is produced and that define and delimit what or who a knowing subject is. In this context, the ambiguity created by the multiple commas in the final couplet of Wheatley's poem, where either Christians or Negros (or both) can be understood as the subject (or object) of imperative address, seems especially apt. The lines issue a stern reminder to white slave owners, as well as to Negro slaves, that the level of a person's spiritual or intellectual enlightenment (whether angelically "refin'd" or "black as *Cain*") has nothing to do with skin color.

WOMEN IN THE PUBLIC SPHERE

The contributions of Astell, de Gouges, Montagu, More, Wollstonecraft, Wheatley, and others clearly demonstrate that, however vigorously dominant Enlightenment ideologies of class, domesticity, and female intellectual deficiency might discourage it, women of different classes and races were actively entering the public sphere. Paradoxically, such activity was in part a function of the very ideological contradictions that thinkers like Astell, de Gouges, and Wollstonecraft were determined to expose. As the historian Joan Scott observes, "Universalist discourses, specifically the discourses of abstract individualism and of social duty and social right, enabled [women] to conceive of themselves as political agents even as those same discourses denied women political agency."[71] Equally paradoxical in light of Enlightenment assertions of confidence in the immanent force of natural law is the amount of prescriptive attention Enlightenment discourse paid to women's conduct. Reflecting on prescriptive writing that pushes women into idealized patterns of behavior through discursive strategies of censure or of praise, Elizabeth Janeway once asked, "Why should anyone be praised for being what she is supposed to be by nature?"[72] One might consider in the context of such a question the tension between the widespread Enlightenment censure of learned women and Rousseau's pronouncement of women's innate intellectual inferiority, or that between his exaltation of the virtues of domesticity and his view of childbearing as a woman's natural role. Such tensions suggest that the amount of ink spilt by Enlightenment political thinkers in asserting and defending gender asymmetry and in disciplining women through explicitly gendered codes of propriety may in fact reflect a tacit, if not anxious, recognition on their part that republican political doctrines were opening possibilities for female agency that needed to be jealously foreclosed, in the hope perhaps of forestalling change that was already beginning to happen.

At the same time that new forms of political thought were opening conceptual spaces for women to think of themselves as knowing subjects and political agents, other cultural transformations were providing them with new economic and creative opportunities. The emergence of a burgeoning literary marketplace driven by the demands of an increasingly literate reading public and open to professional writers who were not classically educated brought many women to writing as a means of livelihood. While for more than a century literary historians traced the origins of the English novel to the innovations of such well-known male writers as Daniel Defoe, Samuel Richardson, and Henry Fielding, current scholars—benefiting from the feminist recovery of work by neglected women writers that began in the 1960s and 1970s—have come to recognize and appreciate the prominent role that women played in the genre's emergence and early development.[73] Aphra Behn, the first Englishwoman to earn a living by her pen, has been credited with having actually inaugurated the genre in the 1680s with the publication of her *Love Letters between a Nobleman and his Sister*.[74] Delarivier Manley's political scandal narrative *The New Atalantis*, a thinly veiled allegory targeting the powerful and controversial Whig statesman the Duke of Marlborough and his famous wife, Sarah, was the most sensational and influential best seller published during the reign of Queen Anne (1702–14) and has been deemed responsible for delivering a fatal blow to the dominance of the Whig Party, which fell from British political power within a year of the book's publication in 1709. Eliza Haywood's novel *Love in Excess; or, The Fatal Enquiry* (1720) rivaled such popular classics as *Robinson Crusoe* (1719) and *Gulliver's Travels* (1726) for preeminence among novels in sales and popularity throughout the 1720s and 1730s.

Thus, whether or not it is possible to determine a single or stable origin of the English novel, it is clear that the emergence of the professional woman writer in the Restoration and the eighteenth century was a development of enormous cultural significance. In 1927 Virginia Woolf celebrated its historical importance when she insisted that "all women together ought to let flowers fall upon the tomb of Aphra Behn . . . for it was she who earned them the right to speak their minds."[75] Indeed, for Woolf, the moment when the middle-class woman began to write professionally constituted a change "of greater importance than the Crusades or the Wars of the Roses."[76]

For a long time, nevertheless, the annals of literary history obscured the magnitude of women's entry into print, in large part because of the way early women writers were represented by their male contemporaries and marketplace competitors. Because of their public visibility and the often outspoken treatment of sex and sexual politics in their work, Behn, Manley, and Haywood were frequently attacked as licentious hack writers. But as William Beatty Warner has shown, it was not at all uncommon for the male writers whose works would come to constitute the British novelistic canon to capitalize on the market for amorous intrigue that their female predecessors had established by incorporating narrative strategies and plot devices from these women's work into their own; far from acknowledging their debt, moreover, writers like Defoe and Richardson actively distanced themselves from the popular work from which they drew, precisely in order to be able to establish their own efforts on more elevated cultural and moral ground.

The new moralism that emerged by midcentury, partly as a result of such competitive bids for dominance in the contested cultural terrain of the early print market, may have succeeded in sullying the reputations of early practitioners like Behn and Manley, but in the long run it did not prevent female novelists from appropriating and exploiting an elevated cultural address for their own purposes. Haywood, in fact, published her best-known works after what is sometimes referred to as her midcareer "conversion" from the explicit eroticism of such early efforts as *Fantomina* (1725) to the more morally decorous didactic prose of *The Female Spectator* (1744–46) and *The History of Miss Betsy Thoughtless* (1751). Over the course of the eighteenth century, women novelists—including Ann Radcliffe, Frances Burney, Maria Edgeworth, and many others—would become a mainstay of the genre in England, gaining popularity throughout Europe and North America and establishing a narrative tradition that would have tremendous influence, perhaps most notably on the novels of Jane Austen.

It is one of the ironies of women's history that the same literary marketplace that generated conduct books relegating women to private life also drew them so insistently into print. As Linda Colley notes in her account of British history, during the eighteenth century "separate sexual spheres were being increasingly prescribed in theory, yet increasingly broken through in practice."[77] Even as Rousseau and Kant were disparaging learned women, French *salonnières* (among them Julie de Lespinasse, Marie-Thérèse de Geoffrin, Suzanne Necker and, later, her daughter Germaine de Staël) in Paris and English Bluestockings (including Elizabeth Montagu, Elizabeth Carter, and Hester Thrale) in London were hosting gatherings whose intellectual culture promoted, among other Enlightenment causes, the transformation of gender roles. The same Enlightenment culture that produced James Fordyce's *Sermons to Young Women* (1766), Rousseau's *Émile*, and the doctrine of separate spheres also produced the feminism of Wollstonecraft and de Gouges—itself a political and intellectual legacy of what Joan Scott has called the "constitutive contradictions" of liberal individualism.[78]

In short, although Kant and other Enlightenment philosophers excluded women from the ranks of rational subjects, many women during the Enlightenment were in fact fulfilling the Horatian dictum for which Kant became so famous (*sapere aude*, "dare to know"), and many communicated their wisdom publicly. Behn, Manley, and Haywood offer a sustained analysis and critique of the sexual double standard and of early modern gender politics; Wheatley exposes the contradictions, the hypocrisy, and the inhumanity of Enlightenment slavery; Wollstonecraft lays bare the inadequacies and corrupting influence of women's education in the period and attacks marriage as a form of legal prostitution; Austen targets the insidiously gendered pretenses of polite society. In distinct but related ways, these women understood the contradictions and costs inherent in their position, as women, in Enlightenment culture. Their penetrating critiques and trenchant ironies mine those contradictions in their own cultural moment, but they also gesture elsewhere, toward other kinds of knowledges, values, and possible futures.

CHAPTER ONE

The Life Cycle: Motherhood during the Enlightenment

KATHLEEN M. BROWN

Every woman too, at certain times, was forbidden to come into a dwelling house, or touch any person, or any thing we ate. I was so fond of my mother I could not keep from her, or avoid touching her at some of those periods, in consequence of which I was obliged to be kept out with her, in a little house made for that purpose, till offering was made, and then we were purified.

—Olaudah Equiano, *The Interesting Narrative of the Life of Olaudah Equiano* (1789)[1]

In order to fulfil the duties of life, and to be able to pursue with vigour the various employments which form the moral character, a master and mistress of a family ought not to continue to love each other with passion . . . an unhappy marriage is often very advantageous to a family, and . . . the neglected wife is, in general, the best mother.

—Mary Wollstonecraft, *A Vindication of the Rights of Woman* (1792)[2]

The Enlightenment was a period of revived intellectual energy for generating, collecting, and classifying new knowledge about humans and the world they inhabited. During this formative time, ideas about the natural world, human societies, and human nature itself all underwent profound change as Enlightenment philosophers and political theorists incorporated information about new lands and indigenous peoples and debated new possibilities that challenged custom and tradition. Significantly, these new ideas emerged in an efflorescence of societies, clubs, academies, coffeehouses, journals, and magazines where men, and occasionally some women, might discuss these matters freely. Among the most important shifts in thinking were those related to sex difference, citizenship, child nurture, education, and the reason for the apparent differences among the various peoples of the world—differences that reshaped the intellectual systems of philosophers, political theorists, theologians, scientists, and artists throughout the Atlantic basin. All of these topics affected how Enlightenment thinkers, and, indeed, many ordinary people, began to envision the duties and natural capacities of human beings in relationship to each other. Central to many of these relationships was the Enlightenment mother—not only in connection with her child but in relation to her spouse, the nation, and the "other" women brought into view by imperial projects. Indeed, motherhood was often at the center of Enlightenment debates about the benefits and perils of civilization, education, the state's relationship to the family, and the plasticity of human nature. From the sexual act that resulted in conception to the mother's responsibilities for the moral and intellectual development of her child, the expectations for mothers and the state's interests in them changed dramatically during the Enlightenment, eventually becoming part of the revolutions and imperial recalibrations that marked the end of the eighteenth century. Although many scholars would date the end of the Enlightenment to this postrevolutionary period, most concede that the ideas it generated had a lasting impact and laid the foundations for the liberal states of the nineteenth century. This is especially true in the case of motherhood, which moved from an Enlightenment ideal for educated, rational child nurture, enriched by a mother's capacity for gaining knowledge intuited through her sensibility, to a more sentimental and embedded Victorian belief in the "civilized" (i.e., white) woman's essential difference from man (and significantly from indigenous, enslaved, or otherwise degraded women) grounded in her greater natural capacity for moral behavior and maternal love. As the English feminist writer and philosopher Mary Wollstonecraft and the self-identified African abolitionist author Olaudah Equiano both recognized, by the age of revolution, motherhood had become the new currency of claims to be recognized as a fellow human being. Although ideals for enlightened motherhood had emerged out of the intellectual ferment resulting from European expansion across the Atlantic and the encounter with New World peoples and terrain, enlightened motherhood also became an important part of the rationale for the European desire to dominate indigenous peoples. In their different ways, both Wollstonecraft, author of *A Vindication of the Rights of Woman* (1792), and Equiano, author of *The Interesting Narrative of the Life of Olaudah Equiano* (1789), realized that the capacity for enlightened motherhood might open the door to other moral and political claims. During the heady moments immediately after the French Revolution, Wollstonecraft contended that middle-class women had the same spiritual and intellectual potential as men. In the reformed world she imagined, that potential might be realized by mothers who were respected and recognized by the state and society. Her contemporary, Equiano, represented himself as one of the millions of victims of the Atlantic slave trade. Claiming African birth rather than the South Carolina heritage he is more likely to have possessed,[3] he sought to give credibility and poignancy to his observations of slavery's cruel stunting of human potential. Whereas for Wollstonecraft, the capacity for rational mother love qualified women to be considered as the equals of men, for Equiano it signified the sensibility and emotional refinement that meant that Africans, too, belonged to the family of civilized human beings.

BECOMING A MOTHER: MEDICAL VIEWS OF SEX, CONCEPTION, PREGNANCY, AND CHILDBIRTH

From the early sixteenth century, European travelers throughout the Atlantic observed with considerable interest that mothers in "civilized" societies—by which they meant Christian, European kingdoms—suffered more debilities and recovered less quickly from childbirth than mothers in so-called savage societies (what Enlightenment *philosophes* would reclassify as primitive societies in their hierarchical vision of all societies passing through different stages of civilization). Citing the birthing, domestic, and child nurture practices of the Gaelic Irish and Native Americans (but almost never of Africans), some medical writers advocated a turn away from the excesses ushered in by civilization. This negative view of the experience of motherhood in Europe framed a larger critique of civilization, especially in its extreme manifestation—luxury—as an enfeebling trend that compromised hardy masculinity. But it also paved the way for seemingly natural approaches to childrearing, housekeeping, and medicine as enthusiasm grew for the wonders of the Americas. The spread of new foods, diets, manners, and habits from the New World to Europe sparked new discussion about what might be the most "natural" regime for human beings who lived in such different climates. What might be appropriate for inhabitants of the torrid zones, where the hot climate had left its imprint on both the constitutions of human bodies and their societies, would not do for Europe's temperate zones. Hot temperatures, physicians such as Thomas Tryon and John Floyer reasoned, made men indolent, reducing their sexual vigor and motivation to labor. "Luxury," as these writers conceived of it, might result from immoderate enjoyment of the pleasures civilization had to offer—overly warm feather beds, hot fires, and stimulating beverages—but it could also occur if Europeans inappropriately adopted the degraded manners and habits of people who inhabited the tropical zones of Africa and the New World.[4] Yet, as many English travelers observed, civilization seemed only to have diminished the constitutions of parturient women. Virginia chronicler William Strachey and others implicitly criticized European habits, asserting that bearing children was natural for women and that only the excesses and errors of civilization had produced the ailments and debilities that led English women and their children to suffer during and after childbirth.[5] The "discovery" of the New World and the peoples who inhabited it coincided with a larger shift in scientific method and philosophy that emphasized the human capacity to understand and manage even the most mysterious and occluded processes in the natural world. Beginning in the 1650s and continuing into the next century, scientific approaches to the reproductive capacities of women began to shift dramatically. Behind this shift was a new faith in the empirical knowledge generated by dissection, in the male practitioners who gathered this knowledge, and in the authority of male doctors—man midwives—to bring improved knowledge and techniques to the birth chamber. Medical writers and others challenged the customary notion that a woman's body was mysterious and could be known only by the woman herself and her female attendants. Rather, they contended, truths about the female body, like those about all bodies, resided inside and could be discovered only through dissection. By the end of the eighteenth century in cities on both sides of the Atlantic, it was no longer true that women dominated the knowledge and practice of childbirth by virtue of their experience and their sex. Male midwives had made a place for themselves as authors of texts explaining conception and as authorities in the birthing chambers of privileged women.[6]

Nicholas Culpeper's *Directory for Midwives* (1651) marks the shift in English medical guides toward a less ritualized birthing chamber (the work of the Protestant Reformation had already cleared the room of "filthy" religious relics and invocations of saints) and an anatomized and therefore male-defined epistemology of women's bodies. In these new birthing spaces, there was no room for superstitious beliefs that the male child's umbilical cord should be cut long because it would determine the length of his penis. Only through dissection and a thorough acquaintance with anatomy could a midwife truly know the body of a patient. The information traditionally acquired by female midwives by touching pregnant women with skilled fingers and hands was now deemed second-rate compared to the knowledge that might be gained by witnessing the dissection of a woman's body. Culpeper's was an early salvo by male doctors and "man midwives" to supplant women's heretofore superior knowledge of the mysteries of the pregnant and laboring woman's body with knowledge produced by male scientists.[7]

Guides to midwifery that introduced the man midwife into the birthing chamber emphasized new family relationships—for example, the father's as well as the mother's relationship to the fetus—and new gender relationships. Medical texts made more ambitious claims for the father's greater physical relevance to the process of conception and fetal development. This paralleled the move by male doctors to claim greater authority over the birth process based not only on their scientific expertise but also on their empathetic relationship to the birthing woman. By the eighteenth century, man midwives were describing themselves as men who felt compassion for their female patients and understood their suffering. Despite a new medical model that posited a distinct anatomy for each sex—overshadowing without completely supplanting the Galenic "one-sex" model of commensurable sex difference in which women were theorized to be imperfectly developed versions of men—the success of male midwives depended in large measure on blurring the emotional distinctions between men and women. But in the tradition of the receipt book, there were still guides to childbirth by women that appealed to women only and contained recipes for enhancing the male libido, regulating the menses, and inducing abortion.[8]

The shifts in scientific approaches to sex and childbirth had political as well as domestic consequences, as historian Lisa Cody notes. The birth of James Francis Stuart to the previously childless James II and Mary of Modena in 1688, monarchs with known Roman Catholic sympathies, produced a crisis of paternity and succession in England. Protestants feared that a successor to James would revive the threat of a future Catholic claimant to the throne. There were no witnesses to the baby's birth, and several close relatives of Mary of Modena disputed the timing of the birth and even the fact of it. Scandal sheets and cartoons questioned the child's paternity and Mary's fidelity to her husband. The subsequent ouster of James II from the throne in a bloodless coup led by William and Mary of Orange, known as the Glorious Revolution, was sparked by this birth and Mary of Modena's achievement of motherhood after a checkered fertility history. In an age of Atlantic encounters that challenged assumptions about women's natural reproductive capacities and of new scientific interventions in the knowledge and practice of childbirth, the unexpected birth of a child to a Catholic queen triggered a seismic political shift that ultimately diminished the power of the English monarchy.[9]

MOTHERHOOD, CIVILIZATION, AND SOCIAL ORDER

Motherhood not only played an important role in this defining moment in national and imperial identity but also became foundational, as the core role and destiny of women, to the emerging philosophical and legal frameworks defining race and slavery in the Americas. Scottish and English philosophers used a civilized society's treatment of its women—gallant manners, chaste morals, and especially the delegation of domestic labor to women as their natural duty—as evidence of its place in the stages of civilization. In this view, the privileges enjoyed by British women and their Anglo-American counterparts—based on their potential to be educated to contribute to polite sociability and to become feeling companions to men—revealed England to be at the peak of civilization, while Native American, African, Turkish, and Chinese women suffered the degraded treatment established by custom in their primitive societies. Politeness and gallantry, however, placed a society on a slippery slope toward becoming overly effeminate, a danger in a world of imperial rivalries and indigenous men capable of mobilizing a fierce form of manhood in war.[10]

Comparisons between Europe's "civilized" Christian mothers and the primitive women of Africa and the Americas anchored racial differences in the legal and cultural contexts of conception, childbirth, and domestic labor. English accounts described Native American women as wanton in their sexual freedom but oppressed in their labor as beasts of burden, forced to work in the fields while their men took their leisure; yet in tension with this portrait was the praise of their beauty and their hardiness in recovering from childbirth. In contrast, African women elicited little praise for their attractiveness or their hardiness but simply appear in English texts as laborers whose capacity for the strenuous work normally done by men went without saying. Wealthy planters in Britain's colonies in Barbados and Virginia began importing African slave laborers in small numbers by the 1640s, sparking legal questions about how they compared to English women in the colonies. Colonial lawmakers resolved the questions by formalizing assumptions about African women's capacity for

grueling field labor and by creating new contexts for their reproductive potential. African women were routinely put to work in the fields—whether the crop
was sugar, tobacco, or, later, coffee, indigo, or rice. Although some English
servant women found that they, too, were expected to hoe rows of tobacco
in Virginia, colony sponsors quickly found it important to define this fate as
unusual except for those too "nasty" and "beastly" to perform the domestic
labor most women preferred.[11]

Unlike mothers in England, enslaved mothers lost their legal claims on male
partners and their rights to their children under a new law defining slave status
in 1662 as following the condition of the mother. With this statute, slave status
passed from mother to child, regardless of the father's status or race. A man,
no matter what his own legal condition, could produce free white children
only if he gained sexual access to a free white woman. Enslaved women became destined to reproduce the master's labor force, even if the father of their
children was the master himself. Indeed, the irrelevance of paternity and the
vulnerability of children whose parents could offer them no protection became
the mark of a slave. While the most privileged English women became the
subjects of midwifery texts that expounded on their suffering during childbirth
and encouraged empathy, laws in Barbados, Virginia, Maryland, and eventually Jamaica and South Carolina detached the motherhood of enslaved women
from fatherhood and family, stripped it of sentiment, and subordinated it to
their role as agricultural laborers.[12]

By the end of the century, even in vastly different colonies in British North
America, motherhood became subject to new laws punishing illegitimacy that
were designed to shore up the social order. In Virginia, which had begun to
import large numbers of enslaved Africans by the 1680s and 1690s, a 1691
statute denouncing the "spurious issue" produced by unions between Anglo
women and African or Indian men prohibited all marriages across racial lines;
this was itself an effort to try to define what race would mean in a colony
where individuals of Anglo-African descent had begun petitioning for their
freedom as early as the 1650s. Denied the right to marry the African or Indian
fathers of their children, Anglo mothers faced extra years of service and, for
a time in Maryland, enslavement for producing such children illegitimately,
while the children themselves bore the burden of long years of servitude. Enslaved women also suffered as a consequence of this law. The prohibition
on legal marriage across the color line did nothing to impede a master's sexual access to an enslaved woman or the profitability of fathering a child by
her but did make it more difficult for her to gain any legal benefit from the
relationship.[13]

Meanwhile, in Massachusetts, an English law on the books since 1624, making a single mother's unwitnessed stillbirth punishable as infanticide, came to public attention in 1691 at the sensational trial and subsequent execution of a young woman who had allegedly killed her illegitimate twins. Elizabeth Emerson was sentenced to die for her crime in 1693, during a decade in which many others—poor, sexually notorious, and usually women of color—swung from the noose for murdering their stillborn infants. Not until the 1730s did a more forgiving legal supposition—that a tenderhearted mother would be unlikely to kill her baby, even when faced with the stigma of single motherhood—replace the harsh Jacobean statute.[14]

Even when it was not the keystone of sexual and racial regulations, motherhood was foundational to the creation of creole societies. In colonial contexts where European goals were less about settlement and more about commerce, European men found few moral strictures constraining their choice of sexual partner—as long as she was a woman. Unions between native women and European men were accepted as a necessary feature of doing business with Indians. In New France and in the territory occupied by Britain's Hudson Bay Company, male fur traders forged long-term relationships with native women and their families and produced *métis* children who moved comfortably between both worlds—a crucial advantage during the period when fur trading provided lucrative incomes. In New Spain north of the Rio Grande River, Indian women and their children were the most likely group to be taken captive and enslaved, a fact that put them at the center of negotiations and violent conflicts between Spaniards and native peoples. Throughout the period, Indian women themselves continued to play diplomatic roles as brokers of peace even after the reconquest of the Pueblo in 1692. Further south, in the Valley of Mexico, Spanish men and Indian women became sexual and economic partners. Their relationships became the subject of numerous "castas" paintings, a pictorial genre that used depictions of populations of mixed-race peoples and that attempted to impose racial and social order on multiracial colonial societies, much as Linneaus had attempted to classify the flora and fauna of the natural world. In these paintings, as in the majority of relationships producing mestizo children, men crossed the color line to partner with darker complected women, but the possibility that light-skinned women might do the same was carefully repressed—a pattern that was to appear throughout the Atlantic basin.[15] Many of the new racial and legal contexts for motherhood were connected to changes in the legal and economic basis for fatherhood. Of special significance was the new link between male political visibility—freedom, belonging to the community of fellow men, and inclusion in the polity—and the ownership of property. Property took on new importance in seventeenth-century England for defining men fraternally as adults, rather than as the childish subjects of patriarchal authority. First articulated by John Locke, this vision of a fraternity of property-holding men spread to North America through Locke's South Carolina constitution, which, though never ratified, was influential in establishing the aristocratic tone of the colony's politics and its slaveholding. Property became especially important to Anglo societies in North America because land was seemingly plentiful for those willing to deceive Indians or shed their blood. The political significance of owning land would seem to have enforced the father's position of dominance in the household (although Locke foreclosed the notion of such influence coming from some divinely sanctioned father right). The reliance on family labor in the northern colonies and the use of unfree laborers everywhere both derived from this patriarchal authority and enhanced it, but the availability of land and the consequent demand for labor limited the authority of fathers. Ultimately, the value of young people's labor and the ease (relative to England) with which they could gain the resources they needed to begin their own households mitigated what was otherwise a stronger North American form of patriarchy. The new importance of land ownership laid the foundation for the difference between men and women within the household as well as in the polity; it also distinguished free men, who could become legally recognized fathers, from enslaved men, who could not.[16]

MATERNAL SENSIBILITY

Several cultural, economic, and religious trends gave new meaning to motherhood during the eighteenth century. The spread of print culture, the consumption of imported goods, and new individualistic theologies and forms of religious expression enabled mothers to expand their influence over children and men. The celebration of sensibility in the world of letters and the impact of evangelical religion encouraged a gentler, more emotionally intense ideal of maternal love and maternal duty to take hold by midcentury. Mothers were no longer confined to achieving respect mainly through their roles as industrious household managers and domestic manufacturers but could now achieve it through tasteful, moderate consumption as well as through the spiritual shepherding and emotional nurturance of children. It was no longer fashionable for men to mock women openly the way the dashing figure of the aristocratic rake was free to do in an earlier era (although women of fashion, who had allegedly let the desire to consume vanquish their common sense and modesty, were still lampooned and ridiculed in the pages of the *Tatler*, the *Spectator*, the *Virginia Gazette*, and the *Pennsylvania Gazette*). Instead, a refined man demonstrated sympathy and gallantry on behalf of "the fair sex," a phrase that reflected the class and racial specificity of this belief in the female capacity for sensibility. Gallantry exhibited a man's refinement and cosmopolitanism but depended on the existence of disparities—emotional, intellectual, and physical—between the sexes. On both sides of the Atlantic between 1730 and 1760, women earned a reputation for tenderheartedness through fervent participation in religious revivals. The revival denominations—Methodists, Baptists, and Presbyterians—made emotional appeals to potential converts and privileged the capacity of the heart to acknowledge sinfulness and receive grace over adherence to catechism or duty.[17]

Somewhat at odds with this emphasis on women's emotional capacity was the new expectation that they would play an important role in teaching their children basic reading skills. In England, books for children—mainly didactic texts that drummed moral lessons into young readers—testified to the new importance of mothers as spreaders of literacy. Mothers had to be educated themselves in order to fulfill this role, but the rationale for female education was to enable mothers to serve the needs of their children and husbands, not to encourage them to pursue individualistic ambitions to become *philosophes* or pedants. Literate mothers could become moral and spiritual guides for their children, a duty enhanced by their special religious sensibility. In fulfilling the role of spiritual and emotional helpmeet as well as industrious housewife, the educated, chaste mother served as a virtuous role model for her daughter and as a loving companion to her husband. Thus, she was a key emotional, spiritual, and intellectual resource for the emerging middle-class household and part of its cultural capital, if no longer manifestly as important to its economy.[18]

Enlightenment ideals of moral sensibility stirred debate about women's essential nature—a discussion that Wollstonecraft transformed by focusing on the condition of women in the socioeconomically "natural" state of the middle class. In her *Vindication of the Rights of Woman*, Wollstonecraft contended that the new expectations for mothers were in actuality consistent with the achievement of women's natural state of morally responsible adulthood. By spurning the artifice of fashion and the distortions of aristocratic manners, women could realize their natural capacities for reason and moral sensibility. In their natural state, she argued, women were prudent and responsible mothers—true adults—rather than vain, childish creatures, trained only to chase pleasure and to please men. If women were allowed to develop these natural capacities for reason and morality, they would be good mothers, and motherhood could define their political relationship to the state and their value and visibility as citizens. This could happen, however, only if men also transformed and learned to value women in their natural state as morally dependable adult companions rather than as childish playthings.

Wollstonecraft's arguments had great resonance for Anglo North America's reading class; more personal libraries in the early United States possessed copies of *A Vindication of the Rights of Woman* than of Thomas Paine's *Common Sense*. In the context of revolution and nation building, her theories about women's natural capacity for reason and moral sensibility found their greatest political use. Known to historians as "republican motherhood," the articulation of an informal cultural role for elite American women in the new nation gave a particular political spin to a broader transatlantic trend defining the moral (as opposed to more purely economic) value of bourgeois womanhood and motherhood. Beliefs that, if they were educated, morally refined, and of the appropriate social position and race, women could bring out the best in men—whether as wives, mothers, or friends—created a seemingly "natural" anchor for the experiment in American republican government. For several decades, elite women like Dolly Madison played important roles in creating the political culture of the nation's capital. Whereas in Britain social critics like Wollstonecraft claimed that only a moral revolution in the upbringing, educations, and relationships of men and women could accomplish the goals of producing virtuous mothers, American readers of Wollstonecraft embraced republican motherhood, confident that, by declaring independence from Britain and creating a new government, they had already experienced the necessary revolution.

MOTHERHOOD IN AN IMPERIAL AGE

Race and imperial ambition were central to resolving the tension between women as civilizers of men and women as unnatural products of the distorting constraints of civilization. In keeping with her focus on the unnaturalness of middle-class women's aping of aristocratic manners, Wollstonecraft never used enslaved women or Native American "squaw drudges" as foils to depict the "wrongs" of women. If she hoped to reveal to readers the unnaturalness of the parasitic, dependent lives of childish women of leisure, it would not do to present overworked drudges, sweating in the fields, as an alternative. So even though she had read and reviewed Equiano's heartrending tale of exploitation and suffering under slavery, she did not present enslaved women as sympathetic female victims. Rather, it was the women of the harem and the seraglio—Eastern women—who provided a foil for the perversity of middle-class women's aristocratic aspirations. Rationally performed duty rather than passion, moral autonomy rather than cloistered dependence, emerged in Wollstonecraft's comparison of English middle-class women to the women of the harem. But even more important, by offering this contrast, Wollstonecraft yoked her vision of the enlightened mother to the imperial ascendance of the West, making it a necessary component of the West's moral, economic, and political domination over the East.[19] Changing ideals for motherhood were accompanied by shifts in medical advice about child nurture according to a logic defined as much by imperialism as by an intensification of maternal sentiment. The population needs of empire produced trends visible around the Atlantic basin. Medical guidebooks linked the individual citizen's health to the health of the body politic, a connection that manifested itself in several ways: in efforts to encourage births and improve child nurture, so as to produce healthy, literate, and productive subjects in imperial Britain and virtuous citizens in the new United States; in the demand for population resources to staff the expanding British empire and to expand the new United States westward into Indian territory; and in a growing interest in the reproductive potential of already enslaved women as antislavery sentiment in Britain grew and eventually led in 1808 to the closing of the Atlantic slave trade to the British Caribbean and the United States.[20]

The burgeoning populations of the British North American colonies ultimately became the most powerful weapon in the eighteenth-century imperial rivalries among Spain, France, and England for control of the continent. In *Observations Concerning the Increase of Mankind* (1751),[21] Benjamin Franklin observed that the population of the North American colonies was doubling every twenty-five years; in fact, it was every twenty-two years, but he was right about the political implications for the balance of power between the metropolis and the colonial mainland. The numerical superiority of Britain's colonial population ultimately helped it to triumph over the French in the Seven Years' War (1754–63) but proved to be a major component of its undoing when, just twelve years later, the discontent of Western settlers over British impediments to the seizure of Indian lands undermined imperial authority and contributed to revolutionary unrest.

The significance of population for imperial might did not go unnoticed by the medical community. Michael Underwood (1736–1820), appointed royal physician to the Princess of Wales, cited his main reason for focusing on infant and child health in his medical guides as the state's need for a population to carry out the work of a vast empire. Citing Underwood, among other medical authorities, American author Mary Tyler picked up on the state's concern for the health of its citizenry in her 1811 *The Maternal Physician*. Despite a lower infant mortality rate in the United States than in Britain, Tyler claimed to be motivated by the tragedy of infant death. She transformed domestic healing into yet another duty of the enlightened republican mother. Not only did the republican mother need to be the rational nurturer of the intellects and morals of her children, but she was charged with their physical nurture and healing as well. The well-being of the nation required that the future citizens entrusted to her care be clean and healthy without falling prey to vanity, fashion, or bodily weakness. Overrefined populations, in Tyler's account, were enfeebled populations in which mothers cared more about fashion and society than about the health of their children. Conversely, if care was based not on reason but on "old wives' tales" and superstition, children also died needlessly. Tyler called for rational, dedicated, observant, and loving mothers to nurture children through both the ordinary trials of infancy and early childhood as well as the deadly threats of epidemic disease and serious injury. Her work joined the advice penned by physicians S. A. Tissot, Bernard Faust, William Buchan, A.F.M. Willich, and others that assigned responsibility for the health of the nation to the mother's stewardship over her household.[22]

Tyler's advice was part of a trend toward natural childrearing that included maternal (rather than wet-nurse) breast-feeding, bathing, fresh air, and freedom from the confines of swaddling. From the middle of the eighteenth century, social commentators and physicians had called on women (by which they meant the well-to-do) to nurse their own babies. Advocates of maternal breast-feeding condemned the hiring of wet nurses as a shirking of the most basic maternal responsibility. As John Gregory noted in his *Comparative View of the State and Faculties of Man with Those of the Animal World* (1765), "men may dispute whether it be proper to let their beards and their nails grow, on the principle of its being natural; but every Human Creature would be shocked with the impropriety of feeding an infant with Brandy instead of its Mother's Milk from an instant feeling of its being an outrage done to Nature."[23] For those who campaigned against wet nurses, maternal breast-feeding appeared as a natural duty of mothers to nurture their children—a duty that seamlessly coincided with imperial aims and population needs.

Yet despite the state's interest in the health and size of its population, women of the most prosperous classes on both sides of the Atlantic began intentionally to reduce the number of children they bore. The average completed family size among white women in the northern states declined by half, dropping from roughly seven children in the 1780s to three and a half children by 1900. Enlightenment ideals for rational companionship and virtuous motherhood helped to usher in the new demographic regime that would eventually come to characterize all developed countries: fewer children than in rural agricultural societies and greater investment in the educations of those children. What is interesting is that women's fertility strategies and family commitments to producing fewer, better-educated children triumphed steadily over the state's interest in expanding the population that could do the work of empire (in the British case) and imperial expansion (in the U.S. case). Even as Underwood decried the high infant mortality of eighteenth-century England and Thomas Jefferson, following in the footsteps of Benjamin Franklin, imagined the cultural, economic, and political transformation of the continent with the "natural" spread of a burgeoning white yeoman population, some American women appear to have been interpreting the legacy of the Enlightenment as supportive of their desires to curb the number of births.[24]

* * *

In the quotations at the beginning of this essay, Wollstonecraft and Equiano both evoke a vision of an exclusive and intensive motherhood as the ideal foundation of the child's future development. Wollstonecraft emphasizes a woman's "soul" equality with men and the corrosive effect of fashion, wealth, and male flattery on her natural capacity for reason and virtue. These negative effects, as she saw them, were the consequence of European society's distorted ideals of maternity and female beauty. In his account of being kidnapped by a slaver, Equiano depicts the bond between a West African mother and child as every bit as emotionally laden as that of white European ideals of maternal sensibility. As he portrays it, the slave trade, an outgrowth of European moral corruption, destroyed the authentic culture and natural bonds between mother and child. Significantly, these two important Enlightenment writers share a vision of the ideal bond between mother and child as the most intense of all familial bonds, more significant even than the bond between spouses. In sharp contrast to contemporary, twenty-first-century wisdom about healthy children being the product of couple-centered families rather than the mother-child dyad, both Wollstonecraft and Equiano idealize motherhood as an exclusive relationship that might trump the bond between husband and wife.

Each of the passages testifies in its own way to the complex cultural significance that motherhood took on during the era of Enlightenment. Enlightenment mothers were the bearers of identity and the reproducers of race, class, and civilization in a world Europeans believed to be filled with yet-to-be-civilized peoples. They were also emblems of the progress of civilization and benchmarks for judging others to be uncivilized. Mothers were at the nexus of the Enlightenment's promise and its complicity in the cultural assumptions underpinning the second British empire. Efforts to redefine women's essential nature, the rational mother's natural duties, and the best way to preserve the health of children were part of the Enlightenment's impact, but they were also instrumental in advancing imperial agendas and giving them the imprimatur of the natural order.[25]

CHAPTER TWO

Bodies and Sexuality: Sex, Gender, and the Limits of Enlightenment

SUSAN S. LANSER

> The theory of the human body is always a part of a world-picture [and] . . . always a part of a *fantasy*.
> —James Hillman, *The Myth of Analysis*[1]

It is a truth almost universally acknowledged that the "West" can date to the age of Enlightenment a striking preponderance of its modern arrangements, from the trivial (eating with forks) to the triumphant (the "rights of man") to the tragic (racial supremacy). The "long eighteenth century" gave us forms of governance built on social contract, an incipient and wildly inequitable global economy dominated by European empires, the stirrings of a self-conscious working class and the claims to power of a rising bourgeoisie, the fashioning of nation-states, the new hegemony of print and the attendant force of public opinion, fealty to empirically tested "nature" as the bedrock of truth, systemic challenges to hierarchies both human and divine, and both a "modern self" and a modern society built along lines of gender that entailed a spectacular failure to extend legal and political rights to women.[2]

As Thomas Laqueur boldly proclaims in his influential *Making Sex: Body and Gender from the Greeks to Freud*, "sex as we know it" was also "invented" in the eighteenth century as the basis for the gender relations that underwrite European modernity.[3] It is the age, as Michel Foucault argued in his pathbreaking *History of Sexuality*, when "a political, economic, and technical incitement to talk" about sexual matters began to forge disciplinary regimes concerned with "the manner in which each individual made use of his sex."[4] It is the age to which Henry Abelove attributes the "invention" of sexual intercourse as the dominant and disciplined sexual practice in an era when pronatalism reigned.[5] And for reasons that I consider intrinsic rather than incidental to these disciplinary projects, the age of Enlightenment also coincides with an intense interest in the implications of female same-sex desires for the emergence of civil society. These convergences remind us that although we tend to think of sex, gender, and sexuality as natural and fixed, modern notions of masculinity and femininity are less than three centuries old; the sexual imperatives with which twenty-first-century cultures are still grappling both shape and are shaped by eighteenth-century contests over nature and power, liberty and authority, desire and duty, human nature and human difference, social order and social mobility—in short, by the Enlightenment's philosophical and political challenges to the predictable workings of the social universe.

It has often been asserted that the age of Enlightenment ushered in a new openness about sexuality. By the century's end, most European countries had abolished capital punishment for sodomy. "Rational" *philosophes* recognized and even celebrated the centrality of (regulated) erotic pleasure for individual happiness and social progress and condemned Christian asceticism as deleterious to both. Denis Diderot, for example, argued for the natural goodness of sexuality in his "Supplément au voyage de Bougainville" (1772) and had one quasi-fictional character, Bordeu, proclaim in the "Suite de l'entretien" (1769) that since "nothing that exists can be against or outside nature," sexual pleasure is equally valid "with a like being, male or female."[6] Even David Hume, writing in the more explicitly Christian ambience of Scotland, argued in his *Enquiry Concerning the Principles of Morals* (1751) that chastity and fidelity were artificial practices grounded in utility rather than natural law and that "Celibacy, Fasting, Penances, Mortification, Self-denial, Humility, Silence, Solitude and the whole Train of monkish Virtues" were actually vices that "serve to no Manner of Purpose," "stupify the Understanding and harden the Heart," and should be rejected by "Men of Sense."[7] Yet Peter Gay is surely right to remind us that Enlightenment thinkers "were still reluctant to engage in a philosophical discussion of sexual behavior."[8] And it is probable that the most significant danger of such a discussion would have been that of under-mining the subordination of women to a sexual contract that bound them legally, economically, and socially to male control.[9] In the eighteenth century's understandings of the female body, female sexuality, and female pleasure we may be able to discern the limits of Enlightenment.

Although this chapter focuses on bodies and sexuality, such topics are only artificially separable from the shapes of domesticity, the constructions of female virtue, and the limitations in women's public power as these were reconfigured across the period. When Laqueur claims that by the late eighteenth century "sex is everywhere precisely because the authority of gender has collapsed,"[10] he means that the new paradigm, in which women are exhorted to "reign" in a domestic sphere dominated by heart rather than head, is alleged to be written on the body, rooted in new understandings of sexual difference that extend from the deepest reaches of individual character to the widest circles of public power. We can see these implications by looking at four related phenomena as they change over the long eighteenth century: the emergent popularity of theories emphasizing sexual differences of body and mind; a newly urgent, pronatalist concept of maternity; changing understandings about female masculinity; and a reconfiguration of patriarchy as *hetero-patriarchy* in tandem with intensified interest both in sapphic subjects and in matters of "choice" in the orientation of female desire. In ways only tangentially addressed here, these developments are often bound up with flexible (if still limited) opportunities for economic and social mobility and the rise of a nonaristocratic elite that will culminate during and after the French Revolution in new understandings of the "rights of man" and in a new class consciousness that will be sharpened in the mid-nineteenth century by social revolution and Marxian thought.

THE BODY OF THE SECOND SEX

As both scientific and popular sources make evident, in early modern Europe the dominant understanding of the relationship between male and female bodies was one of symmetry: that is, of sameness hierarchically understood. In the "great chain of being" that organized living things, women were commonly seen as lesser versions of men. Through the still-prevalent (bio)logic of Aristotle and Galen, every element of the male body had an inferior, but still parallel, female equivalent: menstrual blood was the colder (and unreproductive) counterpart of semen; the clitoris and vagina were versions of the penis; and ovaries were "female testicles" or "stones."

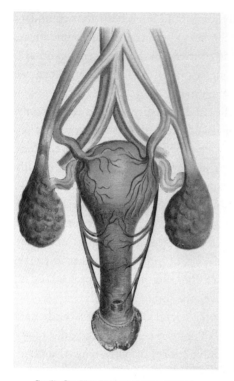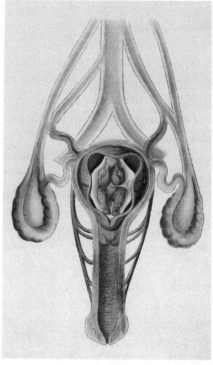

Figur 104a. Die weiblichen Generationsorgane aus dem „Kunstbuche"
von Georg Bartisch. 1575. (Manuscript. Dresdens. C. 291.)

Figur 104b. Die weiblichen Generationsorgane aus dem „Kunstbuche"
von Georg Bartisch. 1575. (Untere Lage.)

FIGURE 2.1: Drawing of the female reproductive organs, by Georg Bartische, "Kunst-buche" (1575). From Fritz Weindler, *Geschichte der gynäkologisch-anatomischen Abbildung* (Dresden: Zahn & Jaensch, 1908), pp. 143 and 145. Credit: Wellcome Library, London. Collection: General Collections, L0043367.

Jane Sharp's *Midwives Book* (1671), the first obstetrical manual written by an English woman, explicitly follows the Galenic path in declaring that "women have all the parts of Generation that Men have, but Mens are outwardly, womens inwardly."[11] Vernacular European languages vividly reflected such assumptions by using common terms for female and male body parts: Sharp describes the "neck of the womb" as simply "a Yard [penis] turned inwards, for they are both one length";[12] the word *vagina* does not even enter English usage until 1682, and the popular and oft-reprinted manual of sex and procreation *Aristotle's Master-Piece* (1690) argues that the clitoris is like the yard in "Scituation [sic], Substance, Composition and Erection" and that the fallopian tubes are "Spermatick Vessels" at each side of the uterus.[13] The doggerel that "women are but men turned outside in," in other words, was the order of the day in scientific as well as in popular literature.

Within this "one-sex" paradigm, moreover, males alone were understood to produce the seeds of generation and thus to carry the full principle of the human soul. The most important (and Aristotelian) medieval theologian, Thomas Aquinas, had asked whether woman should even "have been made in the first production of things" since the very birth of a female was a "mis-begotten" project only made valuable because women were needed as wives and mothers.[14] The full role of the ovum in human reproduction was not understood until the nineteenth century, however; thus *Aristotle's Master-Piece* insists that the ovum is the "Passive Principle" of generation and that "to say that Woman has true Seed, is false and erroneous,"[15] and so philosophers as late as Hegel understood the life principle to reside entirely in males; the female body was a mere receptacle, vulnerable to women's vagaries and to their experiences during pregnancy, but still only the proverbial soil in which the male seed grew. On the other hand, female orgasm was widely considered not merely helpful to but necessary for conception, legitimating female sexuality in a manner that would wane in the nineteenth century.

The belief that women were anatomically lesser versions of men generated parallel assumptions about male and female psychology, morality, and character. When Hamlet famously expostulates of his too-soon-remarried mother, "Frailty, thy name is woman,"[16] he speaks a dominant cultural belief that women are not only physically but also morally, intellectually, and psychologically inferior and, most prominently, less able to control their sexuality. Within this pre-Enlightenment paradigm, women are thus more likely to be unfaithful, more easily tempted by the devil, and less capable of complex moral or intellectual reasoning. The widespread persecutions of women as witches during the early modern period—persecutions under both civil and religious law that persisted into the eighteenth century and involved both Catholic and Protestant communities—found justification in such assumptions about women's moral inferiority.

During the seventeenth century, however, increased literacy (including a dramatic growth in female literacy in the wake of the Protestant Reformation), along with the burgeoning of print culture and the rise of universities, gave a positive potential to the belief that women were copies of men. The concept of male-female similitude became the powerful ground for new arguments that women, afforded men's opportunities for education, could become their intellectual, moral, and spiritual equals. Such arguments, already supported by early Christian thought ("there is neither male nor female . . . in Christ Jesus," as Paul famously wrote in Galatians 3:28), gained attention; the Italian Moderata Fonte, for example, argued in 1600 that "if men and women share the same bodily form, if they are composed of like substance, if they eat and speak in the same way, why should they be thought to differ in courage and intelligence?"[17]

The late seventeenth century witnessed such an intensified accumulation of these arguments that Geneviève Fraisse considers this historical moment to have provided a "fundamental rhetorical break" with the past.[18] François Poulain de la Barre forcefully argued in 1673 that "the mind is no less capable in Women than in Men" since a woman's "brain is altogether like to ours," as are her sensory organs, and that women are thus "as capable as men" of achievements equal to men's in all the arts and sciences.[19] By the early eighteenth century, similar arguments for women's capabilities had become widespread, if not wholly accepted. As Enlightenment thinking flourished and women's education became one of its battle cries, the hierarchical gap between women and men threatened to diminish.

It is in this climate, as Laqueur demonstrates, that biological paradigms of sexual difference began to take hold and the vertical, "one-sex" biology that regarded women as lesser copies of men began yielding to a horizontal "two-sex" system stressing innate differences. Women's bodies and, by extension, women's intellectual and moral qualities came to be seen as distinct from men's in ways that led to a literally sexual politics in which anatomies became "not the sign of but the foundation for civil society."[20] For what better way to co-opt an incipient move toward equality on the basis of sameness than to instantiate as a dominant model the idea of incommensurability between men and women rooted in the body itself? By the end of the eighteenth century, anatomical discourses and representations had shifted, and with them the dominant philosophical and political positions, toward a model that considered men's and women's bodies and minds to be *dissimilar*, each sex naturally tending toward a certain "sphere," with a concomitant shift toward an anatomical vocabulary that emphasized the lack of similitude. The "neck of the womb" was now not a female "yard" but a vagina, the *sheath* for the penis; men's and women's bodies were understood to "fit" together into a heterosexual and more than platonic whole.

Twenty-first-century science has shown us that the two-sex model is no more accurate than its one-sex predecessor, yet the dominant modern understanding, if contested, still emphasizes difference. As Dorothy Sayers quipped in a 1946 essay titled "The Human-Not-Quite-Human," why women are the "'opposite [sex]' I do not know; what is the 'neighbouring sex'?"[21] James Hillman's argument in *The Myth of Analysis* is amply supported by these shifts between sameness and difference: "We see what we believe and prove our beliefs with what we see."[22] Both camps engaged in this kind of circular thinking, but the side that triumphed in the eighteenth century and gave us our modern notions of gender is the side of difference, the side that could posit men as "from Mars" and women as "from Venus." Modern feminisms have likewise embraced both positions, with a "sameness" model dominant in arguments for equality but a "difference feminism" lingering in a range of (conservative) religious and (radical) secular frames.

This recourse to the body as the ground of identity is what Laqueur means when he says that in the eighteenth century biological sex comes to replace social gender as the paradigm for understanding women and men. (Today, by contrast, transgender theory argues for gender to replace sex, on the premise that psychological and social self-definition need not match bodily features.) Although a semantic distinction between sex and gender barely existed in the eighteenth century, arguments for women's equality assumed that differences in social behavior, achievement, or role were socialized differences, the result primarily of a lack of education and opportunity. As women came to prominence as writers, artists, philosophers, classicists, and scientists, biological arguments could preserve male dominance by acknowledging women's intellectual capacities but arguing that women's bodies designed them for different *purposes*. The body itself—not society, not patriarchy—could then become the arbiter and proof of this distinction in roles. Thus, a 1749 English poem, the *Sappho-an*, insists against the evidence of its own narrated acts that "woman was made for man, so nature meant, / And ev'ry fibre answers the intent."[23]

Arguably, no one more fully popularized this idea of incommensurable difference than Jean-Jacques Rousseau. The "egalitarian" promise of Rousseau's influential treatise on education, *Émile* (1762), is that "in the union of the sexes, each alike contributes to the common end, but in different ways." Men and women are "equal" in "what they have in common," but they differ; they are not comparable. "A perfect woman and a perfect man ought not to resemble each other in mind any more than in looks."[24] This promise soon turns out to be only the window dressing for a less balanced arrangement that necessitates women's orientation to men but not men's orientation to women: "One ought to be active and strong, the other passive and weak. One must necessarily will and be able; it suffices that the other put up little resistance. Once this principle is established, it follows that woman is made specially to please man."[25] Indeed, "woman is made to please and to be subjugated"; she "cannot fulfill her purpose in life without [man's] aid, without his goodwill, without his respect." And by virtue of this asymmetrical symbiosis, "every woman wants to please men."[26] In effect, then, women are not women apart from men, and their "power" resides in the informal mechanism of influence. This system by which "the woman [must] obey the man," Rousseau insists, is founded on an "inexorable law of nature," not on "man-made laws,"[27] and so women are powerless to refuse it.

Despite challenges to the Rousseauvian model by men and a few women (of whom Mary Wollstonecraft is the most famous), this notion of sexual complementarity became the bedrock for a domestic and political economy that furthered but also limited the aims of the Enlightenment. Although Catherine Macaulay would argue in 1790 that educated women would "be glad to give up indirect influence for rational privileges; and the precarious sovereignty of an hour . . . for those established rights which, independent of accidental circumstances, may afford protection to the whole sex,"[28] the trend to affirm women's service to a man-made system continued: even as Macaulay was calling for women's "established rights," the German philosopher Johannes Fichte's *The Science of Rights*, written in the 1790s, was advancing a more equivocal argument: Fichte asserts that, since a woman is a "complete human being," she may of course "claim . . . all the rights of men and of citizens which belong to the male sex," but he also suggests that women's orientation of loving service to their husbands must call into question whether "the female sex *can desire* to exercise all her rights."[29] Women are now, in effect, to *choose* the subordination formerly assumed of them, a subordination that Enlightenment thinking could not otherwise fully legitimize. In this way, modernity is able to resolve the contradiction between equality and patriarchy by using discourse to conscript women as subjects of a new but still male-dominant economy that is written on the body itself.

THE REPRODUCTIVE BODY POLITIC

Rousseauvian thought was deeply influential as well in the new politics of reproduction, defining the highest aims of femininity in domestic terms and fostering a sea change in infant care, particularly among the upper classes, by promoting breast-feeding of one's offspring rather than putting children out to nurse. The breast itself was an "unruly signifier" in the age of Enlightenment, as Simon Richter notes; eighteenth-century aesthetic, erotic, and maternalist values converged and conflicted to produce multiple significations for the breast, which was being "colonized" (to use Ruth Perry's term) at once in the new attention to breast-feeding and, conversely, in fashions that emphasized décolletage.[30] And as Madelyn Gutwirth has graphically demonstrated, the breast becomes a primary signifier of liberty in the context of the French Revolution, with the image of a bare-breasted "Marianne" immoralized in

FIGURE 2.2: André Claude Boissier's *Barra couronné par la Liberté* (*Liberty Crowning the [Child Soldier] Barra*) (ca. 1793) deploys a typical image of Liberty as a maiden with bared breast. De Vinck Collection, Biblioteque nationale.

Eugène Delacroix's painting *Liberty Leading the People* (*La Liberté guidant le peuple*, 1830) the most vivid culmination.[31]

Breast-feeding helped to solidify an ideology linking femininity to domesticity and a material practice encouraging women to remain close to home, but it also spoke to concerns about population. Although Rousseau couched his polemic in terms of morals—the breast-fed child was effectively imbibing maternal sentiment—the impetus for feeding one's own offspring responded as well to the high mortality rate of infants suckled by wet nurses, who often

lived in poverty, took in children for remuneration, and may have had a lower
investment than biological parents in any individual child's well-being.[32] The
results in infant mortality were significant; there was an estimated 25 to 40
percent chance that a child sent out to nurse would not return.

This loss of children, especially to the higher classes, caused concern at a
time when population growth seemed imperative. The eighteenth century witnessed a passionate pronatalism as European countries came to recognize the
military, commercial, and industrial value of increased numbers. The number
of single women had risen significantly in the seventeenth century; in the English peerage, for example, well over 20 percent of men and women remained
single, as compared to only 4 percent of males and 9 percent of females for
the cohort born between 1550 and 1574. E.A. Wrigley estimates that about
15 percent of all women in 1680 were single.[33] Beyond long-standing anxieties about women unattached to men—the women most likely, for example,
to be accused of witchcraft—was the perceived urgency for the nation to
reproduce. Britain was especially concerned about population because of a

FIGURE 2.3: Etienne Aubry, *Les adieux à la nourrice* (*Farewell to the Wet Nurse*)
(1776–77). Clark Institute of Art. Photo by Michael Agee.

disadvantageous relationship to the Continent: at 4.9 million around 1700, Britain comprised only 6.8 percent of western Europe's population, while its major enemies, France and Spain, numbered 21.9 million and 8.5 million respectively. Given Britain's interests in an imperialist and mercantile capitalism, the population problem—in terms of workers, consumers, merchants, and military might—was significant. Extraordinary changes in the later eighteenth century testify to British success in reversing its demographic practices. During the second half of the eighteenth century, Britain grew at more than twice the rate of the first half, with the population rising to 11.5 million by 1820; during the same period, France's population grew only to 30.5 million and Spain's to 14 million.

This "population revolution" was primarily a function not of greater health but of greater fecundity. Women's age at first marriage dropped from twenty-six to just over twenty-three, along with a startling 50 percent decrease in the number of women who never married.[34] Illegitimate births rose from 2 percent to 8 percent, with as many as a quarter of first births occurring outside wedlock as opposed to an earlier 10 percent. Abelove has speculated on the basis of these data that "cross-sex genital intercourse" became a much more common practice during the later eighteenth century in correlation with "a dramatic rise in virtually all indices of production," and that disciplinary regimes of production encouraged genital intercourse as a dominant sexual practice where in the past a range of sexual behaviors had been commonplace.[35] Given the epidemic rate of venereal disease in eighteenth-century Europe, the consequences to health were not insignificant.

If we look at the convergence of increased marriage rates, lower age at marriage, higher fertility, more breast-feeding, and probably more genital intercourse not only in England but across the European continent, the consequences for women's bodies are fairly obvious. Women's bodies were serving national economies in ways that not only determined their daily activities but also intensified their vulnerability to illness and death, particularly at a time when physician-managed birth in hospitals, with its attendant dangers of puerperal infection, had begun to displace the assistance of midwives. All of these trends helped to solidify the importance of defining women through the reproductive and maternal body and thereby to intensify the idea of their "natural" difference from men.

It is worth adding that throughout the age of Enlightenment and despite incitements to "libertine" practices, the sexual double standard that more readily ignored adultery and fornication by men while condemning it in women remained relatively fixed. We will never know what most men and women did in bed, of course: only pregnancy, venereal illness, or outright discovery in the act can provide proof positive of sexual behaviors, and none of these of course gives proof of a woman's sexual *desire*. But while a man like James Boswell might leave in his *London Journal* a record of sexual engagements with his "Louisa," the fact that "Louisa" is a pseudonym already suggests how little a woman would want even her heterosexual behaviors outside marriage to be known; Amanda Vickery in *The Gentleman's Daughter* marks the extent to which codes of propriety censored out discussions of sex even from women's private letters to husbands, relations, and intimate friends.[36] Indeed, the notion that the family would now be bonded through amity and serve as a model for civil society arguably made adultery a newly significant *secular* problem rather than only a religious or moral one. Female adultery was especially chastised as decadence came to be associated with the high aristocracy and virtue with the emergent gentry in a new preoccupation, as Foucault noted, with the morality of the classes that ruled.[37] Hence the venom heaped, for example, on Marie Antoinette, whose putative adultery was seen to signify much deeper levels of personal and political corruption; but hence, too, the hostility toward England's Prince Regent for the libertine behaviors that were associated with his mistreatment of his wife. By the end of the century, the notion of virtuous, civic-minded motherhood that spread across Europe and the new United States emphasized women's important—but entirely nonformal—place in the social order, not only revealing but constituting and policing the limits of Enlightenment.

FEMALE MASCULINITY: FROM LEWD TO LESBIAN

Given this new double investment in bodily difference and fecund maternity arguably signified by the specular prominence of the breast, it is not surprising that notions of masculinity in women would also be reconfigured as a component of Enlightenment approaches to the female body and female sexuality and thus to core understandings of gender. In the sixteenth and seventeenth centuries, male effeminacy and female masculinity were parallel and primarily heterosexual ideas. Men became "effeminate" by being too much with women; thus, Romeo laments that Juliet's "beauty hath made me effeminate / And in my temper soften'd valour's steel!"[38] By the same token, the early modern women criticized in the famous English pamphlet *Hic Mulier* (1620) for dressing mannishly in "broad-brimmed hats" and carrying stilettos are charged with behaving "loosely, indiscreetly, wantonly and most unchastely"—toward men.[39] By a similar logic, nearly all the amazons who populate seventeenth-century literature end up with men when they end up with anyone, as do most of the female pirates and soldiers of both history and balladry, even when women fall in love with them.⁴⁰ The cross-dressing Queen Christina of Sweden (1626–89), who left significant evidence of her inclinations for women, was likewise accused in her own day of lewd congress with men.⁴¹ By the same logic, concerns about women who passed as men focused primarily on the threat that male company was assumed to pose to their virginity. And as Sylvie Steinberg notes, the majority of women arrested for cross-dressing were either prostitutes or, more commonly, women seeking a way out of poverty through masculine mobility and employment; the fact of their cross-dressing did not in itself imply anything homoerotic.⁴² In short, within Renaissance logic, female masculinity and the lewdest behavior toward men are more than compatible; women who were accused of being like men were also perceived as desiring them because sexual desire was not yet predicated on polar difference. If this version of female masculinity seems queer to us today, that is because we live on this side of the eighteenth century, when a link between female homoeroticism and female masculinity has been naturalized.

Although female masculinity did not in early modernity normatively connote the homoerotic, female homoeroticism *did* normatively connote female masculinity, usually of a quite literal sort, since biological discourse had long sought in a mannish body the explanation for female same-sex desire. Early modern treatises on hermaphrodites, for example, posit the hermaphrodite as the figure and cause of sexual ambiguities and transgressions, whether they follow the Hippocratic notion of the hermaphrodite as an intermediate sex neither male *nor* female or the Aristotelian model of the hermaphroditic body as genitally male *and* female. Scientists routinely claimed that girls and women, particularly but not only in adolescence, could turn into men through the descent of male genitalia; Antonio de Torquemada's *Jardin de flores curiosas* (1570), for example, enumerates numerous ancient and modern examples of girls and women whose male genitals suddenly became visible.⁴³ Equally prominent was the notion that the "tribade"—the ancient name commonly given to a woman who had sex with women—was endowed with an enlarged clitoris. By this logic, indeed, a woman accused of tribadism might be let off the legal hook if her genitals proved unspectacular: Patricia Crawford and Sara Mendelson report an English case from 1680 in which a lawsuit against a cross-dressing woman for "bigamously" marrying another woman was dismissed after seven midwives found the defendant to have "normal" genitalia.⁴⁴ Importantly, the intense discursive energy expended to account for female–female desire by way of a male body finds scant parallel in discussions about men: the tendency to

equate sex with penetration has the queer consequence of corporeally norma-
tizing sex between men, so that "in order to act like a sodomite, a man did not
have to be different from other men."[45] In the eighteenth century, however, the
pressures of a two-sex model would also bind sexuality and gender to revive
the ancient notion of the "molly"—the man presumed to be the passive and
feminine partner in a male-male alliance.

As eighteenth-century science came to emphasize the incommensurability of male and female bodies, however, the idea that women could turn
into men through the descent of inner organs became discredited. Empirical
skepticism, bolstered by the decline of humoral theory,[46] made it increasingly
difficult to explain female same-sex desire through anatomical masculinity.
Even scientists like James Parsons, who did see the enlarged (or what we
might now call "intersex") clitoris as enabling homoerotic relations, argued
in his *Mechanical and Critical Enquiry into the Nature of Hermaphrodites*
(1741) that women who consorted with women did so not simply "from a
mere natural Inclination" but to avoid the "danger of being expos'd" through
"that Accident, that is the necessary Consequence of dealing with Men."[47]
The Italian anatomist Giovanni Bianchi makes much of the ordinary female
body's capacity for same-sex desire in his *Breve Storia della vita di Catterina
Vizzani* (1744) when he describes Catterina, who dressed as a man and pursued women, as having both "prominent Breasts" and, most important, a clitoris that "was not pendulous, or of any extraordinary Size," as was claimed
in ancient accounts of "all those Females, who, among the *Greeks*, were
called *Tribades* . . .; on the contrary, her's [sic] was so far from any unusual
Magnitude, that it was not to be ranked among the middle-sized, but the
smaller."[48] Yet the genitally unusual female body does not disappear from
European discourse; it is most frequently relocated to racial Others in an intensification of earlier practices. "Some of the *Asiatick*, as well as the *African*
Nations," says Parsons, tend to produce women with enlarged genitals, and
on this basis he thus justifies the cultures that "wisely cut or burn them off
while Girls are young."[49] Sharp's 1671 *Midwives Book* has already suggested
this double standard: "lewd women" who "have their Clitoris greater, and
hanging out more than others have" and who "have endeavoured to use it as
men do theirs" are "frequent" in "the Indies, and Egypt," while Sharp "never
heard but of one in this Country, if there be any they will do what they can
for shame to keep it close."[50] Within this ethnic logic, it is not surprising that,
even as late as 1810, a Scottish judge dismissed the possibility that two British women could have been sexually intimate: "They import the crime of one
woman giving another the clitoris, which *in this country* is not larger than the

nipple of the breast and is, furthermore, immersed between the labia of the pudenda. Therefore, as expressed in language of the Greeks and Romans, it is a crime which, in the general case, it is impossible *in this country* to commit" (my emphasis).[51]

But the erosion of this genital model leaves a disturbing remainder: if there is no anatomical mark of sapphism, then *any* woman is a potential sapphist. It is thus not surprising that, just when anatomical explanations for the tribade falter, there emerges a stronger association of the homoerotic woman with visible masculinity. Where the masculine marker written *in* the body has failed, a new masculine marker gets written *on* that body—a marker through clothing, stature, features, skills—in short, some signifier that sets apart the woman who desires women as manlike and queer and thus allows others to identify and beware of her. In this way, heterosexuality can be maintained and heterosexual desire normalized as a characteristic of gender, and a prototype of the modern sapphic subject-of-representation begins to emerge.

Such a figure is already present in Samuel Richardson's *The History of Sir Charles Grandison* (1754) in the person of Miss Barnevelt, who first enters the text as one of a trio of imperfect women against which the heroine, Harriet Byron, will be the ideal: Miss Cantillon is "very pretty" but "visibly proud, affected, and conceited"; Miss Clements has a "fine understanding" but is "plain"; and Miss Barnevelt is "a lady of masculine features, and whose mind bely'd not those features, for she has the character of being loud, bold, free, even fierce when opposed; and affects at all times such airs of contempt of her own sex, that one almost wonders at her condescending to wear petticoats."[52] This mannish woman—not incidentally also a self-styled intellectual with interest in the masculine field of the classics—is "a fine tall *portly* young lady" who is also manifestly sapphic: "No-body, it seems, thinks of an *husband* for Miss Barnevelt. She is sneeringly spoken of rather as a *young fellow*, than as a woman; and who will one day look out for a *wife* for herself." Indeed, the "odd creature" is soon making passes at Harriet: "Miss Barnevelt said, she had from the moment I first enter'd beheld me with the eye of a Lover. And freely taking my hand, squeezed it."[53] Later, Harriet is "extremely disconcerted," "surpris'd and offended" when Barnevelt praises her body "and then clasping one of her mannish arms round me, she kissed my cheek."[54] At one point, Harriet attempts to limit Miss Barnevelt's possibilities: she imagines Barnevelt with "her Lucy" and immediately decides, "Upon my word I will not let her have a Lucy—She shall have a brother *man* to write to, not a woman, and he shall have a fierce name."[55] Richardson, too, refuses a future for Miss Barnevelt; having served her purpose as a negative example, she falls out of the narrative entirely. Her presence advances not the *plot* but the *message*: women beware woman when that woman is "masculine." Maria Edgeworth's *Belinda* (1801) offers yet another such portrait in the gun-toting Harriot Freke, whose "wild oddity" of "countenance," "dashing audacity," "bold masculine arms," and comfort "in male attire" all mark her as "a young rake" with nothing "feminine about her."[56] Freke is Barnevelt intensified; she "champion[s]" the "Rights of Women," she speaks about the years "when I was a schoolboy—girl—I should say," and she is clearly a woman that "no man of any taste could think of" for a mistress or a wife.[57] But while Miss Barnevelt simply disappears from *Sir Charles Grandison*, Freke must get her comeuppance: her legs cut up in a "man-trap" during one of her mean-spirited escapades, it is "hinted, that the beauty of her legs would be spoiled, and that she would never more be able to appear to advantage in man's apparel": she is, in effect, castrated into femininity.[58]

In this way, the woman who is seen as transgressively masculine in appearance begins to be quite firmly associated with the sapphic rather than with the promiscuously heterosexual, and a bond between gender transgression and homoeroticism begins to cement. By the end of the century, the mere mention that a woman is "masculine" might connote the sapphic in a way that would have been much less likely a century earlier. This shift in understandings of female masculinity thus exposes the very *making* of the relationship between gender and sexuality, supporting David Valentine's claim that this relationship is "ultimately ethnographic and historical rather than purely theoretical."[59]

From early modernity through the eighteenth century and into our own day, however, a crucial constant remains: the association of female masculinity with any transgression of gender role. Thus Kant writes in his *Observations on the Feeling of the Beautiful and Sublime* (1764) that the great classicist Anne LeFèvre Dacier "might as well even have had a beard," since she was engaged in a man's intellectual project.[60] And Rousseau cleverly insists that in order to achieve any measure of equality, women must forgo all behaviors or traits associated with masculinity: "The more women want to resemble" men, Rousseau threatens, "the less women will govern them, and then men will truly be the masters."[61] Under the pressure of a two-body construction of gender, then, female masculinity begins to lose its legendary heroic force; as several scholars have noted, the popularity of female cross-dressing onstage and in popular culture starts to wane toward the end of the eighteenth century; the woman in man's clothes who once performed brave service as a soldier or gave delight as an actress came under the pall of deeper imprecations of deviance.

Yet there remains throughout the eighteenth century a recognition that the "feminine" woman is capable of homoerotic pleasure and must therefore be directed toward relationships with men. A recognition of the sapphic potential in all women helps to explain why eighteenth-century cultural production will continue to grapple with female homoeroticism even, and perhaps especially, in its newest and increasingly popular literary genre, the novel. By the end of the century, the sapphic will play into a political dynamic as well, particularly in France, as contests over female power resolve themselves in a *fraternité* that transforms *ancien régime* paternalism into the rule of men on the basis of their very manhood and relegates women to the supporting role of "republican motherhood."

(NOVEL) LESBIAN SUBJECTS

The changed understandings of bodies that I have been describing support the premise that modernity as the European Enlightenment configured it entailed a necessary reshaping of gender relations to emphasize difference. What has often been erased from the scholarly picture is the agency of female homoeroticism, or what I call the sapphic, in this re-formation. A full understanding of sex, gender, and sexuality in the age of Enlightenment requires a deep look at female homoeroticism both as a flashpoint for gender concerns and as a potential site of resistance.

We will not find what we are looking for, however, in overt and public information from women themselves. As the historian Margaret Hunt reminds us, "the evidence on real flesh-and-blood eighteenth-century lesbians is tantalizingly meager."[62] While a few women did live publicly as couples, as we shall see, I know of only one case outside the coercive context of a legal prosecution in which a woman living in the long eighteenth century acknowledged in writing that she had sex with other women: she is the Yorkshire gentlewoman Anne Lister (1791–1840), and her admissions come in the doubly private form of diary entries written in code. Certainly women did not *declare* themselves to be tribades or sapphists. In contrast to prosecutions of men for sodomy, there were few trials against women in the eighteenth century, and sexual behavior between women rarely took place in public settings. But in published discourse—whether literary, political, scientific, or popular—we find considerable attention to sapphic subjects throughout the Enlightenment.

In fact, cultural investment in female homoeroticism began to burgeon in the late sixteenth century, first in France but soon also in England, Spain, Italy, and the United Provinces.[63] By 1600 writings in a wide range of genres, from travel narratives to legal commentaries to poetry and plays, were already representing women in primary relation to other women, whether explicitly or

implicitly sexual. Some of these representations are sanguine, some condemna-
tory, some simply matter of fact. Some are ethnographic in purpose, survey-
ing with the eye of the explorer one of the strange human phenomena that
Nathaniel Wanley called the "wonders of the little world."[64] Others operate
on a "metamorphic" dynamic in which female–female relations are resolved
into female–male ones, and still others allow female–female relations to prevail.

All of these forms are played out in the genre of the novel, where the sapphic makes a surprisingly strong showing and arguably even underwrites the
novel as a social project. Especially if we attend to narration rather than only
to textual events, it is possible to argue that female same-sex desire shapes
the eighteenth-century novel in unexpected and important ways. Such a claim
might well seem counterintuitive, for scholars have persuasively argued that
the "rise" of the European novel is deeply implicated in the constitution both
of a heterosexual subject and of the "domestic" woman as its fictional linch-
pin. But especially if we recall the gratuitous appearance of Miss Barnevelt in
Richardson's *Sir Charles Grandison*, a more complex textual story—both in
and of the novel—comes to light, suggesting that what Michael McKeon has
called the "secret history of domesticity" may carry the deeper secret of domesticity's dependence on same-sex desire.[65]

It is beyond the possibilities of this essay to trace the full imbrication of
the sapphic and the novel across the long eighteenth century. We would find
a surprising number of early novels in which female–female relations are both
structurally and thematically significant. These range from erotic fictions such
as the early *Académie des dames* (ca. 1680) and *Vénus dans le cloître* (1683),
in which dialogue between women structures a sexual initiation that is both
verbal and physical, to episodic adventure novels in the picaresque tradition
that allow women to pursue other women and often to end up with them.[66]
Of these, perhaps the most unusual is the anonymous 1744 *Travels and Adventures of Mademoiselle de Richelieu, who made the tour of Europe in men's
cloaths.*[67] Reversing the metamorphic pattern in which one woman's desire for
a cross-dressed woman is warded off when the cross-dresser bares her breasts
and reveals her femininity, *Mademoiselle de Richelieu* creates a love story in
which the cross-dressed Alithea bares her breast to the lovely widow Arabella
only to learn to her advantage that Arabella has sworn off men. The two women
acknowledge their love for one another, toy briefly with (fraudulent) marriage,
and travel around Europe disguised as men, eventually resuming female dress
and spending their (aristocratically privileged) lives dividing their time between their respective French estates. Henry Fielding's *The Female Husband*
(1746), following soon thereafter, not only discredits its cross-dressed lesbian

FIGURE 2.4: Illustration of the whipping of Mary Hamilton. The caption reads: "The prisoner being convicted of this base and scandalous crime was sentenced to be publicly and severely whipped four [sic] several times in 4 Market Towns and to be imprisoned for 6 Months." Frontispiece to *The Surprising Adventures of a Female Husband* (London: 1808). The Carl H. Pforzheimer Collection of Shelley and His Circle. The New York Public Library.

character but suggests that cross-dressing is itself a charade whose effectiveness has passed; his fictional Mary Hamilton, loosely modeled on a woman of that name who was prosecuted in England for fraudulent same-sex marriage, is exposed and resoundingly punished not only for marrying another woman but for using that marriage to gain a financial reward and higher status.

The prolific tradition of more or less "philosophical pornography" usually represents sexual relations between women either as circumstantial (a function of the cloister or the sharing of a bed) or as preliminary (they prepare a woman for a man, occur in his presence, or involve him directly). In all these instances the sapphic presents itself as either substitute or supplement. Fanny Hill, the protagonist of John Cleland's *Memoirs of a Woman of Pleasure* (1749), for instance, is quick to tell us after her very satisfying initiation into sex by Phoebe Ayers that once she sees male genitalia, she immediately longs for "more solid food."[68] Yet Phoebe also turns out to have an "arbitrary taste" for young women that compels Fanny, as narrator, to insist, in double negatives, "Not that [Phoebe] hated men or did not even prefer them to her own sex; but when she met with such occasions as this was, a satiety of enjoyments in the common road, perhaps to a secret bias, inclined her to make the most of pleasure wherever she could find it, without distinction of sexes." The circumlocutions in this passage, and its excessive reassurance about Phoebe's heterosexuality, lie in tension here with the extended description of her seduction of Fanny and the suggestion of her "secret bias."[69]

But there is a subtler and more pervasive way in which the sapphic invades the eighteenth-century novel: by setting women in a structurally intimate relationship that is discursively homoerotic insofar as one woman confides her erotic secrets to another. Moreover, several of these novels seem unable to sustain a purely instrumental role for the female confidante, who returns to haunt the novel at its close. And several domestic novels structure their narration to infect a heterosexual love plot; both the playful ending of Marie-Jeanne Riccoboni's *Letters of Juliette Catesby to Her Friend Henriette Campley* (1759) and the tragic resolution of Frances Sheridan's *Memoirs of Miss Sidney Bidulph* (1761) emphasize a resurgence of the female friend.

This imbrication of domestic heterosexuality with the sapphic characterizes—and arguably queers—the mid-eighteenth century's two most famous novels, Samuel Richardson's *Clarissa* (1747–48) and Jean-Jacques Rousseau's *Julie, ou la Nouvelle Héloise* (1762). Each of these epistolary novels includes a female confidante resistant to marriage who professes an excess of love for the heroine. Anna Howe's pledge to Clarissa—"I love thee as never woman loved another"—is repeated throughout Richardson's long text, but the novel effectively rejects the implications of that love on the level of story while requiring it as a narrative device. Separated from Clarissa for 1,500 pages, Anna turns up only when Clarissa is a corpse. In what she herself calls a "wild frenzy," Anna repeatedly kisses Clarissa's lips, as if attempting to bring her back to life.[70] Julie's cousin Claire is likewise set up as a loving confidante in Rousseau's novel, and Claire shares the dying Julie's bed; Julie's husband reports seeing "the two friends motionless, locked in each other's embrace; the one in a faint, and the other expiring"; Claire has to be locked away to stop her from "thr[owing] herself upon [Julie's] body, . . . endeavor[ing] to revive it, press[ing] it, . . . call[ing] it loudly by a thousand passionate names."[71]

Both Anna and Claire attempt to create a kind of posthumous sapphic afterplot. In *La Nouvelle Héloise*'s last letter, Claire insists that Julie lives on, that "her coffin does not contain all of her . . . it awaits the rest of its prey"—Claire

herself—and "it will not wait for long."[72] And Anna imagines that she and
Clarissa "may . . . meet and rejoice together where no villainous *Lovelaces*, no
hard-hearted *relations*, will e'er shock our innocence, or ruffle our felicity."[73]
Thus two of the eighteenth century's most widely read novels embed their heterosexual plots in a sapphic structure that presses beyond the plot's ostensible
closure to turn death into a kind of fantasy of same-sex marriage. Such texts
suggest that the story of the heterosexual subject that the eighteenth-century
novel seems bent on consolidating is also the story of the failure or at least
incompleteness of that task.

This new attention to female homoeroticism within the novel is not manifestly the effect of an increase in same-sex coupling—as far as we know. In
midcentury England, women who lived openly as couples were rare and potentially suspect; thus, Elizabeth Montagu worried about the intimate household
her sister Sarah Scott had formed with Lady Barbara Montagu (no relation)
and wrote to Scott, concerning another couple who had decided to cohabit,
that "making such a parade of their affection" would "add to the jests the
men made on that friendship" and ultimately "give occasion to Lies."[74] But
in 1778 two elite women, Lady Eleanor Butler and Sarah Ponsonby, the "Ladies of Llangollen," made a very public show of their affection by going off
together from Ireland to Wales. Their elopement, to which their families un-
happily acceded after foiling a first attempt, had as a consequence their virtual
abandonment by these relations in terms of financial and moral support, and
their decision to live as a couple in an isolated village in Wales enabled what
may be Britain's first undisguised site for same-sex marriage. In response to
this vulnerable position—one perhaps intensified by their being (Anglo) Irish
rather than strictly English and, in Butler's case, Catholic—the Ladies of Llangollen shielded themselves with an aggressive performance of their upper-class
status and with a political conservatism that was remarkable even for women
of their rank. But they also shared bed, board, and belongings; named one of
their dogs Sapho; signed their correspondence jointly; called each other "my
Beloved" and "my Better half"; and when they went visiting insisted on returning to their "State bedchamber" however late the hour.[75] Although their
elopement caused some scandal in Ireland and sporadic suspicions thereafter,
for most of their forty years of "delicious . . . retirement" these Ladies of
Llangollen lived not simply with impunity but with celebrity, escaping public
suggestion that they were sexually intimate.[76] Their pastoral retreat with its
renowned gardens became a site of pilgrimage; they received dozens of distinguished visitors, corresponded with men and women of rank and of letters, and were iconized in poems, from a sonnet by William Wordsworth to

FIGURE 2.5: Posthumous (1831) engraving of Lady Eleanor Butler and Sarah Ponsonby, the "Ladies of Llangollen." The accuracy of the portraiture has been questioned. The Carl H. Pforzheimer Collection of Shelley and His Circle, the New York Public Library, Astor, Lenox and Tilden Foundations.

Anna Seward's epic "Llangollen Vale." By drawing attention to themselves on their own terms, Butler and Ponsonby effectively turned *themselves* into status symbols of idyllic friendship in an idyllic setting. Within a different class and national framework, the wildly popular French actress Françoise-Marie-Antoinette-Josephe Saucerotte, known as Mademoiselle Raucourt, also lived openly in serial liaisons with the soprano Sophie Arnould, with the German performer Jeanne Souck, and finally with Henriette de Ponty, to whom she left her house and possessions. Although Raucourt was vilified during the early Revolution through her connections with aristocrats, when she died in 1815 admirers stormed the church where a priest had refused her a Catholic burial on the grounds of her sexual transgressions, a sign of public fidelity to France's most famous "tribade."

Raucourt's popularity may be explained in part by a liberating current that underscored the potential of women to form alliances of solidarity across rank. For if sex-as-bodily-difference is replacing gender as the patriarchal bedrock, then a woman who loves another woman is affirming the noncompatibility of men and women and thereby giving an ironic turn to the notion of "natural difference." Significantly, many sapphic texts of the late eighteenth century emphasize a language of similitude: women are "our kind," "my counterparts," "my likenesses," as if men are now a different species. This notion of similitude thus poses the possibility that sapphic sisterhood might also carry a blueprint for a revolutionary equality. The most powerful example among several texts in this vein is the very popular *Confessions d'une jeune fille* or *Confessions de Mlle Sapho*, first published in Pidansat de Mairobert's *Espion anglais* and reprinted at least eight times between 1779 and 1797. In part the compelling first-person narrative of a young girl from the provinces, in part prurient peep show, in part an ethnography so convincing that some scholars continue to see it as a true accounting, the *Confessions* also offers a revolutionary manifesto, running over twenty pages and put in the mouth of Raucourt, that describes a harmonious, peaceful, and disciplined social order responsible for the well-being of all its citizens. Women of every class are admitted, from aristocrats to *philosophes*, actresses, and girls of low birth. Relationships between the women are actively erotic but also tenderly mutual; the society "safeguards the virtue of girls and widows" and offers consolation in old age. Since husbandly philandering, pregnancy and childbirth, and sexual and physical violence are unknown, there are said to be no contradictions "between feelings and faculties: the soul and body march together." The community's moral model is the large happy family: charity toward the unfortunate is a "distinctive characteristic," manners are "gentle and sociable," all goods are held in common, and all distinctions between rich and poor abolished.[77] In short, the community is founded on an equality that is itself premised on likeness. The 1789 *Chevalières errantes, ou les deux sosies femelles* also creates a secret society of "sisters" clearly modeled on the *anandrynes*, and although the young female protagonists eventually marry their male suitors and the "sect" turns out to be a fiction, the suitors are required to join a new secret society in which both men and women must swear to be faithful, loyal, and benevolent.[78]

Yet another 1789 novel, *La Curieuse impertinente*, locates its sapphic sect in a convent, where the happiest of women are also the most considerate, who care for and educate one another in addition to exploring together nature's "hidden mysteries."[79]

From the 1770s, however, virulent representations of the sapphic as a sign of excessive female power began attaching to aristocrats in several countries and especially to the French queen Marie Antoinette and her intimates. Political antisapphism was by no means brand new in the late eighteenth century: there were plenty of murmurs about "dark Deeds at Night" in 1708, for example, when England's Queen Anne banished Sarah Jennings Churchill, Duchess of Marlborough, prominent in Whig circles and the queen's intimate friend since childhood, in favor of a lower-ranked lady-in-waiting, Abigail Masham, whose cousin Robert Harley was an influential Tory member of parliament.[80] But specters of what I call "sapphic separatism" erupted with a vengeance in late eighteenth-century France in what amounted to a national anxiety about female power. The troubles began soon after 1774, when Louis XVI ascended the French throne and the childless Austrian Marie Antoinette became the queen; it was also the year when French women were admitted to the Freemasons, that widespread secret society of powerful men. By 1775 one literary journal was rumoring that there would soon be a "Lodge of Lesbos" with initiations into sapphic rites, and the French order of women masons, dubbed the "English Amazonia," was alleged to require men to "submit to the female order."[81]

In that climate, novels, pamphlets, and caricatures began a campaign of mockery in which highborn women in and beyond France, but particularly those associated with the French court, were represented as sapphists who not only had sex with women but were "persuaded that men were by nature women's inferiors" and who arrogated to themselves both "high privilege" and "limitless power."[82] One early pamphlet portrayed Marie Antoinette's close friend, the Duchesse de Polignac, as ready to wipe out thousands of French citizens in exchange for that power; "Paris is overflowing with people," she says, "let's purge them . . . and ensure our bliss."[83] In a 1789 pamphlet, this same duchess and her "kind" are charged with having "collaborated in swelling the national debt" and turning the state "upside down."[84] In this way the entire complicated financial and political mess of late *ancien régime* France is effectively blamed on sapphic relationships. A particularly scurrilous pamphlet of 1791 lambastes Raucourt as well, calling her "passion for the clitoris" an "insult to nature" and insisting that heterosexuality is "nature's design."[85]

The dramatic shifts in understandings of the sapphic during the later age of Enlightenment are vividly represented in successive entries in the few, mostly French dictionaries that dared to include the term *tribade*. Seventeenth- and early eighteenth-century definitions stressed the individual woman, who is understood to be "imitating" men or "abusing" other women. In 1755 the *Manuel lexique* defines *tribades* collectively, and in sneering terms, as "lascivious women who try to obtain among themselves pleasures they can receive only from the other sex."[86] By the 1780s and 1790s, French–English dictionaries such as *The Royal Pocket Dictionary* and *Chambaud's* define the *tribade* in a more euphemistic but also potentially more political manner as "a woman that loves her own sex";[87] the quick shift in Nugent's *New Pocket Dictionary* from "female sodomite" in 1781 to "woman-lover" in 1787 captures the change.[88] But at the waning end of the Revolution, in 1799, Nugent defines the *tribade* simply and euphemistically as "a bad woman."[89] In a similar spirit, the *Dictionnaire de l'Académie française*, while maintaining its standard definition of *tribade* as a woman who takes advantage of another woman, adds for the first time in 1798 the warning to "avoid this word."[90] As the age of Enlightenment passes and the new two-sex system takes on the role of shaping political as well personal identity, female-female relations thus officially become "matters not fit to be mention'd," as Fielding had called them in 1746.[91]

* * *

Dror Wahrman has persuasively argued that a move from "gender play" to "gender panic" shaped civil society and forged the "modern self."[92] The new polarities of gender that take women into the nineteenth century both refashion and echo formations of earlier periods. Certainly Napoleon repeats Aquinas when he proclaims that women are "but machines for producing children."[93] Yet Napoleon also wrote a legal code that allowed sisters, daughters, mothers, and wives some increase of rights in areas of property, divorce, and inheritance. Such examples remind us that the age of Enlightenment both gave and took away: if it did not grant women legitimate power, it did offer increased literacy, access to education, greater dignity, and some acknowledgment of rights. Only in the twenty-first century are we beginning to emerge from the Enlightenment legacy of a two-sex social order grounded in compulsory heterosexuality and the subordination of women to a domestic economy dominated by men, but we can find in the Enlightenment's ideals, and especially in those values of equality and justice that conflicted with its own treatment of women, a rationale for the increased gender and sexual equality that is now beginning to emerge.

CHAPTER THREE

Religion and Popular Beliefs: Visionary Women in the Age of Enlightenment

PHYLLIS MACK

I told him [Samuel Johnson] I had been that morning at a meeting of the people called Quakers, where I had heard a woman preach. [Johnson replied,] "Sir, a woman's preaching is like a dog's walking on his hinder legs. It is not done well; but you are surprized to find it done at all."
—James Boswell's *Life of Samuel Johnson*, July 31, 1763[1]

This is the story of two women who lived and preached in the parish of Madeley, Shropshire, in the second half of the eighteenth century. Abiah Darby (1716–93) arrived in 1745 as the second wife of Abraham Darby II when he took over the management of the family-owned ironworking company on his brother's death.[2] Her parents were Quaker ministers in Durham, and her relatives were coal fitters and mining engineers, so she was comfortable in the atmosphere of an industrializing town and wrote knowledgeably about the techniques of smelting iron and transporting coal.[3] In 1751 she began traveling as a minister, accompanied by a female friend and occasionally by

her husband. These journeys were carried out mostly on horseback, often for
months at a time, in most parts of England and at all seasons of the year.
Like most eighteenth-century Quaker leaders, she preached at Quaker meetings, conducted family visits, and visited coreligionists who were in prison for
refusing to pay tithes (church taxes). But she also engaged in activities that
were outside the pale for a respectable eighteenth-century woman, Quaker or
otherwise: preaching before army garrisons or town mayors or out of doors at
the market cross. Once she walked into an Anglican church when services were
in progress and upbraided the minister, John Fletcher, for what she called his
"copyhold or priest craft."[4] She also invited him to dinner and lent him books.
Near the end of her life, she wrote to Fletcher, with whom she had pursued a
friendly theological debate over many years, proposing to speak to his congre-
gation after services about a plan to solicit donations and establish a network
of Sunday schools.[5]

Down the hill from the Darby house stood the Anglican and Methodist
church and parsonage,[6] presided over by John and Mary Fletcher. Mary Bosanquet Fletcher (1739–1815) belonged to a wealthy Essex family (her brother
was governor of the Bank of England) and converted to Methodism at age
eighteen.[7] In the following decades she founded and managed an orphanage
and home for impoverished women, sustained a vast written correspondence,
and composed several short works. She was one of the earliest Methodist
women to preach in public and the author of the only extant formal sermon by
a woman. In 1781 she married John Fletcher and moved the following year to
Madeley, where they carried out what amounted to a joint ministry in a parish
of a few thousand people, mainly laborers and colliers (miners). After John's
death in 1785 she continued to run the local Methodist Society, preaching
every Sunday morning before services, conducting parish business, and ap-
pointing ministers, the only female leader in early Methodism to exercise such
authority. She died in 1815.

So we have before us two exceptional women, married to exceptional
men, highly eminent in their respective religious communities, public preachers and published writers, who lived at the center of two momentous historical events, the early Industrial Revolution and the evangelical revival. Both
were wealthy—Mary by birth, Abiah by marriage—and both experienced the
same long widowhood of about thirty years, when they continued to be active as public figures. They knew each other, though their religious habits and
the twenty-two-year difference in their ages probably precluded an intimate
friendship. Mary was apparently intimidated by Abiah's daughter-in-law Deborah Darby (also a preacher), writing in her journal in 1783, "As I was one

MRS. MARY FLETCHER,
Widow of the Revd J. Fletcher
late Vicar of Madely Shropshire

FIGURE 3.1: Portrait of Mary Bosanquet Fletcher as an elderly woman and Methodist preacher. Reproduced with permission from the Methodist Collections at Drew University.

morning at prayer, I thought of one of our neighbours, (a speaker among the Friends,) who was gone to Ireland. It was suggested, [to my mind] should I be called thither, could I resolve to go? It really seemed I could not. The sea, to me ever terrible, appeared then doubly so, and I groaned under the thought,— where is faith and resignation?"[8] Abiah wrote a condolence letter to Mary after John Fletcher's death in eloquent and conventional Quaker language: "I trust thy mind is so center'd upon the living Rock and Jesus, that no storms or oppositions can hurt or molest thy safe hiding place! I salute thee in a degree of that divine love which at seasons the Lord is pleased to touch our hearts with, one towards another . . . [signed, your] very affectionate and sympathizing friend."[9] Five years later, after Mary had been a dinner guest at the Darbys', Deborah remarked that Mary was "a solid and truly pious woman" but "rather too full of conversation."[10]

As exemplars of female leadership in their respective communities, Abiah Darby and Mary Fletcher can teach us a good deal about the relationship between modernization and religion. We can learn how the concerns of middle-class Quakers—technological innovators, traders, and industrialists—differed from those of Methodists, whose legacy, according to some historians, was the creation of a docile laboring class. We can observe how the religious sensibility of a prominent Methodist, whose theology emphasized Jesus's suffering and atonement, differed from that of a Quaker, whose theology emphasized the Inner Light in the depths of every soul. We can compare the public persona of Quakers, who strove for equanimity and emotional control, with that of Methodists, who sought emotional intensity and a heightened sensibility. We can see how two highly prosperous women applied the emerging paradigms of the public and private spheres in their own domestic settings. And we can get a sense of what was at stake for a woman preaching in public in the era of the Enlightenment. Indeed, both women were sensitive to the contemporary stereotypes of women preachers or visionaries as either ridiculous (as in Samuel Johnson's famous squib) or as sexually rampant and hysterical, as in William Hogarth's equally famous engraving Credulity, Superstition and Fanaticism (1762). They were also aware of attempts within their own churches to limit the public activities of women in the later years of the century.[11]

Yet what is, to my mind, most intriguing about Mary and Abiah—so close in spatial terms and so allied in their spiritual vocations, social commitments, and moral values—is that their identities as preachers developed out of two different spiritual epistemologies, two different views of the sources of their own moral authority and agency, and two equally different understandings of the relationship between spirituality and emotion. Like earlier seventeenth-century Quaker prophets, Abiah's impulse to preach or prophesy was felt as an involuntary, almost physical compulsion. She described herself as being seized with the need to speak, experiencing a "distress . . . so great I could have no Peace without giving up to go into the street, to proclaim repentance,"[12] and both her speech and her written works reproduced the language and passion of angry Old Testament prophecy:

FIGURE 3.2: *Credulity, Superstition, and Fanaticism* (1762), William Hogarth's satirical portrait of popular evangelical religion and superstition (see, for example, the notorious case of a woman believed to have given birth to rabbits in the lower left corner).

Oh! Call to remembrance the fatal End of those who were mighty *to drink strong Drink*, who sat *till Wine inflamed them*, who loved *Instruments of Music in their Feasts*, and *chanted to the Sound of the Viol*; who *put the evil Day afar off*, and did not *remember the afflicted*. . . . For these, the Lord declared by his Prophet, *Hell hath enlarged herself, and opened her Mouth without Measure; and their Glory, and their Multitude . . . shall descend into it*. Is the Almighty indeed changed? Doth he

FIGURE 3.3: *Quaker Woman Preaching*. Engraving after a painting by Egbert van Heemskirk. Courtesy Friends House Library, London.

give more Liberty in this Age than he did to these? Have you obtained a Licence to . . . do that which is Right in your own Eyes, to sin with Impunity?

The summons to preach reached Mary not as a kind of mental seizure but through her insights into biblical passages and her own emotions and dreams. Of course, the universal strictures on women's preaching meant that, whatever her religious affiliation, it was impossible for a woman to become an official, ordained minister. Hence any woman who preached publicly in this period had to claim unique, divine inspiration, what John Wesley termed "an extraordinary call"; in this sense, every female minister was a visionary or prophet. But there is a difference between Abiah's biblical language and affect, which implied a kind of spiritual ventriloquism—God speaking through the mouth of the prophet—and the exhortations of Mary, which were consciously crafted essays and meditations, written in her own voice and keyed to the realities of contemporary life. She once produced a set of sermon notes or watchwords, one for every letter of the alphabet. Another of her sermons was taken from Acts 27:29: "They cast four anchors out of the stern, and wished for the day":

> The situation of the ship wherein Paul and his companions were, seems to me to illustrate the state and situation of many of us here. . . . Satan . . . keeps the mind in a continual agitation. Sometimes they are sunk, and almost crushed, under a weight of care; and again raised high in the waves of some expected pleasure. One while they are filled with resentment, on account of some slight from a neighbour . . . while the mind is harassed with the imagination. . . . Sometimes the most idle and extravagant fancies so deeply involve it, that no message from heaven could find any more entertainment than the Saviour could find in the Inn at Bethlehem. By all this, the soul becomes restless. . . . Dear souls, is not this the case with some of you?[13]

Judging by their self-presentation and religious language, Mary's personal agency appears far more developed than that of Abiah. However, if Abiah's prophetic authority was experienced as an involuntary and painful compulsion to speak, her *earthly* authority as a minister depended on no one but herself. The children's catechism she wrote posed the question, "Is the Ministry of Christ confin'd to Men only? Are not Women also call'd to that Work?" The answer is yes, they are, because "Male and Female are one in Christ."[14] She traveled in the ministry with a certificate from her home meeting, and had she needed it, she would have been given funds for her expenses as well. Her second marriage, to Abraham Darby, was a spiritual partnership solemnized at the Friends' Yearly Meeting after she had met him only once. Not only did he support his wife when she became an itinerant minister, but "it was fully understood by Abraham and approved by him," writes her biographer, "that her religious concern counted before all other considerations, even when he or the family were unwell."[15] (Nevertheless, Abraham was the ultimate authority in earthly matters: when he wanted to have their children vaccinated against smallpox, Abiah was terrified and unable to give her full consent; the children were vaccinated anyway.) Mary's authority to preach was bestowed on her primarily by the Methodist leader John Wesley, who gave a small cohort of women permission to tell in public what God had done for their souls, and secondarily by her husband, John Fletcher. Indeed, her life with Fletcher exemplified that new eighteenth-century phenomenon, companionate marriage, an intimate sharing of domestic and religious activities and a merging with and subordination of her psyche and spirit to his; that was how she saw the relationship.[16]

In short, here in this small but seminal place, at a hugely significant historical moment, were two neighbors who knew and respected each other and who shared not only a spiritual and social mission but also a perceived tension between current ideals of feminine domesticity and their own perception of what constituted a meaningful spiritual life. Yet despite their common claim to spiritual authority, their dedication to evangelical religion and social reform, and their willingness to challenge contemporary gender roles, their religious consciousness put them at very different places on the cusp between preindustrial culture and modernity. I suggest that these religious and emotional juxtapositions, these different modes of language, feeling, and consciousness, were characteristic of many encounters in eighteenth-century British culture. More broadly, they reflect the complex processes that scholars have defined as secularization and the creation of the modern self. In the pages that follow, I discuss several aspects of Quaker and Methodist consciousness by analyzing the writings of Mary and Abiah, including their interpretations of dreams, beginning with some general points about eighteenth-century Quakerism.

QUAKERISM AND WOMEN

During his visit to England in 1726–29, the French *philosophe* Voltaire made the acquaintance of a retired Quaker merchant who received and entertained him in his simple country house.

> The Quaker was a hale and hearty old man who had never been ill because he had never known passions or intemperance; never in my life have I seen a more dignified or more charming manner than his. . . . He kept his hat on while receiving me and moved toward me without even the slightest bow, but there was more politeness in the frank, kindly expression on his face than there is in the custom of placing one leg behind the other and holding in one's hand what is meant for covering one's head.[17]

Voltaire admired the man's estate (comfortable but not luxurious), his contempt for the superstitions of Catholics and Jews, and his pacifism, which, in Voltaire's rendition, was expressed with the naive wit of a character in *Candide*, his famous fable about innocence and depravity: "Our god, who has bidden us love our enemies . . . undoubtedly does not wish us to cross the sea to go and slaughter our brothers just because some murderers dressed in red, with a two-foot-high bonnet, enroll citizens by making a noise with two little sticks on tightly stretched ass's skin."[18] So the Quaker takes his place alongside the Incas, Tahitians, and other exotics who provided the *philosophes* with a mouthpiece for debunking their own corrupt society. He also stands as an exemplar of the ideal Enlightenment citizen as seen through the eyes of a premier exponent of Enlightenment values.

While Voltaire was clearly impressed by the graciousness and self-possession of his Quaker host, he was also bemused by the contrast between the old man's rational piety and good common sense and what he saw as certain curious and irrational customs practiced among Quakers at large, particularly their mode of worship, which included preaching by women. In the following passage, he describes a Quaker service:

> [The] silence lasted about a quarter of an hour. Eventually one of them rose, doffed his hat, and after making a few faces and fetching a few sighs he recited, half through his mouth and half through his nose, a rigmarole taken from the Gospels, or so he believed, of which neither he nor anyone else understood a word. . . . "We even let women speak, [he said]. Two or three of our devout women often become inspired at the same time, and then there is a fine old rumpus in the house of the Lord."[19]

Seventeenth-century Quakers had used the language of biblical prophecy to preach to audiences of non-Quakers in places as remote as the Caribbean, Malta, and the forests of the American wilderness. Eighteenth-century Quakers (or Friends, as they called themselves) were both more limited in their preaching and more integrated into the larger community. Indeed, as social reformers and innovators in science, industry, education, medicine, mental health, and the administration of prisons, they seemed to be breathing the clear air of the Enlightenment; the Darbys of Madeley parish were illustrious as pioneers in the early Industrial Revolution that would transform Britain and the world. Yet these same Quakers were also religious seekers striving for self-transcendence, spiritual insight, and radical pacifism, all of which isolated them from the social and political worlds of their contemporaries. Abraham Darby I, inventor of the process of smelting iron ore with coke, was also a Quaker minister. Abraham Darby II, husband of Abiah, who refined the process of smelting and ran the business, was equally devout. He once wrote to an unnamed Friend, *"Jehovah's almighty arm* hath hitherto kept back the destroying Angel. . . . What can be the meaning of this general depravity? Men and women endued with such excellent understandings, to act so diametrically opposite to all sense and reason . . . to all the convictions in their own minds, as if there was no god, no afterlife, no retribution!"[20]

The central principle of Quaker theology was the doctrine of the Inner Light, the existence of a spark of divinity in the soul of every human being.

That Inner Light is the essence of both individual conscience and universal truth, and the source of each person's capacity for moral and spiritual restoration. Seventeenth-century Friends, preaching in the chaos of the Civil War period, expressed these principles by chastising the moral laziness of their neighbors, attacking corrupt institutions, pursuing aggressive missionary activity, and witnessing to Truth by following their own individual "leadings" to speak or act, which often caused them to leave their families, assault the magistrates, or preach naked in the marketplace.[21] A Quaker meeting his social superior on the street would not show deference by removing his hat, but he might well embrace him or begin shouting in his face.

Following the Toleration Act of 1689 (which granted freedom of worship to religious sects), and the ensuing decrease in overt physical persecution, Quakers became businesspeople and family people.[22] English law or their own religious principles prevented them from entering either university or the military, and continued penalties for nonpayment of tithes (taxes to the church) made farming precarious; nor could they engage in luxury trades or the manufacture of products used in warfare. So Friends became involved in the textile and clothing trades, iron foundries, the production of domestic iron ware and porcelain, mining, and banking; by 1802 the largest coal dealer, tea merchant, druggist, tinman, and pewterer in London were all Quakers. Because of strictures against marrying outside the community, all of these enterprises came to be dominated by large manufacturing and trading families, whose kinship ties reinforced Friends' sense of corporate responsibility for solvency and honest dealing, as well as their devotion to private property. In short, by the time Abiah Darby and Mary Fletcher met each other, Quakerism had evolved from a movement of radical visionaries into a community of upstanding citizens with an anxious respect for law and order and a terror of overly emotional behavior or "enthusiasm." As denizens of the English Enlightenment, this new generation of Friends sought reason and emotional balance over passion and enthusiasm, simplicity of manners over unconventional shock tactics (like refusing to remove their hats or show deference), humanitarianism and social stability over contentious politics, family and meeting over public prophecy and missionary work. Salvation was achieved and demonstrated not through asceticism or mystical visions but through the attainment of wisdom and right action: the quality of one's bearing in the world.[23]

Quakers also universalized and depoliticized their conception of their social mission. Their public concerns—pacifism, abolition of slavery, behavior toward native Americans—were articulated as issues of social justice that involved compassion for all humanity (or foreign humanity), not as attempts to disrupt the internal social order or to ally with one social group to criticize another group, as seventeenth-century Friends had allied with the poor and op-pressed to criticize magistrates, king, and clergy. This universalist thinking was not only a path to salvation but also a refuge from a competitive culture where Friends were both professionally active and socially marginalized. Abiah wrote of her husband,

> He . . . had an extraordinary command over his own spirit, which . . . en-abled [him] to bear up with fortitude above all opposition: for it may seem very strange, so valuable a man should have antagonists, yet he had. Those called gentlemen with an envious spirit could not bear to see him prosper; and others covetous, strove to make every advantage by raising their rents of their collieries and lands in which he wanted to make roads; and endeavour'd to stop the works. But he surmounted all . . . and died in peace.[24]

The Irish schoolmaster Richard Shackleton, a guest of the Darbys, confided similar sentiments to his daughter Lydia:

> The friendship which the world professes is, generally, capricious and insincere: their favour is deceitful, and their applause uncertain; but, by commending ourselves to the consciences of all men in our dealings with them, and, in the way of our occupation, doing service to God rather than to man, we shall be upheld over and above the fluctuating tempers of men—over their insidious smiles, as well as their overbearing frowns.[25]

In this dynamic but treacherous external environment, the home assumed equal importance with the meeting for worship as a social and spiritual ref-uge and as a school for character. The busy trader, teacher, or capitalist was elevated to a higher spiritual plane when he retired into his family, divested his mind of all aggression and greed, and transcended class differences by treat-ing his workers, servants, and children as his moral apprentices. Abiah pre-sided over an endless stream of guests and a vast household (walnut trees, a lawn populated with deer, a pond, an island with a summer house) and often preached to guests at dinner. "This is the most extraordinary place I ever was in," wrote Shackleton, "there is such a mixture of religion and worldly busi-ness, human learning and Christian simplicity, among the people; such a wild, native irregularity, subdued and cultivated by art and opulence, about the place."[26] A poem by Shackleton, sent as part of a thank-you note, gave Abiah the credit for redeeming the horrors of early industrialization through her "social, Christian" hospitality:

> Dreadful the view in dusky spires
>   The smokey columns rise
> And fiend like forms stir up the fires
>   Which redden all the skies.
> . . . In dire sounds I heard, I saw with dread
>   The fiery surges swell,
> Aghast I stopp'd by [sic] course and said
>   Oh! Sure this place is hell!
> At last recover'd from my fears
>   I sought the stately dome,
> Where courtesy with kindness cheers
>   And strangers find a home.
> Received, refresh'd and edicted
>   With social Christian Grace,
> Beneath Abiah's roof, I cried
>   "Sure Heaven is in this place."[27]

From Voltaire's perspective, it might have seemed that Friends' religious ideals had been effaced by the secular ideals of the Enlightenment; indeed, many Quaker writings used "God" and "Wisdom," "conscience" and "the Inner Light" as interchangeable terms. From the Quakers' own perspective, their restrained language and behavior was an attempt to formulate a new conception of the right way to discern and express spiritual authenticity. Friends had always believed that salvation—being "in the light"—was expressed through the ordinary gestures of daily life; the earliest Friends were noted for honesty and sincerity as well as for flamboyant public prophecy. For later Friends, who believed that salvation was expressed through calmness, moral clarity, and personal restraint, social behavior had to be both authentic (Voltaire's Quaker still did not remove his hat) and respectable—a model of public virtue rather than a challenge to it; so a male Quaker admired the minister Mary Ridgeway, "in whom were united the seriousness of the minister, and the courtesy of the gentlewoman."[28]

The interdependence and ultimate harmony of money, probity, piety, and a balanced state of mind were all nicely laid out, in color, in the "Map of the Various Paths of Life," shown in Figure 3.4, a kind of moral Monopoly game for the edification of Quaker children, published in 1794. The steady young

tradesman travels a (literally) straight and narrow path through Discreet
County and Courteous Square, building his strength by climbing Manly Hill
along the way. He proceeds through Steady Plains (dutifully pausing at Submission Valley and Diligent Bank) and continues onward to Serenity Province,

FIGURE 3.4: "A Map of the Various Paths of Life" (1794). Photograph of a puzzle,
courtesy Friends House Library, London. (Reproduction of an engraving published in
London by W. Dalton and J. Harvey, May 30, 1794. Tract box LL2/25. Friends House
Library, London.)

where, after inhaling the bracing air of Integrity Level, he is refreshed at a Thriving Farm House, situated just between Competent Close and Economy Precinct. Making an easy descent down Retiring Slope, he comes to rest at Happy Old Age Hall before the final journey to the PEACEFUL OCEAN. The weak young man sneaks out the back door of Parental Care Hall and embarks on a zigzag path to perdition. "Many a young tradesman," says the commentary, "has arrived at the Temple of Fame and yet missed of Esteem Hall; by not keeping a guard over his appetite, he has gone to Feasting Hall . . . and though many are in Perplexity Paris, they will [go on] to Decoy Theatre and Spendthrift Ordinary, which leads to Gambler's Hotel . . . down Losing Vale, by Needy Maze, to Misery Square." Barely avoiding Horror Bog, he finally struggles through Hopeless Slough and no Friend Shed, hurtles into Despair Gulph, is sucked down into the Sinking Sands, and finally disappears into the BOTTOMLESS PIT.[29]

Our young tradesman meets no women on the straight path (except, perhaps, in the kitchen of the Thriving Farm House). In reality, however, Quaker men did not go through life as solitary pilgrims. Not only did women share men's work as farmers, shopkeepers, and merchants; they also civilized the families that formed the manufacturing and trading networks of Friends. The persona of the idealized female Quaker conveyed a gravitas that must have seemed a weighty complement to Voltaire's genial host. Rational, yet sensitive; chaste—even glacial—yet maternal; competent, yet delicate; this was the stock figure of the virtuous Quaker woman found in contemporary plays and magazines. "I think," observed a writer in the *Monthly Magazine*, "that the distinguishing attribute of the sect—Equanimity . . . is now become not a second but an original nature, and is discoverable in that undisturbed regularity of features, particularly among the females—that placidity of countenance . . . an infelt serenity of soul—a deeply charactered composure."[30]

The addition of the domestic matron to the Quaker woman's persona did not imply any diminution of respect for women as ministers or helpmeets. Hundreds of women received certificates to preach, which entitled them to financial support from their home meetings as well as support for the families they left behind; many other hundreds of women were elders, overseeing the pastoral care of their home meetings; and every woman who married participated in a ceremony that was more egalitarian than any other comparable Christian rite.[31] What the new domestic ideology did imply was a prohibition against ecstatic behavior or overt political activity, whether activity in the wider political arena or within the Quaker meeting system. Unlike the ecstatic political prophets of the seventeenth century, a woman could not act like a man in the public spaces now reserved for men alone.[32] On the contrary, it was the physical reserve and quiet authority of women elders and ministers that conveyed an aura of Quaker authenticity, or being "in the light." This created problems of interpretation for the men who listened to Quaker women ministers. Seventeenth-century audiences watching a female prophet disrupting an Anglican church service and shouting at the top of her lungs had to decide whether the prophet spoke with the voice of God or the devil; eighteenth-century audiences listening to the measured tones of a female preacher delivering a sermon had to decide whether she spoke with God's voice or the voice of an ordinary woman using ordinary intelligence to tell men what was wrong with them and what they should do about it.

Relieved of the danger of physical persecution and imbued with the values of both Quakerism and the Enlightenment, Quaker women now struggled to understand themselves and their place in the world in an entirely new language; rather, they struggled to graft a new vocabulary of reason and sensibility onto their original language of Old Testament imagery and bodily signs. In her tract against gambling and other vain pleasures, Abiah's biblical language recalled the angry, provocative rhetoric of seventeenth-century Quaker preaching ("Then *be not Drunk with Wine wherein is Excess, but be filled with the Spirit*: . . Oh! Call to remembrance the fatal End of those who were mighty to *drink strong drink*, who sat *till Wine inflamed them*, who loved *Instruments of Music in their feasts*"). But she also distanced herself from the puritan asceticism of those earlier Friends, writing in the same tract a diatribe against horse racing, cockfighting, throwing at cocks, gaming, plays, dancing, musical entertainments, or any other vain diversions:

[Do not] conclude [that] this Address cometh from a melancholly Enthusiast, who would restrain the Pursuit of proper lawful Liberty and Relaxation, for I can assure you I am not one of those; but am ready and willing, to agree and join in with that Liberty and Freedom the *Truth* doth allow . . . I am not of that Opinion, that we ought to recluse ourselves from the World, but that we keep ourselves from *the Evil* thereof; *using this World as not abusing it*; enjoying the Blessings bestowed, *as good Stewards of the manifold Grace of God*. . . . For the glorious Effects of the *holy Spirit of Truth* in Man, is not confined only to open the spiritual Eye of Faith . . . but also produceth a Change in the natural Capacity; our Understandings as Men will be polished, our Faculties brightened, and qualified for Converse and Commerce among Men. So that in a spiritual and natural Sense, we shall become as *Lights in the World*.[33]

In those two final sentences, the languages of the Inner Light and the Enlightenment finally meet. Later, Abiah wrote in her journal that God expects more from her own generation than from earlier Friends, "For we are favored to live in a much more enlightened age—we enjoying the promises they only saw at a great distance."[34]

The tension between the Quakers' desire to maintain their uniqueness as a group and their equally strong desire to assimilate to the values and customs of Enlightenment society is evident in their private writings. Quaker journals of the period are filled with accounts of preachers straining to recapture the zeal of the earliest Quakers, riding for miles on horseback to meetings but remaining silent before assembled Friends because they did not feel the Light or could not overcome the constraints dictated by their own spiritual inhibitions and good manners. I know of very few Quakers in this period who preached in the marketplace to strangers or standing before the mayor of the town, or who interrupted a church service in order to prophesy, as the earliest Friends did, and as Abiah did on July 14, 1763, when she interrupted the service to prophesy in John Fletcher's church:

> I had the Word to declare with power. The parson (i.e. John Fletcher) heard me patiently and commended what I had said and desired all to take notice of the advice, but objected the points of doctrine I had advanced, which had touched his copyhold on priest craft! I had close work of it for about three hours, but was wonderfully set at liberty to assert the truth of the Gospels, and Scripture proofs were brought to my mind, very fluently. . . . The parson kneeled down and upon the whole he behaved with respect . . . the people were very quiet and after wards I understood one of them said—what shall we choose [sic] one is all for form and the other for no form. Others observed—the parson was often at a nonplus for a reply and seemed at times astonish'd and at a loss.[35]

In 1755 Abiah and her friend Ann Summerland went on a preaching tour to Hertfordshire and Bristol. They carried certificates from their home meeting, and Abraham, Abiah's husband, accompanied them partway. At one meeting she felt oppressed, needing to speak to the leading men of the city. Her companions did not think it was a suitable time, so Abiah gave up the idea but remained "very distressed" all night. The next day, still upset, she went to the mayor's house and asked permission to hold a meeting in the town hall and presented her certificate "that I was no impostor." That night she was very anxious, and the next day she went to the bishop: "I told him . . . I was engaged to come to speak to him from the Holy Spirit, he said 'we don't hear such things'." She wrote to the bishop, urging him to combat vice, but as she recounts in her journal,

> Still my distress was so great I could have no peace without *giving up to* go into the street, to proclaim repentance in the streets—Ann and Friend Coles went with me—Oh it was harder to me than giving up my life—I knew not the way—Ann pointed me down a street, but my mind *was drawn to go forward*, which I did, and *it brought me towards* the market cross—I stop't short before a shop door and lifted up my voice as a trumpet. The people were surprised, one man sprung out to me asking "What is the matter Madam?": but I took no notice and went to another place and spoke and then to the Cross, to the steps leading to the Hall and there I had an open time—again at another place farther, where I also deliver'd my message in great dread . . . the people were quiet and made no objection—some much affected. After being clear I went to the inn, but *a profusion of weeping came over my mind*, and all the way out of town I wept exceedingly for the people, who seemed to sit in darkness.[36]

A letter of 1766 written by a Methodist minister gives an idea of the impression Abiah made on her non-Quaker audience: "[She] was a gentlewoman riding in her carriage going from place to place to visit the people, the other her servant or rather companion." He also wrote that she preached with a truly Christian spirit.[37] Nevertheless, we can see in her own accounts how humbling it was for a respectable lady, well known in the community, to surrender her dignity and position in this way, even though her husband and the Quaker meeting clearly supported her. Her preaching at home to family and guests was apparently just as difficult—and, for her, as socially transgressive—as her public appearances. In 1755 she preached at the dinner table shortly after giving birth: "a great, very great cross to my natural will: but always condemned when I put it by . . . but when I give up, oh the comfort and joy that redounds to my soul, that I then admire how I ever dare disobey—but the next time it's as hard as ever."[38]

In terms of her own subjectivity, Abiah found it extraordinarily difficult to achieve and sustain the equanimity so highly prized as an attribute of female preachers. Clearly, she was affected by the tension between her identity as a wealthy gentlewoman and her vocation as a preacher. She records in her journal that when she was a child her father and his brother argued over an inheritance, and her father surrendered part of his estate to keep the peace.

Her first husband had less material wealth than her own family, and the disapproval of her parents cast a pall over the marriage and increased her guilt at resisting the call to preach: "All the time I was married, which was about two years or upwards—I remained poor and barren in spirit, as one left alone."[39] As the wife of Abraham Darby, she must have experienced an opposite pressure: both a greater scope for good works and a sense of spiritual danger in her life as a lady presiding over a great mansion. Her awareness of the obligations attendant on wealth is apparent in her tract on horse racing, where she basically says, "Take up your burden as exemplars in the community, be vigilant against your own acquisitive nature, teach the values of the Enlightenment to your inferiors, and God will make you wealthy and inviolable":

> To you then, whom the Beneficent Father hath blessed with Affluence, . . . a double Obligation is laid upon you to walk in awful Reverence and Circumspection before your God, as *faithful Stewards* of his manifold Mercies and Grace. . . . Peoples Eyes are upon you, they love to imitate, they conclude ye know better than they, and implicitly follow your steps. . . . [God] expects more from us in this enlightened Age. . . . [If you] obey the holy Will . . . he will bless you in all your Undertakings: The Fields will yield their Increase, and Plenty shall abound in your Dwellings; and nothing shall be permitted to hurt or destroy you.[40]

Abiah may also have felt that her superior position in society required the sacrifice of her self-abasement as a prophet. Certainly her religious temperament was shaped by a particularly intense piety and tendency to self-criticism. As a child, she used to visit a Presbyterian woman to read Scripture and sing psalms, and as a young woman, she felt guilty for letting an impulsive and very brief early marriage divert her from her call to preach. The nightmares she had around this time were remembered and recorded many years later in a journal written for her children. In one dream, she was chased by huge men on horses who threw stones at her; in another, she tried to hide from Christ, who gazed at her in horror. This is the only dream I have found in either Quaker or Methodist records in which God is horrified by the dreamer, and it testifies to her intense feelings of guilt about avoiding the burden of prophecy:

> I had a dream, which showed my state of condemnation. I thought I was in my father's house . . . and one came in and said—Our savior is come to town! I was instantly struck with surprise and great fear, being conscious of my having done sufficient to merit his dreadful resentment!

I thought to myself, I would not be seen by him. . . . But I had no sooner thought—than I saw him passing by the parlor window. . . . In great terror I run up stairs into a chamber to hide myself: when looking towards the window, I saw him at the outside, looking full upon me astonished—I ran into the inner chamber: and at the window, there I saw him standing also. He looked awfully solemn and piercing upon me—with amazement and horror filled.[41]

She finally spoke in 1748 (aged thirty-two) at a Friends' meeting:

I was called upon in our Meeting here and after sitting a long while under the exceeding weighty burden of the word which was alive within me. . . . I finally did speak these words. "My Friends, I am engaged to invite you all to get inward and taste and feel with my soul how good the Lord is." The very same words I should have opened my mouth with when fifteen and seventeen years of age. . . . How I got up, and how I spake I know not, some invisible hand seemed to lift me. I was out of the body . . . so that I for a time hardly knew where I was. But full of joy, I could hardly believe for joy.[42]

It was a month before she spoke again.

METHODISM AND EMOTION

Abiah Darby's concerns about material success are a common affliction among members of successful reform movements, where the second and third generations are both more secure and less single-minded than their forebears. Turning our attention to Methodism and Mary Fletcher, we see a movement younger by almost a century, where there was no shortage of spiritual energy and emotional heat. Eighteenth-century Quakers were modern in terms of their engagement with the world of science and business and their concern for social justice, but they looked backward in attempting to emulate the fervor of the earliest Quakers while eschewing acts of civil disobedience or flamboyant enthusiasm. Methodists were far less sophisticated in terms of their engagement with the secular world, but they were modern in their focus on feelings, tapping into the contemporary concern with sensibility and styles of emotional expression that would later emerge as nineteenth-century Romanticism.

Methodism began in the late 1730s as a renewal movement within the Anglican church led by John and Charles Wesley and a small cohort of ministers, lay leaders, and lay preachers. By the time of John Wesley's death in 1791, the movement had attracted over 72,000 members in Britain and 60,000 in North America.[43] Until the end of the century, Methodists were also Anglicans, remaining within the body of the national church and attending baptism, communion, and so on. Wesley's Methodists were also Arminians: believers in free will but emphasizing the power of Jesus's atonement to justify sinners. In short, Methodism was both a charismatic movement and an organized system of worship, ranging from huge revival meetings to classes of men and women, and small bands or meetings where worshippers were separated by gender and marital status. Most important for our purpose, Methodism, or "heart religion," was a movement that privileged the emotions. Not only did revivalist preaching elicit wildly demonstrative responses; emotional perception was valued above mere reason or intellectual effort. John Wesley once wrote in a moment of desperation, "I do not love God. I never did."[44] Undoubtedly Wesley *believed* in God at that moment, but it was his relationship with God, the affective connection, that was the goal of Methodist worship and discipline.

Mary Bosanquet Fletcher joined the movement when she was about eighteen (her parents having expelled her from their home so that she wouldn't pollute her siblings with her new spirituality and disreputable friends) and quickly became part of a community of women living and praying together in London. From the beginning, her connection to the movement was rooted in her emotional connection to individual members who became her mentors and intimate friends. If Abiah's vocation developed out of her parents' example and feelings of guilt for her daughterly disobedience and current wealth, Mary's spirituality developed out of her parents' lack of sympathy and the intense relationships she cultivated within the movement. One of these relationships was with Sarah Ryan, a woman ten years older who had been a servant, laundress, and bigamist. For many Methodists, Sarah was an embodiment of the primitive, sanctified Christian, whose past suffering and intuitive insight imbued her with an authority out of all proportion to her status as a housekeeper of the Methodist centers in London and Bristol. She and Mary Bosanquet planned to establish an orphanage and haven for poor women. They also exchanged letters of a quite romantic intensity. Mary wrote to Sarah:

> I need not tell you how tenderly I love you nor how thankful I am your stomach is well, though I feel for your nerves. . . . I believe you will return but I observe you never say *when* . . . I must tell you the truth: It was striking the dream you had, that very day I was looking at the hair and ring [you gave me] and thought "if her mind should change before

she returns[,] the contents of this box will ever stand against her," and I know not how it is but I have lost all that assurance I had of your unchangeableness. And don't you remember when you went you said the first letter you wrote or at the least the second, you would assure me of your intention of returning at the time appointed. . . . O Jesus what wouldst thou have me learn by this dispensation? . . . does He now show you anything concerning my soul as he used to do, I shall read your letter over and over and draw out all the honey I can. . . . Tell any who think of your remaining in Bristol "God hath given you to me and I will stand between you and your enemies."[45]

Sarah reassured her,

O my dear your *thoughts* your *thoughts* catch them as they flee bring them into the pure presence of God and there hold them till he hath scattered them by his eye or cleansed them by his holy spirit as to me my dear enjoy me in God look for me in God find me in God love me in God and live with me in God then shall you die with me into God and *we* shall live with God together . . . I am happy very happy.[46]

And in another letter: "When you left me I was able to do but little rested but poorly that night . . . this day I have found you very near my heart . . . but particular at the times of prayer, what union of soul I felt with you I felt your mind as I never did yet so pure so free and so desirous of your being a chaste virgin to Christ for ever. O my love how blest are we . . . one night more . . . [and] we shall meet."[47]

Before her marriage at age forty-two, Mary had repeatedly advised single women to avoid marriage as at best a hindrance to the exercise of piety and at worst a form of tyranny:

How many married persons are at a loss to determine to what length they may oblige their partners in those things not absolutely forbid: and yet such as may be great hindrances in their way. . . . But from all this *you* are free—whatever shines on your soul . . . you are at full liberty to follow it without difficulty or interruption. . . . If you are entrusted with . . . money . . . you can consecrate it all to God. . . . Again, if you are led to cry to God in public, to visit the sick, or in any way to rescue souls from perdition—you have not to ask leave of man. . . . if a man have a bad wife he is still his own master—but the woman is not her own mistress—therefore to these I say take care how you part with the liberty you now enjoy. . . . I say again you are now your own mistress—beware how you become subject.[48]

Nevertheless, she was unwilling to challenge the norm of patriarchal marriage that made such subservience a requirement. Later in life, she writes in terms that would have been anathema to Abiah:

When you are married you can no longer be mistress of yourself—You ought not, for you have made him (whether good or bad, wise or foolish) your superior. . . . [So] let me entreat you never to entertain a thought of taking any man as your head, unless he be such a one as your highest reason chooses to obey—I say your "highest reason" for affection alone will not do here—if you have not a solid ground of esteem . . . you will find it hard . . . always to stand to that submission which will then become your duty.[49]

Perhaps one reason for this conservatism was that her concern for women's moral autonomy coexisted with a powerful desire for those she loved to behave not as equals but as loving parents:

Nov. 12, 1783: [God] showed me he would make his will known to me through that of my dear husband, and that I was to accept his directions as from God, and obey him as the Church does Christ. That I must give myself to his guidance as a child, and wherever we were called, or however employed in the work of God, I should always find protection, and glorify God, while I renounced all choice by doing the will of another rather than my own.[50]

Throughout her life, Mary used dreams and the emotions they elicited as a way to think about the nature of her various roles as teacher, spiritual counselor, wife, and overseer of her late husband's parish. Indeed, dreams were generally important for Methodists as a justification and direct inspiration for female preaching. Unlike Quaker women, whose authority to preach was formalized by a certificate given by the meeting for worship, Methodist women's authority to preach was based on an "extraordinary call," a divine commandment to preach. This commandment did not entitle them to behave either as ordained ministers, preaching from a biblical text, or as political prophets, but only to relate their own personal experience (Mary, we have seen, ignored this rule). Dreams were thus a part of women's public vocation far more than men's. Not only did they convey a visionary authority and a symbolic language that justified and elevated women's preaching; they also implied that the call to preach was both spontaneous and innocuous. Mary often used her own dreams in the same way she used biblical texts; thus she introduced her dream of the Tree of Life as a sermon text that was also a divine message (Mary Taft, a visiting minister, recorded the sermon):

> She thought she saw a large tree, the branches, trunk, and roots, were very beautiful, but all transparent. She saw the sap run in all directions from the root and trunk, through the branches and leaves. . . . She thought the sap run through a part of the branches very swiftly, and that part was very green, lively, and flourishing, but in some part of the branches that ran slowly, and . . . were but languid. . . . She informed us, that the dream was immediately explained to her. She said the trunk and roots, represent God the Father. The human form within the trunk [was] Jesus Christ. The sap represents the Holy Spirit. The branches and leaves the Church. The knots and crooked parts . . . were the remains of unbelief, self will, [and] carnality.[51]

In many of Mary's dreams, she encountered a succession of deceased figures who had been her mentors in life and who assisted her in her struggle to balance her emotional intensity with the detachment of the sanctified Christian whose sole love object is God. The main character in these dreams was John Fletcher, who invariably appeared as counselor and spiritual director, sometimes in a startlingly direct way. Once she dreamed that he shook her shoulder to wake her up when the regular preacher was late. She told the dream to another minister, James Rogers:

> Once when the clergyman Mr. Walters was appointed to meet the people at five in the morning, but over slept himself—Mrs. F[letcher] dreamed about four o'clock that same morning [that] Mr. Fletcher stood at the foot of her bed, and pointing up to the alarm clock placed there, cried—"Arise Polly it is time to get up and go down to our meeting:" and after repeating the same words different times over but she yet continued sleeping— she dreamed, he came to her and gave her a shove on the shoulder with which she was awakened at the exact time to be in readiness to go to the preaching. But as the minister did not come, she prayed and spoke to the attentive audience there waiting—she related to them as much of

the above circumstances as she judged prudent—fully believing that her husband, as well as his and her Lord, were in the assembly.[52]

More often, Fletcher appeared in Mary's dreams as a godlike, parental figure who affirmed his eternal love and concern but cautioned Mary to detach herself from her dependence on him and direct all of her desire toward God. In one dream, unable to think clearly enough to talk to him about religious matters, she could only ask plaintively whether he ever visited her. Characteristically, he responded by reminding her that though he did visit, she should not rely on these visits but on God.

> About the middle of the night I saw my dear husband before me. We ran into each other's arms. I wished to ask him several questions concerning holiness . . . but I found something like a dark cloud on my memory; so that I said in myself, I cannot frame the question I would ask; I am not permitted. At length I asked, My dear, do you not visit me sometimes? He answered, "Many times a day." . . . And may I always know that thou art near me, when I am in trouble, or pain, or danger? He paused, and said faintly, "Why, yes;" then added, "but it is as well for thee not to know it, for thy reliance must not be upon me."[53]

Abiah's relationship to her husband appears to have been one of spiritual equality and immense respect, but the lines of authority between the Darbys were more balanced than between the Fletchers, and the emotional register was more subdued. When Abraham died, Abiah recorded a very moving dream in which he appeared as the suffering Christ:

> I was sitting in a parlor . . . when looking on my left hand I saw a large cross, and a person hanging thereon, with his arms extended. I considered who it should be, and said in my mind, surely it's our savior upon the cross. . . . Then I viewed him earnestly, and presently knew him to be my husband, he had only his shirt on fastened close about him—he took me by the hand, looking upon me with a solid sweet countenance but said nothing . . . [then] the wall and house behind us opened wide, and . . . my husband mounted up . . . I got up and held his hand as far as I could reach, when he gently drew his hand out of mine, and ascended into the air.[54]

Mary also dreamed of her dead husband, but her dream is more gruesome and intimate, and more focused on the lesson he has to teach her:

I thought the side of his tomb was opened . . . and I saw him lying under it, while I lay at his side. . . . He then said, with a sweetness which I cannot describe,—"Put thy arm over me, and feel what companions I have; they must be thy companions too." I put my arm, and felt bones and broken coffins, at which nature seemed to shrink; but I did not speak. He tenderly answered to my thought, "Thou wilt lay thy head upon me."[55]

Not surprisingly Mary's great gift as a writer and preacher was empathy, the capacity to express theological principles in terms of concrete human experience. She wrote in one sermon,

Fix your eye on man. How does he [man] love a stubborn son who will neither serve God nor him? True, he frowns on him, and corrects him. . . . But if that son shed but a tear of sorrow . . . if he but come a few steps, how do the father's bowels yearn towards him! How doth he run to meet him! Now carry the idea a little higher;—are ye not the offspring of God?[56]

CONCLUSION

Compared to the flamboyant religiosity of seventeenth-century visionaries, the scope of Mary Fletcher's and Abiah Darby's religious activities was narrower in spiritual, social, and geographic terms. Abiah preached mainly to other Quakers, and her forays into the non-Quaker world—"a gentlewoman riding in her carriage"—were a perpetual source of anxiety and embarrassment. Mary was attracted by the ascetic practices of the early saints and martyrs, but her own experiments in self-denial were almost ludicrously limited. One night she woke up from a dream about her husband and considered the possibilities for living a more ascetic life:

Last night I dreamed my dear husband wrote a line for me to read. I took up the paper with desire, and read,—"Those who closely follow Jesus Christ, can discern the mark of the thorn in his steps". . . . I see it. If I would walk with Christ, I must know my path by that very mark. . . . Lord, show me how to walk thus! Give me a steady power to rise the very moment the alarm goes off. To watch against sloth all day, and to use more abstemiousness in my food. . . . I am quite clear I have no right to hurt my body. I am not, I think, in any danger of that. . . . I propose to keep a watch over my appetite each day . . . to this I would add, a

shadow . . . of a fast, twice a week. On Mondays and Fridays I would
omit butter in the morning, eating dry bread, and, as usual, rosemary tea
without sugar. For dinner, water gruel, with salt and pepper, and, as on
other days, tea for my supper. This cannot hurt my health, and may be a
kind of remembrancer, that there is such a duty as self-denial.[57]

Note that Mary never imagines here that she could achieve a religious epiph-
any by giving up butter, only that her small sacrifice might serve as "a kind of
remembrancer" of the need to imitate Christ.

That said, it is also true that both women pushed far beyond the limits—
both domestic and spiritual—that constrained religious women in elite
eighteenth-century culture. Abiah continually obliterated the boundaries between the emerging public and the private spheres, prophesying in the street,
preaching at the dinner table to assembled guests, and discussing religious matters with male guests who visited her in her bedroom shortly after she had
given birth. Mary preached at revival meetings and, as John Fletcher's wife,
her preaching and pastoral work paralleled that of her husband. In her widowhood, still resident in the vicarage, she preached twice every three weeks while
the newly incumbent vicar preached only once (she covered for him when he
preached elsewhere in the parish).

In less positive terms, however, Mary and Abiah shared a conflicted and
highly gendered consciousness. Each knew her own importance, if not her own
worth, but each was also constrained by a timidity that was rooted as much
in new attitudes about female domesticity and negative female stereotypes—
the hysterical female, the religious fanatic—as it was in her own individual history. Abiah's behavior as a minister, a hostess, a mother, a community leader,
and a wife was exemplary, and she was not above putting pressure on the
Quaker community to pay for publication of her works. Yet she was intimidated by others less eminent than herself. She describes herself at one meeting as

very low and poor, [having] nothing for myself much less for others. . . .
I should have got to Uxbridge, to attend a funeral—I mentioned it, but
John Elliot was for pressing to London and desirous of our going, so
damped my spirits; but if I had hearkened to the true monitor I should
have gone. I was much distressed. [There was an accident on the road . . .]
we all got safe through . . . but Oh if I had gone to Uxbridge as I ought,
this its likely would not have happened. Oh that I may mind my duty and
not be overperswaded by any one.[58]

After Abraham died she left on a tour of visits to other Quaker families, thinking she could mourn more easily if she were free of her own family's demands, but once again, she hung back: "at meeting engaged in awful prayer, but others being there I hurt myself after, by giving way when it was my place and the other friends having nothing [to say], hurt was done. Oh that I could mind my own business and not look at others."[59]

Mary groomed the younger women in her orbit for spiritual leadership, edited her own writings for publication, and controlled which male curates would be installed in her late husband's parish of Madeley—all this in a period when the leaders of the Methodist Conference were moving aggressively to limit women's sphere of public activity. In her religious and personal writings, she avoided the language of wifely obedience as a metaphor for obedience to God, rather calling herself God's innkeeper, a spiritual mother, and a pillar in God's house. Yet she worried constantly that she would forget her dependence on Christ and thereby lose both her faith and her ability to serve. At age fifty-five, still at the height of her religious activity and eminence, she wrote in her journal, "O how I feel that truth [that] I have merited hell a thousand times over . . . in meeting the class this afternoon I was much humbled everyone seems to get on quicker than me."[60]

Judged in terms of their own spiritual goals, Mary's and Abiah's attempts to achieve both inner peace and a purity of intention clearly failed. But if we consider their efforts in relation to the wider culture, their relentless pursuit of spiritual perfection looks both genuinely impressive and historically significant. The historian Amanda Vickery observes that there was a different meaning of honor for eighteenth-century men and women. For women, honor meant virtue and moral purity, while for men, it meant integrity, being true to one's word. Methodist and Quaker women of this same period were generally less educated and sophisticated than the gentlewomen Vickery describes, but they took as seriously as men the importance of their own moral integrity.[61] In the late eighteenth and early nineteenth centuries, when both Quaker and Methodist leaders continued to oppose women's public leadership, that integrity and a newly unified evangelical culture would generate new movements of religious education, social reform, and missionary outreach, culminating in the campaign for the abolition of slavery and the international movement for women's suffrage, in both of which Quaker and Methodist women were highly active.

Medicine and Disease: Women, Practice, and Print in the Enlightenment Medical Marketplace

LISA FORMAN CODY

Few women hit the early eighteenth-century press like Sarah Wallin. First appearing in London's newspapers during the summer of 1736 as a big-boned, athletic spinster whose strength and dexterity could wrench grown men's twisted spines into proper alignment, "the bonesetter" quickly attracted as much attention for a long list of remarkable orthopedic adjustments as for her flamboyant personality and marital swagger. Her ability to mend dislocated necks and hips drew desperate families to Epsom seeking her aid, but as soon as she spotted a London footman named Hill Mapp, who accompanied one of these customers, she announced that she would marry him and see no patients until they were wed. She set the day. When Sir James Edwards appeared shortly thereafter with the young daughter of a London lawyer, "whose Neck was dislocated, so as to lie double for near two Inches, and is supported by Steel Instruments," Wallin promised to heal the girl but only if she could borrow Edwards's carriage to find a minister and net her groom. According to the newspapers, in early August, at least a day of complete chaos followed, with Wallin speeding back and forth between Epsom, Ewell, Headly, Banstead, and London. She was frustrated by stubborn coachmen, exhausted horses, Anglican ministers with revoked licenses unable to legally marry her to Mr. Mapp, patients pleading for treatment along the way, and a mostly absent bridegroom. Eventually, Sir James arranged for a private carriage to take her to London, where Mr. Mapp was apparently roped into the marriage. While "Mr. Mapp was obliged to walk," Mrs. Mapp took a carriage back to Epsom, where the young girl had been waiting with her dislocated neck. Mrs. Mapp treated the girl and several other patients who had also appeared during the day. The orthopedic successes continued, but rumors also appeared within a fortnight that Mr. Mapp had escaped and absconded with 102 guineas. Mrs. Mapp cheerfully joked about his fickle nature and continued her public service, healing the lame and the crooked. Her marital ups and downs carried on, but so did her consistently remarkable interventions, which attracted the attention of some of the nation's most prestigious physicians and natural scientists, many of whom witnessed her talents throughout the coming months and lauded her contribution to the health of the nation.[1]

The eccentric aspects of Mrs. Mapp's story—from her stunning claims of pulling young girls with scoliosis into properly aligned maidens two inches taller to her dramatic pursuit of a reluctant bridegroom—cannot help but dominate her biography. Sarah Wallin Mapp was a colorful character to be sure, but despite her eccentricity, she probably was not a charlatan, or "quack," which is how she came down in history almost immediately after her sudden, unexpected death in 1737. In her brief moment of national fame, she had gained acclaim and attracted long lines of the desperately disabled, not only because she was eccentric, but also because her purported abilities to heal the disabled were of immeasurable value in a society that relied on all people's physical labor. By correcting the gait of the hobbled, restoring dislocated arms, legs, necks, spines, hands, ankles, fingers, and toes to their rightful configurations, Mrs. Mapp provided the dual benefit of alleviating bodily pain and returning English people back to productivity and work. In her bold personality she was sui generis, but in her ability to alleviate the suffering of disabled bodies, Mrs. Mapp was one of many female practitioners throughout Europe and North America who helped to preserve life and build the diverse labor forces of the eighteenth century.

This characterization of female medical practitioners' positive contribution to Enlightenment-era health care might seem surprising given the broader stereotypes of premodern medicine with its leeches, mercury, and unwashed instruments. After all, before the nineteenth-century developments of anesthesia, sterilization, germ theory, and manufactured antibiotics, doctors and other practitioners surely must have harmed as frequently as they healed. Indeed, eighteenth-century observers frequently lamented the uselessness and pain of many contemporary therapies and interventions. Yet at the same time, they acknowledged that many healers, both male and female, provided dependable and trustworthy care. Not only were there generally reliable practitioners, including midwives, and a variety of useful folk remedies; there were also cutting-edge eighteenth-century developments. These included smallpox inoculation and surgical and chemical lithotomies for kidney stones as well as the acquisition of exotic remedies, such as cinchona bark from the Andes, the only known effective cure for malaria, a disease endemic to both South America and the swampy marshlands of Europe. Although male practitioners developed and promoted many of these effective therapies, so did women, particularly in the first two-thirds of the eighteenth century.

Women had long dominated midwifery, but they also were the keepers of traditional and household medicine. They were the persons most likely to share local pharmaceutical and medical practices in their neighborhoods and when traveling abroad because they had closer contact with servants than their diplomatic and military husbands.[2] Lady Mary Wortley Montagu, the wife of England's ambassador to Turkey, for example, learned of engrafting smallpox when she was in Turkey in the 1710s. And it was the Dutch-German entomologist, botanist, and illustrator Maria Sybella Merien whose precise observations of insect metamorphosis while in the Dutch overseas colonies helped to overthrow theories of spontaneous generation. Merien also brought to Europe from the West Indies knowledge of the "peacock flower" (*Caesalpinia pulcherrima*), which Afro-Caribbean midwives found could induce miscarriages. Her observations about the powers of this gorgeous yellow and orange but toxic bloom were met with silence among male botanists back in Europe:[3] in an age that valued demographic expansion, any substance preventing reproduction was abhorred.

Despite Merien's unsavory investigation of West Indian abortifacients, she was otherwise appreciated among learned Europeans for her lush, detailed, and precise botanical illustrations. Her work was not considered inappropriate, for many contemporaries embraced the notion that women could and should take part in the Enlightenment pursuit of natural knowledge. Philosopher Jean-Jacques Rousseau was among many who considered botany a suitable hobby for females, and scores of journalists and publishers offered accessible explanations of recent botanical, scientific, and medical observations for their female readers.[4] So when such women as Merien and Montagu joined the Enlightenment project of gathering knowledge through observation and experimentation, they were not at odds with men and male practice. Lady Montagu, in fact, worked side by side with her family physician, Charles Maitland, who accompanied her to Turkey, where the two of them investigated Constantinople's medical practices, including the "engrafting" of smallpox pus under the skin of unexposed children. Together they determined it was safe to have Montagu's own son inoculated by a local (unnamed) female expert. Whereas many northern Europeans viewed practices from the exotic East as dirty or dangerous, they more readily accepted such an import given that this aristocratic English mother had endorsed it.[5] Montagu, Maitland, and other proponents of inoculation shared a modern enthusiasm for experimentation and verifiable evidence, categories now considered integral to medical science.

There was another reason why female medical practice and knowledge often flourished during the Enlightenment. Thanks to the dramatic expansion of eighteenth-century print culture, female healers could more readily publish books and pamphlets, advertise their services in the press, and find themselves the subject of journalists' stories as a result of their accomplishments (or eccentricities). In the English case, it is estimated that the number of copies of newspapers expanded from 2.4 million in 1713 to 16 million in 1801.[6] Even within a single newspaper title, in this case the *Gazette van Antwerpen* from the Netherlands, the number of advertisements placed annually exploded: in 1703 the paper printed thirty-one ads for the entire year, but by 1793 published nearly sixteen hundred.[7] Women could put themselves in the public eye in an unprecedented—but acceptable—form as they placed advertisements for their services and medical treatises. They also attracted a national audience, as in the case of Mrs. Mapp. Undoubtedly many readers focused on Mapp's escapades, but sufferers also learned of her wonders and whereabouts through the press. Indeed, one might speculate that her marriage was as much a publicity stunt to guarantee her daily presence in London's press as it was a reflection of true love.

As doctors and elites proclaimed the medical successes of the age, they increasingly drew sharp lines between scientifically informed medicine and other, looser, less formal branches of medical practice. By the last third of the eighteenth century, observers dismissed much of female and folk practice as superstitious and unskilled: female midwives, folk healers, and "she-doctors" like Mrs. Mapp were, and had always been, ignorant, dangerous quacks. Where their cures worked, it was blind luck. Taken seriously by male medical observers in the 1730s, Mrs. Mapp was soon after her death relegated to the loony bin of history; in the words of the eminent physician Percival Pott, she was "an

FIGURE 4.1: Mrs. Sarah Mapp, adapted from William
Hogarth's *The Company of Undertakers* (1736–37).
Author's photograph.

ignorant, illiberal, drunken, female savage" who had deluded the masses with
"the most extravagant assertions."[8]

While Mrs. Mapp may have ended up on the margins, however, her strategies for promoting herself as a life-saving, population-boosting medic were not
so different from those of midwives and female practitioners who managed to
win longer-lasting acclaim in the eighteenth century. For example, as we shall
see, the royal French midwife Madame du Coudray, who established a national
system of midwifery education under the patronage of the Bourbon monarchy,
also exploited the power of print to highlight her contributions to national
health and the growth of the population. Recent historians have tended to
emphasize the extent to which eighteenth-century female healers, especially
midwives, became marginalized as medical men established themselves as "scientists." At the same time, while it is true that the medical authority of women
declined with the advent of the Enlightenment, women were by no means entirely effaced from medical practice, and some established enduring strategies
that ensured the continued involvement of women in health care delivery.

EARLY MODERN MORTALITY, MISERY, AND MEDICAL CARE

Eighteenth-century Europeans believed that a nation's strength depended on its numbers and its ability to expand demographically. But as they looked on the population, they witnessed a sorry state of sickness and disease with few examples of effective cures. They saw numerous cases of suffering and a daunting range of common illnesses, including gout, ague, flu, fever, earaches, scoliosis, smallpox, syphilis, sore throats, thrush, rabies, burns, broken bones, bladder infections, stones, and worms. And they saw that these diseases were only marginally worse than their cures. Mercury, mustard plasters, pulling teeth, and bloodletting had their effects but often fatally so. Given the contaminants of everyday life—from the lead used in winemaking and paint and the mercury used in the making of hats to the omnipresent smoke from hearths; from the human waste and sewage that poisoned water sources to the flour-and-water concoctions fed to newborns whose mothers did not breast-feed—early modern life expectancy was abbreviated. Nearly 10 percent of all babies born in London between 1725 and 1749 died within twenty-nine days.[9] Once babies made it through their first month, they still had on average short and miserable lives ahead of them. Mortality rates and life expectancy varied enormously by region, population density, climate, and class. England's newborn, infant, and childhood mortality rates declined generally after 1750, but the numbers were still fearsome. The industrial town of Colne, Lancashire, suffered an infant mortality rate of two hundred out of a thousand—one out of every five babies—from 1750 to 1820.[10]

Eighteenth-century babies, children, and adults confronted endemic diseases like scarlet fever, dysentery, and many other bacterial and viral illnesses, as well as smallpox, which was endemic in eighteenth-century cities but epidemic elsewhere.[11] In London, Paris, Rome, Kyoto, Cairo, and other cities of hundreds of thousands, lethal microbes wended through the population, exposing nearly every young person. Diseases with high infant and childhood mortality rates eroded urban populations as endemics. Those diseases, such as smallpox, which were significantly more fatal for adults than children, were devastating when they arrived as epidemics rather than lurking endemically in a large city. The worst mortality rates occurred when a disease had not been seen for a decade or more, consequently wiping out both children and adults. On the Japanese island of Tanegashima, a 1737 smallpox epidemic killed approximately a thousand people out of a population of nearly fifteen thousand. In Copenhagen, Denmark, a 1707 epidemic killed eighteen thousand out of fifty thousand residents. And in North America from 1775 to 1783 (during the Revolutionary War), smallpox spread upward from Spanish Mexico and westward from the British North American colonies among entirely unexposed populations, killing nearly 131,000 people, mostly Africans and Native Americans.[12] In remote locations like Iceland and in the European colonies of the Atlantic world, few diseases were endemic, so when smallpox, yellow fever, or other killers arrived they could wipe out more than a quarter of the total population in a few weeks.[13]

In addition to disease caused by microbes, many suffered from congenital defects or malnutrition, including scurvy, rickets, or goiters when vitamin C, vitamin D, or iodine were absent from diets. Accidents and disasters lurked too, in agriculture, fishing, and mining, in workshops and the building trades, and simply around the family hearth or the nearby well. Eighteenth-century newspapers and magazines were littered with lamentable reports of children run over by hackney coaches, men kicked in the face and thrown by horses, and carriages tumbling into ditches, with passengers bruised and maimed. How many were killed or disabled, temporarily or permanently, by these and other accidents is unknown and probably unquantifiable, but the frequency of these types of reports suggests why the services of Mrs. Mapp and other bonesetters were so greatly appreciated by those who otherwise might never walk or work again.[14]

Eighteenth-century men, like men today, could not expect to live as long as women. They faced more dangers at work than women, whether they labored on land or at sea, or worked as common laborers, craftsmen, or even doctors, as we shall see. "Two out of three" men serving the Dutch East India Company "never made it home" at the end of the seventeenth century, with "the trade with Asia . . . costing about six or seven thousand European lives per year."[15] But work at home in Europe was dangerous, too, in several common but lethal trades. White lead was so toxic that one observer described how "an employment of three months" as a paint maker "produces palsy in some of the limbs, commonly a loss of the hand chiefly employed, . . . which rapidly extends, unless the person change his occupation."[16] It was common knowledge that "those who work[ed] . . . in mines of mercury seldom live above three or four years."[17] Medical men's exposure to mercury, other toxins, and their patients' diseases shortened their lives, too. For example, apothecaries' median age at death between 1730 and 1749 in London was forty, while merchants' median age was fifty-two.[18] According to contemporaries, female midwives faced less harm than medical men because they had little contact with mercury and other poisons and because they commonly avoided "the Danger of Infection" contracted from a mother and her bodily fluids by "wash[ing] their Hands in

Water and Vinegar"—a practice that medical men far less often followed until the later nineteenth century.[19]

Women also faced discomforts and dangers. Though few traditionally female occupations involved working with dangerous chemicals, women did suffer exposure to some toxins—for example, the sulfuric gas used to bleach straw in the making of bonnets. But chemical exposure did not sap working women's health as much as did simple overwork. As one early nineteenth-century medical author observed, "The great cause of the ill-health of females . . . is the lowness of their wages. To obtain a livelihood, they are obliged to work in excess."[20] Women's reproductive lives could be painful and fatal, too. Typically, women had about a 1 or 2 percent chance of dying during childbirth or in the forty days of "lying-in" afterward.[21] Considering that mothers gave birth several times during their reproductive lives, they confronted death as a real specter, especially in years of epidemic childbed fever. They also suffered from damaged reproductive organs after difficult labors and from irritating conditions including urinary tract infections and yeast infections, including thrush, which women sometimes shared with their nursing infants. (Wet nurses also feared catching congenital syphilis from their employers' babies.)

In the eighteenth century, there were several categories of health care providers. Some practitioners, namely, physicians, surgeons, and apothecaries, belonged to corporate bodies that had legal privileges and obligations,[22] but other healers worked outside those formal categories. Physicians, the medical elites, relied on their classical educations to write prescriptions in Latin, though they issued bills in their native tongues. They offered explanations for patients' self-described ills and generally avoided having any physical contact with their patients' bodies, although they examined the body's products of urine, feces, saliva, and blood with relish. The unseemly acts of feeling the pulse and letting blood were often left to surgeons, who were in charge of invading the body with instruments from leeches to lancets. (Both of these were used to bleed patients, as ordered by physicians to cure every imaginable ill and manage pain—a reasonably effective strategy, since hemorrhaging induced fainting and thus forgetting.) Apothecaries were the least prestigious medical practitioners, but their preparations of painkillers and panaceas, both real and imagined, were greatly valued by desperate patients.

Most physicians, surgeons, and apothecaries were male, but not universally so. Early modern and eighteenth-century female practitioners worked in each of these medical branches, most commonly in northern Europe and European colonies, where they acquired their expertise as the wives, widows, and daughters of medical men. Although some were fully licensed to practice on their own, they more typically operated as assistants to or as de facto partners of their husbands.[23] It was not at all unusual to hear of a widow carrying on her deceased husband's work. Although most probably continued to wear their own clothes, some adopted the accoutrements of masculinity, as in the case of a "dentist's widow From Limoges [France] who carried on her husband's profession dressed in men's clothes and wearing a false beard."[24] Women even practiced in the male medical branches of physic, surgery, and apothecary in regions that totally prohibited them from doing so—at least in principle. The Italian medical corporations entirely forbade women from any practice other than midwifery, and they policed themselves and interlopers thoroughly; yet they rarely prosecuted rural female healers for practicing surgery and physic because such women were sometimes the only healers in their isolated communities.[25]

Eighteenth-century medical women were often quite talented and in some cases clearly surpassed their fathers or husbands in ability. Consider the case of the fourteen-year-old Catholic Pole Regina Salomea Rusiecki, whose parents forced her to marry an elderly but prominent German doctor and ophthalmologist, Jakob Halpir, in the 1730s. The couple moved to Turkey, where profitable medical opportunities abounded. While in Istanbul, Regina assisted her husband in his cataract operations, but she also sought tutoring from the city's best medical practitioners to learn more techniques. She quickly was recognized for her gifts in curing not only ocular disorders but also urinary tract infections and acne. Like the English bonesetter Sarah Mapp, the young Regina was prodigiously talented as a medical practitioner but cursed in love. Jakob, irritated by her independence and success, abandoned her and absconded with all of their possessions and profits. She carried on, ultimately using new earnings to purchase five prisoners of war—including one who would become her second husband. She made her way back to Poland, obtaining passports and a safe journey by curing the fuzzy vision and pocky visages of European royalty.[26]

In addition to the female practitioners we have met so far, countless more women provided health care in their households and neighborhoods in less formal but no less important ways. European "gentlewomen" had long been expected to help their families, servants, and poorer neighbors by preparing medicine and providing routine care and nursing. The affluent Elizabeth Freke from Norfolk, England, wrote up an inventory in the 1710s of the hundreds of pints of medicines she had prepared for herself, her family, and her friends, suggesting the enormous labor and expertise involved in this expected household duty among elite women.[27] Further down the social scale, women gathered herbs, roots, and other ingredients, which they used in their own preparations or sold to pharmacists. Given that the work of the apothecary overlapped with and resembled much household work, it seemed to cause little stir when women opened their own apothecary shops, as was the case for Elizabeth Greenleaf, who opened her business in Boston in 1727.[28]

In Catholic regions, women provided health care as members of religious orders, including several that had been formed in the seventeenth century as specifically noncloistered communities. The most active and influential of these was the French Daughters of Charity (1633), which gained "a glowing reputation for the sisters as women who got things done without fuss . . . whilst exemplifying the highest level of commitment." By 1700 more than two hundred towns and neighborhoods were served by the Daughters of Charity. The sisters managed hospitals, treated patients, tended to sick prisoners in jails and poorhouses, prepared food and medicine for the poor in their own homes, and even operated dispensaries and pharmacies for the public.[29] They were not the only order committed to healing the world. In 1727 a group of Ursuline sisters traveled to New Orleans to serve as nurses at a military hospital, open a dispensary, and care for the city's residents. New Orleans's population of "destitute men and women deported from the poorhouses of France" was especially vulnerable given the city's tropical climate awash with mosquitoes, parasites, yellow fever, and dysentery.[30] But contemporaries viewed the nuns as contributing far more to the public health of New Orleans than any of the city's medical men, no doubt because they did more to heal than only bleeding and dosing. Unlike the city's doctors, the nuns also fed, washed, and nursed their patients.[31]

Despite corporate restrictions in most European regions limiting women's participation in the medical professions, female healers continued to provide care during the Enlightenment. In rural and isolated regions they performed the work of surgeons, physicians, and druggists as needed and without much intervention from urban, male medical corporations. In towns, many female healers worked alongside male practitioners in complementary roles for the first two-thirds of the century. A cooperative relationship between the sexes also typified medical care within the household, as both wives and husbands felt responsible for the good health of their subordinates and worked together to tend the ill.[32] As we have seen, moreover, some medical husbands and their wives worked in professional partnerships. Despite normative expectations from medical corporations and prescriptive literature about the fundamental differences between the sexes, female and male healers often worked together and in boundary-defying ways. Women sometimes practiced "masculine" surgical techniques, and men, both as doctors and as heads of households, sometimes participated in more "feminine," nurturing roles, including making bandages and poultices, nursing the sick, and cleaning their wounds. Such bending of normative gender expectations seemed to inspire little concern among doctors or the public, except when it came to midwifery.

EIGHTEENTH-CENTURY MIDWIFERY, MATERNITY, AND MALE OBSTETRICS

The most visible and important of all healers in Europe and North America during the early modern period and into the eighteenth century were female midwives. Out of all of the eighteenth-century caretakers of the body, midwives undoubtedly had the most impact on population growth (or decline). By delivering babies, midwives performed the most necessary medical intervention in all communities. For centuries, authorities and laypeople acknowledged and appreciated their contributions—and worried about their deficiencies.

During the seventeenth and eighteenth centuries, female midwives typically managed nearly all births without male medical assistance. Births occurred mostly in women's own homes, and midwives relied on the help of the mothers' friends, relations, and neighbors, all of whom worked together (at least ideally) to physically and emotionally support the woman in labor and to keep the household quiet, ordered, calm, clean, and warm. The midwife herself "caught" the newborn, delivered the placenta, cut the umbilical cord, swaddled the baby, and offered postpartum care to mother and child. In addition to attending births, many midwives advised women (and men) in sexual and reproductive matters. Midwives' responsibilities extended further into the life of the community. In many locales, both Catholic and Protestant, they had been granted the privilege of baptizing unborn and half-born infants. Parish officials and the courts called on them to offer testimony in all sexual and reproductive matters and expected them to give parish officials and clerics the names of illegitimate babies' fathers. These juridical obligations often pitted midwives against mothers and gave them an enormous amount of power within their neighborhoods.[33]

In isolated North American and European regions, midwives of the eighteenth century worked as general practitioners, preparing herbs and roots, making medicines, treating sore throats and diarrhea, dressing wounds, and laying out the dead. In very isolated regions, they might be the only regular medical figures available and thus might be called on to act as surgeons, physicians, or apothecaries. In the West Indies, African midwives were the primary caretakers for their

FIGURE 4.2: *Remarkable Birth of Four Vibrant Live Newborns and One Stillbirth*, watercolor (1719). The midwife Maria Somel and her female assistants have successfully delivered quintuplets in Scheviningen, Netherlands. Reproduced in J. J. de Blécourt and G. C. Nijhoff, *Vijflinggeboorten; een geval van vijflinggeboorte, met eene beschrijving van het praeparaat, en een casuistisch en analytisch overzicht van 27 gevallen van vijflinggeboorte* (Groningen, 1904). Author's photograph.

fellow slaves. They delivered babies, of course, but they also nursed those too sick to work, prepared medicines for the plantations, and provided preventative care, including smallpox inoculation, which they had imported from Africa. They also knew better than Europeans how to manage tropical diseases and parasitic infections caused by chiggers, guinea worms, and other pests.[34]

Despite their expertise and the authority they wielded in households and neighborhoods, early modern midwives rarely operated entirely out of the range of men's control. In both Protestant and Catholic regions, clerics examined and licensed them with the intention of enforcing religious conformity and also preventing their performing abortions. In Italy, clerics meddled in all aspects of their customary duties. Like midwives in most of Europe, Italian *mammane* not only attended births but also carried newborns to baptism (or burial) and participated in the spiritual life of their clients. Though these duties gave midwives power, such activities made them vulnerable to priests who prodded them during holy confession for details about sinning parishioners or peppered them during baptisms as to the identity of illegitimate and orphaned babies.[35]

In the Holy Roman Empire's highly regulated cities, where guilds, town councils, and other corporate bodies policed their citizens, medical men and town councils tracked midwives from apprenticeship to the end of their careers. In Brunswick and other German towns, doctors and burghers determined the exact number of women permitted to practice as midwives, nurses, and apprentices, and they enforced wage controls that were so harsh that German midwifery was barely lucrative for most of the eighteenth century.[36] German cities were exceptional in their extreme control of midwifery, but even the freest urban markets in London, Dublin, Paris, and Boston failed to give female midwives complete control over their work conditions and wages. In all places, midwives were expected to help any woman in travail, no matter how impoverished. This meant that in destitute times and places, midwives might earn little more than a subsistence wage.

In the Caribbean, African midwives enjoyed limited autonomy during the eighteenth century. Plantation owners and others, including Maria Sybella Merien, observed African midwives spreading knowledge about abortifacients and helping to commit infanticides when enslaved mothers could not bear to bring their children into slavery. Planters realized many decades before the abolition of the slave trade (in 1807 in the British colonies and in 1808 in the United States), that the best way to preserve, or even expand, their slave labor force was through good medical care and successful breeding. White doctors, eager to please and profit from their employers, carefully policed African midwives' activities. They also recommended incentives to women to remain pregnant: perhaps a day off every other week might induce a pregnant slave to deliver rather than abort her offspring, suggested Dr. David Collins in *The Practical Rules for Management and Medical Treatment of Negro Slaves in the Sugar Colonies* (1811).[37] Ultimately, however, Collins and others recognized that preventing abortion and infanticide among slaves depended on overseeing and policing enslaved midwives and healers rather than the enslaved mothers themselves.[38]

Surgeons saw midwifery as potentially profitable, especially if they could advertise a special expertise or efficacy that female midwives lacked. Northern European surgeons developed new tools and techniques that helped build a clientele. The seventeenth-century Huguenot Chamberlen family of doctors resident in London developed obstetrical forceps capable of helping poorly positioned babies out of their mothers' pelvic passages; the Dutch surgeon-author Hendrick van Deventer learned of a helpful maneuver from his wife, a midwife, to create more space for an emerging child during birth by pressing the mother's coccyx. Parisian accoucheurs attended elite and charity cases, arranged official appointments to state hospitals and charities, reported their obstetrical findings to scientific societies, and published treatises on reproduction, midwifery, and child care. These seventeenth- and eighteenth-century doctors collectively codified the reproductive and pediatric knowledge that heretofore had been oral and commonplace among women and men. They also emphasized their expertise in saving lives and boosting their nations' population, claims that won them support from philanthropists and statesmen. The historian of medicine Adrian Wilson has suggested further that eighteenth-century doctors' most powerful innovation was to sell themselves not just as emergency practitioners but also as entirely routine birth attendants. These "men-midwives," as they called themselves, appealed to elite pregnant women who believed that these men offered superior care to that provided by female midwives.[39]

As medicine became an increasingly powerful cultural domain during the Enlightenment through its perceived ability to keep people alive and healthy, enterprising men-midwives touted their qualifications while accusing female midwives of lacking the most fundamental skills requisite to deliver the nation's population and provide life-saving care.[40] By the mid-eighteenth century, men-midwives and their supporters openly derided female healers as incompetent and unkind, impatient and unlearned. According to male critics, because the female midwife was eager to earn her pay and return home to sleep, she was apt to yank an oddly positioned unborn baby out of its mother's womb. Should a man-midwife appear, she was likely to lie, pretending to have no idea how she happened to be holding the neonate's headless body while the child's head was trapped, stuck over the mother's pelvis.[41] In fact, such catastrophic deliveries were extremely rare occurrences. Yet scandalous tales of midwives' ignorant and cruel behavior, widely disseminated in men-midwives' treatises and repeated in the contemporary press, helped to establish a growing sense in European and North American cities, from London to Paris to Philadelphia, that male midwives easily outperformed the female competition. One measure of the effect of such stories is that aristocratic and royal mothers began to choose male midwives as birth attendants: Queen Charlotte of England, for example, decided to turn to the society man-midwife William Hunter by the time she was pregnant with her fourth child.[42]

Female midwives did not accept criticism and competition without resistance, of course. As part of their defense, they published works proclaiming their natural authority and extensive experience, but they knew to present their case in Enlightenment terms to appeal to an audience appreciative of observation, science, and reason. Texts by eighteenth-century English midwives

eschewed the superstitious advice and detailed descriptions of sexual parts
and pleasures that seventeenth-century midwives had once offered. Instead,
they flagged their credentials and used case studies pedagogically. They offered
vivid descriptions of potential complications with recommended resolutions.
In other words, they wrote in the style of men-midwives by emphasizing midwifery as a skill mastered through knowledge of anatomy, careful observation,
and hands-on experience.[43]

The most famous eighteenth-century midwife-author, Elizabeth Nihell,
however, took a different approach, attacking men-midwives as "instrument-
wielding," objectifying, and lascivious frauds who entered the profession to
trespass on women's bodies and midwives' livelihoods. She argued that anatomical and medical training was superfluous because midwifery came naturally to women in their innate sympathy for fellow women (and female animals)
in pregnancy and labor. Women's very beings were overcome by a deep need
to help, she explained, because they had "more bowels for women."[44] Though
some have read her work as a protofeminist manifesto for defending childbirth
as a natural experience rather than a medical event to be managed by men,[45]
Nihell's overarching argument about gender was not entirely liberating for
women. Her portrayal of midwives and mothers as creatures driven by passion
and feeling resonated with an emerging Enlightenment view that women were
fragile and emotional, naturally suited for motherhood and maternity but little
else. Without intending it, the content of her argument aligned with the assertion of many men-midwives that women were overly passionate and irrational,
controlled by their nervous sensibilities.[46]

As they pushed more aggressively into this arena long dominated by female midwives, Enlightenment men-midwives and other doctors contributed
to radical new ideas about women's bodies. In part, these experts inherited
a complex, contradictory array of classical, Renaissance, and early modern
beliefs that viewed the female body as dangerously powerful. According to
ancient authorities and aphorisms, women's wombs "wandered" right out
of their pelvises to cause hysterical states of mind. Women's whole beings
reeked with lust and power, and they could cause other women's husbands
to stray, milk to curdle, and enemies' newborns to die. Residues of these beliefs survived into the eighteenth century.[47] At the same time, new arguments
about women's bodies and minds also emerged during the Enlightenment and
were promulgated not only by medical men but also by novelists, journalists,
artists, and philosophers. These ideas positioned women as soft and gentle,
physically vulnerable and emotionally dependent. Women were increasingly
Increasingly depicted by both male and female authors from the 1750s forward

as naturally devoted mothers, obedient daughters and sisters, humble servants, generous neighbors, and tender hearts who were overcome with empathy when they saw a "[bitch] with whelp;" and doctors played up their
ability to help such lovely creatures through their bodily pain and suffering.[48]
These delicate eighteenth-century women, pregnant with supremely valuable
future citizens, were represented as needing scientific expertise and manly
sympathy to carry them safely through the dangers of pregnancy, the trauma
of labor, and the duties of motherhood. Men-midwives described themselves
as peculiarly designed to answer such needs. Their skill at self-promotion
and in interpersonal interactions persuaded both mothers and fathers in elite
households to rely on them as reproductive experts and confidantes. Many
of these doctors also found favor with philanthropists and town councils,
who supported their efforts to establish maternity hospitals and to educate
and regulate female midwives. For example, by the 1730s, town councils in
Edinburgh and Stockholm established lectureships for master obstetricians to
provide training for all the city's midwives, who were required to attend and
pass exams before being permitted to practice their craft.[49]

Finally, in addition to building their reputations as better birth attendants
than traditional midwives, many Enlightenment doctors proclaimed a special
expertise regarding menstruation, vaginal discharge, emotional depression, and
self-stimulation.[50] In other words, at the same time that many midwives were
losing their status and livelihoods, enterprising medical men "discovered" the
troubled female body—or, as some historians have recently proposed, rediscovered ancient and Renaissance versions of female trouble and recast these earlier
models of feminine illness and inadequacy in the form of eighteenth-century
models of sickness. Whether eighteenth-century doctors and scientists had in
fact discovered new territory in the feminine body, they were determined to set
to work conquering or "fixing" it, profiting in the process from its ailments,
real, imagined, and invented.[51]

THE POWER OF PRINT IN THE EIGHTEENTH-CENTURY MEDICAL MARKETPLACE

Eighteenth-century women were not passive, despite claims from doctors and
others that they were, nor did female healers allow themselves to become
fully marginalized during the Enlightenment. Not only did women continue
to practice successfully as midwives and healers, they also took advantage
of an expanding print culture to advertise their skills, to assert their contributions to the population, and to advocate for their medical innovations.

That male practitioners also used the press, public venues, and bureaucratic channels to do these same things and expand their market share, eventually largely sidelining women professionally, does not mean that women were not formidable contenders within the contested arena of the Enlightenment public sphere.[52]

The expansion of print culture helped female practitioners in significant ways. In the case of the press, women had more opportunities to place themselves in the marketplace. After all, eighteenth-century newspapers expanded by every measure: more titles emerged in each major Western city, more provincial and colonial towns established their own local papers, everywhere more copies of each paper were printed, and all papers included more ads annually. Newspapers survived economically not through their sale price but through revenues from advertisers who bought space to advertise everything from runaway slaves and soldiers to unmarried women seeking husbands, from lost banknotes to found pocket watches, from dancing lessons to the evening's opera performance. But medical products, services, and texts were omnipresent, occupying anywhere from "one quarter to one third of all printed space between 1760 and 1820" in the English provincial and metropolitan press.[53]

Medics of both sexes advertised cures for syphilis and therapies for teething babies, but female advertisers focused particularly on these ailments and other assorted domestic and private afflictions. For example, London newspapers during 1769 and 1770 included advertisements for Mrs. Gibson's Medicine, "which causes immediate conception"; a midwife who promised that women with "concealed" pregnancies could secretly reside at her "neat, airy, well furnished house"; and "Specificks for the cure of Secret Disorders and Weaknesses in Women" sold by "The Wife of an eminent Physician." The latter explained that "Modesty . . . obliges us to conceal those disorders, not only where the irregularities of a husband have done us injury, but in many other weaknesses we are liable to from nature." In other words, her "Specific Essence" at five shillings likely combated syphilis, while her "Restorative Drops" at one pound and one shilling likely caused miscarriages.[54] French medics placed similar ads, including one Dame Veros from Marseilles, who promised to cure " 'all secret illnesses' " with "restorative" cures in 1771.[55] These coded advertisements appealing to women's unwanted pregnancies and venereal infections were not to be found everywhere, though. During the colonial period and in the early republic, American midwives and female healers advertised their expertise or the commodities they sold at their shops, but they appear not to have offered thinly disguised clandestine services.[56]

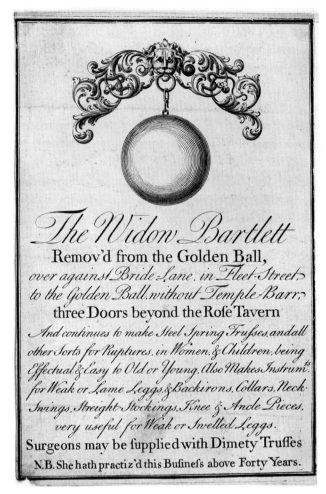

FIGURE 4.3: Trade card advertising "The Widow Bartlett,"
who made trusses and other orthopedic devices in eighteenth-
century London. Wellcome Library, London. M0015860.

Eighteenth-century female healers took advantage of Enlightenment print
culture by publishing medical books and pamphlets not only in the fields of
midwifery, as we have seen, but also in domestic and household medicine,
including herbals and "medical cookery." Out of thirty-five new eighteenth-
century household guides printed in England, eighteen were written by women
and another eleven were published anonymously, with many running into
multiple editions.[57] Eliza Smith's *The Compleat Housewife; or, Accomplished
Gentlewoman's Companion* appeared in eighteen editions between 1727 and
1773.[58] European cookbooks produced in the first two-thirds of the century

included recipes for regular meals and dishes as well as household supplies and medical remedies for coughs, fevers, worms, rashes, and more. But as historian of gender and science Londa Schiebinger has noted, this medical advice disappeared after the 1750s, and female authors revised their works as pure cookbooks.[59] Late eighteenth-century author Elizabeth Raffald explicitly promised that she left all such medical recipes to " 'the physicians . . . whose proper province they are.' "[60] As Smith's *The Compleat Housewife* saw its final printing in 1773, Dr. William Buchan's *Domestic Medicine* (first edition, 1769) was on its way to becoming the most popular medical blockbuster in the British Isles and North America for the next century.[61] Although certainly a populist text in its encouragement of laypeople to manage their health, Buchan's work swamped the competition, including that by female medical experts.

These trends in eighteenth-century print culture reflected parallel transformations in the household and professional arenas. In the early modern and early eighteenth-century European world, the household was more than a domestic retreat. It was ideally a self-sufficient space where its inhabitants produced food, clothing, and medications for themselves. Few households in reality provided entirely for themselves, but prescriptive literature advised wives to make remedies and manage their families' health in addition to all of their other domestic obligations. As a space that provided for all needs, the household was both an occupational and a familial space, with women and men taking part in cooking and chemistry, housework and healing. Early modern men could proclaim a legitimate expertise in household medicine, and women as well as men could publish works in chemistry.[62] By the early eighteenth century, however, spaces and occupational expertise began to separate. By the mid-eighteenth century, as scientific societies flourished, work in natural philosophy typically occurred outside the home. Natural philosophers, doctors, and the learned gathered together not at their residences but at their colleges, clubs, societies, and coffeehouses—all spaces from which women were excluded either explicitly or by force of custom.

Despite the transformations in British household and professional practice that limited women's medical opportunities, midwives and female medics in the Netherlands, France, and the new United States expanded their opportunities, ultimately by conforming to men's professional and bureaucratic expectations. In the Netherlands—and eventually in other northern European regions with strong bureaucratic infrastructures—eighteenth-century midwives did not resist municipal regulations and policing. Instead of defending midwifery as a solely domestic occupation that only women had the natural right to practice, as English midwives did, Dutch midwives accepted working with medical men and bureaucrats who might regulate their practice. By working within a system that linked domestic, private concerns of birth and family to public health and order, and by highlighting the cleanliness and healthfulness of home births managed by women, Dutch midwives were able to protect a culture of midwifery in the home and gain the trust of medical men to perform basic obstetrical surgeries themselves without calling on a doctor. To this day, nearly 70 percent of Dutch childbirths are handled entirely by female midwives without requiring intervention by either midwife specialists or obstetricians.[63]

In France, female midwifery was improved and elevated during the Enlightenment thanks to the extraordinary work of one single woman: the royal midwife, Angélique Marguerite Le Boursier du Coudray, who capitalized on the French crown's fear of national depopulation. Well connected and well trained, du Coudray authored the *Abrégé de l'art des accouchements* (The art of obstetrics) in 1759, which initially functioned as a sort of advertisement of her expertise and her Enlightenment point of view. She petitioned Louis XV to be granted the privilege of teaching scientific midwifery to the rural midwives of France. With the help of carefully crafted and detailed stuffed mannequins of mothers and fetuses that she built out of wicker, cloth, and leather, she spent three decades traveling and teaching women throughout France the nature of childbirth. Du Coudray trained midwives on the ground, but she also knew that she must train instructors to carry on the tradition of female midwifery. Among her talented protégés, her niece, Madame Marguerite Coutanceau, became a master midwife and author herself and weathered the Terror and Napoleon to train yet more generations of French midwives. As in the case of Dutch midwives, du Coudray worked within the constraints of a highly bureaucratic state, rather than trying to work outside of it. She faced stiff competition and rabid hostility from contemporary men-midwives, but her ambition, energy, and unmarried, childless status permitted her to travel and train at least ten thousand French midwives. Her male critics and competitors kept to their comfortable lives in Paris and other cities, but in so doing they failed to influence the thousands of practitioners on the ground that du Coudray met and educated.[64] By establishing a national, state-sponsored system of enlightened midwifery education, du Coudray ultimately kept child delivery in the hands of women. Just as important, she disseminated outstanding obstetrical knowledge across the nation, which her biographer, Nina Gelbart, argues may have been one of the root causes of France's declining infant mortality rates after the 1750s.[65]

The new American republic, with its tenuously linked states and pronounced lack of bureaucracy and regulation at both the federal and local levels, offered

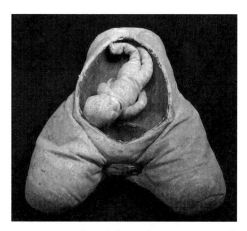

FIGURE 4.4: An eighteenth-century French obstetrical model. Dittrick Medical History Center, Case Western Reserve University.

medical entrepreneurs of both sexes fresh opportunities. Medical colleges, so-cieties, and schools of thought popped up across the country, particularly as the United States expanded westward. Male and female medics took advantage of this vast market, and, without having to worry about defying medical cor-porations as in the European case, women could style themselves "doctresses." Both sexes openly advertised medical solutions to menstrual "obstructions" from the late 1790s forward, as many Americans sought to limit the size of their families. And quite unlike the English case, where female authors confined their household manuals to cooking and cleaning, American women took up the tradition of publishing encyclopedic guides on all aspects of household care and sustenance, including medical remedies. Early nineteenth-century Ameri-can women were not as marginalized as their British sisters were in popular health care: not because they worked within a bureaucratic system as French and Dutch midwives did, but because there was no such bureaucracy in the expansive and expanding United States.[66]

At the end of the Enlightenment, then, women's professional status was far more varied than it had been a century earlier. In 1700 women had worked across Europe and its colonies as midwives; in rural areas they practiced fairly independently and broadly, serving as family-care practitioners. Early eighteenth-century women were also expected to prepare medications in the home and to know which plants healed or harmed, and consequently were appreciated for their natural and therapeutic knowledge. But by 1800 many places, especially in the British Isles, saw the exclusion of women from medical knowledge and practice. In contrast, midwives in France and the Netherlands shored up their authority, and in the new United States, enterprising female authors and practitioners flourished, despite stiff competition from men.

As for the state of health across the eighteenth century, infant mortality rates had declined in London and several other capital cities and the countryside. Enlightenment midwives and medical men were both eager to take credit for such advances. Mortality from smallpox declined thanks to the practice of inoculation (and, after the late 1790s, vaccination). Women had no small hand in contributing to these demographic advancements. Women had been at the center of inoculation practice in Asia and Africa when Montagu discovered their work and shared the news in the Western world.

The Enlightenment is rich with dynamic female healers, from Mrs. Mapp to Madame du Coudray. And as different as these two figures are—one a dramatic flash in the pan, the other a devoted public servant who criss-crossed France in order to educate all her nation's midwives—the two shared the entirely Enlightenment goal of growing the population by birthing babies and returning the maimed to work.

The eighteenth century is typically viewed as the period in which women's medical authority declined in the West, and female practitioners are sometimes portrayed as the victims of the cunning machinations of medical men who supplanted their traditional authority. That depiction is not entirely false, but it warrants a more nuanced assessment. Female healers did survive in this period. As they had in times past, women continued to work as medics and midwives, most particularly on the geographic and cultural periphery of the countryside. In the Netherlands and in prerevolutionary France, moreover, they negotiated ways to establish authority in male-dominated bureaucracies and patronage systems, and they did so in institutionally rooted ways that extended their influence throughout their lifetimes and beyond.

CHAPTER FIVE

Public and Private: Public and Private Lives in Eighteenth-Century France

JOAN B. LANDES

There is no question that the Enlightenment, as an intellectual and social movement, possessed universal aspirations. In practice, as this volume demonstrates, it transcended national boundaries. Yet perhaps no country is as closely associated with the Enlightenment as France. While the English authors Francis Bacon, John Locke, and Isaac Newton are rightly credited with laying the scientific and moral foundations of the movement, and the German philosopher Immanuel Kant acknowledged for famously asking "Was ist Aufklärung?" ("What Is Enlightenment?"), it was the authors and image makers of prerevolutionary and revolutionary France who most insistently deployed the contrasting imagery and iconography of the Enlightenment as a conflict between *lumières* (light) and *tènèbres* (darkness).[1] The *philosophes*— the French scientists, journalists, and authors most closely associated with the Enlightenment—would have greatly enjoyed the paradox of attributing the movement's greatest achievements to France, a country they much decried for its autocratic institutions and religious orthodoxy. Moreover, as this chapter shows, there is a further irony in associating the French Enlightenment with the birth of modern notions of public and private spheres, for in fact the categories of the public and the private remained ill defined as a feature of daily existence throughout the eighteenth century. While it may be accurate to say that modern notions of public and private life emerged from the intellectual challenges and final political cataclysm that shaped French life during this century, it is also important to understand that the later (essentially nineteenth-century) understanding of these categories as distinct, gender coded, and defined by the boundary that separates the inside from the outside of the household was still only in the process of formation during the Enlightenment.

During this age, France and other western European societies experienced urban expansion tied to a developing market economy and communication networks linking not just elites but also ordinary people and goods across increasing distances. At the same time, however, many households still operated according to a traditional economic model in which domestic units were also sites of production. Working men did not need to leave the home to secure their livelihood when the house was itself a workplace, and adult and child family members worked alongside servants, journeymen, and employees.

The private, domestic realm within aristocratic households was also a complex and often public affair in composition, function, and visibility. Among the elites, personal life had an aura of publicity. We have all heard stories about the peculiarities of early modern royal households, where in a holdover of medieval courtliness the king's ministers retained intimate access to his majesty's bodily functions, where a royal marriage was consummated before courtiers, and where queens were expected to give birth before an audience. Noble homes showcased wealth and rank, which also depended on an ethos of public visibility before others of one's rank. Concerning such grand households, the French novelist and pamphleteer Louis-Sébastien Mercier observed later in the eighteenth century, "Once a house is constructed, hardly anything is finished; only a quarter of the expenses have been laid out. Yet to arrive are the carpenter, the upholsterer, the painter, the gilder, the sculptor, the furniture-maker &c. The inside occupies three times more time than the construction of the building: antechambers, staircases, hallways, amenities, all of it is never ending."[2] The interiors of grand homes were also the site of highly publicized intellectual and social gatherings, such as the famous Enlightenment salons, which were often hosted by a woman in her home. Interestingly, such assemblies had their origin in the *ruelle*, a seventeenth-century morning social or literary gathering in the bedroom of a fashionable lady.[3]

FIGURE 5.1: Jean-Michel Moreau the Younger, *Have No Fear, My Good Friend* (1775). J. Paul Getty Museum 85.GG.416. The interior scene of an opulent household. A finished version of this drawing appeared in the series *Monument du costume* of 1776: a record of moral and social behavior and contemporary taste in clothing and furnishings. Reclining on a daybed in a mirrored alcove, an apprehensive young woman is reassured by her friend about her first pregnancy.

Indeed, what for us is private, even secretly guarded, might during this period have been an open secret. For example, as arranged marriages remained the rule among the propertied classes of prerevolutionary France, intimate affairs were typically forged outside rather than inside of the domestic unit, as were cross-sex intellectual friendships. Nor were such affairs private in the contemporary sense of being conducted in secret, outside of the public gaze. Mistresses might accompany their lovers in social company, and husbands and wives often worked out arrangements to afford them time to spend with their lovers. In addition, public and private space was not delineated or bordered in familiar ways; or, it might make sense to say, the concepts of public and private were only just beginning to acquire many of their present-day meanings, thereby suggesting a less strict division between public and private spheres than is suggested by the most influential theoretical models linking the emergence of public and private spheres to the Enlightenment. It is to the latter that we first turn, as a prelude to a fuller exploration of the many ways in which early modern, purportedly private life had—what to modern sensibilities would be—a very public character. We also address the forces contributing to an increasingly gendered production of space.

THEORIZING THE EIGHTEENTH-CENTURY PUBLIC AND PRIVATE SPHERES

In what sense was a change in outlook on public and private life connected to the Enlightenment? And how, additionally, were ideas about the public and the private influenced by the new material and social circumstances associated with enlightened landscapes? No work has been more influential in answering these questions than Jürgen Habermas's account of the structural transformation of the public sphere, which is tied to an insightful understanding of the structure of private life during this age.[4] Habermas is indebted to Kant, who famously defined Enlightenment as "mankind's exit from its self-incurred immaturity" by man's use of his own reason, a difficult and dangerous process, involving the rejection of prejudices and the courage to use one's own reason without guidance by another.[5] Like Kant, Habermas conceives of the Enlightenment as a process, not a completed project. He also celebrates the rise of critical reason, locating its emergence in the rise of what he calls an oppositional or bourgeois public sphere—beyond the sphere of official state and aristocratic court culture. Within the public sphere, he finds the emergence of an ideal of equality, insofar as the authority of the better argument could assert itself against the social rank of the speaker and insofar as, in principle, everyone had to be *able to participate*.

According to Habermas, the oppositional or bourgeois public sphere of the eighteenth century arose in opposition to the absolutist state and aristocratic court society, in tandem with changes in the social organization and communication networks of early modern territorial states: the growth of urbanism, capitalist commerce and stock markets, new systems for news and the mail, and, finally, state administrations for taxation and "policing" of subject populations. Thus, Habermas complements the oft-noted privatization of economic production in the emerging modern era with an analysis of the role performed by a new set of cultural institutions flourishing in urban centers: coffeehouses, clubs, reading and language societies, lending libraries, concert halls, salons, and, above all, journals and the commercial press. He casts the bourgeois public sphere as a sphere of private people coming together as a public through the "historically unprecedented" public use of their reason. Interestingly, he also links the emergence of the cultural and political dimensions of the new public sphere to new expressions of privateness, which were joined in turn to the emergence of a new form of the private sphere—the patriarchal conjugal family and its domain of intimacy—and the intensification of processes of (psychological) individualism.

FIGURE 5.2: Louis Léopold Boilly, *The Arcades at the Palais Royal* (ca. 1804). Pen and black ink, and brush and gray wash, gray gouache over black chalk. Art Institute of Chicago. Worcester Sketch Fund, 19963.558. The arcades of the Palais Royal in Paris were a fashionable site of public leisure associated with gambling, shopping, sexuality, and "free" opinion. Boilly emphasizes the gendered dimension of public space, where a woman's virtue was potentially at risk. Note also in the extreme right foreground a turbaned man and a bare-breasted woman with a tied headscarf as worn by Caribbean blacks, suggesting the greater social heterogeneity of public in contrast to private company.

Who were the private individuals who constituted the oppositional bourgeois public, and what was the character of the private sphere of which Habermas speaks? Habermas is aware of the practical limitations of the bourgeois
model of the oppositional public sphere. Family life and the principles of privacy were distorted by the system of private property and the requirements of
the market. Put differently, the private individuals associated with the bourgeois
public sphere were burdened by the conflict between their position as property
owners and their realization of their common humanity with others irrespective of property lines. In short, not all individuals were able to acquire property.
Class and all its accoutrements (property, income, literacy, and cultural background) were major barriers to full participation in the bourgeois public sphere.
In addition, and most pertinently for our purposes, with few exceptions the
bourgeois or oppositional public sphere remained primarily a restricted male
preserve. Habermas recognizes the limitations on women's freedom and equality. Although women and dependents were factually and legally excluded from
the political public sphere, he is nevertheless impressed by their place within
the nonpolitical spaces of the oppositional public sphere, including as salon
hostesses or readers of literary works. As he observes, "Female readers as well
as apprentices and servants often took a more active part in the literary public
sphere than the owners of private property and family heads themselves."[6]

To better understand the gendered character of the division between public
and private life, we follow Habermas's intuition that women's lesser fortunes
in both the political and literary public spheres were in large measure a consequence of their position within an intensifying patriarchal form of the family.
We thus turn next to consider the crucial institution of the family in France,
about which Habermas gave only the barest outline in his influential study of
the structural transformation of the public sphere.

THE INSTITUTION OF THE FAMILY

In Catholic France, marriage was regarded as a sacrament, indissoluble by nature and pleasing before God. The free, unconstrained agreement of all the parties, including the parents, was a significant feature of both canon and secular
law.[7] In the realm of secular law and the royal courts, marriage was a contract,
entered into by husband and wife for the purpose of procreation. Marriage
was deemed "the first, the simplest form of society, and the one which is the
nursery of human kind."[8] As the foundation of civil society, the family was a
legal unit by means of which property could be transmitted from generation to
generation.[9] It was an institution with complex ramifications, of both a public

and a private sort. As the French Renaissance scholar Michel de Montaigne remarked, "We do not marry for ourselves, whatever we say; we marry just as much and more so for our posterity, for our family."[10] Indeed, not only but especially among the propertied classes, arranged marriage remained the rule in prerevolutionary France.

In practice, however, not all families proved to be indissoluble, and separations might occur due to a husband's abandonment or, less frequently, a mutual decision to separate without legal ratification. Whereas a husband could consign an intractable or violent wife to a convent, the bar was higher for women. A woman who sought a legal separation would need to establish her husband's culpability on the grounds of severe ill treatment, aggravated adultery, extreme and dangerous debauchery, false accusations of adultery or other grave assaults on her honor, deadly hatred, or attempted murder.[11] Overall, the legal grounds for separation of property and person were strict, and especially if initiated by a woman, proof would need to exceed evidence of ordinary maltreatment. Despite these barriers, both customary and Roman law regimes in different regions of France gave women greater latitude in demanding separation than many other European women of the period.[12] Still, French women, like their peers elsewhere, were constrained by the power of fathers and husbands over their daily existence, and that power was most directly exercised in the intimate corridors of family life. The obedience of the child toward the father was modeled on the subject's relation to the sovereign, and to a large extent so was the obedience of the wife toward her husband, who possessed the so-called *puissance maritale* prescribed by civil law.

WOMEN AND PRODUCTIVE LABOR

For those with limited or no property, family life embraced both production and reproduction. Households typically required the labor of at least one adult male and one adult female. Artisanal women worked alongside their husbands and children in a domestic workplace located within the household. Because of the value of domestic female labor, remarriage after the death of a wife was likely. At the same time, domestic production was increasingly linked to a growing market economy. In important respects, women provided the connections that made the integration of urban and rural existence possible. According to Merry E. Wiesner,

> rural women in western Europe did have some control over what they produced and sold. They made soap, butter, and cheese, gathered nuts,

herbs, eggs, and manure, raised geese, rabbits, and chickens, and then sold these in market towns and cities to gain cash in order to fulfill their tax and rent obligations; unlike the sale of grain, which was restricted to harvest time, these products were sold year-round, making them a particularly important part of the household economy. Women thus served as an important human link between the rural and urban economies, with rural women traveling to town to sell their products or their labor, and urban women going out to the rural areas to buy products to sell or to work on parcels of land that were often still owned by their families.[13]

Domestic households in eighteenth-century France bore little resemblance to the stripped-down nuclear family model, which in later centuries came to be regarded as a characteristic of a private sphere managed solely by women. Women conducted a goodly amount of the buying, selling, and trading of goods in the marketplace, and these transactions were intimately tied to the household economy. In families without access to land, single and married women's wages were essential to the family's livelihood, although women were always paid less than men, even for the same work. The family household, moreover, often provided income to non-kin. Even in modest households, the domestic unit might include servants and other unrelated persons. Both rural and poor urban women often supplemented their household's economy by acting as wet nurses for young children from the privileged classes, whose mothers either could not or preferred not to nurse their infants. Servants and other women from modest backgrounds might send their newborn children to a wet nurse, and small children were often sent into service or were trained to help around the house, while adolescents were assigned to apprenticeships.[14] Thus, among the children resident in peasant households were children who were boarding until the age of three or four, when they returned to their families of origin. In elite families, alongside domestic servants and retainers, the household included governesses or tutors, hired to supervise the child's first schooling. In sum, women's position in the household economy required them to negotiate life inside and outside the family, thereby often bridging what would later be seen as distinct public and private spheres.

As early as the seventeenth century, nevertheless, many master's wives who had once taken an active role in production were increasingly consigned to more domestic tasks, including the running of a household that could include unmarried apprentices and journeymen. Women's domestic location was further guaranteed by extrafamilial institutions, such as guilds or associations of craftsmen in a particular trade. Although some women, notably seamstresses,

did become guild members, most women were excluded from guild membership.[15] Women working outside the home were typically found in crafts not
regulated by the guilds or in the new protocapitalist industries beyond guild
control. They worked in hospitals, infirmaries, and orphanages, as midwives,
wet nurses, and healers. As for guild labor, the eighteenth century marked a
transformative point, in that guilds were temporarily suspended during the
1770s and then finally abolished in 1791 during the French Revolution. Daryl
Hafter's comparison of women's work in different French cities analyzes the
impact of guild membership on women's access to public and private opportunities. In Rouen women could become members and even masters in a number
of guilds (of which eight were associated with textile production). In contrast,
in Lyon, women did work in the famous silk industry but as auxiliary workers, sometimes legally and sometimes illegally, primarily preparing thread for
master silk weavers. Hafter concludes that the privileges associated with guild
labor took precedence over the legal disadvantages of gender. In Rouen the
guild women were all *marchande publique*, the French equivalent of the English category of *femme sole*, meaning they were allowed to act as legal persons
on their own, without male approval, even if they were married. After the
revolutionary dissolution of the guilds in 1791, women cloth workers never
again achieved the status they had once had in Rouen. Yet even in this case, the
Rouen guild women were a small group, and their situation in no way represented a golden age of women's work.[16]

TRANSFORMATIONS IN PRIVATE SPACE
AND ITS MEANINGS

What we have come to think of as the "private sphere" was not a static reposi-
tory of domestic values or social reproduction. As we have begun to see, the
very same market forces affecting social labor and the household economy
worked over time to institute less permeable boundaries between public and
private life. New material circumstances encompassed by what is termed the
consumer revolution of the eighteenth century, for example, seem to have al-
tered the meaning of the private domain.[17] By filling the home with the increasingly available objects of material culture, domesticity itself was becoming
infused with emerging notions of intimacy and psychological interiority. In
a remarkable piece of historical research, the late Annik Pardailhé-Galabrun
and her team of fifty-one graduate students scrutinized some three thousand
probate inventories, documenting the changing physical and material environ-
ments of eighteenth-century Parisians of different social ranks, including the

spatial layouts of homes (the number and kinds of rooms) and their material contents (furniture, clothing, books, religious objects).[18] On the basis of this imposing evidence, Pardailhé-Galabrun identifies a revolution in the manner of living that she associates with the birth of intimacy. Homes became more spacious, interior spaces more rationally ordered and specialized by functions. In place of kneeling kitchens, upright kitchens were designed; the number of chairs increased, as did social games and the popularity of serving coffee. Formerly multipurpose spaces were converted to intimate premises: *cabinets* to satisfy bodily functions in private, *secretaries* for storing private objects, *chambers* with fewer occupants and more private beds. Stoves replaced fireplaces for more even heat; color-coordinated decors were used to enhance the attractiveness of domestic spaces. While most Parisians continued to live in cramped spaces, across the century inhabitants nevertheless experienced an increase in space compared to those living in the preceding century. "The average occupation density on the eve of the Revolution was about two main rooms for three

FIGURE 5.3: Jean-Baptiste Greuze, *The Paternal Blessing, or the Departure of Basile* (ca. 1769). Pen and black ink, and brush and gray wash, gray gouache over black chalk. Art Institute of Chicago. Worcester Sketch Fund, 19963.558. In this scene from Greuze's novel in pictures, *Basile et Thibault, ou les Deux Educations*, the virtuous Basile prepares to leave home to defend his country.

persons. The way the number of secondary and outlying rooms burgeoned, prompted by the desire for greater privacy and comfort, also helped to contribute to expanding the habitable living area."[19] For Pardailhé-Galabrun, "the innovations constituted the Enlightenment in action, for many brought rationality, order, and the pursuit of happiness into daily experience."[20]

The middle and upper class's widening embrace of the value of feeling, or sensibility, also buttressed enlightened styles of living. Originating in philosophical and scientific writings, the concept of sensibility became popular in the emergent literary genre of the sentimental novel, which dramatically portrayed emotionally moving experiences and linked sentimentality with virtue.[21] Indeed, the *philosophe* Denis Diderot is reported to have preferred that his daughter die than that she fail to cry over the tragic persecution of so virtuous a heroine as the English author Samuel Richardson's Clarissa.[22] In the visual arts, too, sensibility emerged as a theme, which had much to do with the intensifying values attached to private life. The French artist much favored by Diderot, Jean-Baptiste Greuze, was renowned in his day for his mastery of sentimental subjects, which were often set within domestic dramas of filial piety involving prodigal sons and worthy patriarchs.[23]

ENLIGHTENED PERSPECTIVES

Even as it was shaped by patriarchal norms in law, religion, and tradition, the family—and, in related fashion, the logic of private life—became an object of enlightened scrutiny. Thus, in his contribution to the *Encyclopédie* on the term *femme* (wife), the Chevalier Louis de Jaucourt examined the reasoning behind male domination:

> The supreme being having judged that it was not good for man to be alone, conceived a desire to unite him in close society with a companion, and this society is made through a voluntary accord between the parties. As this society has as its principal goal the procreation and protection of the children it produces, the father and mother of necessity devote all their energies to nourishing and properly rearing the fruits of their love up until the time when they are able to care and judge for themselves.
>
> But although the husband and the wife have fundamentally the same interests in their marriage, it is nevertheless essential that governing authority belong to one or the other: now the affirmative right of civilized nations, the laws and the customs of Europe give this authority unanimously to the male, being the one endowed with the greatest strength

of mind and body, contributing more to the common good in matters of sacred and human things; such that the woman must necessarily be subordinated to her husband and obey his orders in all domestic affairs. This is the belief of the ancient and modern jurists and the formal decision of legislators.[24]

Having presented the theological, legal, and customary arguments for male superiority, Jaucourt next proceeded in true enlightened fashion to dismantle them. In this respect, he joined the chorus of *philosophes* in embracing the institution of the family as the oldest and most natural of human societies but in wishing to transform its character: from brute patriarchy to a sentimental unit where loving affection, not power, is the glue that binds members together, and where respect and natural obligation, not blind obedience, maintain whatever hierarchy is necessary for the proper raising of children. If marriage is freely contracted, he argued, then it also ought to be freely dissolved by the consent of both partners. Thus, like Paul-Henri Thiry, Baron d'Holbach; Claude Adrien Helvétius; and Voltaire, Jaucourt spoke in favor of the freedom to divorce. According to Jaucourt, neither nature nor utility "demands that the husband and wife be obliged to remain together for the rest of their lives, after having raised their children and left them with what they need to maintain themselves."[25] Furthermore, as he maintained in his article "Family," "the reasons we've just listed for marital power are not without rejoinder, humanely speaking; and the character of this work allows us to boldly enunciate them."

It appears first of all that it would be difficult to demonstrate that the authority of the husband comes from nature; because this principal is contrary to the natural equality of men; and just because one is suited for commanding doesn't mean that it is actually one's right to do so: 2. Man does not always have greater strength of body, wisdom, spirit or conduct than woman: 3. Scriptural precepts being established in punitive terms, indicates as well that there is only a positive right. One can therefore claim that there is no other type of subordination in marital relations than that of the civil law, and as a consequence, the only things preventing change in the civil law are particular conventions, and that natural law and religion do not determine anything to the contrary.[26]

During the years leading up to the French Revolution, *philosophe* arguments on the family began to achieve a wider publicity for a new generation in a series of legal cases that touched on women's role in marriage. The publication of lawyers' judicial memoirs, written to sway both judicial and public opinion on behalf of their clients, and the subsequent republication of the most illustrious legal cases in collections of causes célèbres were among the most popular reading materials for women as well as men, rivaling even the sales of popular novels. As King Louis XVI's secretary of state Guillaume-Chrétien de Lamoignon de Malesherbes remarked in 1774, "Has anyone reflected on the gradual progress that printed mémoires have made on minds over the past twenty years? Women who once read only novels now read them." As numerous scholars have suggested, these cases set the stage for the revolutionary laws concerning the family.[27] Similarly, Enlightenment writings emphasizing the cultural variety of family customs and law, the utility of such outlawed practices as divorce, and the idea of sentiment as the basis for marriage and family laid the groundwork for the political consideration during the Revolution of legal changes concerning such matters as divorce, paternal privilege, inheritance, and parental authority.[28]

Before considering the transformations in public and private life that took place in the century's final revolutionary decade, we pause to consider some loving relationships among France's enlightened elite, focusing in particular on how at least one enlightened couple forged a domestic union of exceptional equality and sexual fidelity. As we shall see, the intimate relationships forged by other prominent enlightened figures were more in keeping with standard practices of the day, according to which marriage was typically by arrangement. The women considered in the next section are exceptional in having acquired an education, which afforded them opportunities as scientists, novelists, hostesses, or diarists. In Old Regime France, access to educational institutions varied by sex. Typically, only boys were sent to formal schools outside the home, *pensions* or *collèges*. In contrast, although girls might at some point attend a convent school, the curriculum of such schools was designed primarily to prepare the girl for her future duties as a wife and mother. Toward the latter part of the century, new boarding schools for young ladies independent of the church sprang up, but they too promoted the aim of making women more useful members of society in their principal roles as women.[29] The best-educated women of the age would have had to acquire their education by private rather than public means. Their rare accomplishments are comprehensible, however, in an age in which autodidacticism was widely pursued, more often by men not otherwise advantaged in their access to established institutions of knowledge, like the Royal Academies, or by those who willfully defied church- and state-authorized curricula.[30]

LOVE AND MARRIAGE AMONG FRANCE'S
ENLIGHTENED ELITE

In 1786, at the age of forty-two, Marie-Jean-Antoine-Nicolas de Caritat, the Marquis de Condorcet, known to posterity as the last *philosophe*, married the 22-year-old Sophie de Grouchy, with whom he forged a loving relationship based on shared political convictions and an enduring intellectual partnership. An inspired proponent of human rights, Condorcet moved from his first achievements in mathematics into public service. Through educational and constitutional reforms, he hoped to create a liberal, rational, and democratic polity. He authored defenses of women's rights and the rights of enslaved Africans, proposing the abolition of slavery in France's overseas colonies. Condorcet published actively throughout the 1780s and later drafted numerous legislative bills for the National Assembly on the question of colonial reform and the slave trade. In addition, he advocated for freedom of commerce, the rights of religious minorities, and criminal-law reform. He considered neither sodomy nor suicide as crimes, writing that they "do not violate the rights of any other man," unlike rape, which "violates the property which everyone has in her person."[31]

Condorcet's most extensive arguments on women's rights appear in two essays. The first was authored in 1787; the second, "On the Admission of Women to the Rights of Citizenship" ("Sur l'admission des femmes au droits de la cité") was published in 1790 in the *Journal of the Society of 1789*—both prompted by broader discussions about appropriate constitutional arrangements. In addition, a commitment to women's rights informs his poignant testament to his daughter and is not forgotten in the section of the *Sketch for a Historical Picture of the Progress of the Human Mind* known as the *Fragment on the New Atlantis*, where he again objects to using allegations about physical or intellectual inferiority to justify political exclusion.[32] In his 1791 *Memoirs on Public Instruction*, he demands that public education be open to women and men and that women not be excluded from any curriculum, including science.[33] He believed in the right of a woman to plan her pregnancies, and he would have provided for women's admission to all professions for which they showed talent. In the tenth stage of the progress of the human mind in his posthumously published final work, *Sketch for a Historical Picture of the Progress of the Human Mind*, he boldly affirms that "among the causes of the progress of the human mind that are of the utmost importance to the general happiness, we must number the complete annihilation of the prejudices that have brought about an inequality of rights between the sexes, an inequality fatal even to the party in whose favour it works."[34] Comparing the disfiguration that tyranny in the political order wreaks on tyrants as much as their victims, Condorcet argued that men would be infinitely better off once they accepted the full equality of women. He never relinquished his conviction that a woman not only could but should prepare vocationally for her own independence. In his advice to his infant daughter, he advised that she prepare for all circumstances by having an occupation: "Get into the habit of working, so that you are self-sufficient and need no external help," he wrote. "Though you may become poor, you will never become dependent on others." Such work should not be routine or menial but rather "a type of work which does not occupy the hands alone, but engages the mind without straining it; something which compensates your efforts by the pleasure it gives you." Were she to lose her mother as well as her father, he asks her guardians to prepare his daughter for a great deal more than "the usual ladylike accomplishments," advising, "I should like my daughter to learn to draw, to paint and to engrave well enough to be able to earn a living without too much difficulty or repugnance. I should like her to learn to read and to speak English."[35]

It is clear that Condorcet drew inspiration from his wife on questions of public and private life and female emancipation. Like her husband, de Grouchy was committed to bringing about major judicial and political reforms in France, and she shared his antipathy toward the church and his commitment to secular values. The two met through their common interest in the defense of three peasant victims of judicial error and legal abuse, the *roués de Chaumont*.[36] In addition to collaborating frequently on Condorcet's writings, de Grouchy translated the works of Adam Smith and Thomas Paine. During the most violent phase of the French Revolution, the Terror, Condorcet composed his most famous work, *Sketch for a Historical Picture of the Progress of the Human Mind*, while she also wrote an optimistic text known as *Letters to Cabanis on Sympathy*, devoted to achieving "a society of happiness" and linking sensibility and affect to the progress of social justice.[37] Throughout her lifetime, de Grouchy also hosted a series of salons. Her first salon, in 1775, was attended by many foreign visitors—including Thomas Jefferson, Thomas Paine, and the Marquis de Beccaria—as well as the writers Pierre de Beaumarchais and Madame de Staël and the playwright and pamphleteer Olympe de Gouges (author of the 1791 *Declaration of the Rights of Woman and the Female Citizen*). After 1789, during the early liberal phase of the Revolution, the Condorcet salon attracted members of the Girondin revolutionary faction, and it hosted meetings of the Social Circle, one of the revolutionary clubs most supportive of women's participation and women's rights.[38] Following Condorcet's untimely death in 1794, de Grouchy worked assiduously to publish her late husband's oeuvres. She also revived her salon, which provided a meeting place for dissenting republicans under the consulate and the empire.[39]

Like his views on women's rights and abolition, Condorcet's marriage appears to have been exceptionally forward-looking and, for its time and place, a rare fulfillment of the most utopian expressions of domestic bliss advocated by many eighteenth-century *philosophes*, whose own conjugal relations were usually far from this ideal. The mathematician and coeditor (with Diderot) of the *Encyclopédie*, Jean le Rond d'Alembert, himself an illegitimate child of the *salonnière* (the French term for salon hostess) and author Claudine Guérin de Tencin, was the intimate friend (but apparently only frustrated lover) of the *salonnière* Julie de Lespinasse, in whose home he came to reside. In contrast, Diderot married against his parent's wishes but did not find happiness in the union; he entered into affairs with the writer Madeleine de Puisieux and later Sophie Volland, with the latter relationship lasting from 1755 until her death in 1784.[40]

At the age of thirty-nine, the brilliant and celebrated author Voltaire entered into a liaison with the brilliant Marquise du Châtelet, a 29-year-old married mother of three, an author and translator of works in mathematics and physics. With her husband's acknowledgment, they lived together at Cirey, the Châtelet country estate. Châtelet had been married by arrangement at eighteen to an aristocratic military officer twelve years her senior, and throughout her married life she took lovers, with her husband's acceptance. He also accepted paternity for the child she bore to her final lover, the poet Jean François de Saint-Lambert, with whom she began an affair in 1748. She gave birth on September 3, 1749, to a daughter but died a week later at the age of forty-two, followed not long thereafter by the child. Her husband, Saint-Lambert, and Voltaire all intensely mourned her passing.[41] It is also noteworthy that Châtelet received support for her intellectual accomplishments not only from Voltaire, who boasted about many of her achievements, such as her ability to learn English in merely fifteen days, but also from her husband. As her biographer Judith Zinsser notes, "Despite his lack of interest in what she was reading, [her husband] the marquis never wavered in his support of her unorthodox choices," even to the extent of defending her inclusion of Voltaire in her household.[42]

A final example, with less happy outcomes, of a couple's attempt to forge an enlightened union in the manner of the Condorcets brings us back to the final decade of the century. The memoirist, *salonnière*, revolutionary supporter, and subsequent victim of the radical revolution Manon Philipon, best known by

Mᵐᵉ. DU CHATELET.

d'après le Tableau original de Drouais.

H. Grevedon.   Lith. de Demanne.

FIGURE 5.4: Gabrielle Émilie Le Tonnelier de Breteuil, Marquise du Châtelet-Lomont. Library of Congress LC-USZ62-62124.

her married name Madame de Roland, freely elected to marry a man twenty years older, and they both struggled to win their respective families' consent to the match. Despite this, Roland never achieved the conjugal happiness of which she dreamed.[43] Although she remained faithful to her husband, in her last years she drew close romantically to François Buzot, a member of her husband's political faction in the republican legislature. Within days of her execution by guillotine during the Terror, her grief-stricken husband took his own life; Buzot was found dead some months later.

CONCLUSION: PRIVATE AND PUBLIC MATTERS
AT THE END OF THE EIGHTEENTH CENTURY

By any measure, the decade of the 1790s in France deserves its renowned place in modern history. After all, it is largely to France that we owe our modern concept of revolution, and the events in France are to the present day still rightly termed the "great revolution," one of the most important historical episodes of all times. The Revolution's core principles—liberty, equality, fraternity— were more than slogans, and the changes wrought during the Revolution shook not only France but also the whole established order of Europe. It encompassed a profound reorganization of society, culture, and politics from which no one was exempt. Religious minorities were granted rights, the nobility was abolished, serfdom and remaining feudal obligations were suppressed, the Catholic Church was reorganized, republican rule was established, and a war commenced that would eventually spread to much of Europe, the Caribbean, and the Near East. During the popular phase of the republican revolution, all men in France (irrespective of former rank or present status) were granted the right to vote, and, in response to the historic slave uprising in Saint-Domingue (present-day Haiti) and abolitionist feelings on the mainland, in 1794 the French legislative assembly declared the abolition of slavery in all of France's colonies.

In contrast, under the new constitutions of the liberal monarchy and republican France, *all* women were deprived of equal political rights, and French women did not achieve suffrage until 1944. In Old Regime France, women were certainly deprived of educational and political opportunities—including being barred by Salic Law from ascending to the throne, which was possible in other countries of old Europe. However, aristocratic and haute-bourgeois women of Old Regime France did enjoy many opportunities denied to less well-born men. Thus, rank as well as gender shaped a woman's possibilities in prerevolutionary France. What is striking about the revolutionary decade is how women as a category were newly defined and newly excluded from equal rights. Indeed, what Condorcet termed "the admission of women to the rights of citizenship" (in his 1790 essay by that name) was widely opposed on the grounds that women possessed distinctive natures that perfectly suited them to the fulfillment of their domestic duties.[44] Women were deemed unqualified for the realm of public affairs because of their alleged greater susceptibility to sensations, flawed rationality, and weaker sense of justice. For the first time, sex was introduced as a constitutional condition in France for the possession of political rights, even as rights were proclaimed to be universal and inalienable.

Yet women were not quiescent during the Revolution. In the first years of the Revolution, women like men were politicized, expressing their enthusiasm for the new order by joining popular clubs and participating in demonstrations. The English revolutionary sympathizer Mary Wollstonecraft and the French playwright Olympe de Gouges authored eloquent defenses of women's rights, while other women made the case for women's equality in grievances sent to the king at the outset of the Revolution and subsequently before assemblies of revolutionary men inside clubs and associations. Surprisingly, Condorcet, the early advocate of women's voting rights, remained silent on the issue during the constitutional debate that took place in 1793 before the nation's new legislative body, the Convention. As the chair of a committee on the draft constitution, he did not publicly advocate for women's equal inclusion in the body of citizens, thereby reinforcing the Convention's decision to deny women full citizenship on the basis of their sex. Under the republic, created in September 1792, the distinction was eliminated between passive and active voters, which had been a feature of France's first postrevolutionary constitution in 1791. The latter categorized citizenship according to property, measured by the ability to pay a given level of taxes, and also denied the full exercise of rights to servants or household dependents. By eliminating the barriers to male citizenship, including emancipating slaves in 1794, the revolutionary legislature made the denial of women's rights more explicitly than ever a matter of sexual difference rather than of property or class status. During the same period, women's popular activism was met increasingly by a campaign against activist women in the revolutionary press. In the fall of 1793, the Convention voted to proscribe women's political participation in clubs and their presence in the galleries of political assemblies, proclaiming that women's nature made them suited to domestic, not political, life.[45]

In contrast to their place in public affairs, French women fared much better in the domain of social and civil existence during the Revolution. While they did not get the right to vote or to serve as political representatives, they demanded and benefited from often substantial changes in the realm of private life. Republican women were accorded respect as *citoyennes* (female citizens), and they benefited from many positive changes in civil law, such as the granting of divorce and more egalitarian inheritance rights. Building on earlier criticisms of the family mounted by pamphleteers, lawyers, jurists, and *philosophes*, as Suzanne Desan has shown, the Revolution "attempted a veritable overhaul of intimate conjugal dynamics and the legal practices of marriage."[46] The revolutionaries sought to instantiate within the family a new bond between public and private life, which in turn directly affected the way in which men and women, parents and children related to each other, their wider kin and neighbors, the community at large, and the public authorities.[47] As Desan summarizes,

> The revolutionaries reduced parental authority over marriage, took legal control of conjugal matters out of the hands of the Catholic Church, created civil marriage, gave civil rights to children born out of wedlock, and, perhaps most controversially, legalized divorce. Some forty to fifty thousand divorces occurred during the Revolution. Hoping to institute greater liberty and equality within marriage, the Convention even voted in principle to grant wives equal control over communal marital property; this innovation never fully became law. Yet, if the revolutionaries launched a whole-scale attack on arranged and indissoluble marriage, they also deeply valued this institution as a site of patriotic regeneration and social cohesion. Male and female revolutionaries alike glorified romantic love as a patriotic act, urged wives to convert their husbands and children to republicanism, and encouraged couples to create affectionate marriages as a foundation for the republic's social unity. As Nicolas de Bonneville stated in his *New Conjugal Code* in 1792, "Marriage is the social bond that unites the citizen to the fatherland [*patrie*] and the fatherland to the citizen." In the new regime, as in the old, marriage with all its complexities continued to structure intimacy, undergird economic arrangements and family alliances, and inform basic practices of gender and authority.[48]

Just as revolutionaries like Bonneville had singled out the family and the bond of marriage as the glue of the social order, so too did conservatives in challenging the Revolution's most radical reforms, including the civil rights of natural (i.e., illegitimate) children, egalitarian inheritance, divorce, and other attacks on *puissance paternelle*, or the authority of fathers. The efforts of jurists to strengthen the father's position was at the heart of a new system of family unity and honor within the imperial regime created after Napoleon's 1799 coup d'etat, and the latter took place within a counterrevolutionary context where slavery was reestablished and men's democratic political rights were also attacked. In the 1804 Civil Code, widely known after 1807 as the Napoleonic Code, patriarchal control of women's sexuality was reinforced and women's domestic rights were limited as measures were undertaken to strengthen the family-based order of private property.

In conclusion, the contours of public and private life were shaped over the course of the eighteenth century by economic, political, juridical, and ideological forces, as well as by the efforts of men and women to alter the circumstances of their intimate and public lives. The Enlightenment played a part in these changes, yet most inhabitants of France, no matter their rank, hardly lived their public and private lives as strictly segregated territories. In particular, by modern standards, the private sphere had an especially public cast, whether by virtue of the economic roles and activities of family members or the publicity that attended private matters. Along with economic transformations like the consumer revolution of the period, enlightened critiques of inherited forms of patriarchal family life offered possibilities for individual fulfillment within the private realm and described new ways of distinguishing public from private existence. The marriage of the Marquis de Condorcet and Sophie de Grouchy demonstrates how a few exceptional individuals were able to forge marriages of relative equality and mutual respect. During the early Revolution, some of the more egalitarian implications of enlightened critiques were implemented, especially those affecting women's roles within the family, if not the state, only to be constrained or entirely abandoned under Napoleon's rule. It was at the end of the century, however, that many of the gendered features of public and private existence began to emerge in their modern expression.

CHAPTER SIX

Work and Education: The Case of Laboring Women Poets in England, Scotland, and Germany

SUSANNE KORD

During the age of Enlightenment, women stopped working. Or, to put it somewhat differently, during the age of Enlightenment, "women" stopped "working."

"WORK"

Into the strife
Of busy life
The man must rush, must work and toil,
And plant and build,
Must wake and watch,
And hoard and snatch,
And dare the peril for the spoil.
Wealth pours in its plenteous streams,
With wealth are bent the garner's beams;

His house's widen'd rooms with wealth are fill'd;—
That house the home of comfort; there
The matron-mother plies her care,
Versed in every saving art;
Well she plays the housewife's part:
To the girls imparts her skill,
Keeps the boys from doing ill;
Directs with well discerning eye
The busy hand of industry;
With art to win, and care to keep,
Adding to the gather'd heap.
The sweet-scented drawers with treasures she fills,
She twirls the spun thread round the quick flying wheels,
Collects in the clean and well order'd chest
The smooth shining wool, the linen snow white,
And makes every thing there look polish'd and bright,
And is never at rest.[1]

In England, Scotland, and Germany, the countries under discussion here, the age of Enlightenment engendered major philosophical shifts in attitudes toward women's education and coincided with major economic shifts, among them the Industrial Revolution.[2] The move from predominantly agricultural to predominantly industrial societies resulted in the dissociation of gainful employment from the domestic sphere. Particularly the educated middle class, which rose to new prominence during the Enlightenment, distinguished between work performed by the man outside of the house and housework performed by the woman inside. The new bourgeois understanding of work as segregated by both space and gender enabled a far greater hierarchization (the understanding of remunerated work performed by men/outside being more valuable than unremunerated work done by women/inside) than would have been practicable in times when men and women worked side by side in house, barn, and field and very often performed the same tasks.[3] This new framework is not merely economic but also conceptual; it describes a changed view not only of work but also of women. Once middle-class women had been defined in philosophy and literature as "Beautiful Souls," as embodied in Friedrich Schiller's ethereal creatures who joyously and effortlessly fulfill their "feminine destiny,"[4] it became impossible to see them as workers. Once the house had become identified with the private sphere, as the safe haven to which the middle-class man returns after a hard day at "work and toil," the very idea of work was banished from it. In the economic realm, this meant the eradication of women's gainful employment; in fact, the bourgeois male's ability to keep his wife at home (not "working") became one of the surest indicators of his economic success.[5] Conceptually, the understanding of the house as a "home" necessitated the redefinition of women's (house)work as something other than work. Although the prompt and flawless performance of housework became one of the most defining aspects of the perfect middle-class housewife, she was expected, to employ a phrase from the poem by Schiller quoted earlier, to "ply

FIGURE 6.1: Ernst Erwin Oehme, illustration to Friedrich Schiller's "Das Lied von der Glocke" ("The Song of the Bell") (1872–77). Courtesy of Kurt Kramer, www.glocken-online.eu.

her care," not work. Graceful, charming, gentle, and refined, the Beautiful Soul may be responsible for the success of the six-course dinner for forty, but she must not, under any circumstances, permit her efforts to *appear* as work—in front of the guests, she cannot even be seen to supervise the servants.[6]

The Enlightenment, in other words, marks the first stage of two fundamental conceptual shifts, one radically redefining ideas of work, the other radically redefining ideas of femininity. In the context of the Industrial Revolution, "work" becomes something performed outside of the house for money, associated with strife and contrasted with the peace reigning in the house. "Women" are viewed as innocuously gracious creatures whose function it is to turn the house into the home of comfort and thriftily preserve the wealth amassed by their men. Women soothe and care, they collect and preserve, they teach and direct. They make everything look polished and bright. What they do *not* do, under any circumstances, is work.

In the age of Enlightenment, women stopped "working."

"WOMEN"

Well, children, whar dat is so much racket der must be something out o' kilter. I tink dat 'twixt de niggers of de Souf and de women at de Norf all a talkin 'bout rights, de white men will be in a fix pretty soon. But what's all dis here talkin' 'bout? Dat man ober dar say dat women needs to be helped into carriages, and lifted ober ditches, and to have de best places—and ain't I a woman? Look at me! Look at my arm! . . . I have plowed and planted and gathered into barns, and no man could head me—and ain't I a woman? I could work as much as any man (when I could get it), and bear de lash as well—and ain't I a woman? I have borne five children and I seen 'em mos all sold off into slavery, and when I cried with a mother's grief, none but Jesus hear—and ain't I a woman?[7]

The answer to the rhetorical question posed by the abolitionist and former slave Sojourner Truth would evidently have to be a resounding "No." For although she was biologically a woman, she was not perceived as such by her contemporaries. She was perceived as a worker, more specifically—in this case—as a black and a slave.

Woman was a term that indicated not only whiteness but also middle-class status, a term that implied privileges as well as a (different) kind of oppression. Identity, a stable category for members of a dominant culture/class/gender and expressible in a single name (Goethe = Goethe; Shakespeare = Shakespeare),

FIGURE 6.2: Photographic image of Sojourner Truth on carte de visite with inscription, "I sell the shadow to support the substance, Sojourner Truth" (1864). Still image. Part of the Alfred Withal Stern Collection of Lincolniana. Library of Congress, Rare Book and Special Collections Division.

is variable for members of other cultures/classes/genders. The variability of Sojourner Truth's identities (a slave, a woman, a sojourner, a teller of truth) expresses itself in a plethora of names (Isabella van Wagener = Sojourner Truth's name after the family who owned her; Isabella Baumfree = Sojourner Truth's possible birth name or that of her owners previous to the van Wageners; Sojourner Truth = her self-given name describing her self-determined identity as a religiously motivated abolitionist).[8] Variable identities are unstable because they are subject to interpretation by members of the dominant culture, in whose view single aspects of identity may inflate to appear as the whole ("Sojourner Truth is a slave") and other aspects may vanish entirely ("Sojourner Truth is no woman").

Sojourner Truth's words, delivered in December 1851 at the Women's Convention in Akron, Ohio, would make no sense were it not for the understanding, fashioned during the Enlightenment and broadly accepted at the time of her speech one hundred years later, that a woman is implicitly white and middle class. Neither of these ideas, though, furnished Sojourner Truth with her principal point of attack and call for reconceptualization. Instead, she focused on the idea that may well have been, for her, the most profound paradox of all: the notion that as a worker, she could not be a woman because "woman" was understood to mean a soothing presence, a preserver of wealth, a beautiful soul, an angel in the house.

In the age of Enlightenment, "women" stopped working.

EDUCATION

Of course, even as "women" of the age stopped "working," women of the age continued to work. Lower-class women labored in a wide range of occupations, as spinners, seamstresses, washerwomen, milkmaids, cowherds, and domestic servants; paid work available to middle-class women was largely limited to three occupations—governess, actress, and writer.[9] My focus in what follows will be on lower-class women writers,[10] with only a brief coda on their middle-class colleagues, for two reasons. The simplest one is that we have many more written sources about women writers than about women in any other eighteenth-century profession. The more complex one is that the concepts with which this essay is most centrally concerned—ideas of work and education as they were applied to women in and beyond the age of Enlightenment—intersect most significantly in the writing by and about lower-class women. These documents thus provide us with ideal test cases for changing ideas about women and work during the epoch, specifically for the degree to which working women accepted or contested these ideas and in which context(s) they chose to do either.

For lower-class women poets of the age, work and education were central themes. Their representation as "unlettered" or "natural" geniuses in mid- to late eighteenth-century bourgeois aesthetics was predicated largely on their assumed ignorance of the aesthetic and philosophical background or poetic rules.[11] Only the lower-class poet's lack of formal education could guarantee the naturalness and authenticity of her poetic output. "Elizabeth Bentley had no education; she read only by accident; but from the moment she did read, she felt in herself a power of imitation, and a faculty of combining imagery, together with a facility of poetical expression."[12] To her patron, the Scottish dairywoman Janet Little "betrays no one indication that I could discover of ever having opened a book or tagged a rhyme."[13] The Scottish domestic servant Christian Milne appears as a poet writing "without *external* aid from birth or education" who could not be judged by the standards applied to middle-class poets: "Let no stern critic . . . / talk of *rules*, when *rules* are all unknown" (emphasis in the original).[14] The English cottager Ann Candler's utter lack of schooling showed "that her Poems are more the spontaneous productions of genius than the work of memory or education."[15] And the work of the English domestic servant Mary Leapor was presented to readers "as a convincing Proof of the common Aphorism, *Poeta nascitur, non fit*" (a poet is born, not made).[16]

This "born" genius, then, writes spontaneously rather than painstakingly, aided not by book learning but by an astonishing "natural" ability to recall snippets of erudition that have haphazardly ("innocently") come her way. Several poets of the age were famous for their extraordinary abilities to recall text passages verbatim; the Scottish alehouse keeper Isobel Pagan, for example, although illiterate, could supposedly recite the entire Bible, word for word, from memory. In such depictions of the poet's mnemonic powers, her presentation as an unlettered genius clearly intersects with her characterization as a poor rural worker, for it is this unusual memory that enables the poet to write despite the constant interruptions that are part and parcel of her life. The image of the poet from the laboring classes, in other words, hinges centrally on both her complete lack of education and the fact that she continued to work physically. Milne composed her poetry while employed at physical labor throughout the week and remembered it all, verbatim, until she finally had a chance to write down her compositions on Sunday evenings. As Milne described the creative process,

> Though the profits of my little book and the patronage of the worthiest people have been very sweet to me; yet those blessings have been much embittered by the ridicule and contempt with which I have been treated, by those among whom I am obliged to live, because I have been so idle as to write rhymes. But those respectable ladies and gentlemen whose names I have mentioned can witness that I have not been the more idle on that account; for I have composed my poems, such as they are, when I was most busily employed about my washing, baking, or when rocking the cradle with my foot, the ink-stand in one hand, the pen in the other, and the paper on my knee, with my children about me. When busy at work, I laid the paper and ink-stand beside me, and wrote the stanza as it came into my mind, and then to my work again.[17]

In Milne's narrative, the discourse of the humble laborer and that of the natural genius inform each other: on the surface, the statement is designed to protect the poet from accusations of "idleness" (by which is meant both the process of writing, which does not, in this narrative, count as real work, and the neglect of her household and wifely duties due to her writing). Her self-defense against this accusation, her failure to describe her creative occupation as work and therefore respectable, indicates agreement with her accusers as to where her real duties lay and indirectly defines her as a peasant and housewife, rather than a poet. But the self-definition as a poet, and a "natural" poet at that, subtly injects itself into the narrative in her description of her writing as unconscious: poetic creation takes place at moments when she is "most busily employed," surrounded by either the wash or the children, at moments when her mind is clearly on other things. Milne's evocation of the unconscious creative process is strongly reminiscent of descriptions of the same process by the washerwoman Mary Collier, the first known eighteenth-century woman peasant poet, who conceived her verse "as on my Bed I lay, / Eas'd from the tiresome Labours of the Day": in a state between waking and sleep, during "moments of meditation that border on dream-work."[18]

As these examples readily show, the aesthetic theory of the uneducated genius, originally advanced in the theoretical work of middle-class men, often turned into coercive practice in the poetic or autobiographical work of lower-class women. Given that middle-class aesthetic theorists were very often also the patrons under whose protection lower-class authors wrote and published, this is hardly surprising. One of the more eloquent examples of the coerciveness of the natural genius idea is the case of Anna Louisa Karsch and her patrons. Karsch, a German cowherd without formal schooling, began her literary career as a local celebrity who entertained guests at village festivities, marriages, and funerals with impromptu poetry performances. Two months after she was discovered by the Baron von Kottwitz, who spirited her away to Berlin in his coach, Johann Georg Sulzer, one of the century's most important aesthetic theorists, wrote to his friend Johann Jakob Bodmer:

> Here in Berlin, there has been an extraordinary apparition in circles of taste: a poetess formed by Nature alone, who, taught only by the muses, promises great things. . . . it is nothing to her to produce the finest thoughts on every subject and express them in excellent verse. I doubt very much that anyone has ever had language and rhyme as much in his power as this woman. She sits down in a large social gathering and amidst the chatter of twelve or more persons writes songs and odes of which no poet would need to be ashamed.[19]

Sulzer, who later claimed in his foreword to her poems that "poets are not formed through erudition and rules, but receive their calling and capacity from

Nature alone,"[20] cited as evidence Karsch's unconsciousness when writing, her spontaneity and speed, her utter lack of formal education, and therefore her guaranteed lack of contact with poetic rules.[21] His assessment of Karsch corresponds closely to his remarks in theoretical writings on the subjects of poetic inspiration, originality of invention, and poetic genius.[22] Just as Sulzer, in his aesthetic works, views genius as a gift of nature, unattainable through training or education and closely linked with "physical circumstances,"[23] so in his foreword to her poems he takes Karsch's biography as proof of the authenticity of her genius:

> How indubitably our poetess has received her calling from Nature alone
> is evinced most clearly from all circumstances of her life. For in this
> life we find nothing, aside from natural inclination, that could possibly
> have instigated, artificially, her urge to write poetry, not a single circum-
> stance that could lead us to surmise that erudite rules, in her case, take
> the place of genius.[24]

Karsch's literary career, in other words, centrally depended on her continued ability to embody bourgeois theories of "natural" poetic genius. Indications are that she was quite aware of this and did what she could to conform to this image by frequently emphasizing her humble origins and lack of formal education and by minimizing her exposure to reading whenever she could. "Art has no part of it," she claimed of her own writing, "and reading has only here and there added a touch."[25] After first hearing of Edward Young's theory of natural genius, she professed herself a dedicated follower of his aesthetic and defined herself on his terms.[26] The story of her early and insatiable desire to read and write that is a staple in the life stories of many of the century's peasant poets appears in her biography as well, complete with a touching account of strenuous parental opposition to her reading and writing.[27] If Sulzer views the original impetus for her urge to write poetry as rooted in "Nature," Karsch makes an effort to place it as close to "Nature" as possible: according to her autobiographical letters, her love of poetry was first awakened by a young herdsman who read literature out loud to a circle of breathlessly listening peasant children.[28] In letters to her patron Johann Wilhelm Ludwig Gleim, she frequently invokes the natural genius theory and self-applies it by emphasizing, as the primary traits of her writing, her speed and spontaneity, the tremendous memory for which she was already famous in the context of her impromptu performances, and the compulsion she felt to write poetry: her claim, in one of her last letters, that she wrote poetry in her sleep[29] directly echoes the mandate

of unconscious poetic production issued in aesthetic treatises. Her letters to
Gleim and others often contain impromptu verse passages, and she countered
Gleim's objections to her rhymed letters and his requests for proper prose epis-
tles with apologies that are themselves, cheekily enough, written in verse:

> Prose letters should I write, you say,
> But can I, with my wayward thoughts?
> Dear friend, your quarrel's not with me,
> My habit brings all pains to nought,
> Habit, this force of Nature strong
> Compels me to relentless verse
> And it's in verse that I, in my last song
> Will greet you even from my hearse.[30]

In this depiction of herself as "compelled to verse," as literally unable *not*
to write, she skillfully evokes the aesthetic discourse of the poet as medium,
helpless in the grip of the muse. Paradoxically, Karsch, who insisted that her
letters were private documents and repeatedly refused to have them published,
thus thwarted Gleim's attempts to make her letters appear more "private" and
autobiographical (with an eye to potential publication) by deleting the rhymed
interludes that might make the letters appear more "literary."

If the phenomenon of Anna Louisa Karsch was instrumentalized, at least
initially, as the exemplification of natural genius theories, this image of her did
not result in either poetic or financial autonomy for the actual poet. Although
her first volume of poems was an unprecedented success, earning her the record honorarium of two thousand talers, she had no control over the capital, which was invested on her behalf by her patrons, Gleim and Sulzer, who
acted as her legal guardians. When Karsch died in 1791, she left her children
3,600 thalers, but during her lifetime, she meagerly subsisted on the interest
of this investment and depended on the patronage of various supporters for
her survival and the education of her children. As in the cases of other peasant
poets, this financial dependence had poetic consequences because it defined
the reasons for publishing her work as not literary but financial: the goal
of the edition, as stated by Sulzer in the foreword, was to "rescue [Karsch]
from the direst poverty."[31] Karsch herself, taking her cue from him, often
defined her writing as occasional poetry written exclusively for financial gain.
In letters to Gleim, she repeatedly tried to influence the manner in which her
patrons provided for her financially; her patrons, conversely, considered her
financially unreliable and wasteful and for this reason controlled the capital

FIGURE 6.3: Portait of Anna Louisa Karsch, painted by Karl
Christian Kehrer (1791). Oil on canvas. Courtesy of the
Gleim-Haus Halberstadt.

all the more tightly. On the one hand, then, Karsch's patrons characterized
their charge as an exemplification of natural genius and employed a rhetoric
in which she appears as deserving of literary patronage; on the other hand,
via their firm control over Karsch's finances, they defined that patronage as
charity to the pauper.

WORK AS A POETIC THEME

I assure you that there are moments when Art almost attains to the
dignity of manual labour.

—Oscar Wilde[32]

Poetic representations of physical labor constitute a tradition that most obviously contravenes the pastoral, ousting the Arcadian shepherd from the text to

make room for the laboring peasant.[33] In contrast to the rather overdetermined pastoral tradition, these poems are characterized by a marked absence of literary context. Unlike the pastoral, they portray physical labor. Unlike the georgic, they do not present a positive or heroic view of labor.[34] Unlike the nineteenth-century tradition of workers' literature, these earlier poems, while they depict the living and working conditions of the lower classes in the harshest possible terms, do not draw political or social conclusions; they cannot be considered "protest" literature in a sense that would align them with the proletarian tradition.

The two poems I discuss in this section treat physical labor or rural life in a way that can be considered neither "literary" (if literary implies fictional as opposed to factual) nor "personal" (if personal implies private as opposed to social or political). To be sure, Mary Collier's "The Woman's Labour" and Anna Louisa Karsch's "Schlesisches Bauerngespräch" ("Silesian Peasant Talk") use a literary form (meter and verse) and place themselves in a literary tradition; Collier's "Woman's Labour" is ostentatiously a response to another poem, Stephen Duck's "The Thresher's Labour." Yet both document experiences that transcend "fiction" in three major ways: through their depiction of rural labor or working/living conditions that cannot be contained in either the pastoral or the georgic traditions; through their refusal to limit themselves to the "subjective" that has its place in "fiction" and can comfortably be contrasted with "objective fact"; and, finally, through their clear positing of the individual not as separate from or opposed to society but as its symbol and representative.

Collier's poem "The Woman's Labour" (1739), written in response to Duck's "The Thresher's Labour" (1730, 1736),[35] is the first published documentation of female rural labor by a woman laborer, provoked in part by Duck's depiction of female field hands sitting idly by, busily employing their tongues rather than their hands, while the men break their backs in the field. Collier's objective, then, is not merely the depiction of women's work, but its depiction as unnoticed and scorned (by men in general and Duck in particular). In the opening lines of the poem, Collier draws a clear distinction between herself and Duck: whereas Duck, formerly a laborer himself, has now ascended to the status of "Immortal Bard" and "Fav'rite of the Nine," not to mention favorite of the queen, who granted him her patronage, Collier "ever was, and's still a Slave," her life "always spent in Drudgery."[36] Hers is a response written by a laborer during her rare minutes of leisure between the endless rounds of physical work she describes in the poem, a response addressed to someone for whom physical labor is, at most, a remembered experience. Implicit in this initial drawing of lines is Collier's distrust of Duck's selective remembrance, even her suspicion that he may have deliberately falsified the facts to embroider his fiction:

> on our abject State you throw your Scorn,
> And Women wrong, your Verses to adorn.[37]

Duck's concern, Collier asserts, is clearly no longer with work (its accurate representation as experienced reality) but with his verse (its embellishment for the benefit of his bourgeois and aristocratic readers). Her poetic reply therefore tries to eradicate this discrepancy between fact and fiction, and it is this aspect of Collier's poem, her dissociation of her own work from Duck's, that makes it possible to read her poem as a self-conscious documentary of work rather than a "poem" in the literary sense.

In what may well be the first description of the female double shift as full-time worker and housewife/mother,[38] Collier documents a series of tasks performed by women in the fields, washhouse, and scullery and, finally, in their own homes. Emphasized throughout her elaborate depiction of haymaking, raking, plowing, reaping, gleaning, charring, washing, brass and pewter cleaning, beer brewing, cooking, bed making, swine feeding, and child and husband tending are the length and frenzy of a woman's workday and general work conditions (extremes of heat and cold), the physical injuries women undergo in the performance of labor (raw and bleeding hands), and the exploitation of women by upper-class men who underpay them and lower-class men who profit from but underappreciate their work. Repeatedly, a man's work conditions are explicitly contrasted with a woman's: the men, coming home from the fields, are finished for the day, waiting to be fed and go to sleep, whereas women returning from the fields

> find our Work but just begun;
> So many Things for our Attendance call,
> Had we ten Hands, we could employ them all.[39]

Charwomen regularly rise at midnight to do the lady's washing,

> While you on easy Beds may lie and sleep,
> Till Light does thro' your Chamber-windows peep.[40]

Collier's repeated examples of women's work performed while the men are asleep is, of course, a direct refutation of Duck's accusation of female idleness; her summing up

Our Toil and Labour's daily so extreme,
That we have hardly ever *Time to dream* (emphasis in the original)[41]

again emphasizes to what extent the longer workday of women encroaches on
their sleep and simultaneously takes up Duck's statement that work follows the
laborer into his dreams. While Collier's description of field labor is comparatively brief, she elaborates on those areas of work that are specific to women,
such as washing: in this, as well, she deliberately pits the woman's work against
the man's ("So many Hardships daily we go through, / I boldly say, the like *you*
never knew" [emphasis in the original][42]). A washerwoman's day begins in the
middle of the night, when

O'ercome with Sleep; we standing at the Door
Oppress'd with Cold, and often call in vain,
E're to our Work we can Admittance gain.[43]

The arduous work of scrubbing, washing, laying out, and bleaching, and the treatment of sensitive materials like ruffles, lace, and fringes, are interrupted only by
the mistress's admonishments to save on soap and firewood. This work goes on

Until with Heat and Work, 'tis often known,
Not only Sweat, but Blood runs trickling down
Our Wrists and Fingers; still our Work demands
The constant Action of our lab'ring Hands.[44]

Collier's poem ends on a grim note: the laborer is paid off with "Six-pence
or Eight-pence"; the future holds nothing for the laborer but "*Old Age* and
Poverty" (emphasis in the original) and continuous exploitation by "sordid
Owners [who] always reap the Gains."[45] Her concluding image of women laborers as the daughters of Danaus, with which she answers Duck's comparison
of the male field hand with Sisyphus,[46] characterizes the poem's author simultaneously as a poet and as a washerwoman. A literary allusion to Greek mythology in a poem about labor by a laborer who, in its opening lines, describes
herself as completely uneducated could be considered a rather incongruous
motif. And yet it is paradoxically this highly literary image of the eternal washerwomen, endlessly employed in filling the bottomless tub, that most succinctly
reiterates Collier's description of women's labor as never-ending and thankless.
    Collier's poem, ostentatiously concerned with gender as well as class, an-
swers Duck's work (and foreshadows Sojourner Truth's insight) in another way

as well. Whereas Duck, in his elaborate description of women as uselessly prattling gossips, can be said to accentuate traditional views of femininity, Collier's response obscures the femininity of female workers who, covered with soot, dirt, and filth at the end of their workday, can no longer be recognized as women:

> Colour'd with Dirt and Filth we now appear;
> Your threshing *sooty Peas* will not come near.
> All the Perfections Woman once could boast,
> Are quite obscur'd, and altogether lost. (emphasis in the original)[47]

Collier's elimination of femininity from the image of rural womanhood is reiterated in the comments of bourgeois observers, who frequently bemoaned the fact that many rural women looked like men and lacked the feminine qualities of virtue and ladylike reticence as they walked behind the plough. An observer of women's field labor in 1794 found it positively

> painful . . . to behold the beautiful servant maids of this country toiling in the severe labours of the field. They drive the harrows, or the ploughs, when they are drawn by three or four horses; nay, it is not uncommon to see, sweating at the dung-cart, a girl, whose elegant features, and delicate, nicely-proportioned limbs, seemingly but ill accord with such rough employment.[48]

How laboring women appear to the male observer is also a substantial part of, indeed furnished the provocation for, Collier's poem, where the elimination of femininity serves a distinct purpose: it negates the male view of women (either as beautiful and delicate or as useless, lazy, and gossipy) and identifies work as the defining aspect of a woman's existence. Woman, in her description, is no longer recognizable as a woman but merely as a worker. Nevertheless, and this seems to be Collier's implicit conclusion, the view of this worker as a woman persists, and must persist, for it is this distinction that makes it possible to pay her even less for her labor than the already insufficient male wage and to saddle her with a workload that is described as double that of the male worker. Collier's poem is thus, as Landry has read it, a protofeminist work;[49] it is class identified in its clear indictment of the exploitation of the rural laborer through upper-class employers, but it simultaneously furnishes one of the earliest examples of a gendered critique of the exploitation of lower-class women not only by the upper classes but also by men of their own class.

FIGURE 6.4: Peasant women working in the fields. Jean-François Millet (1814–75), *Des glaneuses* (*The Gleaners*) (1857). Musée d'Orsay, Paris.

Anna Louisa Karsch's "Schlesisches Bauerngespräch zwischen Vetter Hanß und Muhm Ohrten, gehalten zu R . . . bei Großglogau im November 1758" (Silesian peasant talk between Cousin Hans and Aunt Ohrte, which took place in R . . . near Großglogau in November 1758)[50] makes us privy to a discussion between two peasants on the impact of the Seven Years' War on the rural population. The conversation progresses from complaints about heavy taxation and the mistreatment of peasants in times of war to the praise of rural life in peacetime, finally ending in a panegyric on Frederick the Great. The poem deliberately mixes public with private spheres (in its intertwining of larger political and social concerns and personal matters in the conversation) and literary concerns with rural reality. Written in the Silesian dialect, it is one of the earliest dialect poems in the German language and clearly attempts to emulate real-life conversation in other ways as well, particularly in the unmotivated changes of subject and the interspersing of seemingly irrelevant news, such as Cousin Lehne's preparations for her brother's visit. In addition, the exact designation of time and place in the poem's title establishes a claim to realism by anchoring the conversation in a specific historical context: the reader's position as a consumer of didactic literature is obscured by the intimated role of someone listening in on a private conversation. At the same time, the employment of alexandrine meter[51] throughout the poem places it into a literary tradition; Ernst Josef Krzywon, for instance, has read the poem as an example of the political poetry of the German baroque (*Bauernklage*) and linked Karsch's usage of literary form to both Martin Opitz and Johann Christoph Gottsched.[52] While the deliberate (mis)use of the "heroic" alexandrine meter would seem to hint at a subversive evocation of literary traditions, both the panegyric on the king and the portrayal of peasant life in peacetime evoke other literary traditions, including pastoral and georgic forms, without a trace of irony. Rural reality, as it appears in Hanß's description, is characterized by health, piety, hard work, a loving family life, and a delight in plain rustic fare, all of which are elaborately contrasted with the city dweller's corruption, hypocrisy, lavish eating habits, and frequent illnesses.

Although labor supposedly dominates this idyllic life, only four lines out of sixty-two in his speech even mention physical work;[53] the rest of Hanß's report is given over to philosophical and religious ruminations about the virtues and pleasures of country life. In this respect, one might be inclined to read this poem as indebted to the traditional pastoral and/or georgic, and not, as Helene M. Kastinger-Riley has done, as a "mirror of the true rural milieu"[54] or as based in any way on Karsch's "vivid personal experience."[55] But if Karsch, rather than describing work as she knew it, fell into the pastoral trap, she simultaneously negates a literary tradition: in claiming the pastoral for the peasant, she ostentatiously defies the bourgeois depiction of the literary peasant as coarse, unrefined, and ridiculous, the comic character of rural literature.[56] She does this not only by usurping the Arcadian shepherd's space for the peasant but also by hinting at an—albeit imagined—reality. For Hanß's initial complaints about the heavy taxation during wartime—peasants in times of war paid between 33 and 45 percent of their total income in taxes directly to the armies[57]—are trumped by Ohrte's account of the unimaginable suffering visited on the peasant under enemy occupation. Ohrte's fiction within a fiction, her act of imagining potential disasters destroying the pastoral idyll that poses as "fact" within the poem, is paradoxically the passage that comes closest to evoking rural reality: the peasant's farm is burned down, his seeds destroyed, his grain, livestock, and household goods stolen.

This attempt to represent real suffering disintegrates at the point where the suffering is perceived as so extreme that it can no longer be contained in the pastoral or georgic form that provides the poem's frame. Whereas Karsch manages to convey highly affecting images of the peasant being beaten by troops and his barn and stables being emptied, the experience of rape in wartime is rather mincingly hinted at:

> And many a man has had to witness, stand amazed
> As soldiers treat his wife in most improper ways
> One does not like to speak of it. But really, it's a fright
> To hear of things the Russians do to young women at night.
> One listens to these things, it is no laughing matter,
> And your wife, Hanß, is pretty, the village has none better,
> Cossacks would gladly take her, their hours to while away,
> And you'd be spitting mad, and there'd be hell to pay.[58]

At this point, Karsch's attempt to convey rural reality in the pastoral form breaks down, form proving woefully inadequate to content. This painful inappropriateness is expressed in euphemisms that demote a crime to "improper" behavior, helplessness and despair to a childish tantrum ("spitting mad"; in the original: "Du argertest Dich närsch"), and the destruction of lives to "no laughing matter." In a literary world that is engaged in an aestheticization of rural reality, as Hanß is in the elaborate description of his workday, such experiences are beyond the words available to the genre.

Karsch's "Schlesisches Bauerngespräch" is a good test case for what happens when the pastoral meets rural reality in a text that is primarily concerned with the latter rather than the former. Her poem tries to adapt the traditional pastoral and georgic to a different purpose, one that is not, like a mock-pastoral would be, strictly literary. The didactic purpose of the poem is essentially conservative, as expressed in both Hanß's idyllicization of rural life and the elaborate apotheosis of the king. Nonetheless, Karsch attempts, as Kastinger-Riley has noted, to give the peasant his due: in contrast to bourgeois portrayals of the peasant as the klutzy comical character, peasants in this conversation appear as the backbone of rural society as well as of Frederick's war.[59] Without question, Karsch portrays it that way; at the same time, it is difficult to overlook the aestheticization inherent even in this acknowledgment of the peasant's vital role: in a precise parallel to the denial of labor and the depiction of unworked-for rural bounty in the traditional pastoral, the peasant's forced contributions appear, in her poem, as voluntary offerings. Karsch's poem thus seems essentially torn. On the one hand, it aestheticizes rural life and glorifies the king with the help of traditional poetic forms (the pastoral and the georgic). On the other hand, its employment of dialect, the attempts to emulate real-life conversation in the frequent jumps, non sequiturs, unmotivated subject changes, and the relation of seemingly unimportant details seem to express a social purpose, namely, the realistic portrayal of lower-class concerns. Where rural reality threatens the pastoral idyll, as it does in the rape story, the pastoral is quickly reasserted in the refusal to engage reality ("One does not like to speak of it") and in the conformist conclusion that peasants should recognize that, compared to such horrors, their current hard lives are a veritable bed of roses:

> That pittance of a tax is all you suffer now
> And trifle that it is, you whine and make a row.[60]

Despite her radically different perspective, Karsch's poem can be read from within the tradition of women's labor poems. Like Collier, she attempts to describe rural reality from within a literary form. Whereas she rather downplays the labor theme, she emphasizes exploitation in her assessment of the consequences of war for the rural population. Both Collier and Karsch express their understanding of exploitation as the essence of lower-class experience, represented in Collier's poem in the class-encompassing "we" and in Karsch's in the exchange between two different people with two distinct perspectives (Hanß complains, Ohrte appeases). Whereas Collier's work demonstrates both class consciousness and class solidarity in the depiction of the servants' exploitation, Karsch tries to find a way to map the pastoral sense of contentment onto the rural reality she describes, accordingly downplaying and negating the fact of exploitation that Hanß, at the outset of the poem, protests so vigorously, and turning this protest into praise of the king in the peasant's mouth.

POVERTY IN POETRY: WORK AND EDUCATION REVISITED

In one of her letters to her patron Bridget Freemantle, Mary Leapor imagines herself a successful poet:

> If our scheme succeeds, I intend to shew my public spirit: . . . I shall erect a few Almshouses; and have some thoughts of founding a hospital for indigent or distracted poets. I presume this will take up as much of my superfluous wealth as I can spare from the extravagance of a gay retinue and splendid equipage, in which I intend to abound. Amidst all this, I shall not be ingrateful, though perhaps somewhat haughty. Yet my

chariot or landau shall ever be at your service, and ready to convey you
to my country-seat, or to my house in *Hanover-square*.[61]

What Leapor lampoons here is the prejudice against which the common discourse of the humble cottager, content in her station, was intended to serve as
defense: the fear, obsessively expressed in the writing of bourgeois patrons,[62]
that elevating peasants above their "stations" would invariably result in their
transformation into idle, haughty, luxury-loving, and ungrateful wretches.
Leapor's charitable intentions of erecting "almshouses" and hospitals for "in-
digent or distracted poets" are also an unmistakable comment on the nature of
patronage, here perceived precisely in the way in which Gleim and Sulzer practiced it on Karsch: as charity to the pauper rather than patronage of the poet.

    And yet Leapor's satire is an uncomfortable one, her dream of "superflu-
ous wealth" all too obviously implying its reverse, which is of course the main
reason why the peasant poet requires patronage (the secondary reason being
the opportunity to write and publish). In the work of lower-class poets, poverty is a regularly recurring theme. Christian Milne's "The Wounded Soldier"
describes a starving family in heartrending terms; Ann Candler's "Reflections
on My Own Situation" provides a glimpse of the author as a pauper living on
meager alms "with the dregs of human kind."[63] An untitled impromptu poem
by Karsch, inserted seamlessly into a letter to Gleim, depicts similar circumstances:

> oh dearest Gleim see fathers hurry, in vain to work for just a little bread,
> meanwhile beset by cold and hunger's dread, the children cry, redoubling
> his worry, they cry like dogs deprived of mother's breast, their mothers
> roam the streets full of despair, the children are abandoned everywhere,
> like little ravens flung out of the nest, they hope for bread from morning
> until night, and many sick and poor lie on the straw, not even granted
> water in their plight, whereas the rich do shove into their maw, the most
> delicious foods till they are ill, I see this sadly, much against my will,
> my spirit bids me forget nevermore, that I myself was hungry, cold and
> poor.[64]

    The question of what could lift the poet out of poverty, a term that in poems
may indicate physical penury or intellectual deprivation, is often answered by
pointing at the lower-class poet's forbidden fruit: education. Numerous poets
who, in poems and autobiographical writing produced for public consumption
(such as forewords to their editions), strategically adopted the self-image of

the unlettered poet, expressed, in personal letters, profound regret at having been denied a formal education. Karsch, for example, often lamented the fact that her mother removed her from her uncle's tutelage at a crucial stage in her learning: "I am still upset that my mother did not leave me with my old uncle; he would have taught me Latin and I could now read Flacchus and Virgil."[65] The same indictment is levied in her poem "Ann meine Mutter in jene Wellt geschrieben den dritten Juny 1785" (To my mother, written to her in the other world on the third of June 1785), but in this poem, she sarcastically turns blame into gratitude for the ignorance in which she was kept:

> But upon further contemplation
> I am quite certain that your daughter
> Would not be seen as a sensation
> If you had more than German taught her
> For if you had, then folks would say
> That I pilfered from him, or him
> Who wrote poetry in the ancient days
> That must be why it was your whim
> To save me from Latin and erudition,
> Accept, dear Mother, my contrition,
> Your nagging thus my thanks has earned
> 'Tis my good fortune I'm unlearned.[66]

Karsch's ironic self-image as "unlearned" implies an obvious conundrum: in her letters, Karsch regretted her limited education, particularly her ignorance of foreign languages, to the end of her days; simultaneously, she was well aware that it was this ignorance that enabled her entire career as a "natural" poet. For lower-class ("uneducated") women writers, education constituted an irresolvable paradox.[67] On the one hand, it stood for the (for them, tabooed) erudition of the male, middle-class writer. On the other hand, it alone distinguished the "author" from the hack, the career writer from the literary nine-day wonder.

Work as a subject in these poems is beset by a similar ambiguity, simultaneously implying physical labor performed under threat of poverty ("work") and the more genteel exertions of the poet at her escritoire ("the work"). The work (at times also known as "poetic idleness"; see Christian Milne) is, in fact, what enables the poet to stop working. In Karsch's "Meine Zufriedenheit" (My contentment), poverty is a personal experience shudderingly remembered but now thankfully in the past:

My fingers now no longer tear the flax,
I, now so used to wine, am never parched
With thirst, laboring under the distaff's arch,
And never does the sun melt me like wax.

When Sirius's flame in vale and glade
Burns up the thresher, tires the walking boy,
Then I sit bless'd with bounty and with joy,
In plenty do I rest, and in the shade.

O friend! and when the spinner's hand
Laboriously tears and rents the cotton wool,
Then I now play my undemanding role
Which often wins me praise throughout the land![68]

At its most obvious, Karsch describes poetry as a ticket out of poverty, but there is more here. There is, in fact, an implication that poverty contextualizes poetry in a way that negates bourgeois claims of the transcendence and nobility of literature. Poetry written from within poverty, past or present, accentuated or submerged, can make no such claim. The business of poetry is rather prosaically downgraded to easy (rather than arduous) labor, performed in the shade rather than under the scorching sun. This depiction of writing as easy work is predicated on the understanding of writing *as* work, a simultaneous violation of four mandates: the pastoral tradition that excludes labor from literary representation, the new bourgeois understanding of bourgeois literature as transcendent and written for posterity, the interpretation of lower-class poetic occupation as "idleness," and the aesthetic/critical view of the peasant poet as spontaneously inspired and therefore, by implication, incapable of (poetic) work (such as editing or rewriting). Peasant poets' literary aspirations, at least as presented in their poetry, are often neither prompted by a sense of themselves as "natural geniuses" nor inspired by bourgeois-style dreams of posthumous fame but are instead simply aroused by a desire for an improvement in their working conditions.

While in laborious toil I spent my hours,
Employ'd to cultivate the springing flowers:
Happy, I cry'd, are those, who leisure find
With care, like this, to cultivate their mind.[69]

In this poem, Leapor views intellectual labor "like this," in other words: as comparable to physical work rather than as its antithesis, as indeed Karsch did in her poem on contentment. The difference, as both Karsch and Leapor knew, lay in the kind of work and in the circumstances under which it was performed, not in a contrast between (physical) work and (poetic) idleness. Unlike the cultivation of a garden, the cultivation of a mind may be performed in the shade; it may, as Leapor states, sport the appearance of "leisure." The poet thus employed may, as Karsch has said, seem to be merely "resting," but writing is nevertheless, in a marked deviation from the assumptions of bourgeois and pastoral discourses, recognized as work.

CODA: WORK AND "THE WORK"

It is perhaps this aspect that marks the most extreme difference between the writing of lower-class women and that of middle-class women of the Enlightenment. Middle-class women writers regularly denied that their work was "work," in more or less the same manner in which lower-class women writers strategically self-applied the natural genius theory. Luise Adelgunde Gottsched, for example, one of the century's most highly educated women and most prolific writers, defined much of her work as legwork in support of her husband's literary and bibliographic projects.[70] Dorothea Schlegel, who published her novel *Florentin* anonymously (it was, in fact, widely believed to have been written by her husband), insisted, once her authorship was known, that she regarded the book not as an artistic undertaking but as a financial one: its sole purpose, she claimed, was to round out the family income so that her husband, thus somewhat relieved of the necessity to provide for the family, could concentrate on his art.[71]

These two examples, to which many others could be added,[72] show that both education and work assumed highly ambivalent meanings in women's writing that moreover clearly relate to the class context in which the terms were used. Lack of education was often perceived, by lower-class writers, as an obstacle to their advancement into the realm of the (middle-class) writer, which—to them—also represented the realm in which it was no longer necessary to work (physically) for one's survival. Too much education, on the other hand, could ruin both the career of the "natural genius" and the reputation of the bourgeois housewife. Thus, both groups regularly misrepresented their work as unlettered, unerudite, and unintellectual. "Work," as well, assumes a class-specific ambivalence when used by women writers. If lower-class women classed their oeuvre as work, albeit easy work by comparison to physical labor, middle-class women were often extremely careful to cast their literary activity as purely supportive of their husbands' more important literary projects. Their work, in other words, is redefined as housework; the author becomes the literary equivalent of Schiller's housewife, who collects, preserves, and "adds" but does not actually "work."

For the past two hundred years, readers of women's literature have had to contend with these ideas. They are perpetuated, for example, in the seemingly irreparable rift between male writers (commonly assumed to be dedicated to their art) and female writers (commonly assumed to be in it for the money). To contest this and other assumptions about men's versus women's literature, as feminist criticism has done since at least the 1970s, leads straight into yet another dilemma: the question of whether women's writing can be fairly considered within a tradition of philosophical and literary movements and cultural contexts shaped by men or whether it should be read "on its own terms."[73] Readers of women's literature are thus faced with an unappetizing alternative, that of either ghettoizing women's literature or applying to it aesthetic and philosophical criteria that social and cultural histories of literature have shown to be largely or entirely inapplicable. Either way, reading women's writing still involves considering questions that women writers of the Enlightenment indirectly asked of their readers two hundred years ago. Among these, we might find the following: Can the work's reception overcome its inception? Is literature that was so resolutely diminished, undercut, and belittled, by both its authors and its critics, eligible for a reception as Great Art, with all the unassailable certainties and claims to transcendence this implies? Can the aesthetic criteria of the past be rethought to a degree that would make such an understanding possible? Can work that has been disparaged as easy work, legwork, or housework ever become "the work"?

CHAPTER SEVEN

Power: Varieties of Women's Political Power in Enlightenment England

CHARLOTTE SUSSMAN

In her *Vindication of the Rights of Woman*, Mary Wollstonecraft famously writes, "I do not wish [women] to have power over men; but over themselves."[1] Social power fascinated Wollstonecraft, and she uses the word frequently in her polemic. But what does she mean by it here? The sentence seems to make its point by juxtaposing two quite different kinds of power: the sort that women should hold "over themselves," which we might understand in terms of the Enlightenment ideals of moral restraint, disinterestedness, and self-control; and the sort women might wield over men. But when Wollstonecraft disavows the prospect of women having "power over men," is she rejecting the sexual sway women might have over men in private life, or is she referring to the possibility that women might aim for some more public, more political form of power? This short, vehement sentence is as provocative and ultimately as hard to parse today as it must have been in 1792, perhaps even more so. It succinctly raises many of the questions that circle around the word *power* when we think about

the concept with regard to gender. We are all Wollstonecraft's daughters in this
respect, and even now, when we consider male power, I suspect we still think
first of political and economic power. In contrast, when we think about female
power, we immediately think not of those categories but rather of the moral
power Wollstonecraft suggests here, or of the sexual power she disavows.

This chapter aims to trace the intersection and entanglement across the Enlightenment of these latter two forms of power: the power that derives from the
female body and the power that derives from feminine moral authority. Given
the space I have here, I am able to offer only a partial and incomplete view of a
complicated question. Nevertheless, I hope to revisit some of the still perplexing
issues Wollstonecraft raises in her *Vindication*. I begin by tracing the shift that
took place over the course of the eighteenth century from privileging women's
sexual power to celebrating their moral power. I then consider how both those
aspects of femininity were deployed in the more explicitly political arena of
parliamentary politics. I conclude with two examples of such deployment, both
fairly well known: Georgianna, Duchess of Devonshire's involvement in the
Westminster elections of 1784, and the activities of ladies' antislavery societies
in the first decades of the nineteenth century. Both cases demonstrate how questions of female power were nuanced by class during this period and also how
shifting standards of feminine physical propriety affected political involvement.

Wollstonecraft begins her investigation of the subjugation of women on
a personal note. "After considering the historic page, and viewing the living
world with anxious solicitude," she writes,

> the most melancholy emotions of sorrowful indignation have depressed
> my spirits, and I have sighed when obliged to confess that either Nature
> has made a great difference between man and man, or that the civiliza-
> tion which has hitherto taken place in the world has been very partial.

She concludes, at least in this opening paragraph, that the cause of her distress
is the "false system of education" put forward in books written by men,

> who, considering females rather as women than human creatures, have
> been more anxious to make them alluring mistresses than affectionate
> wives and rational mothers; and the understanding of the sex has been so
> bubbled by this specious homage, that the civilized women of the present
> century, with a few exceptions, are only anxious to inspire love, when
> they ought to cherish a nobler ambition, and by their abilities and virtues
> exact respect.[2]

Wollstonecraft's most important legacy to Western feminism is often thought to be the distinction she makes here between women "as females" and as "human creatures"—between a vindication of women's rights based on their difference from men and one based on their equality.

At the same time, however, she articulates a theory of female power—or, rather, she sketches out a history of female power, one that was very important to Enlightenment thought. Despite the advances of civilization, she suggests, women remain in thrall to the "specious homage" they are given because of their ability to "inspire love." In other words, in the eyes of the world, feminine power is tied to feminine sexuality; women's power is indistinguishable from sexual sway. For Wollstonecraft, however, true civilization will occur only when women rely on "their abilities and virtues [to] exact respect"—in other words, when they leave the temptation to hold sexual sway over men behind. This is her idea of Enlightenment progress.

FIGURE 7.1: Portrait of Mary Wollstonecraft by John Opie (ca. 1790–91). Tate Gallery, London/Art Resource, New York.

Even this brief dissection of the opening paragraph of the *Vindication*, however, reminds us of what a difficult word *power* is to define, particularly with regard to what Wollstonecraft calls her "weak and wretched" "fellow-creatures"[3]—women—who have always been excluded from most conventional definitions of the concept. Yet while women were securely outside the franchise during the eighteenth century (out of it, of course, until the beginning of the twentieth century), they were still involved, in surprising ways, with England's political landscape during this era. In the pages that follow, I look at the way the Enlightenment narrative of feminine progress—women's progress from being creatures reliant on their sexual wiles for what little power they had to being individuals of a higher order who influenced others through moral force—intersects with women's involvement in British politics.

In the late seventeenth and early eighteenth centuries, British culture was still heavily invested in the power of female beauty. When the Empress in Margaret Cavendish's *The Blazing World* wants to subdue her enemies, for instance, she simply dresses up:

> The Emperess [sic] appeared upon the face of the Water in her Imperial Robes; in some part of her hair she had placed some of the Star-Stone, near her face, which added such a lustre and glory to it, that it caused a great admiration in all that were present, who believed her to be some Celestial Creature, or rather an uncreated Goddess, and they all had a desire to worship her; for surely, said they, no mortal creature can have such a splendid and transcendent beauty, nor can any have so great a power as she has, to walk upon the Waters, and to destroy whatever she pleases, not only whole Nations, but a whole World.[4]

The word *power* shows up here too, but in quite a different sense than how it is used in the *Vindication*. The Empress has powers the way Superman has powers—to walk on water, to destroy nations and worlds. She could rule those around her by sheer force, but she doesn't need to, because her appearance inspires a "desire to worship her" in all who encounter her, who are awed by her "splendid and transcendent beauty." Despite Cavendish's characteristic hyperbole, we can see here the cultural force attributed to feminine display, particularly as embodied by an aristocratic woman.[5]

As the eighteenth century progressed, this form of feminine power became more suspect. The poet Alexander Pope, for example, is fascinated by women's capacity to inspire desire and wreak destruction. And yet such displays are always viewed with suspicion. His mock-epic *The Rape of the Lock*, for instance, acknowledges the power of feminine beauty, albeit ironically, when, rivaling the sun's beams, the poem's glittering heroine, Belinda, "launches" into her day by sailing down the Thames.[6] Like Cavendish's Empress, she subdues all before her: "Fair Nymphs, and well-drest Youths around her shone, / But ev'ry Eye was fix'd on her alone. / On her white Breast a sparkling *Cross* she wore, / Which *Jews* might kiss, and Infidels adore."[7] The poet apologizes for the power Belinda seems to wield: "If to her share some Female Errors fall, / Look on her Face, and you'll forget 'em all."[8] Using the subjunctive, the poet first raises the possibility of female duplicity and then subordinates it to the power of surface beauty. Femininity here joins an alluring, distracting surface with an unknowable sexual "error" that may lie beneath. The poem deems this combination provocative. When Belinda's erstwhile suitor, the Baron, stealthily clips a lock of her hair—the "rape" that instigates the conflict of the poem—he is motivated by his "admiration" of her locks. It is this motivation that spurs his ambition "by force to ravish or by Fraud betray."[9] Unlike *The Blazing World*, Pope's poem is uneasy about the power of Belinda's beauty and its tendency to invite disaster.

By the second quarter of the century, women's "power" was firmly relegated to the private sphere, at least in theory. As Pope says in his "Epistle to a Lady," addressing his friend Martha Blount,

> in Public Men sometimes are shown,
> A Woman's seen in Private life alone:
> Our bolder Talents in full light display'd,
> Your Virtues open fairest in the shade.[10]

Pope seems to separate the spheres quite clearly here: public/private, light/dark, talent/virtues. A woman is sequestered—an image rather than an actor—seemingly removed from the question of power altogether. Yet when he comes to describe what it is that women actually do in private life, Pope finds himself engaging with the discourse of power nevertheless. The perfect, "private" woman is

> She, who ne'er answers till a Husband cools,
> Or, if she rules him, never shows she rules;
> Charms by accepting, by submitting sways,
> Yet has her humour most, when she obeys.[11]

The syntax here recalls the lines describing Belinda, with "if she rules" replacing "if she have faults"—both disturbing ideas that Pope can apparently put forward only with an "if" in front to give himself an alibi, so to speak. He introduces the possibility of feminine power inside the home through the subjunctive—"if she rules him . . ."—and then tells us that such power, if it does exist, will never be visible. The next line combines the language of sexuality—"charms"—with vocabulary that can be both sexual and political—"sways." Paradoxically, woman "has her humour most"—is either most herself or most easily gets her own way—when she obeys. And yet the second line of the couplet does make us forget the images of "swaying" and "charming" provided by the first line. The way the couplet joins "sway" and "obey" as a rhymed pair of words highlights the tension between the ideas of the first line and the ideas of the second. Clearly, the domestic arena is not removed from questions of power; nor is it one in which power relations are clearly established. Rather, it is a place where complex power relations are negotiated, where domestic variations on "ruling" and holding sway are played out.

For Wollstonecraft, as for Pope, the dynamics of power in domestic settings are analogous to those in political settings. Women believe that their only chance to wrest control over their lives is to manipulate others' perception of their weakness.

> Women . . . sometimes boast of their weakness, cunningly obtaining power by playing on the *weakness* of men; and they may well glory in their illicit sway, for, like Turkish bashaws, they have more real power than their masters; but virtue is sacrificed to temporary gratifications, and the respectability of life to the triumph of an hour.[12]

Using the same word, *sway*, Wollstonecraft too implies that such power is illegitimately obtained, comparing it to the subterfuge of Middle Eastern courts in a way that would have had negative connotations for the xenophobic English. Furthermore, she firmly associates such suspect political power with female sexuality—with its need for triumphal gratification—in sharp contrast to the virtue and respectability she hopes for women.

But what did any of these things have to do with political power? As Amanda Vickery reminds us,

> All the institutions of the eighteenth-century state were dominated by men . . . women could not be Members of Parliament, nor could they hold office of state. Women played no direct role in county government or in the administration of criminal justice, as they could not serve as

Justices of the Peace, deputy lieutenants, or high sheriffs. Indeed, women
could not even serve as ordinary jurors until 1919.[13]

And yet women did find extraparliamentary ways to participate in politics.
Perhaps the earliest, and most obvious, intervention was through the medium
of printed scandal and political writing. One writer who intervened in this way
was Delarivier Manley, a contemporary of Pope's.

Manley lived during the first blossoming of political parties in England and
dedicated most of her literary career to that conflict. She was a party writer
for the Tories during the reign of Queen Anne, turning scandal and gossip into
thinly veiled allegory and "fiction." She once received fifty pounds from Robert Harley, the Tory prime minister, but claimed that was "all I ever received
from the public for what some esteem good service to the cause."[14] Yet her par-
tisanship is certainly what brought her success, and was the motivation for her
best-known work, *Secret Memoirs and Manners of Several Persons of Quality
of Both Sexes. From the New Atalantis, an Island in the Mediterranean,* better
known simply as *The New Atalantis* (1709). Manley turned to writing party
propaganda after being duped, at an early age, into a bigamous marriage with
her cousin, John Manley. This relationship left her a fallen woman with an illegitimate child, as scandalous a figure as most of those about whom she wrote.
In addition to *The New Atalantis*, Manley wrote several other scandalous al-
legories, including one on the career of Sarah Churchill, Anne's favorite and
a Whig, called *The History of Queen Zara and the Zarazians* (1705); several
plays; and an autobiographical narrative, *The Adventures of Rivella* (1714),
as well as taking over the editorship of the *Examiner* from Jonathan Swift
in 1711. These profitable ventures into print earned her the epithet "Scan-
dalosissima Scoundrelia."[15] Swift, with whom she enjoyed a collegial working
relationship, seems to be describing Manley in his poem "Corinna," which
imagines a baby girl blessed by both Cupid and a satyr: "While the poor child
lay fast asleep / Then Cupid thus, 'This little maid / Of love shall always speak
and write' / 'And I pronounce,' the satyr said, / 'The world shall feel her scratch
and bite.' "[16] And Manley's writing does demonstrate the effects that a woman's scratching and biting words could have in the political realm.

The New Atalantis recounts the journey of Astrea, the goddess of justice,
to the island of Atalantis and its capital city of Angela (England and London,
respectively) to gather information to help her in tutoring the island's next
ruler.[17] Once there, she meets her "mother," Virtue, and the two are given a
tour of the principal people and places of the kingdom by Lady Intelligence,
"first lady of the bedchamber to the Princess Fame," whose "garments are

all hieroglyphics."[18] The three travel invisibly, and Lady Intelligence conveys the elaborate, scandalous histories of the people they encounter. Occasionally, another character will speak directly to the three women: most importantly, Mrs. Nightwork, a midwife who knows particularly intimate details about the shocking sexual exploits of the Atalantians and whose presence links the birth of (illegitimate) babies to the "birth" of scandal. Despite their collegial relationship, the main narrators have different reactions to the stories they hear. While the goddesses, Astrea and Virtue, tend to draw moral lessons from the information they take in, Lady Intelligence seems interested in covering as much scandalous ground as possible. Intelligence, indeed, seems at times to lose patience with her more celestial charges. She also competitively defends her role, telling Mrs. Nightwork, "I'm afraid you are taking my province from me, and engrossing all the scandal to your self."[19] This may be because both Lady Intelligence and Mrs. Nightwork know that their livelihoods, unlike that of the goddesses, depend on the retail of gossip. As Nightwork says, "We should be but ill company to most of our ladies, who love to be amused with the failings of others, and would not always give us so favourable and warm a reception, if we had nothing of scandal to entertain them with."[20] Giving the reader multiple perspectives on the action allows Manley to oscillate between two configurations of femininity: an ancient preconception of female interlocutors as gossips and an emerging idea that women should serve as the moral censors of social interaction. Although most critics believe that Manley has a closer allegiance to Lady Intelligence than the goddesses, her inclusion of both allows the reader to avoid choosing between moral judgment and the pleasures of scandal.

The New Atalantis was so successful that the first volume had gone into three editions by the time the second was published. The piece as a whole went into six editions in ten years, making it the "bestselling novelistic fiction of the decade."[21] The extent to which its numerous readers recognized the characters of *The New Atalantis* as real people is open to dispute. Keys that "identified" characters were published separately, but they do not definitively link each character to an actual person.[22] For the text to work as scandal, then, the reader must already know at least part of the story being told allegorically and must enjoy hearing it told again. Some in power certainly did read it as a political intervention: Manley, the publishers, and printers of the text were indicted for seditious libel in October 1709, but she was discharged without sentence after her trial in February 1710. In a more general sense, however, the work was certainly political, as it participated in, and helped shape, the transition between politics imagined as the private doings of royalty, ministers, and military men and politics imagined as public knowledge discussed by the general reader. Thus, even if the average reader does not know that Count Fortunatus is supposed to be the Duke of Marlborough, he or she can consider and discuss that character's method of doing political business. Ironically, this transmission from the private to the public sphere is enabled by the traditionally debased mode of women's gossip. Much of *The New Atalantis*, then, seems to work on two levels: as scandal and as autonomous novelistic anecdotes—stories focusing on the passions and sensations of love, which the literary critic Ros Ballaster has dubbed "amatory fiction."[23] The description of the "new cabal," a group of aristocratic women who dress as men and conduct affairs with other women, has also raised the question of whether Manley envisaged a feminine utopia in the midst of the corruption and scandal of Atalantis. A number of other episodes deal with incest, polygamy, and infanticide and raise the more abstract and "novelistic" question of whether an individual has the right to break society's moral laws. Those who do so usually are punished in the text, and yet the narrators consistently express sympathy for characters who feel driven to commit these crimes. On one level, Manley suggests that the sexual transgressions of the Whigs are symptoms of their political corruption, linking public and private through the retail of scandal. On another level, however, she pushes prose narrative into a new role in public life, by making private sexual choices the material for public discussion.

In *The New Atalantis*, when women come together, they are assumed to be plotting sexual misdeeds: "these ladies are of the new Cabal, a sect (however innocent in it self) that does not fail from meeting its share of censure from the world. Alas! What can they do? How unfortunate are women? If they seek their diversion out of themselves and include the other sex, they must be criminal? If in themselves (as those of the new Cabal), still they are criminal?"[24] Sexuality thus has a place in the public sphere, while politics infiltrates the private sphere. "You are a politician, I find, Madam, as well as a midwife," Lady Intelligence tells Mrs. Nightwork when the latter tells her the details of a nobleman's political alliances—all learned in the bedchamber, of course.[25] Such supposedly feminine spaces are not separated from the political after all.

Despite Pope's blithe assurance that women will stay in the shade, of course they did not, particularly aristocratic women from "politically active families," who, according to Vickery's gloss on the work of Elaine Chalus, "had little choice but to be involved throughout the political process," albeit mostly through social activities, taking up a "drudgery of pleasures . . . between elections in order to maintain and consolidate family influence in the constituency—attendance at balls, assemblies, breakfasts, dinners, and race meetings was obligatory."[26]

And yet these political activities were quite circumscribed. The case most often presented to explain the limits of women's active intervention in parliamentary politics is that of Georgianna, Duchess of Devonshire's canvassing for the flamboyant Whig Charles James Fox in the Westminster election of 1784. Georgianna's somewhat unconventional participation in the campaign seems to have been one of the things that secured the election for Fox, but it is the opprobrium heaped on her efforts by the opposition, led by then prime minister William Pitt, that has survived in historical memory.

One thing that seems to have secured the opprobrium that has surrounded Georgianna's efforts was her willingness to cross class lines. Not only did she urge the artisans and laborers of Westminster to vote, but she also offered them rides to the polls in the ducal carriage. Furthermore, she descended from that carriage and mixed with the hoi polloi on foot. The shine, the glitter of aristocratic display seems to have been blunted when she closed the distance between the audience and the object of admiration. One Thomas Rowlandson caricature of the duchess shows her embracing a plebian man, probably the butcher she was rumored to have actually kissed. She is the taller of the two figures to begin with, but she is made even more imposing by the fronds and feathers of her enormous hat. The duchess and the plebe are embracing, their lips touching; due to the height difference, the man's eyes are tilted up toward her face. He looks both awestruck and somewhat stupefied. Behind them, another woman cheers them on, with a word balloon reading "Huzza—Fox forever."

One thing the election shows us, Judith S. Lewis points out, is that "the notion that 'family' belongs in the private sphere and 'politics' in the public sphere makes little sense. It was not merely that women refused to stay home, but also that politics refused to stay 'in public.' Politics, like charity, often began at home."[27] Historians have long assumed that Georgianna was attacked on the basis of her sexuality for entering the political fray, positing evidence such as the following doggerel rhyme purported to be written by "Lovers of Truth and Justice":

> I had rather kiss my Moll than she,
> With all her paint and Finery;
> What's a Duchess more than Woman?
> We've sounder flesh on Portsmouth Common.[28]

These lines do depict the duchess as sexually loose, but they also depict her as lower class and thus suggest that she was being attacked for her disregard for class as well as gender boundaries. The female "flesh" one might expect to

FIGURE 7.2: Thomas Rowlandson, *The Devonshire, or Most Approved Method of Securing Votes* (1784). Metropolitan Museum of Art. The Elisha Whittesley Collection, the Elisha Whittesley Fund, 1959 (59.533.57).

meet on Portsmouth Common would be that of a prostitute, a woman making her living by selling her sexuality; a "Moll" was also a sexually loose woman. The doggerel's statement that the duchess is actually more degraded, physically less "sound," than either type of woman implies that her activities have done more than trouble the class hierarchies of British society—they have reversed them, turned them topsy-turvy. As Linda Colley points out, to be a "public woman" was the linguistic equivalent of being a prostitute. The duchess had extended her "attachment" beyond her own family (and her family's boroughs) to proclaim her allegiance to Fox—an allegiance based on ideas rather than blood. For many observers, this automatically opened her activities to charges of sexual misconduct.[29] The Borough of Westminster was one in which all rate payers could vote, and to win their support, the duchess shared conversation and beers with artisans and butchers. Her behavior seemed too democratic by far, especially for an aristocrat.

Thus, once again, we find the deployment of female sexuality in the public arena of politics to be a vexed and difficult issue. This is particularly true, according to Lewis, at the intersection of class and gender:

Standards of decency were being contested: standards of decency that conveyed political meaning in a particular political context. It was not so much what a woman did as how she did it . . . When appearing "in publick," [Georgianna's mother, the dowager Lady Spencer] advised her younger daughter, Harriet Lady Duncannon, in 1786, it was essential "to maintain a certain dignity that should belong to your station in life." So the critique [of Georgianna] was at least as class-specific as it was attached to gender.[30]

Because she was an aristocratic woman, certain kinds of public display were acceptable for the duchess, even required; she, like many aristocratic women from politically active families, was required to be seen—and to be seen displaying the clothes and bearing suitable for her class—at various public assemblies, as a way of making her family's status visible. And yet other activities—those deemed overly sexual or below her "station"—were considered improper. Of course, one might argue that Georgianna was able to have the impact she did on Fox's campaign by being aware of those limitations and playing against them. But it has been the criticism directed at her—not the nature of her political strategies—that has been most remembered.

The aspects of the duchess's behavior that were specific to her aristocratic status come into sharper relief when we compare them to the activities of a group of middle-class women who also hoped to have an impact on British politics: the women of the ladies' antislavery societies, which were active at the beginning of the nineteenth century. As we have seen, we can understand the way Georgianna wielded power only if we take both her gender and her class into account. The duchess seems to have been extremely conscious of the social mores surrounding the public visibility of aristocratic women, who were expected to spend considerable time in the public eye, visible but not otherwise accessible to the classes below them. Georgianna exploited such visibility by thwarting those expectations; her willingness to close the distance between herself and the plebian masses, to let them touch as well as see her, made her visibility that much more striking and forceful. She achieved much of her impact and nearly all of her notoriety, that is, by *working against* the expectations of how aristocratic women were supposed to wield power through the public display of their bodies. Ladies' antislavery societies did the opposite. They *worked within* the class-inflected limits on their gender roles—in this case the very different expectations for middle-class women—to access what political power was available to them in the public sphere. Indeed, they often used those very limits—the injunction to morality and empathy, for example—to their advantage.

In the early nineteenth century, the qualities Wollstonecraft desired for women allowed them to become central figures in the British antislavery campaigns, primarily under the aegis of ladies' antislavery societies. The emergence of the British antislavery movement is one of the great puzzles of Enlightenment historiography; its eventual success is even less explicable. At the beginning of the eighteenth century, almost all Britons regarded chattel slavery as an unpleasant but necessary part of enjoying the fruits of an overseas empire. By the end of the century, that same broad segment regarded slavery as a moral outrage that could not be tolerated in a modern nation. In 1807 Britain abolished its slave trade; in 1833 it emancipated its slaves. From a contemporary perspective, this story is puzzling on two counts. We can't help but ask how so many people could have cared so little about the horrors of slavery for so long. And if that was indeed the case, why did so many people change their ethical ideals so completely in such a relatively short amount of time? One answer has to do with new forms of extraparliamentary political agitation, much of it by evangelical groups.[31] Among the new forms of social activism fostered by such organizations was the emergence of ladies' antislavery associations. These groups, along with a number of other women's philanthropic associations formed at the turn of the century, transformed a growing cultural reliance on middle-class women's moral rectitude into a vehicle for political activities outside the home.

F.K. Prochaska has found that approximately 160 religious, moral, educational, and philanthropic associations were founded in England between 1700 and 1830: "About one hundred and thirty of these were established in the years 1790–1830."[32] By the 1830s women's longtime involvement in the antislavery movement had led them to form their own philanthropic associations to focus on this issue; "in 1825 three women's antislavery societies were formed, at Birmingham, Sheffield and at Calne in Wiltshire; by the end of the decade there were over forty others."[33] The political activities of such groups were very different than those of aristocratic women like Georgianna, who came from a tradition of political influence. For one thing, the membership of such associations was formed primarily of middle-class religious women and "evolved out of their already accepted roles in religious philanthropy and the religious societies aimed at the expansion of evangelical Christianity. Philanthropy and religious work were accommodated as extensions of women's caring and domestic functions, part of the *status quo* of gender relationships."[34] In a full-length study of women's involvement in the abolitionist movement in Britain, Clare Midgley concludes that it was "the first large-scale political campaign by middle-class women, and the first movement in which women aroused the opinion of the female public in order to put pressure on Parliament," making important "interconnections between domestic and political life and between public and private activities."[35]

But that line between the privacy of the domestic sphere and the publicity of political engagement had to be negotiated carefully by these groups, as we have already seen with activities by aristocratic women like Georgianna. By and large, women confined even their political activities to the domestic sphere; "in most [philanthropic groups], women worked only with women. If they addressed mixed-sex meetings, they did not speak in public but at 'drawing room' or 'parlour' meetings of invited guests."[36] Yet even these activities sometimes seemed too openly political for their male colleagues. William Wilberforce, an evangelical and leader of the abolitionist cause, once told a friend that "for ladies to meet, to publish, to go from house to house, stirring up petitions—these seem to me proceedings unsuited to the female character as delineated in scripture."[37] What bothers Wilberforce is women's public participation in politics—going door to door, attending meetings. As with the objections to Georgianna's activities, the question is not *whether* women should be involved in politics but *how* they should be involved.

Clearly, the more middle-class women could keep their bodies—particularly the sexual aspects of their bodies—out of the public eye, the better. The late eighteenth and early nineteenth centuries saw an increasing sensitivity to women deploying any kind of sexual display for political ends, and yet the same era witnessed a pronounced rise in the level of organized female intervention into cultural affairs. In retrospect, these activities often look quite "public." Indeed, the ideology of separate spheres—a rhetorical insistence that women's role was to run the household and ensure their families' physical and spiritual health while men managed the worlds of business and politics—could be a double-edged sword, used by some to caution women against public behavior and by others to render such behavior appropriate and perhaps even obligatory, as in this exchange from an abolitionist pamphlet entitled "A Dialogue between a Well-Wisher and a Friend to the Slaves in the British Colonies":

> B. But I really think women ought not to interfere in this business, on account of its being a political question: for women have nothing to do with such subjects; they are quite out of their province, and I think it is not consistent with propriety and hardly with feminine modesty, that they should put themselves forward on this occasion.
>
> A. I own I have never been able to affix any clear meaning to the expression you have just used, and which I have often heard before, that

this is a political question. It appears to me to be peculiarly a religious and moral question.[38]

That is, in order for women to intervene in the antislavery debates—which of course also took place on the level of parliamentary politics—they had to code their activities as part of the feminine "realms" of religion and morality. In this way, women were able to access a kind of agency in the world outside the home that had more to do with the cultural force of private domestic practices than with overtly political actions—though they were able to influence those as well. Indeed, Elizabeth Heyrick, in her "Apology for Ladies' Anti-Slavery Associations" (1828), proposes that the exclusion of women from the political arena actually gives them an advantage:

> Though *we* have no voice in the senate, no influence in public meetings,—though no signatures of ours are attached to anti-slavery petitions to the legislature,—yet we have a voice and an influence in a sphere, which, though restricted, is no narrow one. To the hearts and consciences of our own sex, at least, we have unlimited access. By dispelling their ignorance, disseminating among them correct information of the nature and consequences of West Indian slavery, and dissuading them from all participation in its guilt, by a conscientious rejection of its produce, we may withdraw its resources and undermine its foundations.[39]

After elaborating on the ways in which women cannot exercise political power, Heyrick goes on to argue that the "hearts and consciences" of women are a powerful tool in the destruction of the slave trade.

More typically, ladies' antislavery societies emphasized the power women's moral sense might exert over men's political decisions. The descriptions given by such groups of their own activities often underline the potential efficacy of influence, rather than the necessity for public arguments. As Heyrick, the author of "Appeal to the Hearts and Consciences of British Women" (1828), explains,

> [A woman] may . . . exert a powerful influence over public opinion and practice without violating that retiring delicacy which constitutes one of her loveliest ornaments. The peculiar texture of her mind, her strong feelings and quick sensibilities, especially qualify her, not only to sympathise with suffering, but also to plead for the oppressed, and there is no calculating the extent and importance of the moral reformations which

might be effected through the combined exertion of her gentle influence and steady resolution.[40]

This statement works to align femininity and abolitionist actions. A woman's qualities of "strong feelings," "quick sensibilities," "gentle influence," and "steady resolution"—in short, the qualities that were beginning to define her gender identity—demand her involvement in the antislavery campaign. Even a woman's lack of public political power is mobilized here as a moral asset; a woman is thus qualified to "plead for the oppressed." The author of the passage is careful to deploy domestic sentiments toward the public good while at the same time protesting that women are uninterested in manipulating actual parliamentary decisions. The woman lending her voice to the cause of the suffering slaves has no stake in the economic or political consequences of her actions; her only concern is with her personal moral rectitude, and that of the people around her. An "Appeal to the Christian Women of Sheffield" also argues for the enormous, though apolitical, force of moral influence:

> We are met by the question, "What can *Women* do in this cause?" . . . We are happily excluded from the great theatre of public business, from the strife of debate, and the cares of legislation; but this privilege does not exempt us from the duty of exerting our influence, in our own appropriate and retired sphere, over that public opinion, without which no important moral reformation can be accomplished . . . it is ours to shew what may be effected by the combined exertion of gentle influence and steady resolution. Is it assuming too much, to say, that no cruel institutions, or ferocious practices, could long withstand the avowed and persevering censure of the women of England?[41]

Statements such as this avow both the value and the power of the domestic sphere. Such retirement is not relief from civic duties but rather requires its own kinds of activities—influence and censure. Male antislavery activists usually courted and relied on the strength of feminine influence. Sir James McKintosh observed that "in proportion as they possessed the retiring virtues of delicacy and modesty, those chief ornaments of women, in that proportion had they come forward to defend the still higher objects of humanity and justice."[42]

Since their inception, the activities of ladies' antislavery societies have been seen in the context of a history of emancipation—first of men and women of African descent, then of white, middle-class British women themselves.

By the end of the nineteenth century, the *Westminster Review* could look back and note that

> The reign of Queen Victoria and the progress of emancipation began to-gether, and have flourished side by side. It was inevitable, when a woman sat on the throne, that the thoughts of other women should turn towards a wider sphere of influence than that previously known; while the spread of education, the development of railways, and the increase of wealth all tended in the same direction. The public work of women began appro-priately enough with the antislavery agitation, when William Wilberforce then prophesied that the step thus taken by them would lead to their own emancipation.[43]

The author's conviction that the "public work" of white middle-class women in the antislavery cause led to political action on their own behalf has been reinforced by a number of recent studies of women's involvement in abolition-ist activities. Many of these authors, however, focus on the way abolitionist activity fostered the administrative skills and political self-awareness crucial to such women's fight for their own rights later in the nineteenth century, rather than emphasizing any necessary link between abolition and women's politi-cal power. Kenneth Corfield points out that despite the practical knowledge they gained, the members of ladies' antislavery societies "made no explicit claims for their sex's rights."[44] Nevertheless, Louis and Rosamund Billington conclude that "feminism [drew] upon the more radical elements of abolition-ist ideology, and the experience of a network of women working within the reform milieu. In this sense, as later feminists recognized, the activities of their mothers, grandmothers and aunts in the antislavery movement laid the foun-dations of feminism."[45] These explanations highlight the political utility of the connections white, middle-class women were able to forge among themselves within the framework of the antislavery movement. The privacy of the do-mestic space was converted into a new site for political involvement. In this context, it is perhaps significant that the writer in the *Westminster Review* highlights the connection between the thoughts of politically minded women and the ascension of Queen Victoria; the empowerment of middle-class women may have been enabled by their identification with the most politically power-ful British woman of the period.

We can come back now to Wollstonecraft's heartfelt wish that women achieve "power over themselves" rather than "power over men." This was clearly an influential model for the way the Enlightenment dealt with the relationship between women and social power: women were supposed to master their own affect and their own sexuality, and to model that mastery to others, influencing the behavior of those around them to moral ends that were only contingently political. It was a worthy goal, and one that allowed women a surprising amount of agency in the public arena at the end of the eighteenth and the beginning of the nineteenth century.

To conclude, however, it is worth thinking not only about the ways that the sexual power exercised by the duchess and the moral power deployed by the ladies' antislavery societies differed from each other but also about the ways in which they might have been similar. Both, in their way, are rooted in the body: the display of the body in the case of sexual power; the regulation and control of the body—one's own as well as those of the family under one's management—in the case of moral or domestic power. And both seem to preclude, in practice, if not in theory, the exercise of the forms of masculine power I noted at the beginning of this essay: economic and overt political power. While women have made great strides in both areas since Wollstonecraft's day, not least in winning the right to vote, it is chastening to realize that women still have less of a claim on these kinds of power than do men. As of 2008 women in the United States earned only 79.9 percent of what men earned.[46] In 2010 only 16.8 percent of congressional seats in the United States were held by women, and women had been elected to just 22 percent of the elected executive offices across the country. The Enlightenment changed many things about the way women wielded and experienced power, but in some ways it did not change very much at all. Women's power to a surprising degree remained circumscribed within the bounds of their own bodies and did not extend to the more abstract realms of representative politics or the newly far-flung capitalist networks of the era.

I thus close with a quote from Virginia Woolf's *A Room of One's Own*, which succinctly links women's intellectual impoverishment with their financial impoverishment. Having dined at a fictional women's college at "Oxbridge," the narrator and her friend discuss the plainness of the meal they've received:

> We burst out in scorn at the reprehensible poverty of our sex. What had our mothers been doing then that they had no wealth to leave us? . . . If only Mrs. Seton and her mother and her mother before her had learnt the great art of making money and had left their money, like their fathers and their grandfathers before them, to found fellowships and lectureships and prizes and scholarships appropriated to the use of their own sex . . . [But] to endow a college would necessitate the suppression of

families altogether . . . Consider the facts, we said. First there are the
nine months before the baby is born. Then the baby is born. Then there
are three or four months spent in feeding the baby. After the baby is fed
there are certainly five years spent in playing with the baby. You cannot,
it seems, let children run about the streets. People who have seen them
running wild in Russia say the sight is not a pleasant one.[47]

Woolf's ironic tone is inimitable, but the point is clear: women have been
blocked from economic power. For Woolf, that power is something that allows
not only material comforts in one's own lifetime but also the ability to make an
impact on institutions across time by, for example, endowing colleges and setting up named scholarships. Women have been prevented from wielding such
power by the pressing demands of maintaining a family: not simply the biological demands of bearing children and feeding them, but the moral demands
of "civilizing them." The moral and sentimental authority the ladies' antislavery societies deployed so deftly to achieve their goals finds its limit here, in the
unremunerated labor of keeping children from running wild in the streets.

CHAPTER EIGHT

Artistic Representation: The Famous Ballads of Anna Gordon, Mrs. Brown

RUTH PERRY

When one thinks of the Scottish Enlightenment, one imagines men striding up the craggy peak adjoining Holyrood Park in Edinburgh, arguing and gesticulating, or reading one another's works by candlelight, or sitting over whiskey or beer in largely male company. But there were, of course, women who participated in the intellectual ferment of that period. Among other things, women were an important part of the traditional song culture that interested Scottish intellectuals as the antiquarian remains of a precious national culture. Indeed, as Robert Burns and Sir Walter Scott knew, women were often crucial in transmitting and preserving this stream of Scotland's literary history. Thus, while learned written and printed investigations were pouring forth from the four universities of Scotland, with reverberations all over the Western world, Scottish scholars and philosophers were eagerly collecting and sharing whatever records they could find of a traditional culture that was essentially oral and popular and carried forward largely by working people and occasionally by their own mothers and aunts. This is the story of the most famous of these women, Anna Gordon, whose repertoire of ballads was the first ever to be tapped and written down by antiquarians and literary scholars, at a time when scholars feared that the oral tradition was in danger of disappearing forever.

* * *

Songs in eighteenth-century Scotland were the treasures of the poor and the casual possessions of the rich. Traditional music in Scotland had a long history of playing and singing going back at least to early medieval times, despite invasion and civil war, and was fully integrated into the culture as a whole. An unusually musical society, Scotland also had, for a number of reasons, a very permeable interface between the classical and popular traditions, between "high" and "low" culture, which added to the widespread popularity of traditional music.[1] People of all ranks played and sang and whistled it. There was (and is) an enormous repertoire of traditional music in the form of both songs and tunes, the bulk of the latter usually composed for fiddle and for the pipes. The illiterate carried this fund of pleasure in their memories, to make their work go faster and to enliven the long, dark nights. With the advent of print, the cultivated classes collected broadsides and songbooks, created musical manuscripts, and foraged for lost examples of songs and instrumental compositions to add to their national heritage.

In the eighteenth century, intellectuals and scholars turned to this unique repertoire as a particular object of study. Significant figures of the Scottish Enlightenment—Dr. William Tytler, Dr. James Beattie, Dr. John Gregory, Dr. Benjamin Franklin, and Henry Home, Lord Kames—all wrote treatises on the unique melodic qualities of Scottish song; and literary men such as Dr. Robert Anderson, Robert Jamieson, Sir Walter Scott, and Joseph Ritson wrote about the simple but magnificent poetry of the old ballads.[2] These men were investigating what we would now call historical sociology, the history of societies and cultures, as well as the antecedents of their own national heritage.

Aberdeen, the city of "Bon Accord" as it came to be known, a city with "as many musicians as magistrates" according to a secular songbook published in 1662, boasted one of the oldest "sang schools" in the country, established by James VI in an act of 1579, designed to keep alive "the art of music and singing" following the Reformation.[3] The city elders were charged with supporting this school and paying a music master, and it survived late into the eighteenth century, providing musical instruction for young people, girls as well as boys. As early as 1698, the town council of Old Aberdeen, the academic enclave to the north of the main part of the city, tried to ban private music teachers (both women and men) from teaching vocal or instrumental music in an attempt to protect the monopoly of the burgh's St. Nicholas sang school on teaching music.[4] The city also had an official, licensed dancing master in residence from the early eighteenth century on. And on the streets of the city, itinerant ballad singers sang their wares and sold them for pennies.[5]

This was the city into which Anna Gordon was born in 1747. It was one of the largest in Scotland—a university town with two old and reputable colleges and its own newspaper, the *Aberdeen Journal*. Anna Gordon's father, Thomas Gordon, was a professor of humanity—Greek and Latin—at King's College. Her mother was Lilias Forbes, daughter of the satirist and composer William Forbes. Between the Gordons and the Forbes's, perhaps the commonest surnames in the area, Anna Gordon was related to half the gentry of the northeast.

We have no direct evidence of how Anna Gordon Brown was educated, but grammar schools for girls existed in eighteenth-century Aberdeen.[6] Literacy was highly valued in Presbyterian Scotland in the eighteenth century—one had to be able to read and interpret scripture without an intermediary; it was one of the most educated populations in Europe.[7] Besides, Aberdeen was a college town and one that gave women as well as men access to higher learning, however informally. For example, Patrick Copland's public lectures in mechanics, hydrostatics, electricity, magnetism, and astronomy were attended by women as well as men. Private classes were also available for women in modern languages, classics, and music.[8] Anna Gordon's sister Elizabeth, who was two years older and with whom she was raised and educated, was said to have had a college education although neither college officially admitted women.

FIGURE 8.1: King's College, Old Aberdeen, where Anna Gordon's father, Thomas Gordon, was professor of humanity. Photo by Neal Murray.

It is likely that the Gordon girls both sat in on their father's tutorial sessions, for professors often supplemented their incomes at that time by boarding and/ or tutoring students in their homes.[9] The few letters of Anna Gordon Brown's that have survived display an educated mind. In one, she shows her familiarity with the epic poet Ossian and refers to his understanding of "grief in joy"; in another, she thanks her correspondent for sending her a copy of *Oberon* by the German poet Christoph Martin Wieland—whether in German or English we do not know.

One wants to know about the extent of Anna Gordon's learning because she was the carrier, the vessel, the transmitter of a large repertoire of magnificent Scottish ballads for which everyone in the English-speaking world is, or ought to be, grateful. She claims to have learned them as a child, from her mother and her maternal aunt and a servant in their natal household, without any recourse later to the ballad collections of Thomas Percy or David Herd or any other printed versions.[10] Because her ballads are remarkable for their artistry, their power, and their direct simplicity—with many wonderful aesthetic touches—there has been some question about whether to believe her claim that

FIGURE 8.2: Humanity Manse, Old Aberdeen, where Anna Gordon lived for her first forty years. Photo by Neal Murray.

her ballads were unimproved from outside sources and that she sang them as she learned them. The ballads she carried in her mind are more complete, more thoroughly beautiful, with consistently purer diction, more poignant details and occasional exquisite touches, than have been found in other versions of the same ballads. The repertoire as a whole is of such a high caliber, with so little dross, that it shows a highly selective literary sensibility at work. Francis James Child, the great ballad collector of the nineteenth century, wrote on the first page of his magisterial compilation: "No Scottish ballads are superior in kind to those recited in the last century by Mrs. Brown, of Falkland."[11]

The quality of these ballads of Anna Gordon's—later Mrs. Brown—was apparent to collectors in her own time as well. Robert Anderson, a Scottish literary scholar and biographer, interested in old ballads as were many of the Scottish literati in his day, sent transcriptions of several of Anna Gordon's ballads to Bishop Percy, the famous English collector, copied from a manuscript made in 1783 for one of her father's friends, William Tytler. Tytler had been deeply immersed in Scotland's musical past and was the author of the *Dissertation on Scottish Music*. It was at his request that Anna Gordon's ballads had been recorded in writing in the first place. His son, Alexander Fraser Tytler, then loaned the manuscript to Anderson, who copied parts of it to send to Thomas Percy. His transmission to Percy was accompanied by the following note:

> It is remarkable that Mrs Brown . . . never saw any of the ballads she has transmitted here, either in print or M.S, but learned them all when a child by hearing them sung by her mother and an old maid-servant who had been long in the family, and does not recollect to have heard any of them either sung or said by any one but herself since she was about ten years. She kept them as a little hoard of solitary entertainment, till, a few years ago, she wrote down as many as she could recollect, to oblige the late Mr W. Tytler, and again very late[ly] wrote down 9 ballads more to oblige his son the Professor [Alexander Fraser Tytler].
>
> Mr Jamieson[12] visited Mrs Brown, on his return here from Aberdeen, and obtained from her recollection 5 or 6 ballads more and a fragment. If this treasure excite your Lordship's curiosity, I shall transmit to you the titles of the ballads, with the first stanza, and number of stanzas of each. The greater part of them is unknown to the oldest persons in this country. I accompanied Mr Jamieson to my friend Scott's house in the country, for the sake [of] bringing the collectors to a good understanding.[13] I there took onus [on] me to hint my suspicion of modern manufacture in which

Scott has secretly anticipated me. Mrs. B. is fond of ballad poetry, writes verses, and reads every thing in the marvellous way. Yet her character places her above the suspicion of literary imposture, but it is wonderful how she should happen to be the depository of so many curious and valuable ballads.[14]

So we have Anderson sending copies of Anna Brown's ballads to Bishop Percy and going with Jamieson—another admirer of Mrs. Brown—to visit Scott, where they discussed her "hoard of solitary entertainment" and its provenance. Scott then included some of her ballads in his *Minstrelsy of the Scottish Border*, published a few years later. These literary men, Anna Brown's contemporaries, were struck with the quality of the ballads that she carried in her memory. They noted the literary cast of her mind—that she wrote poetry, read marvelous tales, and so on. But in the end they did not believe that she *consciously* improved the ballads she sang and recited—unlike Percy, for instance, or Matthew "Monk" Lewis or Sir Walter Scott, who famously *did* tinker with the ballads that they transmitted to the public.

They did not think that Anna Brown would prevaricate when she said she had not changed the ballads since she learned them as a child. The reason they suspected her at all was because it was not the habit at that time of literary scholars who collected and published ballads to simply present them as they were collected. Percy, Lewis, and Scott found it irresistible not to "improve" these anonymous narratives that seemed to belong to no one, that were lacking a single, authoritative version, and that were couched in such deceptively simple language. They could not help but feel that their educated, poetic intuitions were superior to the effusions of the illiterate people from whom these song texts were assumed to derive. Scott and Lewis even edited those versions of Mrs. Brown's texts that they obtained from William Tytler and Robert Jamieson.[15] Confronted with her entire magnificent repertoire, Scott and Anderson naturally assumed that she had rewritten these ballads that she had gathered through oral transmission from singers who had, in turn, learned them aurally.

Another point to remark from Anderson's letter to Percy is the excitement that the discovery of Anna Gordon's ballads prompted in these men of letters. These ballads represented to them what remained of the earliest known poetry in English. For the Scots especially, Scottish ballads were evidence of a continuous literary tradition independent of, aesthetically superior to, and more ancient than that of England.[16] Traditional music and song in Scotland carried national significance for everyone, regardless of class; ballads were part of their literary heritage—their literature was never thought of as a separate category from their song. "The greater part of them is unknown to the oldest persons in this country," Anderson had written of Anna Gordon's ballads, treating them as rediscovered excavated treasures from the literary history of their country. Alexander Fraser Tytler himself had remarked this to Anna Brown in 1800 when she sent him a set of her remembered texts: "They are indeed consummately beautiful and I regard them as a high acquisition to the Stock of our Old National Poetry."[17]

In a broader sense, of course, this interest in balladry and the oral traditions they represented was part of a movement that changed the course of literary history. Their beguilingly fresh diction, neither colloquial nor formal, fired an entire generation of writers and poets for whom Augustan conventions had become stale. The stark emotional content of the ballads and their unadorned clarity of voice swept away the cobwebs of neoclassicism, opened the floodgates of romanticism, and pointed the literary endeavor in a whole new direction. It is no simple coincidence that the collection that inaugurated this new literary movement was called the *Lyrical Ballads* and that the diction and prosody of this new way of writing borrowed much from the traditional ballad idiom. William Wordsworth and Scott were deeply influenced by the ballad collections published by antiquarians that they read in their youth, and their imaginations were formed by these materials. As Maureen McLane writes, "It is not an overstatement to say that, in the last decades of the eighteenth and the first of the nineteenth centuries, almost every major British literary poet found him- or herself engaging with oral tradition, as well as with the figure of the oral poet, his work, his cultural position, and his method of composition."[18]

Treasure troves like Anna Gordon Brown's suggested a whole substratum of literary history, a vast underground wellspring of popular poetry, largely untapped, that had never found its way into print but that still lived on in the partial memories of the old or the illiterate. Some, like Anna Gordon, were lucky enough to hear them sung, although few were able to retain them after hearing them just once or twice. As Anderson had said in his note to Percy, "It is wonderful how she should happen to be the depository of so many curious and valuable ballads," unable to entirely allay his suspicions about the scope and quality of what Anna Brown remembered.

The truth is that she was in the right place at the right time, an unexpected heir to a rich tradition. The northeast of Scotland is to this day famous for its wealth of ballad lore, and many ballads have been collected in Aberdeenshire since Anna Brown's time. The Glenbuchat manuscript, for example, transcribed onto paper watermarked 1814, 1815, 1816, and 1817 but only recently edited, contains sixty-eight ballads that were collected, it is thought, by Robert

Scott, the minister of the parish.[19] Even a century later, in the early twentieth century, Gavin Greig, a school master in Aberdeenshire, collected hundreds of versions of songs and ballads still being sung by people living in that part of Scotland, now published in eight volumes.[20]

What is more remarkable is that Anna Gordon had the native intelligence and taste as a girl to want to learn these splendid ballads when they were sung to her. As her father explained to Alexander Fraser Tytler, the son of his old friend, she learned many of them from her mother's sister, who had lived her married life on a remote estate near Braemar. Thomas Gordon wrote the following letter to Alexander Fraser Tytler about this source:

> An Aunt of my children, Mrs. Farquherson now dead, who was married to the proprietor of a small estate near the sources of the Dee, in the division of Aberdeenshire called Braemar, a sequestered, romantic pastoral country; if you ever went to your estate by the way of the castle of that name, you are not such a stranger to it as need a description. This good old woman, I say, spent her days, from the time of her marriage, among the flocks & herds at Allan a quoich, her husbands seat, which, even in the country of Braemar is considered as remarkable for the above circumstances. She has a tenacious memory, which retained all the songs she heard the nurses & old women sing in that neighborhood. In the latter part of her life she lived in Aberdeen, & being maternally fond of my children when young, she had them much about her, & was much with us. Her songs & tales of chivalry & love were a high entertainment to their young imagination. My youngest daughter Mrs Brown, at Falkland, is blessed with a memory as good as her aunts, & has almost the whole store of her songs lodged in it. In conversation I mentioned them to your Father [i.e., William Tytler], at whose request my Grandson Mr Scott, wrote down a parcel of them as his aunt sung them. Being then but a meer novice in musick, he added in his copy such musical notes as he supposed, notwithstanding their correctness, might give your father some imperfect notion of the airs; or rather lilts, to which they were sung. Both the words & strains were perfectly new to me, as they were to your father, & proceeded upon a system of manners, & in a stile of composition, both words & music, very peculiar, & of which we could recollect nothing similar. . . . Mrs. Farquherson, I am sure, invented nor added nothing herself.[21]

So Anna Gordon had the interest, the memory, and the access to an unusual repertoire of old ballads while they were still being heard and sung.

She was undoubtedly drawn both to the ballad poetry and to the melodies, for elsewhere she mentions the plaintive melodies of Scottish songs. This ballad repertoire seems to have existed in a woman's tradition that crossed class lines, for her father did not know them although he was very musical; that is, he was an early member of the Aberdeen Musical Society and a flute player. As he wrote to Alexander Fraser Tytler, "the words & strains were perfectly new to me, as they were to your father, & proceeded upon a system of manners, & in a stile of composition, both words & music, very peculiar, & of which we could recollect nothing similar." Anna Gordon's mother and her aunt were well born, but the maid servant from their family from whom she reports that she also learned some of her ballads, and the Scots-speaking staff on her aunt's country estate in Allan a quoich—"nurses & old women"—belonged to the laboring class that seems to have retained the old ballads the longest as a living tradition. Young Anna Gordon absorbed their ballads like a sponge and she did it aurally, probably singing them along with the older women.

The manuscript that was being passed around among Anderson, Percy, Scott, and Jamieson had been penned by Anna Brown's nephew, Robert Scott, who took down the words and music to the ballads as his aunt sang them at Tytler's request in 1783. That is, Mrs. Brown was not a passive copyist of the ballads that she heard from her relatives and laboring women but learned them as a singer does and had them in her memory as songs. And like any ballad singer, she never sang a ballad exactly the same way twice. Some of her ballads were collected from her several times, with a number of years intervening between sessions, and there are significant differences between these versions. Folklorists have spilt a good deal of ink about these differences and have asked whether they mean that she simply memorized the ballads imperfectly or rather that she "recreated" the ballads each time she sang them by an oral formulaic method, like that of the "singers of tales" of Yugoslavia described by Albert Lord.[22] In this method, which used a combination of memory and oral composition, the narrative sequence of the verses and some of the ending rhyme words would be remembered; but the exact wording of the lines might vary quite a bit as the singer drew on a more or less conventional stock of phrases and images, improvising as she went along. According to some ballad theorists, that is how ballads in the popular tradition came to be perfected in the first place—by small evolutionary improvements made by each practitioner, then saved by the next singer and added to, with a concomitant dropping away of the awkward phrases that did not work or were not memorable.[23]

In emphasizing that Anna Gordon Brown learned her repertoire as a singer, I am suggesting that she did not consciously alter the ballads that attracted her attention in her youth but that as a singer with an exquisite sensibility she may have unconsciously improved on what she learned as she sang them. In the present era, tied as we are to print, we associate poetry making with an exact sequence of words that has been written down rather than with improvisation on a theme. But oral improvisation was an art form very much alive in Anna Gordon Brown's day. Illiterate as well as literate men and women sang ballads on the streets, at feasts and fairs and in taverns, for a few pence and food and drink.[24] Traveling peddlers—who sold ballads door to door in the form of slips, chapbooks, and broadsides—would often pick them up aurally and sing them as well, and this was a Europe-wide phenomenon. One of the most popular novels of the early nineteenth century, *Corinne, ou, L'Italie* by Madame de Stael, features a heroine famous for her ability to improvise oral poetry who is adored and celebrated by the people of Rome for her spectacular gift.[25]

We cannot, at this distance, disentangle Mrs. Brown's artistry from that of the generations that had sung these ballads before she heard them. All that can be said with certainty is that the ballad was a significant art form in eighteenth-century Scotland, prized by scholars and intellectuals, and that Anna Gordon Brown's extensive and excellent repertoire of them was the first to be recorded from a living person. When Alexander Fraser Tytler wrote to her in 1800 to urge her to try to remember more ballads, he called them "precious morsels of Genius and Feeling which are perhaps preserved in the memory of one or two of the present generation, who like yourself, have taste to cherish them."[26] This suggests that most of "the present generation"—by which Tytler meant people of his (and Mrs. Brown's) own class—no longer had the desire, capacity, or opportunity to learn the old ballads aurally. No one had yet thought to tap the memories of laborers or artisans, as ballad collectors were just beginning to do at the turn of the century. People of fashion at this time seem to have been more eager to imitate the tastes and habits of continental Europe than to learn the old ballads that their older relatives or servants might know. As John Ramsay of Ochtertyre complained in 1807, irritated at what he considered a hypocritical taste for Italian opera and French cooking among the Scottish beau monde: "Few of our modish Ladies can understand, much less relish a Scots song."[27] As for himself, he felt that "our sweet Scots melodies *married* to Allan Ramsay's verse, suit our northern *lugs* better" than Italian art songs "warbled" by Madame Catalini "in a celestial strain."[28]

Anna Gordon learned her ballads when she was too young to care about what was sophisticated or prized by the fashionable people of her country. Moreover, she came from a musical family with a prior interest in Scottish song. Her maternal grandfather, William Forbes, was a musician and composer

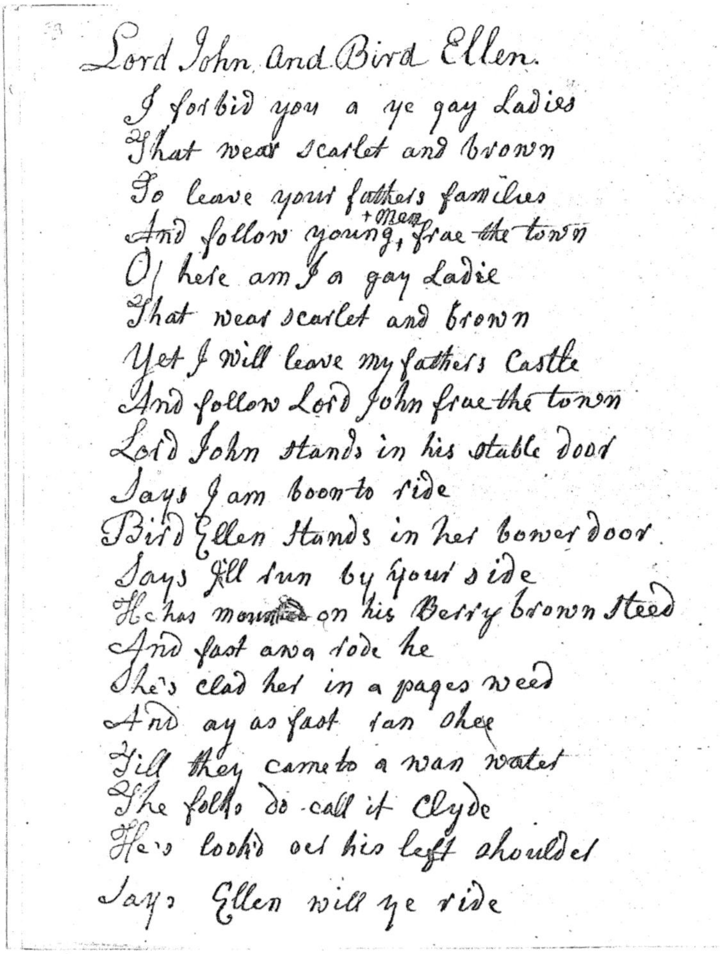

> Lord John, and Bird Ellen.
>
> I forbid you a ye gay Ladies
> That wear scarlet and brown
> To leave your fathers familes
> And follow young, frae the town
> Of here am I a gay Ladie
> That wear scarlet and brown
> Yet I will leave my fathers Castle
> And follow Lord John frae the town
> Lord John stands in his stable door
> Says I am boon to ride
> Bird Ellen stands in her bower door
> Says I'll run by your side
> He has mounted on his Berry brown steed
> And fast away rode he
> She's clad her in a pages weed
> And ay as fast ran shee
> Till they came to a wan water
> The folks do call it Clyde
> He's look'd out his left shoulder
> Says Ellen will ye ride

FIGURE 8.3: Mrs. Brown's 1800 transcription for Alexander Fraser Tytler of "Lord John and Burd Ellen." With permission of the National Library of Scotland. Note the differences compared to the text of this ballad taken from his aunt's singing by Robert Eden Scott in 1783, given in the text.

and a fierce Scots nationalist, who wrote polemical satires against the Act of Union in the early eighteenth century. With the usual Scottish combined interest in folk and classical musical traditions, he set traditional Scottish tunes in classical baroque forms—such as the sonata—and composed Scottish tunes for the fiddle. When he died in 1740, he left behind an enormous collection of musical instruments and music books and manuscripts. It was his daughters, and a maid servant who worked in his household, who sang the ballads that Anna Gordon learned as a girl.

Her own father, Thomas Gordon, joined the Aberdeen Musical Society (begun in 1748 by a handful of gentlemen who liked to play music together) in 1750. His older brother, George Gordon, professor of Oriental languages at King's College, Anna Gordon's uncle, joined the society in 1749. Indeed, the Musical Society had many distinguished members: John Gregory, James Beattie, and Alexander Gerard; with a few exceptions, most of the members of the Aberdeen Philosophical Society were also members of the Aberdeen Musical Society.[29] Two professional musicians were also founding members of the society: Alexander Tait, the organist at St. Paul's Episcopal Chapel, and Francis Peacock, the town's dancing master and an adept on the cello and fiddle. In 1762 Peacock published *Fifty Favourite Scotch Airs for a Violin, German Flute and Violoncello, with a Thorough Bass for the Harpsichord*, a volume that included such classic tunes as "Yellow-Haired Laddie," "The Lass of Patty's Mill," and "The Broom Cowdenknows." Thomas Gordon was on the subscription list for this book, along with most of the rest of the Aberdeen Musical Society, and so we know that this songbook must have been one that Anna Gordon grew up with. Although none of the tunes for "her" repertoire of ballads are among these airs in Peacock's collection—for they are from a different, although related, branch of the vernacular musical tradition—it bespeaks a general interest in music in her family and at least some knowledge of traditional folk song.

Very soon after it was formed, the Aberdeen Musical Society began to offer public concerts that ladies could attend, with tickets available only through members of the society. It was stipulated that these concerts would have three acts, that some piece of Arcangelo Corelli's music would be played in each part, and that each act would end with a Scottish song. These concerts were very popular and became more frequent as the years passed. Again, it is likely that Anna Gordon and her sisters and their mother would have attended these concerts. The content of a typical program can be inferred from the music owned by the society, a mix of Scottish, English, German, and Italian composers that included Arne, J. C. Bach, Barsanti, Corelli, Geminiani (including his settings of Scottish tunes), Handel, Haydn, Oswald, Rameau, and Scarlatti, among others.[30] The shape of the public concerts, with their stipulated Corelli and Scottish songs, the mixture of classical music and Scots vernacular music, "high" and "low," is typical of the range of musical taste in eighteenth-century Scotland.

But, of course, the ballads that Anna Brown preserved for us lie outside both of these traditions, the classical idiom and the vernacular songs of eighteenth-century songbooks. They are neither "high" nor "low." In their diction, narrative complexity, and cultural meaning they do not resemble the brief, light Scottish lyric songs that finished each part of the musical society's concerts and whose airs Peacock collected and published in 1762. Although ballads are also in the folk tradition, they come from a different cultural dimension—heroic in their stature, grand in their narrative reach, ballads can be said to resemble nothing so much as abbreviated epics. Their sophisticated narratives, use of dialogue, formulaic imagery, dramatic ellipses, plot structure, details, historical allusion, patterns of alliteration, and so forth locate the poetry of ballads in a different, more involved, and more haunting world than Allen Ramsay's or even Robert Burns's songs.

Musically, ballad melodies are often modal and pentatonic, intensified by their narrow compass, and have a stark simplicity compared with the more elaborate and decorative lyric melodies of the classic eighteenth-century Scottish songs. Ballad tunes are made to carry complex narratives, and so they are strong and often hypnotic—"lilts" rather than "airs" in Thomas Gordon's telling distinction. When these plaintive melodies are combined with the powerful verse tales that they carry, the effect can be overwhelmingly intense. As the *piobaireachd*, or classical music of the bagpipes, is to the light music of the pipes—marches, strathspeys, and reels—so the narrative ballads, sometime called the "muckle" or big songs, are to the simpler Scots lyrics. In these latter, lighter songs, the beautiful and sometimes ornate melodies are the chief source of their appeal. But in the ballads, the tunes—or lilts—must carry narratives of great weight and force without distracting from these words; they must provide for their texts a frame and a solid foundation.

Despite our later interest in the melodies of ballads, it was Anna Gordon Brown's ballad poetry that earned her a place in the history of literature. The nearly three dozen short epic texts that were recorded from her singing memory and celebrated by the scholars and literati of her day established a paradigm for the ballad that has prevailed ever since. As Thomas Pettitt remarked, "Our inherited notions of what a ballad ought to be are based precisely on . . . the models furnished by Mrs. Brown in particular."[31] Their literary qualities have been cataloged and enumerated by ballad scholars from Gerould to Buchan,[32] beginning with the impersonal, Olympian point of view characteristic of the epic. There is no psychologizing, no individual subjectivity, no interiority developed for any of the characters, and almost no explicit judgment on the part of the narrator. This impassive exposition alternates with the formulaic and often repetitive dialogue of the characters; the frequent use of incremental repetition creates a rhythm of hypnotic crescendos.

What happens passes in front of our eyes like a silent movie, one scene dissolving into the next without comment or summary. This narrative movement from one scene to another in ballads has been felicitously called "leaping and lingering"—for ballad narratives leap over great swathes of time (seven years at a time) and enormous spaces (oceans and continents) in order to linger in the complications of a single scene. These scenes, which constitute the dramatic cruxes of the ballad, generally occur more than halfway through the dramatic action, like the third or fourth act in a play whose opening acts are given in synopsis but for which we are not present. In one ballad, this central scene begins when a woman's sweetheart returns from the sea on her wedding day and tests her fidelity to him; in another, a woman knocks on her lover's door with their baby in her arms on a windy night and is not answered by him—he is sleeping—but by his mother, who does not let her in. The movement in ballads from one scene to another is swift and unexplained, as it happens in dreams; one finds oneself in vivid and powerful scenes without it mattering how one got there.

The diction of ballads is simple and stately, the diction of oral poetry. Other features of oral poetry are the frequent use of incremental repetition, formulaic imagery ("gray steed and the brown," "skin as white as milk"), internal assonance as well as end rhymes, quatrains with a predictable rhyme scheme (such as abcb), and extensive alliteration, mixing the music of language with the music of the melody. There are supernatural portents and signs—rings that change color, talking birds, ghosts, and fairies and an altogether pre-Christian attitude toward magic and the hypernormal. These are the features of Anna Brown's ballads. Whether they are more fully developed linguistic features of the ballads from the northeast of Scotland or elements that Anna Brown especially remembered or elaborated, we will never know, but in our own day, they are known as characteristics of the "classic" ballad.

What follows is a transcription of one of the most beautiful of Anna Gordon Brown's ballads, taken down from her singing or recitation by her nephew, Robert Scott, around 1783.[33] This magnificent ballad cannot be fully apprehended if one simply reads the words on the page. The pace set by the melody, the relentlessness of the tale, the stately way it unfolds, the way the language rhymes and reverberates—these require it to be heard rather than read.[34]

To begin with the title that Anna Brown gives it, "Burd Ellen": John Jamieson, antiquarian and philologist, and the compiler of the first *Etymological Dictionary of the Scottish Language* in 1808, wrote that "burd is still used as an appellation of complacency by superiors to women of lower degree."[35] So the complete title, "Lord John and Burd Ellen," may imply a difference of class between the two main characters.

Burd Ellen

1 I warn ye all ye gay ladies That wear scarlet an brown
   That ye dinna leave your father's house To follow young men frae town.

2 O here am I a lady gay That wears scarlet & brown
   Yet I will leave my fathers house An follow Lord John frae the town[36]

3 Lord John stood in his stable door Said he was bound to ride
   Burd Ellen stood in her bow'r door Said she'd rin by his side.

4 He's pitten on his cork-heal'd shoon[37] An fast awa' rade he
   She's clade hersel in page array An after him ran she

5 Till they came till a wan[38] water An folks do ca it Clyde
   Then he's lookit oer his left shoulder Says Lady can ye wid.[39]

6 O I learn't it *i my father house* [superscript: wi my bowerwomen]
   I learn't it for my weal
   Wheneer I came to a wan water To swim like any eel.

7 But the firstin stap the Lady stappit The water came til her knee
   Ohon alas! said the lady This water's oer deep for me.

8 The nextin stap the lady stappit The water came till her middle
   An sighin' says that gay lady I've wet my gouden girdle

9 The nextin stap the lady stappit The water came till her pap[40]
   An the bairn that was in her two sides For caul[41] began to quake

10 Lye still lye still my ain dear babe Ye work your mither wae
    Your father rides on high horseback Cares little for us twae

11 O about the midst o' Clydes water There was a yeard fast stane[42]
    He lightly turn'd his horse about An took her on him behin

12 O tell me this now good Lord John An' a word ye dinna lee
    How far it is to your Lodgin' whare we this night maun be

13 O see you nae yon castle Ellen That shines sae fair to see
   There is a lady in it Ellen Will sunder you & me

14 There is a lady in that castle Will sunder you and I
   Betide me well betide me wae I sal go there & try

15 O my dogs sal eat the good white bread An ye shall eat the bran
   Then will ye sigh and say alas That ever I was a man

16 O I sal eat the good white bread An your dogs sal eat the bran
   [superscript: Sin food that love is fed upon is neither bread nor bran;]
   And I hope to live an bless the day That ever you was a man

17 O my horse sall eat the good white meal An ye sall eat the corn
   Then will ye curse the heavy hour That ever your love was born.

18 O I sall eat the good white meal An your horse sall eat the corn
   [superscript: I may, I may, Lord John what eer I eat Or meal or corn]
   An I sall bless the happy hour That ever my love was born.

19 O four & twenty gay Ladies Welcom'd Lord John to the ha'
   But a fairer Lady than them a' Led his horse to the stable sta'

20 An four & twenty gay Ladies Welcom'd Lord John to the green
   But a fairer Lady than them a' At the manger stood alane[43]

21 Whan bells were rung & mass was sung An a' man boun to meat
   Burd Ellen at a bye table Amo' the footmen was set

22 O eat & drink my bonny boy The white bread an the beer
   The never a bit can I eat or drink My heart's sae full of fear.

23 O eat an drink my bonny boy The white bread an the wine
   O I canna eat nor drink master My hearts sae full o' pine

24 But out it spake Lord John's mother An a wise woman was she
   Whare met ye wi that bonny boy That looks sae sad on thee?

25 Sometimes his cheek is rosy red An sometimes deadly wan
   He's liker a woman big wi bairn Than a young lords serving man

26 O it makes me laugh my mother dear The words to hear frae thee
 He is a squires ae dearest son That for love has follow'd me. [superscript:
 That I got in the high countree]

27 Rise up rise up my bonny boy Gi my horse corn and hay
 O that I will my master dear As quickly as I may.

28 She's ta'en the hay under her arm The corn intill her han'
 An she's gane to the great stable As fast as e'er she can

29 O room ye roun my bonny brown steeds / O room ye near the wa'[44]
 For the pain that strikes me thro my sides Full soon will gar me fa

30 She's lean'd her back against the wall Strong travail seiz'd her on
 An even amo the great horse feet Burd Ellen brought forth her son

31 Lord John mither intill her bow'r Was sitting all alone
 When in the silence o the night She heard fair Ellens moan

32 Won up won up my son She says Go se how a does fare
 For I think I hear a womans groans An a bairn greeting sair

33 Oh hastily he gat him up Stay'd neither for hose nor shoone
 An he's taen him to the stable door Wi' the clear light o' the moon

34 He struck the door hard wi' his foot An' sae has he wi' his knee
 An iron locks an' iron bars. Into the floor flung he
 Be not afraid Burd Ellen he says Thers nane come in but me

35 Up he has taen his bonny young son An gard wash him wi the milk
 An up has he taen his fair lady Gard row[45] her i the silk

36 Cheer up your heart Burd Ellen he says Look nae mair sad nor wae
 For your marriage & your kirkin[46] too Sal baith be in ae day

This elaborate ballad happens in five scenes of varying length and complexity. The first two verses suggest that we are with one of the principals, a "gay" lady (that is, a spirited and lively lady) who wears both scarlet and brown (that is, expensive clothes dyed with rare scarlet dyes as well as homespun). But the unusual first person is dropped after these verses, and the ballad resumes the more common third-person narrative. Lord John is standing in his stable door, and he announces that he is about to leave, to ride away; Burd Ellen, from her bower door, says she will run by his side. Then he puts on cork-heeled shoes—expensive shoes not meant for walking any distance out of doors—and she puts on page's clothes and runs after him. That is all we know about the principals at the outset: she is determined to go with him, on foot if need be.

The next scene occurs when they come to the Clyde river. Lord John looks over his left shoulder, the negative side, and asks if she can wade across. She says that she can swim. But when she tests the water, she finds it is very deep and very cold, and the child that she is pregnant with begins to quake within her. This is the first we learn of her condition. Then she complains to her unborn child that its father cares little for either of them, but Lord John turns his horse around and takes her up behind him. The situation has gotten denser: a determined pregnant woman of the lower orders is apparently chasing after her lover, who is trying to desert her.

She then asks him where they are going, and he points to a castle shining in the distance and tells her that there is a lady in that castle who will keep them asunder. One does not know if the dangerous and mysterious lady is a prior wife, a witch, or a relative. There follows a sequence of rapid exchanges between Lord John and Burd Ellen that are like the stichomythia of archaic drama. Lord John threatens her that better food will be fed to his horses and dogs when they reach the castle—white bread—while she will be fed only bran. Her reply is feisty and combative: "O I sal eat the good white bread An your dogs sal eat the bran." Lord John repeats his threat of bad treatment: "O my horse shall eat the good white meal An ye shall eat the corn," and she makes another cocky comeback. Her replies establish her pluck and hopefulness.

The third and most elaborate sequence begins when they arrive at the castle. Four and twenty gay ladies welcome Lord John, while Burd Ellen, although more beautiful than any of them, takes his horse to the stable in the guise of his page. After the bells are rung and the mass is sung—a refrain line common to ballads from this part of Scotland—everyone goes in to eat and Burd Ellen is seated with the footmen. There, Lord John urges her to eat white bread and to drink beer or wine, in direct antithesis to his earlier threat of bad food, but she tells him her heart is too full of fear and pain to be able to eat anything. Lord John's wise mother speaks up and asks where he found his page, whose color keeps changing and who looks so sad; "he's liker a woman big wi bairn," she says, than a young lord's page boy. Lord John protests that he is the precious only son of a squire who follows him out of love. Then he commands Burd Ellen to feed his horse, and she obeys him with alacrity.

The fourth scene is in the stable, where Ellen enjoins the horses to move over and make room for her against the wall, for she is in great pain. And there she delivers her child, among the great horses' feet, as the ballad describes it, leaving the listener with the image of a tender newborn baby lying dangerously close to the huge hooves of horses in a stall.

Lord John's mother hears Ellen's groans in childbirth and the baby's cry and sends her son to investigate what is happening in the stable. Her instruction to him implies her knowledge and approval of the situation, contradicting Lord John's earlier warning that the lady of the castle would "sunder" them. He races down to the stable, without stopping to put on his shoes and socks, and kicks open the door, calling out to Burd Ellen not to be afraid. Then he takes his son and washes him in milk and takes his fair lady and enfolds her in silk— formulaic phrases implying loving, lapping luxury—and assures her that he will marry her on the next day that she goes into church, probably the same day that they christen the child.

Like many of Anna Brown's ballads, this one ends triumphantly with a woman getting what she wants despite serious obstacles. A great deal is left to the imagination: how these two met and became lovers in the first place, what led to Lord John's leaving her, why Burd Ellen is so stubborn in sticking with him—whether the hope of a highborn marriage or her love for him— none of that is spelled out. We have no idea what any of the principals feels until the final scene in which Lord John kicks open the stable door and takes up his newborn son to wash him in milk. Similarly, we do not know why he assumes that his mother will object to the match or why he threatens that Burd Ellen will be mistreated in the castle. The listener can conjecture many different motivations, evolving from many different scenarios, but all of it is simply conjecture. We fill in these details as we hear the ballad, based on our own hopes and fears and expectations, and the blankness of the ballad can accommodate many different fantasies. This is one of the reasons these tales have lasted so long; their flexibility enables many differently satisfying projections. As discussions following ballads always demonstrate, people imagine the scenes differently, conjuring up images in different places in the song and making different assumptions about the histories of the characters and their reasons for behaving as they do. There is a great deal of room for varying interpretations.

In a different genre, the novel, for example, the thoughts and feelings of the three main characters would be spelled out, as well as the scenery and weather, in a fully contextualized, realistic account. But the ballad form gives only the barest outline of a story of attempted betrayal and the triumph of fidelity. It might be constructed by the listener as the story of a brave woman who did not give up and who, in the end, got what she wanted. Some have heard this ballad as the story of a cruelly exploitative and cowardly man; still others are struck by the story of the wise old mother who wants her line perpetuated and who therefore accepts a daughter-in-law of lower degree once she has proven fertile. And these are only some of the possibilities. This open-endedness, this capacity of the ballad narratives to be adapted to many different story lines, has led to their not infrequent use over the centuries as plots for plays, prose fiction, and, in our own day, graphic novels.

Ballads, of course, were still being sung in the fields and on the streets of England and Scotland when the novel was in its infancy. They are one of the oldest literary forms, probably dating from the Middle Ages, a recent relative of the oral epic, and they provided stories for the imagination to dwell on long before more modern forms of literary fiction. The ballad has been defined as a folktale set to music—and if a tale is a short story with the mental proportions of an epic, then ballads are tales.

Ballads are everywhere in the cultural landscape of eighteenth-century Britain once we start looking for them. One sees visual depictions of ballad singers and ballad sellers in the works of William Hogarth and other print-makers. Ballads are sung on the pages of fiction by Tobias Smollet, Oliver Goldsmith, Mrs. Griffith, Laurence Sterne, Jane Austen, Walter Scott, and Elizabeth Gaskell. They are the reading matter of Cathy and Hareton in Emily Brontë's *Wuthering Heights*. Ballad singers appear in works by Eliza Hay-wood, Frances Burney, and, of course, Thomas Hardy. They are referred to casually in the seventeenth-century letters of Dorothy Osborne and the eigh-teenth-century letters of Lady Mary Wortley Montagu, Mrs. Delany, Eliza-beth Montagu, and Amelia Opie. The seeds of much of Walter Scott's fiction and narrative verse can be found in the ballads he collected for a delighted readership in 1802–3. Plays like Nicholas Rowe's *Jane Shore* (1714) and John Home's *Douglas* (1756) are based on ballads. Many eighteenth-century writ-ers wrote ballads—among them, Swift, Prior, Smollett, Wordsworth, and Southey. Similarly, it was a form to which a number of aristocratic and middle-class Scotswomen turned their hands: Lady Grisell Baillie, Alison Rutherford Cockburn, Susanna Blamire, Lady Anne Barnard, and, most famous of all, Caroline, Baroness Nairne.[47]

FIGURE 8.4: William Hogarth, *The Enraged Musician* (1741). A ballad singer is standing under a musician's window and singing from a broadside of "The Ladies' Fall." Tate Gallery, London; Art Resource, New York.

Elsewhere I have written about the gendering of songs and ballads in eighteenth-century Scotland and how the association of women with the preservation and transmission of traditional ballads intensified the nationalistic meaning of this art form.[48] Anna Gordon, or Mrs. Brown of Falkland as she has been called after Child's usage, is perhaps the most important exemplar of this association. Although our print-conscious age hardly regards the ballad with literary interest any longer, it was of intense interest in the eighteenth century as a record of the earliest known vernacular poetry. In Scotland in particular, for all the reasons of national specificity and cultural interest that I have indicated, ballads were of interest to scholars and antiquaries and ordinary people alike. That the ballad tradition was a women's tradition—in the sense that it was carried in a female line, remembered by women and taught by women to other women and girls—has not been sufficiently emphasized. This

FIGURE 8.5: *A Ballad Singer* (ca. 1750). An image
of decent poverty. Photo credit: Rischgitz. Getty
Images, Hulton Archive.

ancient poetic form, at least as it was preserved in living tradition in Scotland
until the eighteenth century, appears to have been maintained by the musical
and poetic talents of women from all ranks of life.[49] Then as now, cultural
historians told one another the story of Anna Gordon Brown, who became the
conduit for our common literary and musical heritage—our "best" ballads in
English—in the golden age of balladry.

NOTES

Introduction

Many thanks to my editorial assistant Melissa Byl for her dedicated and careful work in the preparation of this volume in its early stages.

1. Peter Gay, *The Enlightenment: An Interpretation*, vol. 1, *The Rise of Modern Paganism* (New York: Knopf, 1966), p. 3.

2. Ibid., p. 10. *Philosophe*, the French word for philosopher, is the term used to refer to French Enlightenment thinkers.

3. See, for example, Jonathan Israel, *Radical Enlightenment: Philosophy and the Making of Modernity 1650–1750* (Oxford and New York: Oxford University Press, 2001); Margaret Jacob, *Living the Enlightenment: Freemasonry and Politics in Eighteenth-Century Europe* (New York: Oxford University Press, 1991); Carla Hesse, *The Other Enlightenment: How French Women Became Modern* (Princeton, NJ: Princeton University Press, 2001); Sankar Muthu, *Enlightenment against Empire* (Princeton, NJ: Princeton University Press, 2003); Roy Porter, *The Creation of the Modern World: The Untold Story of the British Enlightenment* (New York: W. W. Norton, 2000); and Emma Rothschild, *Economic Sentiments: Adam Smith, Condorcet, and the Enlightenment* (Cambridge, MA: Harvard University Press, 2001).

4. Linda Colley, *Britons: Forging the Nation, 1707–1837* (New Haven: Yale University Press, 1992), pp. 240–41.

5. On British consumer protests, see Charlotte Sussman, *Consuming Anxieties: Consumer Protest, Gender and British Slavery, 1713–1833* (Stanford: Stanford University Press, 2000). On Parisian market women, see Hesse, *Other Enlightenment*, pp. 3–30.

6. For the origin of the term "Black Atlantic" to refer to the intellectual culture of the African diaspora, see Paul Gilroy, *The Black Atlantic: Modernity and Double Consciousness* (Cambridge, MA: Harvard University Press, 1993).

7. Mary Astell, *Reflections Upon Marriage, The third edition. To which is added a preface, in answer to some objections* (London, 1706; originally published in 1700 as *Some Reflections Upon Marriage* and better known by that title).

8. John Locke, *Two Treatises of Government*, ed. Peter Laslett (London: Cambridge University Press, 1960), bk. 1, chap. 5, sec. 48, p. 192. According to William Blackstone, the status of married women under the law in eighteenth-century England was that of the *feme-covert*: "By marriage, the husband and wife are one person in law: that is, the very being or legal existence of the woman is suspended during the marriage, or at least is incorporated and consolidated into that of the husband: under whose wing, protection, and cover, she performs every thing; and is therefore called in our law-french a feme-covert." *Commentaries on the Laws of England* (Oxford: Clarendon, 1765–69), bk. 1, chap. 15, sec. 3, p. 430, the Avalon Project: Documents in Law, History and Diplomacy, Yale University, available at: http://avalon.law.yale.edu/18th_century/blackstone_bk1ch15.asp (accessed July 25, 2010).

9. Astell, *Reflections*, preface.

10. Ibid.

11. Olympe de Gouges, *The Declaration of the Rights of Woman*, in *Women in Revolutionary Paris, 1789–1795: Selected Documents*, trans. Darline Gay Levy, Harriet Branson Applewhite, and Mary Durham Johnson (Urbana: University of Illinois Press, 1979), p. 89.

12. Ibid., p. 93.

13. For further discussion of de Gouges, see Joan Wallach Scott, *Only Paradoxes to Offer: French Feminists and the Rights of Man* (Cambridge, MA: Harvard University Press, 1996), pp. 19–56; and pp. 18–19 this volume.

14. Quoted in Janet Todd, *Mary Wollstonecraft: A Revolutionary Life* (New York: Columbia University Press, 2000), p. 179.

15. Mary Wollstonecraft, *A Vindication of the Rights of Woman*, ed. Deidre S. Lynch (New York and London: W. W. Norton, 2009), p. 7.

16. Ibid., pp. 10, 12, 25, 24, 40–41.

17. Among other notable advocates of women's education during the Enlightenment were Catherine Graham Macaulay in England and Judith Murray Sargent in North America. Several prominent men during the Enlightenment, including the Marquis de Condorcet in France and Theodor Gottlieb von Hippel in Germany, also defended women's right to public education.

18. See, for example, Londa Schiebinger, "Skeletons in the Closet: The First Illustrations of the Female Skeleton in Eighteenth-Century Anatomy," *Representations* 14 (1986): 42–82; and Londa Schiebinger, *The Mind Has No Sex? Women in the Origins of Modern Science* (Cambridge, MA: Harvard University Press, 1989), esp. pp. 189–213.

19. Jean-Jacques Rousseau, *Émile; or, On Education*, trans. Allan Bloom (New York: Basic Books, 1979), pp. 361, 358, 365.

20. Ibid., p. 362.

21. See Madelyn Gutwirth, *The Twilight of the Goddesses: Women and Representation in the French Revolutionary Era* (New Brunswick, NJ: Rutgers University

Press, 1992), esp. pp. 58–66; and Ruth Perry, "Colonizing the Breast: Sexuality and Maternity in Eighteenth-Century England," *Journal of the History of Sexuality* 2 (2) (1991): 204–34.

22. Rousseau, *Émile*, p. 46.

23. Among them, Henry and Sarah Fielding, Frances Sheridan, Frances Brooke, and, by some accounts, a reformed Eliza Haywood. See Janet Todd, *The Sign of Angelica: Women, Writing and Fiction, 1660–1800* (New York: Columbia University Press, 1989).

24. Quoted in Perry, "Colonizing," pp. 229–30.

25. Quoted in ibid., p. 228.

26. Madelyn Gutwirth astutely observes that "the powerful male nursling in her left arm nearly strangles her with his embrace," in "Suzanne Necker's Legacy: Breastfeeding as Metonym in Germaine de Staël's *Delphine*," *Eighteenth-Century Life* 28 (2) (2004): 17–40, at p. 25.

27. Mary D. Sheriff, *Moved by Love: Inspired Artists and Deviant Women in Eighteenth-Century France* (Chicago: University of Chicago Press, 2004), p. 219. According to Sheriff, Diderot attributed the husband's satisfaction in Greuze's painting to "his vanity at having produced this pretty swarm of brats" (quoted on p. 219).

28. Perry, "Colonizing," p. 206.

29. Ibid., p. 231.

30. Ibid.

31. On domestic ideology as a strategy of class consolidation, see Nancy Armstrong, *Desire and Domestic Fiction: A Political History of the Novel* (New York: Oxford University Press, 1987).

32. Susan C. Greenfield, "Introduction," in *Inventing Maternity: Politics, Science, and Literature, 1650–1865*, ed. Susan C. Greenfield and Carol Barash (Lexington: University Press of Kentucky, 1999), p. 18.

33. Toni Bowers, "'A Point of Conscience': Breastfeeding and Maternal Authority in *Pamela*, Part 2," in Greenfield and Barash, *Inventing Maternity*, pp. 138–58, at p. 142.

34. Immanuel Kant, "An Answer to the Question: What Is Enlightenment?" trans. James Schmidt, in *What Is Enlightenment? Eighteenth-Century Answers and Twentieth-Century Questions*, ed. James Schmidt (Berkeley: University of California Press, 1996), p. 58; and Immanuel Kant, *Observations on the Feeling of the Beautiful and Sublime*, trans. John T. Goldthwait (Berkeley: University of California Press, 1960), p. 79.

35. Rousseau, *Émile*, p. 409.

36. Mary Astell, *A Serious Proposal to the Ladies*, parts 1 and 2, ed. Patricia Springborg (London: Pickering and Chatto, 1997), p. 22.

37. Astell, *Reflections*, preface.

38. Robert Halsband, ed., *The Complete Letters of Lady Mary Wortley Montagu*, 3 vols. (Oxford: Clarendon Press, 1965–67), vol. 1, p. 45.

39. Ibid., vol. 3, p. 22.

40. Kant, *Observations*, p. 78. For further discussion of Kant on women, see Robin May Schott, "The Gender of Enlightenment," in *Feminist Interpretations of*

Immanuel Kant, ed. Robin May Schott (University Park: Pennsylvania State University Press, 1997), pp. 319–37.

41. Kant, "Answer," p. 58.

42. Philip Dormer Stanhope, *The Letters of Philip Dormer Stanhope, Earl of Chesterfield, with the Characters*, ed. John Bradshaw (1774; New York: Scribner, 1892), p. 141, available at: http://www.archive.org/stream/cu31924103071613/cu31924103071613_djvu.txt (accessed June 18, 2010).

43. Michele Le Doeuff, *The Sex of Knowing*, trans. Kathryn Hamer and Lorraine Code (New York and London: Routledge, 2003), pp. 26–27.

44. Dorinda Outram, *The Enlightenment*, 2nd ed. (Cambridge: Cambridge University Press, 2005), p. 80.

45. Article 110 of *The Fundamental Constitutions of Carolina: March 1, 1669*, the Avalon Project: Documents in Law, History and Diplomacy, Yale University, available at: http://avalon.law.yale.edu/17th_century/nc05.asp (accessed June 18, 2010).

46. C.B. Macpherson, *The Political Theory of Possessive Individualism: Hobbes to Locke* (Oxford: Clarendon, 1962).

47. See Susan Buck-Morss, "Hegel and Haiti," *Critical Inquiry* 26 (4) (2000): 821–65; and David Brion Davis, *The Problem of Slavery in Western Culture* (New York: Cornell University Press, 1966).

48. Locke, *Two Treatises*, p. 159. Videos of contemporary performances of "Rule, Britannia!" are available online at http://www.youtube.com/watch?v=yDE3yavXs-A (accessed January 20, 2010).

49. Jean-Jacques Rousseau, *The Social Contract*, trans. G.D.H. Cole (London and Toronto: J.M. Dent and Sons; New York: E.P. Dutton and Co., 1913), p. 5.

50. For recent historical work on the exploitation of the productive and reproductive labor of women of African descent in colonial slavery, see Jennifer L. Morgan, *Laboring Women: Reproduction and Gender in New World Slavery* (Philadelphia: University of Pennsylvania Press, 2004).

51. Felicity A. Nussbaum, *Torrid Zones: Maternity, Sexuality, and Empire in Eighteenth-Century English Narratives* (Baltimore: Johns Hopkins University Press, 1995); and Kord, chapter 6, this volume.

52. See on this matter Denise Riley, *"Am I That Name?" Feminism and the Category of "Women" in History* (Minneapolis: University of Minnesota Press, 1988).

53. Although England outlawed slave trading in 1807, colonial slavery itself was not abolished throughout the British Empire until 1833.

54. Edward Said, *Culture and Imperialism* (New York: Knopf, 1993), p. 93; and Susan Fraiman, "Jane Austen and Edward Said: Gender, Culture, and Imperialism," *Critical Inquiry* 21 (4) (1995): 805–21, at p. 810.

55. Fraiman, "Jane Austen," p. 821.

56. See, for example, Ruth Perry, "Austen and Empire: A Thinking Woman's Guide to British Imperialism," *Persuasions* 16 (1994): 95–106; and Ellen Pollak, *Incest and the English Novel, 1684–1814* (Baltimore: Johns Hopkins University Press, 2003), pp. 162–99.

57. See most notably Margaret W. Ferguson, "Juggling the Categories of Race, Class, and Gender: Aphra Behn's *Oroonoko*," in *Women, "Race," and Writing in the Early Modern Period*, ed. Margo Hendricks and Patricia Parker (New York: Routledge, 1994), pp. 209–24; and Susan B. Iwanisziw, ed., *Troping Oroonoko from Behn to Bandele* (Burlington, VT: Ashgate, 2004).

58. de Gouges, *Declaration*, p. 96.

59. Ibid., p. 93.

60. Christopher L. Miller, *The French Atlantic Triangle: Literature and Culture of the Slave Trade* (Durham, NC: Duke University Press, 2008), p. 116.

61. Whitefield had been the chaplain of the English aristocrat and religious leader Selina Hastings, countess of Huntingdon, to whom Wheatley's elegy was addressed and who would later become a sponsor of Wheatley's work.

62. Julian D. Mason Jr., ed., *The Poems of Phillis Wheatley*, rev. ed. (Chapel Hill: University of North Carolina Press, 1989), p. 48.

63. Henry Louis Gates Jr., *The Trials of Phillis Wheatley: America's First Black Poet and Her Encounters with the Founding Fathers* (New York: Basic Books, 2003), p. 5.

64. Ibid.

65. Ibid., p. 7.

66. Mason, *Poems of Wheatley*, p. 83.

67. Ibid., p. 53.

68. See, for example, Albertha Sistrunk, "The Influence of Alexander Pope on the Writing Style of Phillis Wheatley," in *Critical Essays on Phillis Wheatley*, ed. William H. Robinson (Boston: G.K. Hall, 1982), pp. 175–88.

69. W.E.B. Du Bois, *The Souls of Black Folk*, ed. Farah Jasmine Griffin (1903; New York: Barnes & Noble Classics, 2003), p. 9.

70. Astell, *Reflections*, preface.

71. Scott, *Only Paradoxes*, p. 15.

72. Elizabeth Janeway, *Man's World, Woman's Place: A Study in Social Mythology* (New York: William Morrow, 1971), p. 52.

73. The classic work on the early English novel is Ian Watt's *The Rise of the Novel: Studies in Defoe, Richardson and Fielding* (Berkeley: University of California Press, 1957). For more recent studies detailing women's prominence in the novel's early development in England, see Rosalind Ballaster, *Seductive Forms: Women's Amatory Fiction from 1684 to 1740* (Oxford: Clarendon, 1992); Cheryl Turner, *Living by the Pen: Women Writers in the Eighteenth Century* (London: Routledge, 1992); Catherine Gallagher, *Nobody's Story: The Vanishing Acts of Women Writers in the Marketplace, 1670–1820* (Berkeley: University of California Press, 1994); Paula McDowell, *The Women of Grub Street: Press, Politics, and Gender in the London Literary Marketplace, 1678–1730* (Oxford and New York: Clarendon, 1998); and William B. Warner, *Licensing Entertainment: The Elevation of Novel Reading in Britain, 1684–1750* (Berkeley: University of California Press, 1998). For corresponding studies in the French context, see Joan DeJean, *Tender Geographies: Women and the Origins of the Novel in France* (New York: Columbia University Press, 1991); and Joan Hinde Stewart, *Gynographs: French Novels by Women of*

the Late Eighteenth Century (Lincoln: University of Nebraska Press, 1993). For recent reflections on the challenges still facing scholars of Enlightenment women writers in French studies, see also Joan DeJean, "And What about French Women Writers?" Eighteenth Century: Theory and Interpretation 50 (1) (2010): 21–24.

74. Judith Kegan Gardiner, "The First English Novel: Aphra Behn's Love Letters, the Canon, and Women's Tastes," Tulsa Studies in Women's Literature 8 (2) (1989): 201–22.

75. Virginia Woolf, A Room of One's Own, ed. Susan Gubar and Mark Hussey (1929; Orlando, FL: Harcourt, 2005), p. 65.

76. Ibid., p. 64.

77. Colley, Britons, p. 250.

78. Scott, Only Paradoxes, p. 18.

Chapter 1

1. Olaudah Equiano, The Interesting Narrative of the Life of Olaudah Equiano, ed. Vincent Caretta, rev. ed. (London: Penguin, 2003), p. 42.

2. Mary Wollstonecraft, A Vindication of the Rights of Woman, ed. Deidre S. Lynch (New York and London: W. W. Norton, 2009), p. 34.

3. Vincent Caretta, Equiano, the African: Biography of a Self-Made Man (Athens: University of Georgia Press, 2005).

4. Thomas Tryon, A Treatise of cleanness in meats and drinks of the preparation of food, the excellency of good airs and the benefits of clean sweet beds; also of the generation of bugs and their cure (London: Printed for the Author and sold by L. Curtis, 1682); Thomas Tryon, The Good Housewife made a doctor, or Health's choice and sure found friend (London: Printed and sold by Andrew Sowle, in the Holloway-Lane, near Shoreditch, 1685); and John Floyer, An enquiry into the right use and abuses of the Hot, Cold, and Temperate baths in England (London: Printed for R. Clavel, 1697).

5. William Strachey, The Historie of Travell into Virginia Britania (1612), ed. Louis B. Wright and Virginia Freund (London: Printed for the Hakluyt Society, 1953).

6. Adrian Wilson, The Making of Man-Midwifery: Childbirth in England, 1660–1770 (Cambridge, MA: Harvard University Press, 1995); and Thomas Laqueur, Making Sex: Body and Gender from the Greeks to Freud (Cambridge, MA: Harvard University Press, 1990).

7. Mary E. Fissell, Vernacular Bodies: The Politics of Reproduction in Early Modern England (Oxford: Oxford University Press, 2004); and Laqueur, Making Sex.

8. Fissell, Vernacular Bodies, p. 191.

9. Ibid., pp. 230–31; and Lisa Forman Cody, Birthing the Nation: Sex, Science, and the Conception of Eighteenth-Century Britons (Oxford: Oxford University Press, 2005).

10. Barbara Taylor, "Feminists versus Gallants: Manners and Morals in Enlightenment Britain," in Women, Gender, and Enlightenment, ed. Sarah Knott and Barbara Taylor (New York: Palgrave, 2005), pp. 30–52; Sylvia Sebastiani, " 'Race,' Women, and Progress in the Scottish Enlightenment," in Knott and Taylor, Women, Gender,

and Enlightenment, pp. 75–96; Anna Bryson, *From Courtesy to Civility: Changing Codes of Conduct in Early Modern England* (Oxford: Oxford University Press, 1998); Inga Clendinnen, "Fierce and Unnatural Cruelty: Cortes and the Conquest of Mexico," *Representations* 33 (Winter 1991): 65–100; Juliana Barr, *Peace Came in the Form of a Woman: Indians and Spaniards in the Texas Borderlands* (Chapel Hill: University of North Carolina Press, 2007); and Ann M. Little, *Abraham in Arms: War and Gender in Colonial New England* (Philadelphia: University of Pennsylvania Press, 2007).

11. Susan D. Amussen, *Caribbean Exchanges: Slavery and the Transformation of English Society, 1640–1700* (Chapel Hill: University of North Carolina Press, 2007); and Kathleen M. Brown, *Good Wives, Nasty Wenches, and Anxious Patriarchs: Gender, Race, and Power in Colonial Virginia* (Chapel Hill: University of North Carolina, 1996), 88.

12. Amussen, *Caribbean Exchanges*, pp. 134–35; Jennifer L. Morgan, *Laboring Women: Reproduction and Gender in New World Slavery* (Philadelphia: University of Pennsylvania Press, 2004); Brown, *Good Wives*, pp. 132–33.

13. Brown, *Good Wives*, pp. 197–201.

14. Peter C. Hoffer and N.E.H. Hull, *Murdering Mothers: Infanticide in England and New England, 1558–1803* (New York: New York University Press, 1984), pp. 20, 33–40; and Cornelia Hughes Dayton, *Women before the Bar: Gender, Law, and Society in Connecticut, 1639–1789* (Chapel Hill: University of North Carolina Press, 1995), pp. 207–15.

15. Patricia Seed, *To Love, Honor, and Obey in Colonial Mexico: Conflicts over Marriage Choice, 1574–1821* (Stanford: Stanford University Press, 1988); Barr, *Peace Came*; María Elena Martinez, *Geneaological Fictions: Limpieza de Sangre, Religion, and Gender in Colonial Mexico* (Stanford: Stanford University Press, 2008); and Verena Martinez-Alier, *Marriage, Class, and Colour in Nineteenth-Century Cuba: A Study of Racial Attitudes and Sexual Values in a Slave Society* (London: Cambridge University Press, 1974).

16. Carole Shammas, *A History of Household Government in America* (Charlottesville: University of Virginia Press, 2002).

17. Rebecca Hartkopf Schloss, *Sweet Liberty: The Final Days of Slavery in Martinique* (Philadelphia: University of Pennsylvania Press, 2009); Susan Juster, *Disorderly Women: Sexual Politics and Evangelicalism in Revolutionary New England* (Ithaca, NY: Cornell University Press, 1994); Janet Moore Lindman, *Bodies of Belief: Baptist Community in Early America* (Philadelphia: University of Pennsylvania Press, 2008); and Anna M. Lawrence, *One Family under God: Love, Belonging, and Authority in Early Transatlantic Methodism* (Philadelphia: University of Pennsylvania Press, 2011).

18. Nicole Eustace, *Passion Is the Gale: Emotion, Power, and the Coming of the American Revolution* (Chapel Hill: University of North Carolina Press, 2008); Lawrence, *One Family under God*; Juster, *Disorderly Women*; Phyllis Mack, *Visionary Women: Ecstatic Prophecy in Seventeenth Century England* (Berkeley: University of California Press, 1992); Ruth H. Bloch, "Changing Conceptions of Sexuality and Romance in Eighteenth-Century America," *William and Mary Quarterly*

60 (1) (2003): 13–42; and Jan Lewis, "The Republican Wife: Virtue and Seduction in the Early Republic," *William and Mary Quarterly* 44 (4) (1987): 689–721.

19. Mary Wollstonecraft, review of Equiano, *Analytical Review*, May 1789; and Wollstonecraft, *Vindication*, chap. 4.

20. Morgan, *Laboring Women*; Barbara Bush, *Slave Women in Caribbean Society, 1650–1838* (Bloomington: Indiana University Press, 1990); Trevor G. Burnard, *Mastery, Tyranny, and Desire: Thomas Thistlewood and His Slaves in the Anglo-Jamaican World* (Chapel Hill: University of North Carolina Press, 2004); and Christopher Leslie Brown, *Moral Capital: Foundations of British Abolitionism* (Chapel Hill: University of North Carolina Press, 2006).

21. "America Past and Present Online," http://wps.ablongman.com/wps/media/objects/28/29569/primarysources1_5_1.html.

22. Kathleen M. Brown, *Foul Bodies: Cleanliness in Early America* (New Haven: Yale University Press, 2009), pp. 224–30.

23. Quoted in Mary Catherine Moran, "Between the Savage and the Civil: Dr. John Gregory's Natural History of Femininity," in Knott and Taylor, *Women, Gender, and Enlightenment*, pp. 8–29; the Gregory quote is on p. 15.

24. Susan E. Klepp, *Revolutionary Conceptions: Women, Fertility, and Family Limitation in America, 1760–1820* (Chapel Hill: University of North Carolina Press, 2009).

25. Felicity A. Nussbaum, *Torrid Zones: Maternity, Sexuality, and Empire in Eighteenth-Century English Narratives* (Baltimore: Johns Hopkins University Press, 1995); Brown, *Good Wives*; Amussen, *Caribbean Exchanges*; and Brown, *Foul Bodies*.

Chapter 2

1. James Hillman, *The Myth of Analysis* (Evanston, IL: Northwestern University Press, 1972), p. 220.

2. By the "long eighteenth century," I mean the years from about 1660 to 1815 or 1820 that scholars tend to see as a holistic period. As we know, historical events, let alone trends and tendencies, do not map neatly onto round-number periods. On gender and the "modern self," see Dror Wahrman, *The Making of the Modern Self: Identity and Culture in Eighteenth-Century England* (New Haven: Yale University Press, 2004).

3. Thomas Laqueur, *Making Sex: Body and Gender from the Greeks to Freud* (Cambridge, MA: Harvard University Press, 1990), p. 149.

4. Michel Foucault, *The History of Sexuality*, trans. Robert Hurley (New York: Random House, 1980), vol. 1, pp. 23, 26.

5. Henry Abelove, "Some Speculations on the History of Sexual Intercourse during the Long Eighteenth Century in England," *Genders* 6 (1989): 125–30.

6. Denis Diderot, "Suite de l'entretien," in *Oeuvres philosophiques* (Paris: Garnier frères, 1964), p. 379 (my translation).

7. David Hume, *An Enquiry Concerning the Principles of Morals* (London: A. Miller, 1751), p. 174.

8. Peter Gay, *The Enlightenment: An Interpretation*, vol. 2, *The Science of Freedom* (New York and London: Norton, 1977), p. 201.

9. See Carole Pateman, *The Sexual Contract* (Stanford: Stanford University Press, 1988).

10. Laqueur, *Making Sex*, p. 156.

11. Jane Sharp, *The Midwives Book. Or the whole Art of Midwifry Discovered* (London: Simon Miller, 1671), p. 40.

12. Ibid.

13. *Aristotle's Master-Piece; or, The Secrets of Generation Display'd in all the Parts thereof* (London: J. How, 1690), pp. 99, 104.

14. Thomas Aquinas, *Summa Theologica*, trans. Fathers of the English Dominican Province (London: Burns, Oates, and Washbourne, 1920), vol. 4, p. 274.

15. *Aristotle's Master-Piece*, p. 15.

16. William Shakespeare, *Hamlet*, act 1, scene 2.

17. Moderata Fonte, *The Worth of Women: Wherein Is Clearly Revealed Their Nobility and Their Superiority to Men*, ed. and trans. Virginia Cox (Chicago: University of Chicago Press, 1997), p. 262.

18. Geneviève Fraisse, *Les Femmes et leur histoire* (Paris: Gallimard, 1998), p. 11 (my translation).

19. François Poulain de la Barre, *The Woman As Good as the Man; or, The Equallity of Both Sexes. Written Originally in French, And Translated into English by A.L* (1673; London: N. Brooks, 1677), pp. 87, 84.

20. Laqueur, *Making Sex*, p. 157.

21. Dorothy L. Sayers, *Are Women Human?* (Grand Rapids, MI: Eerdmans, 1971), p. 53.

22. Hillman, *Myth of Analysis*, p. 221.

23. *The Sappho-an. An Heroic Poem, of Three Cantos* (London: Cha. Brasier, 1749), p. 47.

24. Jean-Jacques Rousseau, *Émile; or, On Education*, trans. Allan Bloom (New York: Basic Books, 1979), p. 358.

25. Ibid.

26. Ibid., p. 329.

27. Ibid., p. 324.

28. Catherine Macaulay, "On the Idea of a Sexual Difference in the Human Character," *The Aberdeen Magazine, Literary Chronicle, and Review*, 3 vols. (Aberdeen: J. Chalmers, 1788–90), vol. 3, p. 583.

29. Johann Fichte, *The Science of Rights*, trans. A. E. Kröger (Philadelphia: Lippincott, 1869), p. 440.

30. Simon Richter, *Missing the Breast: Gender, Fantasy, and the Body in the German Enlightenment* (Seattle: University of Washington Press, 2006), p. 15. See also Ruth Perry, "Colonizing the Breast: Sexuality and Maternity in Eighteenth-Century England," *Journal of the History of Sexuality* 2 (2) (1991): 204–34.

31. Madelyn Gutwirth, *The Twilight of the Goddesses: Women and Representation in the French Revolutionary Era* (New Brunswick, NJ: Rutgers University Press, 1992).

32. George D. Sussman, "Parisian Infants and Norman Wet Nurses in the Early Nineteenth Century: A Statistical Study," *Journal of Interdisciplinary History* 7 (4) (1977): 637–53.

33. E. A. Wrigley, *People, Cities, and Wealth: The Transformation of Traditional Society* (Oxford and New York: Blackwell, 1987), p. 260.

34. On the effects of pronatalism in England, particularly on representations of never-married women, see Susan S. Lanser, "Singular Politics: The Rise of the British Nation and the Production of the 'Old Maid,'" in *Singlewomen in the European Past 1250–1800*, ed. Judith M. Bennett and Amy M. Froide (Philadelphia: University of Pennsylvania Press, 1999), pp. 297–323.

35. Abelove, "Some Speculations," pp. 128, 136.

36. Amanda Vickery, *The Gentleman's Daughter: Women's Lives in Georgian England* (New Haven: Yale University Press, 1998), p. 11.

37. Foucault, *History of Sexuality*, p. 123.

38. William Shakespeare, *Romeo and Juliet*, act 3, scene 1.

39. *Hic Mulier; or, The man-woman: being a medicine to cure the coltish disease of the staggers in the masculine-feminines of our times. Exprest in a briefe declamation* (London: Printed for I. Trundle, 1620), n.p.

40. See, for example, Dianne Dugaw, *Warrior Women and Popular Balladry, 1650–1850* (Chicago: University of Chicago Press, 1989); and Kathryn Schwarz, *Tough Love: Amazon Encounters in the English Renaissance* (Durham, NC: Duke University Press, 2000).

41. See, for example, Urbain Chevrau, *A Relation Of the Life of Christina Queen of Sweden: with Her Resignation of the Crown, Voyage to Bruxels, and Journey to Rome* (London: Henry Fletcher, 1656).

42. Sylvie Steinberg, *La Confusion des sexes: le travestissesment de la Renaissance à la Révolution* (Paris: Fayard, 2001), pp. ix, 40.

43. Antonio de Torquemada, *Jardin de flores curiosas, enque se tratan alginas materias de humanidad, philosophia, theologia y geographia* (Salamanca: Juan Baptista de Teranova, 1570).

44. Patricia Crawford and Sara Mendelson, "Sexual Identities in Early Modern England: The Marriage of Two Women in 1680," *Gender and History* 7 (3) (1995): 362–77.

45. Helmut Puff, *Sodomy in Reformation Germany and Switzerland 1400–1600* (Chicago: University of Chicago Press, 2003), p. 35.

46. Humoral theory, dominant from the classical through the long early modern period, attributed physical and mental characteristics to the individual body's balance among four fluids (black bile, yellow bile, blood, and phlegm). A dominance of one humor was associated with qualities of temperament (respectively, melancholic, choleric, sanguine, and phlegmatic), and imbalances were also held responsible for deviations and disabilities, including those of gender.

47. James Parsons, *A Mechanical and Critical Enquiry into the Nature of Hermaphrodites* (London: J. Walthoe, 1741), p. 22.

48. Giovanni Bianchi, *An Historical and Physical Dissertation on the Case of Catherine Vizzani*, trans. John Cleland (London: W. Meyer, 1751), pp. 37, 43–44.

49. Parsons, *Mechanical and Critical Enquiry*, pp. 10–11.

50. Sharp, *Midwives Book*, pp. 44, 45.

51. Cited in Lillian Faderman, *Scotch Verdict: Miss Pirie and Miss Woods v. Dame Cumming Gordon* (1983; repr., New York: Columbia University Press, 1993),

p. 65. Faderman is citing the testimony of Allan Maconochie, Lord Meadowbank, serving as Lord Ordinary to the libel suit brought by Pirie and Woods.

52. Samuel Richardson, *The History of Sir Charles Grandison* (Oxford: Oxford University Press, 1986), p. 42.

53. Ibid., p. 43.

54. Ibid., p. 57.

55. Ibid., p. 69.

56. Maria Edgeworth, *Belinda* (Oxford: Oxford University Press, 1994), pp. 43, 49, 47.

57. Ibid., pp. 229, 231, 233.

58. Ibid., pp. 311, 312. For a fuller discussion of sapphism in *Belinda*, see Lisa Moore, *Dangerous Intimacies: Toward a Sapphic History of the British Novel* (Durham, NC: Duke University Press, 1997).

59. David Valentine, "The Categories Themselves," *GLQ: A Journal of Lesbian and Gay Studies* 10 (2) (2004): 215–20, at p. 219.

60. Immanuel Kant, *Observations on the Feeling of the Beautiful and Sublime*, trans. John T. Goldthwait (Berkeley: University of California Press, 2004), p. 78.

61. Rousseau, *Émile*, p. 327.

62. Margaret Hunt, "The Sapphic Strain: English Lesbians in the Long Eighteenth Century," in Bennett and Froide, *Singlewomen*, pp. 270–96, at p. 277.

63. I explore the dynamics and possible reasons for this configuration of sapphic representations in "Mapping Sapphic Modernity," in *Comparatively Queer: Crossing Time, Crossing Cultures*, ed. Jarrod Hayes, Margaret Higonnet, and William Spurlin (London: Palgrave Macmillan, 2010), pp. 69–89.

64. Nathaniel Wanley, *The Wonders of the Little World; or, A General History of Man in Six Books* (London: T. Bassett, 1673).

65. See Michael McKeon, *The Secret History of Domesticity: Public, Private, and the Division of Knowledge* (Baltimore: Johns Hopkins University Press, 2005).

66. I explore the picaresque tradition in Susan S. Lanser, "Sapphic Picaresque, Sexual Difference and the Challenges of Homo-Adventuring," *Textual Practice* 15 (2) (2001): 251–68.

67. *The travels and adventures of Mademoiselle de Richelieu: Cousin to the present Duke of that Name. Who made the tour of Europe, dressed in men's cloaths, attended by her Maid Lucy as her Valet de Chambre*, 3 vols. (London: M. Cooper, 1744).

68. John Cleland, *Fanny Hill; or, Memoirs of a Woman of Pleasure* (Harmondsworth, UK: Penguin, 1985), p. 71.

69. Ibid., pp. 49–50.

70. Samuel Richardson, *Clarissa; or, The History of a Young Lady* (Harmondsworth, UK: Penguin, 1985), p. 1402.

71. Jean-Jacques Rousseau, *Julie, or the New Heloise: Letters of Two Lovers Who Live in a Small Town at the Foot of the Alps*, trans. Philip Stewart and Jean Vaché (Hanover, NH: University Press of New England, 1997), p. 602.

72. Ibid., p. 612.

73. Richardson, *Clarissa*, p. 1403.

74. Elizabeth Montagu, letter of 18 [September 1750] to Sarah Robinson [Scott] (Huntington Library, Montagu MSS MO 5719), quoted in Gary Kelly, "Introduction,"

in *Bluestocking Feminism: Writings of the Bluestocking Circle, 1738–1785,* ed. Gary Kelly (London: Pickering & Chatto, 1999), vol. 5, p. xii.

75. Eva Mary Hamilton Bell, ed., *The Hamwood Papers of the Ladies of Llangollen and Caroline Hamilton* (London: MacMillan, 1930), p. 103 and passim.

76. Ibid., p. 80.

77. [Pidansat de Mairobert], *Confessions d'une jeune fille,* in *Espion Anglois* (London, 1778), p. 227 (my translation).

78. *Chevalières errantes, ou les deux sosies femelles* (Paris: Maradan, 1789).

79. *La Curieuse impertinente, traduite de l'anglois* (London, 1789), p. 101 (my translation).

80. [Arthur Maynwaring], "A New Ballad. To the Tune of Fair Rosamond" (London, 1708), p. 1.

81. *Les Imitateurs de Charles IX* (Chantilly, 1789), p. 110 (my translation).

82. Honoré Gabriel Riquetti, Comte de Mirabeau, *Erotika Biblion* (Rome, 1783), pp. 92–93.

83. *Les Imitateurs de Charles IX,* p. 110 (my translation).

84. *Confession et repentir de Mme de P*** ou la nouvelle Madeleine convertie,* reprinted in Hector Fleischmann, *Madame de Polignac et la Cour galante de Marie-Antoinette* (Paris: Bibliothèque des curieux, 1910), p. 130 (my translation).

85. *La Liberté ou Mlle Raucour à toute la secte anandryne assemblée au foyer de la comédie française* ([Paris], 1791), n.p. (my translation).

86. *Manuel lexique ou dictionnaire portatif des mots françois dont la signification n'est pas familière à tout le monde,* ed. l'abbé Prévost (Paris: Chez Didot, 1755), vol. 2, p. 502 (my translation).

87. Lewis Chambaud, *Chambaud's Dictionary, French and English and English and French* (London, 1787), p. 299.

88. Thomas Nugent, *The New Pocket Dictionary of the French and English Languages,* 3rd ed. (London, 1781), p. 231; and Nugent, *New Pocket Dictionary,* 5th ed. (London, 1787), p. 276.

89. Thomas Nugent, *The New Pocket Dictionary of the French and English Languages* (London, 1799), p. 326.

90. *Dictionnaire de l'Academie française,* 5th ed. (1798) (my translation).

91. Henry Fielding, *The Female Husband; or, The Surprising History of Mrs. Mary, alias Mr. George Hamilton* (London: M. Cooper, 1746), p. 5.

92. Wahrman, *Making of the Modern Self,* pp. 34, 39, and passim.

93. Napoleon Bonaparte to Gaspard Gourgaud, July 9, 1817, quoted in *The St. Helena Journal of General Baron Gourgaud,* trans. Norman Edwards (London: John Lane, 1932), p. 119.

Chapter 3

Portions of this material appeared originally in *Signs: Journal of Women in Culture and Society* 29 (1) (2003), pp. 164–65 (Copyright: University of Chicago Press), and is reproduced here with the kind permission of the publisher; and Phyllis Mack, *Heart Religion,* p. 169 (Copyright © 2008 Phyllis Mack), reprinted with the permission of Cambridge University Press.

1. James Boswell, *Life of Johnson* (1791; repr., Harmondsworth, UK, and New York: Penguin Books, 1979), p. 116.

2. Rachel Labouchere, *Abiah Darby: 1716–1793, of Coalbrookdale, Wife of Abraham Darby II* (York, UK: William Sessions, 1988), p. 39.

3. T. S. Ashton, *Iron and Steel in the Industrial Revolution* (Manchester: Manchester University Press, 1924), pp. 249–52.

4. Labouchere, *Abiah Darby*, p. 129.

5. Abiah Darby to John Fletcher, 22/6th month/1784, John Rylands Library, MSS. MAM Fl 2.7/1.

6. Until the death of John Wesley in 1792, Methodism was officially a branch of the Anglican church, and members were encouraged to attend both Anglican and Methodist services and to receive communion from Anglican ministers. With the exception of John Wesley, John Fletcher, Charles Wesley, and a few others, most Methodist ministers were unordained lay preachers who did not administer the sacraments.

7. Henry Moore, *The Life of Mrs. Mary Fletcher, Consort and Relict of the Rev. John Fletcher, Vicar of Madeley, Salop*, 6th ed. (London: J. Kershaw, 1824).

8. Ibid., p. 146.

9. Abiah Darby to Mary Fletcher, n.d., John Rylands Library, MAM Fl 2.7/3.

10. Labouchere, *Abiah Darby*, p. 242.

11. On Methodists, see Phyllis Mack, *Heart Religion in the British Enlightenment: Gender and Emotion in Early Methodism* (Cambridge and New York: Cambridge University Press, 2008), pp. 290ff. In 1803 the Methodist Central Conference at Manchester formally disavowed female preaching. On Quakers, see Phyllis Mack, "Religion, Feminism, and the Problem of Agency: Reflections on Eighteenth-Century Quakerism," *Signs: Journal of Women in Culture and Society* 29 (1) (2003): 149–77. Quaker women campaigned in vain to restore the women's Yearly Meeting from 1746 until 1783.

12. Journal of Abiah Darby, p. 70; Abiah Darby, "An Expostulatory Address To all who frequent Places of Diversion and Gaming, etc." (Shrewsbury: by A. Darby of Coalbrooke-dale, printed by Mr. Cotton, Salop, 1765), p. 14.

13. Moore, *Mary Fletcher*, p. 405.

14. Abiah Darby, *Useful Instruction for Children, By way of Question and Answer* (London: Luke Hinde, 1763), p. 40.

15. Labouchere, *Abiah Darby*, p. xx.

16. On companionate marriage in the eighteenth century, see Ruth Perry, *Novel Relations: The Transformation of Kinship in English Literature and Culture 1748–1818* (Cambridge and New York: Cambridge University Press, 2004). Perry argues that the emphasis on the couple and the nuclear family was accompanied by a loss of autonomy for women, who were no longer supported by their connections with female relatives.

17. Voltaire, *Letters on England*, trans. Leonard Tancock (1734; London: Penguin, 1980), p. 23.

18. Ibid., p. 26.

19. Ibid., p. 27.

20. Letter from Abraham Darby II, Friends House Library, London, MSS. Port 38 No. 2.
21. Phyllis Mack, *Visionary Women: Ecstatic Prophecy in Seventeenth-Century England* (Berkeley: University of California Press, 1992).
22. On Quakers in business, see Arthur Raistrick, *Quakers in Science and Industry: Being an Account of the Quaker Contributions to Science and Industry during the 17th and 18th Centuries* (London: Bannisdale, 1950); and James Walvin, *The Quakers: Money and Morals* (London: John Murray, 1997).
23. Mack, "Religion," p. 161.
24. Copy of a Letter from Mrs. Darby, circa 1775, in T.S. Ashton, *Iron and Steel in the Industrial Revolution* (Manchester: Manchester University Press, 1924), Appendix, pp. 249–52.
25. Richard Shackleton to Lydia Shackleton, Waterford, 17/7th month/1779, quoted in Mary Leadbeater, *Memoirs and Letters of Richard and Elizabeth Shackleton*, 2nd ed. (London, printed for Harvey and Darton, Grace-church Street, 1823), p. 139.
26. Richard Shackleton to his wife, quoted in Labouchere, *Abiah Darby*, p. xiii.
27. La Bouchere, Abiah Darby, xiii.
28. James Jenkins, *The Records and Recollections of James Jenkins*, ed. J. William Frost (1776; New York and Toronto: Edwin Mellen, 1984), p. 90.
29. "A Map of the Various Paths of Life" (London: W. Darton & J. Harvey, May 30, 1794), Friends House Library, Tract Box LL2/25.
30. *Monthly Magazine* 12 (1804), article on Quaker women, quoted in Patricia Howell Michaelson, "Religious Bases of Eighteenth-Century Feminism: Mary Wollstonecraft and the Quakers," *Women's Studies* 22 (3) (1993): 281–95, at p. 285.
31. On traveling women ministers, see Rebecca Larson, *Daughters of Light: Quaker Women Preaching and Prophesying in the Colonies and Abroad, 1700–1775* (New York: Knopf, 1999).
32. Mack, "Religion," p. 161.
33. Darby, "Expostulatory Address," pp. 15, 16.
34. Journal of Abiah Darby, 1744–69, Friends House Library, London, p. 119.
35. Labouchere, *Abiah Darby*, p. 129.
36. Journal of Abiah Darby, pp. 70–71.
37. Labouchere, *Abiah Darby*, p. 149. On Abiah's thinking on class, see Edwina Newman, "Abiah Darby and the Tradition of Quaker Women's Prophetic Writings in the Mid-Eighteenth Century," unpublished paper, 2009.
38. Journal of Abiah Darby, p. 49.
39. Ibid., p. 17.
40. Abiah Darby, "An Exhortation In Christian Love, To All Who Frequent Horse-Racing, Cock-Fighting, Throwing At Cocks, Gaming, Plays, Dancing, Musical Entertainments, Or Any Other Vain Diversions," 3rd ed. (Newcastle: I. Thompson, 1770), pp. 18, 19, 26, 38.
41. Journal of Abiah Darby, p. 17.
42. Labouchere, *Abiah Darby*, p. 47.
43. David Hempton, *Methodism: Empire of the Spirit* (New Haven and London: Yale University Press, 2005).

44. Henry D. Rack, *Reasonable Enthusiast: John Wesley and the Rise of Methodism* (1989; repr., Nashville, TN: Abingdon, 1992), p. 546.
45. Mary Bosanquet to Mrs. Ryan, n.d., Fletcher/Tooth Collection MAM Fl 37/7.
46. Sarah Ryan to Mary Bosanquet, n.d., Fletcher/Tooth Collection MAM Fl 6/9/17.
47. Sarah Ryan to Mary Bosanquet, 1763, Fletcher/Tooth Collection MAM Fl 6/9/7.
48. Mary Bosanquet Fletcher, "Watchwords," Fletcher/Tooth Collection MAM Fl /27/4/18.
49. Madeley Society Business, Fletcher/Tooth Collection MAM Fl 38.4.
50. Moore, *Mary Fletcher*, p. 153.
51. Zachariah Taft, *Biographical Sketches of the Lives and Public Ministry of Various Holy Women*, 2 vols. (Leeds: H. Cullingworth, 1828), vol. 1, pp. 26–27.
52. James Rogers, Autobiography, Diaries Box, John Rylands Library.
53. Moore, *Mary Fletcher*, p. 260.
54. Journal of Abiah Darby, p. 127.
55. Moore, *Mary Fletcher*, p. 243.
56. Ibid., p. 408.
57. Ibid., pp. 280–81.
58. Journal of Abiah Darby, p. 98.
59. Ibid., p. 117.
60. Mary Fletcher, Journal, January 27, 1795, Fletcher/Tooth Collection MAM Fl 39/5/72.
61. Amanda Vickery, *The Gentleman's Daughter: Women's Lives in Georgian England* (New Haven: Yale University Press, 1998).

Chapter 4

I am grateful to Ellen Pollak for her kind patience and astute suggestions. I also thank my research assistant Meagan Biwer for her work using the Burney newspaper collection, accessed online; all British articles cited within this essay were accessed between November 2009 and December 2010. Many thanks to Brian Davidson, David Harley, Katherine Norris, and Red York for checking some references.

1. My descriptions are drawn from the *London Daily Post* from August 5, 1736, on, and throughout 1736 in the *London Evening Post*, the *London Daily Post*, the *Daily Journal*, *Read's Weekly Journal*, the *Old Whig*, the *Daily Gazette*, the *Universal Spectator*, the *Grub Street Journal*, and the *Weekly Miscellany*. See also T.A.B. Corley, "Sarah Mapp," in *Oxford Dictionary of National Biography*, ed. Colin Matthew, Brian Harrison, and Lawrence Goldman (Oxford: Oxford University Press, 2004), available at: http://www.oxforddnb.com.ezproxy.libraries.claremont.edu/view/article/56037 (accessed June 29, 2010).
2. Harold J. Cook, *Matters of Exchange: Commerce, Medicine, and Science in the Dutch Golden Age* (New Haven: Yale University Press, 2007), p. 204.
3. Londa Schiebinger, *Plants and Empire: Colonial Bioprospecting in the Atlantic World* (Cambridge, MA: Harvard University Press, 2004), pp. 101–4 (on Montagu) and pp. 105–93 (on abortifacients and the peacock flower).

4. Jean-Jacques Rousseau, *Lettres sur la botanique élémentaires à Madame de L[essart]* (Neuchâtel, 1771–73, Paris: Poincot, 1789); Ann B. Shteir, *Cultivating Women, Cultivating Science: Flora's Daughters in England, 1760–1860* (Baltimore: Johns Hopkins University Press, 1996); and Paula Findlen, "Translating the New Science: Women and the Circulation of Knowledge in Enlightenment Italy," *Configurations* 3 (2) (1995): 167–206.

5. Schiebinger, *Plants*, pp. 103–4.

6. Jeremy Black, *The English Press in the Eighteenth Century* (Aldershott, UK: Greg Revivals, 1991), p. 105.

7. Dries Lyna and Ilja Van Damme, "A Strategy of Seduction? The Role of Commercial Advertisements in the Eighteenth-Century Retailing Business of Antwerp," *Business History* 51 (1) (2009): 100–21, at p. 103.

8. Percival Pott, *Some Few General Remarks on Fractures and Dislocations* (London: L. Hawes, W. Clarke, and R. Collins, 1769), p. 2.

9. E.A. Wrigley, R.S. Davies, J.E. Oeppen, and R.S. Schofield, *English Population History from Reconstitution* (Cambridge: Cambridge University Press, 1997), table 6.4, p. 226.

10. Steven King and Alan Weaver, "Lives in Many Hands: The Medical Landscape in Lancashire, 1700–1820," *Medical History* 45 (2) (2000): 173–200, at p. 177n20.

11. S.R. Duncan and Susan Scott, "Smallpox Epidemics in Cities in Britain," *Journal of Interdisciplinary History* 25 (2) (1994): 255–71; and Margaret DeLacy, "Puerperal Fever in Eighteenth-Century Britain," *Bulletin of the History of Medicine* 63 (4) (1989): 521–56.

12. Ann Bouman Jannetta, *Epidemics and Mortality in Early Modern Japan* (Princeton, NJ: Princeton University Press, 1987), p. 101; A.J. Mercer, "Smallpox and Epidemiological-Demographic Change in Europe: The Role of Vaccination," *Population Studies* 39 (1985): 287–307, at p. 305; and Elizabeth Fenn, *Pox Americana: The Great Smallpox Epidemic of 1775–82* (New York: Hill and Wang, 2001).

13. Ólafur Bjarnason, "Epidemics in Iceland in the Eighteenth Century," *Nordisk Medicinhistorisk Aarsbok* 6 (1980): 76–81; and Trevor G. Burnard, "'The Countrie Continues Sicklie': White Mortality in Jamaica, 1655–1780," *Social History of Medicine* 12 (1) (1999): 45–72.

14. For a typical chronicle of accidents involving horses and vehicles, see "Remarkable Domestic Events. October 1791," *The Historical Magazine, or, Classical Library of Public Events* 3 (1791), p. 378, which lists four human and two equine deaths and at least a dozen serious injuries for October alone throughout England. One historian tentatively suggests that as high as 20 percent of accidental deaths may have been attributable to horses or horse-drawn vehicles in the late eighteenth century; see P.E.H. Hair, "Deaths from Violence in Britain: A Tentative Secular Survey," *Population Studies* 25 (1) (1971): 5–24, at pp. 9–10.

15. Cook, *Matters of Exchange*, p. 178.

16. Review of *Malvern Hills: A Poem*, by Joseph Cottle, *The Monthly Review; or Literary Journal*, new ser., 28 (1799): 21–25, quote on p. 23.

17. On mercury mines, see William Buchan, *Domestic Medicine; or, A Treatise on the Prevention and Cure of Diseases*, 11th ed. (London, 1790); the quotation is on p. 39.

18. Bernardino Ramazzini, *A Treatise of the Diseases of Tradesmen, Shewing the Various Influence of Particular Trades upon the State of Health* (London, 1705), pp. 22–25 (on exposure to mercury); and Peter Earle, *The Making of the English Middle Class: Business, Society and Family Life in London 1660–1830* (Berkeley: University of California Press, 1989), p. 310 (on median ages of death).

19. Ramazzini, *Treatise*, pp. 108–9 (on syphilis), pp. 101–7 (on midwives' good health); the quotation is on p. 107 (on washing).

20. C. Turner Thackrah, *The Effects of the Principle Trades, Arts, and Professions*, 2nd ed. (London: Longman, Rees, Orme, Brown & Green, 1831); the quote on pp. 30–31.

21. Adrian Wilson, *The Making of Man-Midwifery: Childbirth in England, 1660–1770* (London: UCL Press, 1995), p. 19.

22. Laurence Brockliss and Colin Jones, *The Medical World of Early Modern France* (Oxford: Clarendon, 1997), pp. 480–621; and Mary Lindemann, *Health and Healing in Eighteenth-Century Germany* (Baltimore: Johns Hopkins University Press, 1996), pp. 164–71.

23. Celeste Chamberland, "Partners and Practitioners: Women and the Management of Surgical Household in London, 1570–1640," *Social History of Medicine* 24 (3) (2011): 554–69; Deborah Harkness, *The Jewel House: Elizabethan London and the Scientific Revolution* (New Haven: Yale University Press, 2007); Anthony Fletcher, *Gender, Sex and Subordination in England 1500–1800* (New Haven: Yale University Press, 1995), pp. 232–38; and Brockliss and Jones, *Medical World*, p. 175.

24. Margaret Hunt, *Women in Eighteenth-Century Europe* (London: Longman, 2010), p. 194. For more examples, see Matthew Ramsey, *Professional and Popular Medicine in France, 1770–1830: The Social World of Medical Practice* (Cambridge: Cambridge University Press, 1988).

25. David Gentilcore, "Charlatans, the Regulated Marketplace and the Treatment of Venereal Disease," in *Sins of the Flesh: Responding to Sexual Disease in Early Modern Europe*, ed. Kevin Sienna (Toronto: Centre for Reformation and Renaissance Studies, 2005), pp. 57–80, at p. 64.

26. Janina M. Konszacki and Kurt Alterman, "Regina Salomea Pilsztynowa, Ophthalmologist in Eighteenth-Century Poland," *Survey of Ophthalmology* 47 (2) (2002): 189–95.

27. Elaine Leong, "Making Medicines in the Early Modern Household," *Bulletin of the History of Medicine* 82 (1) (2008): 145–68.

28. Metta Lou Henderson, *American Women Pharmacists: Contributions to the Profession* (Binghamton, NY: Haworth, 2002), p. 2.

29. Brockliss and Jones, *Medical World*, pp. 267–71; the quotation is on p. 269.

30. Emily Clark, " 'By All the Conduct of Their Lives': A Laywomen's Confraternity in New Orleans, 1730–1744," *William and Mary Quarterly*, 3rd ser., 54 (4) (1997): 769–94; the quotation is on pp. 777–78.

31. On Sister Xavier Herbert's work running the dispensary, see Henderson, *American Women Pharmacists*, p. 2; and Jack D. L. Holmes, "Medical Practice in New Orleans: Colonial Period," *Alabama Journal of Medical Sciences* 6 (4) (1969): 433–41, at p. 433 (on doctors' bad reputation).

32. Lisa Smith, "The Relative Duties of Man: Domestic Medicine in England and France, ca. 1685–1740," *Journal of Family History* 31 (3) (2006): 237–56; and Kathleen M. Brown, *Good Wives, Nasty Wenches, and Anxious Patriarchs: Gender, Race, and Power in Colonial Virginia* (Chapel Hill: University of North Carolina Press, 1996), p. 347.

33. David Cressy, *Birth, Marriage and Death: Ritual, Religion, and the Life-Cycle in Tudor and Stuart England* (Oxford: Oxford University Press, 1997), pp. 15–94; Jacques Gélis, *History of Childbirth: Fertility, Pregnancy and Birth in Early Modern Europe*, trans. Rosemary Morris (Boston: Northeastern University Press, 1991); Laurel Thatcher Ulrich, *Good Wives: Image and Reality in the Lives of Women in Northern New England, 1650–1750* (New York: Knopf, 1980), pp. 126–45; and Hilary Marland, "The *'burgerlijke'* Midwife: The *stadsvroedvrouw* of Eighteenth-Century Holland," in *The Art of Midwifery: Early Modern Midwives in Europe*, ed. Hilary Marland (London and New York: Routledge, 1993), pp. 192–213; for conflicts between women, see Laura Gowing, *Common Bodies: Women, Touch and Power in Seventeenth-Century England* (New Haven: Yale University Press, 2003), pp. 43–51; and Brown, *Good Wives*, pp. 97–98, 100.

34. Laurel Thatcher Ulrich, *A Midwife's Tale: The Life of Martha Ballard, Based on Her Diary, 1785–1812* (New York: Knopf, 1990); and Karol K. Weaver, *Medical Revolutionaries: The Enslaved Healers of Eighteenth-Century Saint Domingue* (Urbana and Chicago: University of Illinois Press, 2006), pp. 48–60.

35. Nadia Maria Filippini, "The Church, the State and Childbirth: The Midwife in Italy in the Eighteenth Century," in Marland, *Art of Midwifery*, pp. 152–75.

36. Lindemann, *Health and Healing*, pp. 194–214.

37. "A Planter" [Dr. David Collins], *The Practical Rules for Management and Medical Treatment of Negro Slaves in the Sugar Colonies* (London: J. Barfield, 1811), p. 147.

38. Eddie Donoghue, *Black Women; White Men: The Sexual Exploitation of Female Slaves in the Danish West Indies* (Bloomington, IN: Authorhouse, 2006), pp. 198–99.

39. Wilson, *The Making of Man-Midwifery*, pp. 161–83.

40. Liann McTavish, *Childbirth and the Display of Authority in Early Modern France* (London: Ashgate, 2005); and Lisa Forman Cody, *Birthing the Nation: Sex, Science, and the Conception of Eighteenth-Century Britons* (Oxford: Oxford University Press, 2005), pp. 186–96.

41. William Smellie, *A Treatise on the Theory and Practice of Midwifery*, 3 vols. (London, 1752–64), vol. 3, pp. 252–53.

42. Cody, *Birthing the Nation*, p. 215; Olwen Hedley, *Queen Charlotte* (London: John Murray, 1975), pp. 74–75, 100, 114; and Judith Schneid Lewis, *In the Family Way: Childbearing in the British Aristocracy, 1760–1860* (New Brunswick, NJ: Rutgers University Press, 1986).

43. For eighteenth-century examples, see Sarah Stone, *A Complete Practice of Midwifery* (London, 1737); and Margaret Stephen, *Domestic Midwife; or, The Best Means of Preventing Danger in Child-Birth Considered* (London, 1795). For the more anecdotal style of early modern midwifery texts, see Jane Sharp, *The Midwives Book. Or the whole Art of Midwifry Discovered* (London: Simon Miller, 1671).

44. Elizabeth Nihell, *A Treatise on the Art of Midwifery* (London, 1760), p. 90.

45. Mary Daly, *Gyn/Ecology: The Metaethics of Radical Feminism* (Boston: Beacon, 1978), p. 224; and Jo Murphy-Lawless, *Reading Birth and Death: A History of Obstetric Thinking* (Bloomington: Indiana University Press, 1998), pp. 50, 60, 66.

46. Laurinda S. Dixon, *Perilous Chastity: Women and Illness in Pre-Enlightenment Art and Medicine* (Ithaca, NY: Cornell University Press, 1995), pp. 221–45; and G. J. Barker-Benfield, *The Culture of Sensibility: Sex and Society in Eighteenth-Century Britain* (Chicago: University of Chicago Press, 1992).

47. Helen King, *Hippocrates' Woman: Reading the Female Body in Ancient Greece* (London: Routledge, 1998), esp. pp. 205–50; Lyndal Roper, *Oedipus and the Devil: Witchcraft, Religion, and Sexuality in Early Modern Europe* (London: Routledge, 1994); Mary E. Fissell, *Vernacular Bodies: The Politics of Reproduction in Early Modern England* (Oxford: Oxford University Press, 2004); and Marie-Hélène Huet, *Monstrous Imagination* (Cambridge, MA: Harvard University Press, 1993).

48. Quote from a letter writer to the *Gazetteer and New Daily Advertiser* (April 22, 1772); Cody, *Birthing the Nation*, pp. 144–47; and Toni Bowers, *The Politics of Motherhood: British Writing and Culture, 1680–1760* (Cambridge: Cambridge University Press, 1996).

49. Hunt, *Women*, p. 102; Vincent de Brouwere, "The Comparative Study of Maternal Mortality over Time: The Role of Professionalisation of Childbirth," *Social History of Medicine* 20 (3) (2007): 541–62, at pp. 545–46; and Christopher Hoolihan, "Thomas Young, M.D. (1726?–1783) and Obstetrical Education at Edinburgh," *Journal of the History of Medicine and Allied Sciences* 40 (1985): 327–45.

50. Samuel Tissot, *Avis au people sur la santé* (Paris, 1761); and Alexandra Lord, "The Great 'Arcana of the Deity': Menstruation and Menstrual Disorders in Eighteenth-Century British Medical Thought," *Bulletin of the History of Medicine* 73 (1) (1999): 38–63.

51. Alexander Hamilton, *A Treatise on the Management of Female Complaints* (Edinburgh, 1792); Monica Green, *Making Women's Medicine Masculine: The Rise of Male Authority in Pre-Modern Gynaecology* (Oxford: Oxford University Press, 2008); and Ornella Moscucci, *The Science of Woman: Gynaecology and Gender in England, 1800–1929* (Cambridge: Cambridge University Press, 1990).

52. Colin Jones, "The Great Chain of Buying: Medical Advertisement, the Bourgeois Public Sphere, and the Origins of the French Revolution," *American Historical Review* 101 (1) (1996): 13–40.

53. Hannah Barker, "Medical Advertising and Trust in Late Georgian England," *Urban History* 36 (3) (2009): 379–98, at p. 384.

54. All three advertisements are collected in Sir John Cullum, Miscellaneous Newspaper Cuttings, 1712–1785, British Library, Shelfmark1890.c.7: the Mrs. Gibson clipping (1768) is on fol. 1, the midwife's private lying-in establishment clipping (1770) on fol. 2, and the secret disorders clipping (1770) on fol. 3. Mrs. Gibson placed an advertisement at least eighteen times between January 3, 1765, and August 3, 1769, in the *Gazetteer and New Daily Advertiser* and the *Public Advertiser*.

55. Lindsay Wilson, *Women and Medicine in the French Enlightenment: The Debate over "Maladies des Femmes"* (Baltimore: The Johns Hopkins University Press,

1993), pp. 118–20. Madame Veros's advertisement, which Wilson translates, is in note 60 on pp. 200–201.

56. My description of American female healers' advertisements is based on keyword searches of *Readex: America's Historical Newspapers* (accessed November 17 and December 20, 2010); after the late 1790s, American advertisements frequently advertised abortions and other family-planning measures. See Janet Farrell Brodie, *Contraception and Abortion in Nineteenth-Century America* (Ithaca, NY: Cornell University Press, 1994).

57. Londa Schiebinger, *The Mind Has No Sex? Women in the Origins of Modern Science* (Cambridge, MA: Harvard University Press, 1989), p. 115.

58. Eliza Smith, *The Compleat Housewife; or, Accomplished Gentlewoman's Companion* (London, 1727).

59. Schiebinger, *The Mind Has No Sex?* pp. 112–16.

60. Elizabeth Raffald, *The Experienced English Housekeeper, For the Use and Ease of Ladies, Cooks, etc.* 2nd ed. (Manchester, 1769), preface, quoted in Schiebinger, *The Mind Has No Sex?* p. 115.

61. William Buchan, *Domestic Medicine, or, The Family Physician: being an attempt to render the medical arts more useful* (Edinburgh: Balfour, Auld, and Smellie, 1769).

62. Mary Trye, *Medicatrix, or the Woman-Physician* (London, 1675); and Marie Meurdrac, *La Chymie charitable et facile, en faveur des dames* (Paris, 1666).

63. M.P. Amelink-Verburg, S. P. Verloove-Vanhorick, R. M. Hakkenberg, I. M. Veldhuijzen, J. Bennebroek Gravenhorst, and S. E. Buitendijk, "Evaluation of 280,000 Cases in Dutch Midwifery Practices: A Descriptive Study," *British Journal of Obstetrics and Gynaecology* 115 (5) (2008): 570–78.

64. Angélique Marguerite Le Boursier du Coudray, *Abrégé de l'art des accouchements* (Paris, 1759; followed by six more editions printed throughout France); Marguerite Guillaumanche Coutanceau, *Eléments de l'art d'accoucher en faveur des sages-femmes de la généralité de Guienne* (Bordeaux, 1784); Marguerite Guillaumanche Coutanceau, *Instructions théoriques et pratiques à l'usage des élèves de Mme Coutanceau* (Bordeaux, 1800); and Nina Gelbart, *The King's Midwife* (Berkeley: University of California Press, 1998).

65. Gelbart, *King's Midwife*, p. 277.

66. Paul Starr, *The Social Transformation of American Medicine: The Rise of a Sovereign Profession and the Making of a Vast Industry* (New York: Basic Books, 1982), pp. 30–78; popular female authors who incorporated medical advice in their domestic treatises included Lydia Maria Child, *The American Frugal Housewife* (Boston, 1829; 33rd ed., New York, 1855) and Mrs. A.L. Webster, *The Improved Housewife* (Hartford, 1843; 21st ed., Boston, 1858).

Chapter 5

1. See Rolf Reichardt and Deborah Louise Cohen, "Light against Darkness: The Visual Representations of a Central Enlightenment Concept," *Representations* 61 (1998): 95–148. On the French contribution to the Enlightenment, see Dan Edelstein, *The Enlightenment: A Genealogy* (Chicago and London: University of Chicago Press, 2010).

2. Louis-Sébastien Mercier, *Tableau de Paris*, 12 vols. (Amsterdam: 1782–88), vol. 1, chap. 89, p. 283. Unless otherwise noted, all translations from primary or secondary French sources are my own.

3. Jolanta T. Pekacz writes, "According to Verena von der Heyden-Rynsch, the term *salon*, meaning social gathering for the purpose of conversation, appeared for the first time in 1807, in Mme de Staël's *Corinne*. . . . In the seventeenth century what later came to be called *salon* was referred to as *ruelle, cabale, cabinet, réduit, al-côve, compagnie, société, cour littéraire, cercle, assemblée*, and *chambres*; in the eighteenth century as *souper, diner*, or *bureau d'esprit*." *Conservative Tradition in Pre-Revolutionary France: Parisian Salon Women* (New York: Peter Lang, 1999), p. 1. See also Verena von der Heyden-Rynsch, *Salons européens. Les beaux moments d'une culture feminine disparue*, trans. Gilberte Lambrichs (Paris: Gallimard, 1993), p. 13.

4. Jürgen Habermas, *The Structural Transformation of the Public Sphere: An Inquiry into a Category of Bourgeois Society* (1962), trans. Thomas Burger with Frederick Lawrence (Cambridge, MA: MIT Press, 1989). Among many feminist critiques of Habermas's work, see my "The Public and the Private Sphere: A Feminist Reconsideration," in *Feminism, the Public and the Private*, ed. Joan B. Landes (Oxford: Oxford University Press, 1998), pp. 135–63.

5. Immanuel Kant, "An Answer to the Question: What Is Enlightenment?" (1784) in *What Is Enlightenment? Eighteenth-Century Answers and Twentieth-Century Questions*, ed. and trans. James Schmidt (Berkeley: University of California Press, 1996), pp. 58–64, at p. 58.

6. Habermas, *Structural Transformation*, p. 56.

7. Indeed, in both state and church law, the early modern period saw an increasing emphasis on parental consent. Following the Council of Trent, tolerance of the practice of clandestine marriages by couples was replaced by an emphasis on the publication of banns, ceremonial officiation by a priest, and paternal consent. Similarly, the French state attempted to extend parental control over the marriage of children to age twenty-five or thirty. For an essential overview, see James F. Traer, *Marriage and Family in Eighteenth-Century France* (Ithaca, NY: Cornell University Press, 1980).

8. Louis, chevalier de Jaucourt, "Mariage (Droit naturel)," in *Encyclopédie, ou dictionnaire raisonné des sciences, des arts et des métiers*, ed. Denis Diderot and Jean le Rond D'Alembert, vol. 10, pp. 104–6, available through the University of Chicago and ARTFL Encyclopédie Projet, ed. Robert Morrissey, at: http://encyclopedie.uchicago.edu/ (accessed August 3, 2010).

9. On the family economy, see Natalie Zemon Davis, *Society and Culture in Early Modern France* (Stanford, CA: Stanford University Press, 1975); Natalie Zemon Davis, "Women in the Crafts in Sixteenth-Century Lyon," in *Women and Work in Pre-Industrial Europe*, ed. Barbara A. Hanawalt (Bloomington: Indiana University Press, 1986); Louise A. Tilly and Joan W. Scott, *Women, Work, and Family* (New York: Holt, Rinehart and Winston, 1978); Olwen Hufton, *The Prospect before Her: A History of Women in Western Europe, 1500–1800* (New York: Vintage, 1998); Olwen Hufton, "Women and the Family Economy in Eighteenth-Century France," *French Historical Studies* 9 (1) (1975): 1–22; Olwen Hufton, "Women, Work, and Marriage in Eighteenth-Century France," in *Marriage and Society: Studies in the*

Social History of Marriage, ed. R.B. Outhwaite (New York: St. Martin's, 1981); Gay Gullickson, *Spinners and Weavers of Auffay: Rural Industry and the Sexual Division of Labor in a French Village, 1750–1850* (Cambridge: Cambridge University Press, 1986); and Tessie Liu, *The Weaver's Knot: The Contradictions of Class Struggle and Family Solidarity in Western France, 1750–1914* (Ithaca, NY: Cornell University Press, 1994).

10. Montaigne, "On Some Verses of Vergil," in *The Complete Essays of Montaigne*, trans. Donald Frame (Stanford, CA: Stanford University Press, 1965), pp. 645–46, cited in Suzanne Desan, "Making and Breaking Marriage: An Overview of Old Regime Marriage as a Social Practice," in *Family, Gender, and Law in Early Modern France*, ed. Suzanne Desan and Jeffrey Merrick (University Park: Pennsylvania State University Press, 2009), pp. 1–25, at p. 3.

11. See Boucher d'Argis, "Séparation," in Diderot and D'Alembert, *Encyclopédie*, vol. 15, p. 60.

12. "In England, common law strictures gave husbands control over wives' property, and William Strahan, an eighteenth-century jurist, noted that in comparison to France there was 'no such' separation of goods in England. Even in other customary law regions, such as the German territories, separate property provisions were often refused to women. Protestant regions, including England, Switzerland, and some German territories, introduced divorce in principle in the sixteenth century, but in practice women had great difficulty in securing decisions in their favour. In Venice, where church courts retained jurisdiction over separations of person and property, either spouse could seek such actions, and people of all social classes seem to have had some prospect of using them successfully to remedy their marital woes." Julie Hardwick, *Family Business: Litigation and the Political Economics of Daily Life in Early Modern France* (Oxford and New York: Oxford University Press, 2009), p. 26.

13. Merry E. Wiesner, "Spinning Out Capital: Women's Work in Preindustrial Europe, 1350–1750," in *Becoming Visible: Women in European History*, ed. Renate Bridenthal, Susan Mosher Stuard, and Merry E. Wiesner, 3rd ed. (Boston and New York: Houghton Mifflin, 1998), pp. 203–31, at p. 212.

14. As a consequence, Margaret Hunt concludes that child care was often less of a problem for the early modern woman than for contemporary women; see *The Middling Sort: Commerce, Gender, and the Family in England, 1680–1780* (Berkeley: University of California Press, 1996). Regarding servants' use of wet nurses, Nancy Locklin recounts a 1768 case in which a servant, Petit Pain, and his wife returned to Nantes, leaving their baby with a wet nurse in Paris without meeting the wet nurse's requirement to have paid the entire bill in advance. Nancy Locklin, *Women's Work and Identity in Eighteenth-Century Brittany* (Aldershot, UK, and Burlington, VT: Ashgate, 2007), pp. 23–24.

15. On women in all-female and mixed guilds, see Clare Haru Crowston, *Fabricating Women: The Seamstresses of Old Regime France, 1675–1791* (Durham, NC: Duke University Press, 2001); Cynthia Truant, "Parisian Guildswomen and the (Sexual) Politics of Privilege: Defending Their Patrimonies in Print," in *Going Public: Women and Publishing in Early Modern France*, ed. Elizabeth Goldsmith and

Dena Goodman (Ithaca, NY: Cornell University Press, 1995), pp. 46–61; Daryl Hafter, *Women at Work in Preindustrial France* (University Park: Pennsylvania State University Press, 2007); and Elizabeth C. Musgrave, "Women in the Male World of Work: The Building Industries of Eighteenth-Century Brittany," *French History* 7 (1) (1993): 30–52.

16. Hafter, *Women at Work.*
17. See Neil McKendrick, John Brewer, and J.H. Plumb, *The Birth of a Consumer Society: The Commercialization of Eighteenth-Century England* (Bloomington: Indiana University Press, 1982); John Brewer and Roy Porter, eds., *Consumption and the World of Goods* (London: Routledge, 1993); John Brewer and Ann Bermingham, eds., *The Consumption of Culture, 1600–1800: Image, Object, Text* (London and New York: Routledge, 1995); Maxine Berg and Helen Clifford, eds., *Consumers and Luxury: Consumer Culture in Europe 1650–1850* (Manchester: Manchester University Press, 1999); Robert Fox and Anthony Turner, eds., *Luxury Trades and Consumerism in Ancien Régime Paris* (Aldershot, UK: Ashgate, 1998); and Carolyn Sargentson, *Merchants and Luxury Markets: The Marchands Merciers of Eighteenth-Century Paris* (London and Malibu: Victoria and Albert Museum in conjunction with the J. Paul Getty Museum, 1996).
18. Annik Pardailhé-Galabrun, *The Birth of Intimacy: Privacy and Domestic Life in Early Modern Paris*, trans. Jocelyn Phelps (Philadelphia: University of Pennsylvania Press, 1991). Because the English version of the French original is considerably truncated, see also Pardailhé-Galabrun, *La naissance de l'intime: 3000 foyers parisiens, XVIIe–XVIIIe siècles* (Paris: Presses Universitaires de France, 1988). In addition, see Daniel Roche's rich account of the lives of eighteenth-century Parisian wage earners and servants: *The People of Paris: An Essay in Popular Culture in the Eighteenth Century*, trans. Marie Evans with Gwynne Lewis (Berkeley: University of California Press, 1987). On the social meaning of consumption in domestic interiors and the latter's relationship to polite sociability, domesticity and privacy, see Katie Scott, *The Rococo Interior: Decoration and Social Spaces in Early Eighteenth-Century Paris* (New Haven, CT: Yale University Press, 1995); Rochelle Ziskin, *The Place Vendôme: Architecture and Social Mobility in Eighteenth-Century Paris* (Cambridge: Cambridge University Press, 1999); Mark Girouard, *Life in the French Country House* (New York: Knopf, 2000); Mimi Helman, "Furniture, Sociability, and the Work of Leisure in Eighteenth-Century France," *Eighteenth-Century Studies* 32 (4) (1999): 415–45; and Dena Goodman and Kathryn Norberg, eds., *Furnishing the Eighteenth Century: What Furniture Can Tell Us about the European and American Past* (New York: Routledge, 2007).
19. Pardailhé-Galabrun, *Birth of Intimacy*, p. 51.
20. As summarized by Carolyn Lougee, review of *La naissance de l'intime*, *American Historical Review* 98 (1) (1993): 175–76, at p. 176.
21. On sensibility, see David J. Denby, *Sentimental Narrative and the Social Order in France, 1760–1820* (Cambridge and New York: Cambridge University Press, 1994); Anne Vincent-Buffault, *The History of Tears: Sensibility and Sentimentality in France* (1986; repr., London: Macmillan, 1991); Anne C. Vila, *Enlightenment and Pathology: Sensibility in the Literature and Medicine of Eighteenth-Century*

France (Baltimore: Johns Hopkins University Press, 1998); Jessica Riskin, *Science in the Age of Sensibility: The Sentimental Empiricists of the French Enlightenment* (Chicago: University of Chicago Press, 2002); G. J. Barker-Benfield, *The Culture of Sensibility: Sex and Society in Eighteenth-Century Britain* (Chicago: University of Chicago Press, 1992); and Paul Goring, *The Rhetoric of Sensibility in Eighteenth-Century Culture* (Cambridge: Cambridge University Press, 2005).

22. Vincent-Buffault, *History of Tears*, p. 10. See also Samuel Richardson, *Clarissa; or, The History of a Young Lady* (1748; repr., Harmondsworth, UK: Penguin, 1985).

23. See Emma Barker, *Greuze and the Painting of Sentiment* (Cambridge: Cambridge University Press, 2005); and Bernadette Fort, "The Greuze Girl: The Invention of a Pictorial Paradigm," in *French Genre Painting in the Eighteenth Century*, ed. Philip Conisbee (Washington, DC: National Gallery of Art; New Haven, CT: Yale University Press, 2007). For discussion of Greuze's *The Well-Beloved Mother*, see the Introduction in this volume.

24. Louis, chevalier de Jaucourt, "Wife," trans. Naomi Andrews, in *The Encyclopedia of Diderot & d'Alembert Collaborative Translation Project* (Ann Arbor: Scholarly Publishing Office of the University of Michigan Library, 2005), available at: http://hdl.handle.net/2027/spo.did2222.0000.444 (accessed August 3, 2010), originally published as "Femme," in *Encyclopédie* (Paris, 1756), vol. 6, pp. 471–72.

25. Jaucourt, "Mariage," vol. 10, p. 106. For similar arguments, see Paul-Henri Thiry, Baron d'Holbach, *La Morale universelle, ou les devoirs de l'homme fondés sur sa nature*, 3 vols. (Amsterdam: Marc Michel Rey, 1776), sec. 5, chap. 1, pp. 5–6; Claude Adrien Helvétius, *De l'Homme, de ses facultés intellectuelles et de son éducation*, (London: La Société Typographique, 1773), 410–13; and Voltaire, "du Divorce," in *Oeuvres complètes*, ed. Louis Moland, 52 vols. (Paris: Garnier Frères, 1877–85), vol. 17, pp. 68–70.

26. Louis, chevalier de Jaucourt, "Family," trans. J. E. Blanton, in *Encyclopedia of Diderot & d'Alembert*, available at: http://hdl.handle.net/2027/spo.did2222.0000.444 (accessed August 3, 2010), in *Encyclopédie*, vol. 6, pp. 390–91.

27. Malesherbes, cited by David A. Bell, *Lawyers and Citizens: The Making of a Political Elite in Old Regime France* (New York: Oxford University Press, 1994), p. 155. On gender issues in the causes célèbres, see Mary Trouille, *Wife-Abuse in Eighteenth-Century France* (Oxford: Voltaire Foundation, 2009); Tracey Rizzo, *A Certain Emancipation of Women: Gender, Citizenship, and the "Causes Célèbres" of Eighteenth-Century France* (Selinsgrove, PA: Susquehanna University Press, 2004); Sarah Maza, *Private Lives and Public Affairs: The "Causes Célèbres" of Prerevolutionary France* (Berkeley: University of California Press, 1993); and Jeffrey Merrick, "Sexual Politics and Public Order in Late Eighteenth-Century France: The Mémoires secrets and the Correspondance secrète," *Journal of the History of Sexuality* 1 (1) (1990): 68–84.

28. For an excellent overview of these different emphases in Enlightenment writing on the family, see Traer, *Marriage and Family*, pp. 48–78.

29. See Dena Goodman, *Becoming a Woman in the Age of Letters* (Ithaca, NY: Cornell University Press, 2009), pp. 63–99; Roger Chartier, Dominique Julia, and Marie-Madeleine Compère, *L'éducation en France du XVIe au XVIIIe siècle* (Paris: Société d'édition d'enseignement supérieur, 1976); and Martine Sonnet, "A Daughter to Educate," in *A History of Women in the West*, vol. 3, ed. Natalie Zemon Davis and Arlette Farge (Cambridge, MA, and London: Belknap Press of Harvard University Press, 1993), pp. 101–31.

30. In a review of Londa Schiebinger's *The Mind Has No Sex? Women in the Origins of Modern Science* (Cambridge, MA: Harvard University Press, 1989), Lorraine Daston astutely observes that "the strong feminine presence in 18th-century Parisian salons . . . had less to do with the peculiarly feminine stamp of Enlightenment intellectual life than with the rampant autodidacticism, from which provincials and parvenus profited as much as women." Lorraine Daston, "Presences and Absences," *Science*, new ser., 246 (4936) (1989): 1502–3, at p. 1502. For the classic account of the Parisian Grub Street, see Robert Darnton, *The Literary Underground of the Old Regime* (Cambridge, MA: Harvard University Press, 1982).

31. J.-A.-N. Condorcet, "Notes on Voltaire" (1789), in *Oeuvres complètes de Condorcet*, ed. A. Condorcet O'Connor and M.F. Arago, 12 vols. (Paris: Didot, 1847–49; repr., Stuttgart: F. Frommann, 1968), vol. 4, pp. 561, 563, 577, cited in Iain McLean and Fiona Hewitt, eds. and trans., *Condorcet: Foundations of Social Choice and Political Theory* (Aldershot, UK, and Brookfield, VT: Edward Elgar, 1994), p. 56.

32. Condorcet, "On Giving Women the Right of Citizenship (1790)," in McLean and Hewitt, *Condorcet*, pp. 335–40. See also Condorcet, "Works Written in Hiding: Condorcet's Advice to His Daughter [1794]," and "Letters from a Freeman of New Haven to a Citizen of Virginia on the Futility of Dividing the Legislative Power among Several Bodies (1787)," in McLean and Hewitt, *Condorcet*, pp. 284–91, 292–334; and J.-A.-N. de Condorcet, *Sketch for a Historical Picture of the Progress of the Human Mind* (1795), trans. June Barraclough (New York: Noonday Press, 1955). See also Catherine Fricheau, "Les femmes dans la cité de l'*Atlantide*," in *Condorcet: mathématicien, économiste, philosophe, homme politique*, ed. Pierre Crépel and Christian Gilain (Paris: Minerve, 1989), pp. 355–69. My account here is drawn from a more in-depth discussion of the work and lives of the author and his wife in Joan B. Landes, "The History of Feminism: Marie-Jean-Antoine-Nicolas de Caritat, Marquis de Condorcet," in *The Stanford Encyclopedia of Philosophy*, ed. Edward N. Zalta, Spring 2009 ed. (Stanford, CA: Metaphysics Lab at Stanford University, 2009), available at: http://plato.stanford.edu/archives/spr2009/entries/histfem-condorcet/. See also my earlier, somewhat contrasting account of Condorcet in Joan B. Landes, *Women and the Public Sphere in the Age of the French Revolution* (Ithaca, NY: Cornell University Press, 1988), pp. 112–17.

33. See Condorcet, *Cinq mémoires sur l'instruction publique* (1791), available at: http://classiques.uqac.ca/classiques/condorcet/cinq_memoires_instruction/cinq_memoires.html; and Catherine Kintzler, *Condorcet: L'Instruction publique et la naissance du citoyen* (Paris: Le Sycomore, 1984).

34. Condorcet, *Sketch*, p. 193.

35. "Condorcet's Advice to His Daughter (1794)" and "Condorcet's Testament (March 1794)," in McLean and Hewitt, *Condorcet*, pp. 284, 290.

36. De Grouchy's uncle, the magistrate Charles Dupaty, president of the parliament of Bordeaux, had taken up the cause of the condemned.

37. *Les "Lettres sur la sympathie" (1798) de Sophie de Grouchy: philosophie morale et réforme sociale*, ed. Marc André Bernier and Deidre Dawson (Oxford: Voltaire Foundation, 2010).

38. For more on this club, see Gary Kates, *The Cercle Social, the Girondins, and the French Revolution* (Princeton, NJ: Princeton University Press, 1985).

39. In 1793 Condorcet came under a political order of proscription because of his views and his opposition to the political leadership during the Reign of Terror. During his eight months in hiding, he composed his unfinished *Sketch for a Historical Picture of the Progress of the Human Mind*. He was arrested on March 27, 1794, and imprisoned in Bourgla-Reine, where he was found dead in his prison cell on March 29. The cause of his death remains unknown.

40. See Alice M. Laborde, *Diderot et Madame de Puisieux* (Saratoga, CA: Anma Libri, 1984); and Denis Diderot, *Diderot's Letters to Sophie Volland*, selected and trans. Peter France (London: Oxford University Press, 1972).

41. See Judith P. Zinsser, *La Dame d'Esprit: A Biography of the Marquise du Châtelet* (New York: Viking, 2006); and Judith P. Zinsser, "Volume Editor's Introduction," in *Selected Philosophical and Scientific Writings*, by Emilie du Châtelet, ed. Judith P. Zinsser, trans. Isabelle Bour and Judith P. Zinsser (Chicago: University of Chicago Press, 2009).

42. Zinsser, *La Dame d'Esprit*, p. 37.

43. Dena Goodman attributes Manon Roland's unhappiness to the impossibility of coming to terms with the demands of women's subordination in marriage: "When Manon finally found someone whom she believed to be her intellectual superior and married him, she discovered that such superiority did not justify the power he exercised over her." Dena Goodman, "Marriage Choice and Marital Success," in Desan and Merrick, *Family, Gender, and Law*, pp. 26–61, at p. 47. See also Gita May, *Madame Roland and the Age of Revolution* (New York: Columbia University Press, 1970).

44. Condorcet, "Sur l'admission des femmes au droits de la cité," *Journal de la Société de 1789*, no. 5 (July 3, 1790), translated Hewitt and McLean as "On giving Women the Right of Citizenship (1790)."

45. The literature on women and the Revolution is extensive: see, especially, Darline Gay Levy, Harriet B. Applewhite, and Mary Durham Johnson, eds. and trans., *Women in Revolutionary Paris, 1789–1795: Selected Documents* (Urbana: University of Illinois Press, 1979); Landes, *Women and the Public Sphere*; Joan B. Landes, "The Performance of Citizenship: Democracy, Gender, and Difference in the French Revolution," in *Democracy and Difference: Contesting the Boundaries of the Political*, ed. Seyla Benhabib (Princeton, NJ: Princeton University Press, 1996), pp. 295–313; Joan B. Landes, *Visualizing the Nation: Gender, Representation, and Revolution in Eighteenth-Century France* (Ithaca: Cornell University Press, 2001);

Dominique Godineau, *The Women of Paris and Their French Revolution*, trans. Katherine Streip (1988; repr., Berkeley: University of California Press, 1998); Lynn Hunt, *The Family Romance of the French Revolution* (Berkeley: University of California Press, 1992); Geneviève Fraisse, *Reason's Muse: Sexual Difference and the Birth of Democracy*, trans. Jane Marie Todd (1989; repr., Chicago: University of Chicago Press, 1994); Christine Fauré, *Democracy without Women: Feminism and the Rise of Liberal Individualism in France*, trans. Claudia Gorbman and John Berks (Bloomington: Indiana University Press, 1991); Suzanne Desan, *The Family on Trial in Revolutionary France* (Berkeley: University of California Press, 2004); Jennifer Ngaire Heuer, *The Family and the Nation: Gender and Citizenship in Revolutionary France, 1789–1830* (Ithaca, NY: Cornell University Press, 2005); Joan Wallach Scott, *Only Paradoxes to Offer: French Feminists and the Rights of Man* (Cambridge, MA: Harvard University Press, 1996); Olwen Hufton, *Women and the Limits of Citizenship in the French Revolution* (Toronto: University of Toronto Press, 1992); and Anne Verjus, *Le cens de la famille: Les femmes et le vote, 1789–1848* (Paris: Belin, 2002).

46. Desan, "Making and Breaking Marriage," p. 19.
47. For an excellent account of the accomplishments of the early Revolution, as well as the retreats, limitations, and reversals in family law during the Directory and Napoleonic regimes, see Desan, *Family on Trial*. For a probing account of paternity as a category of family history, see Rachel G. Fuchs, *Contested Paternity: Constructing Families in Modern France* (Baltimore: Johns Hopkins University Press, 2008).
48. Desan, "Making and Breaking Marriage," p. 19.

Chapter 6

1. Friedrich Schiller, "The Song of the Bell," in *The Song of the Bell. Translated from the German of Frederick von Schiller. With the Original*, trans. Samuel Taylor Coleridge (London: Treuttel and Würtz, 1827), pp. 13–15. All translations from primary or secondary German sources used in this essay are my own unless otherwise noted; page attributions refer to the corresponding German text passages.
2. Since these developments did not take place concurrently in different countries, the chronological placement of the Enlightenment differs considerably, with various start and finish dates between 1650 and 1800 commonly used. My focus in this essay is on the period between 1739 and about 1800.
3. On the Industrial Revolution and its impact on concepts of work and gender during the Enlightenment, see Joyce Burnette, *Gender, Work and Wages in Industrial Revolution Britain* (Cambridge and New York: Cambridge University Press, 2008); and Karin Hausen, "Die Polarisierung der 'Geschlechtscharaktere'—Eine Spiegelung der Dissoziation von Erwerbs- und Familienleben," in *Sozialgeschichte der Familie in der Neuzeit Europas*, ed. Werner Conze (Stuttgart, Germany: Ernst Klett, 1976), pp. 363–93.
4. Friedrich Schiller, "Über Anmut und Würde," in *Werke in drei Bänden*, ed. Gerhard Fricke and Herbert Göpfert (Munich: Carl Hanser, 1966), vol. 2, pp. 382–424, passim.

5. Ute Frevert, *Women in German History: From Bourgeois Emancipation to Sexual Liberation*, trans. Stuart McKinnon-Evans, with Terry Bond and Barbara Norden (Oxford: Berg, 1989).

6. For the Enlightenment, see Barbara Duden, "Das schöne Eigentum: Zur Herausbildung des bürgerlichen Frauenbildes an der Wende vom 18. zum 19. Jahrhundert," *Kursbuch* 47 (1977): 125–40; for later periods, see Sibylle Meyer, "Die mühsame Arbeit des demonstrativen Müßiggangs: Über die häuslichen Pflichten der Beamtenfrauen im Kaiserreich," in *Frauen suchen ihre Geschichte: Historische Studien zum 19. und 20. Jahrhundert*, ed. Karin Hausen (Munich: Beck, 1983), pp. 180–84; and Marion A. Kaplan, *The Making of the Jewish Middle Class: Women, Family and Identity in Imperial Germany* (New York and Oxford: Oxford University Press, 1991), pp. 27–31.

7. Sojourner Truth, "Ain't I a Woman?" cited in Donna Haraway, "Ecce Homo, Ain't (Ar'n't) I a Woman, and Inappropriate(d) Others: The Human in a Post-Humanist Landscape," in *Feminists Theorize the Political*, ed. Judith Butler and Joan W. Scott (New York and London: Routledge, 1992), pp. 86–100, at pp. 90–91.

8. On the various names and differing life dates of Sojourner Truth, see, among others, Gerda Lerner, *The Creation of Patriarchy* (New York and Oxford: Oxford University Press, 1993), pp. 105–6; and Jennifer S. Uglow and Frances Hinton, eds., *The International Dictionary of Women's Biography* (New York: Continuum, 1982), pp. 470–71.

9. I do not concern myself with aristocratic women in this essay, partly due to limitations of space and partly because the Enlightenment, for reasons that would lead too far afield here, did not have the same impact on their working conditions as it did for women of the middle and lower classes. On women writers, authorship issues, and class difference, see, for example, Bridget Hill, *Women, Work and Sexual Politics in Eighteenth-Century England* (London: UCL Press, 1994); and Linda V. Troost, ed., *Eighteenth-Century Women: Studies in Their Lives, Work and Culture* (New York: AMS Press, 2001). For aristocratic women of later epochs, see Muireann O'Cinneide, *Aristocratic Women and the Literary Nation, 1832–1867* (Basingstoke, UK: Palgrave Macmillan, 2008).

10. On this group of authors, see Susanne Kord, *Women Peasant Poets in Eighteenth-Century England, Scotland, and Germany: Milkmaids on Parnassus* (Rochester, NY: Camden House, 2003); Donna Landry, *The Muses of Resistance: Laboring-Class Women's Poetry in Britain, 1739–1796* (Cambridge: Cambridge University Press, 1990); and Moira Ferguson, *Eighteenth-Century Women Poets: Nation, Class, and Gender* (Albany: State University of New York Press, 1995).

11. See the chapter "Back to Nature: Bourgeois Aesthetic Theory and Lower-Class Poetic Practice," in Kord, *Women Peasant Poets*, pp. 19–47. This was a class-specific assumption. Uneducated middle-class women were never labeled "natural geniuses"; instead, they were often denigrated as hacks for their lack of erudition. Whether and to what degree middle-class women should be educated was lengthily debated in eighteenth-century "Moral Weeklies" in both England and Germany. See, for example, Andrew F. Brown, *On Education: John Locke, Christian Wolff, and the "Moral Weeklies"* (Los Angeles: University of California Press, 1952); and Wolfgang Martens, *Die Botschaft der Tugend: Die Aufklärung im Spiegel der deutschen Moralischen Wochenschriften* (Stuttgart, Germany: Metzler, 1971).

12. From the unpaginated preface to Elizabeth Bentley, *Genuine Poetical Compositions on Various Subjects, by E. Bentley* (Norwich, UK: Crouse and Stevenson, 1791).

13. Frances Dunlop in a letter to Robert Burns, July 13, 1789, in William Wallace, ed., *Robert Burns and Mrs. Dunlop: Correspondence Now Published in Full for the First Time*, 2 vols. (New York: Dodd, Mead, 1898), vol. 1, p. 274.

14. From the preface to Christian Milne, *Simple Poems on Simple Subjects. By Christian Milne, Wife of a Journeyman Ship-Carpenter, in Footdee, Aberdeen* (Aberdeen: J. Chalmers, 1805), pp. 10–11 and p. 9, respectively.

15. Anon., "Memoirs of the Life of Ann Candler," Ann Candler, *Poetical Attempts, by Ann Candler, a Suffolk Cottager; with a Short Narrative of Her Life* (Ipswich: John Raw, 1803), p. 3.

16. Bridget Freemantle, "To the Reader," in *Poems upon Several Occasions. By Mrs. Leapor of Brackley in Northamptonshire* (London: J. Roberts, 1748), n.p.

17. From an autobiographical statement by Christian Milne, quoted in Elizabeth Spence, "Letters from the Northern Highlands," in *Sketches of Obscure Poets, with Specimens of Their Writings* (London: Cochrane & McCrone, 1833), pp. 178–90, at pp. 185–86.

18. Citation of Collier's verse and discussion in: Donna Landry, "The Resignation of Mary Collier: Some Problems in Feminist Literary History," in *The New Eighteenth Century: Theory, Politics, English Literature*, ed. Felicity Nussbaum and Laura Brown (New York and London: Methuen, 1987), pp. 99–120, at p. 102.

19. Johann Georg Sulzer, letter to Johann Jakob Bodmer, 1761, quoted in *Die Karschin: Friedrichs des Großen Volksdichterin. Ein Leben in Briefen*, ed. Elisabeth Hausmann (Frankfurt/M.: Societäts-Verlag, 1933), p. 74.

20. Sulzer, "Vorrede," in Anna Louisa Karsch, *Auserlesene Gedichte* (1764), ed. Barbara Becker-Cantarino (Karben: Petra Wald, 1996), pp. vii–viii.

21. Ibid., pp. vii–xxi.

22. For example, in Johann Georg Sulzer, "General Theory of the Fine Arts (1771–74): Selected Articles," trans. and ed. Thomas Christensen, in *Aesthetics and the Art of Musical Composition in the German Enlightenment: Selected Writings of Johann Georg Sulzer and Heinrich Christoph Koch*, ed. Nancy Kovaleff Baker and Thomas Christensen (Cambridge: Cambridge University Press, 1995), pp. 3–108.

23. Johann Georg Sulzer, "Entwickelung des Begriffs vom Genie," in *Vermischte philosophische Schriften 2 Theile in 1 Band* [2 vols. in 1] (Leipzig: Weidmanns Erben & Reich, 1773), pp. 307–22, at p. 319.

24. Sulzer, "Vorrede," pp. xi–xii.

25. Anna Louisa Karsch and Johann Wilhelm Ludwig Gleim, *"Mein Bruder in Apoll": Briefwechsel zwischen Anna Louisa Karsch und Johann Wilhelm Ludwig Gleim*, vol. 1, ed. Regina Nörtemann; vol. 2, ed. Ute Pott (Göttingen, Germany: Wallstein, 1996), vol. 1, p. 361. This and all further quotations from Karsch's letters are in my translation; page numbers refer to the German original (this edition).

26. Ibid., vol. 1, pp. 91–93.

27. Karsch and Gleim, *"Mein Bruder in Apoll,"* vol. 1, pp. 341–63. For similar stories in the biographies of other poets, see Kord, *Women Peasant Poets*, pp. 104–59.

28. Karsch and Gleim, *"Mein Bruder in Apoll,"* vol. 1, p. 345.

29. Hausmann, *Die Karschin*, p. 381.

30. Karsch and Gleim, *"Mein Bruder in Apoll,"* vol. 2, p. 173.

31. Sulzer, "Vorrede," p. xxiv.

32. Oscar Wilde, "The Model Millionaire," n.d., available at: http://www.wilde-online. info/the-model-millionaire.html (accessed June 1, 2009).

33. The pastoral tradition, based on the poems of Virgil or Theocritus, depicts the lives of shepherds in an idyllicized rural landscape, typically contrasting the innocence and serenity of country life with the corruption and wretchedness of life in the city and/or at court.

34. Georgic poems, modeled on Virgil's *Georgika*, describe practical aspects of rural work or agricultural affairs.

35. Both texts have been reprinted in Stephen Duck, *The Thresher's Labour (1736)* and Mary Collier, *The Woman's Labour [Mary Collier] (1739)*, introd. by Moira Ferguson, Augustan Reprint Society Publication, no. 230 (Los Angeles: UCLA William Andrews Clark Memorial Library, 1985). All further references to the poems are to this edition.

36. Collier, *Woman's Labour*, pp. 5–6.

37. Ibid., p. 7.

38. See Deborah Simonton, *A History of European Women's Work, 1700 to the Present* (London and New York: Routledge, 1998); on Collier's take on the "double burden," see particularly pp. 70–75.

39. Collier, *Woman's Labour*, p. 10.

40. Ibid., p. 12.

41. Ibid., p. 11.

42. Ibid., p. 12.

43. Ibid.

44. Ibid., p. 14.

45. Ibid., pp. 15, 17. The difference in pay could well, as Landry has assumed, allude to the gendered wage gap ("Resignation," p. 106).

46. As related in Homer's *Odyssey*, Sisyphus was punished by the gods by having to spend eternity rolling a heavy stone up a hill only to have it roll down again as soon as he had brought it to the summit; the daughters of Danaus were likewise punished for disobedience by being condemned to the endless task of filling a bottomless vessel with water. Cf. Edith Hamilton, *Mythology* (Boston and London: Little, Brown, 1998).

47. Collier, *Woman's Labour*, p. 16.

48. Andrew Pringle's *General View of the County of Westmoreland* (1794), cited in Bridget Hill, ed., *Eighteenth-Century Women: An Anthology* (London: George Allen & Unwin, 1984), p. 186.

49. Landry, "Resignation," p. 117.

50. Anna Louisa Karsch, "Schlesisches Bauerngespräch zwischen Vetter Hanß und Muhm Ohrten, gehalten zu R . . . bei Großglogau im November 1758," in *Gedichte. Nach der Dichterin Tode herausgegeben von ihrer Tochter Caroline Luise von Klencke* (1792), ed. Barbara Becker-Cantarino (Karben: Petra Wald, 1996), pp. 376–88. All passages from the poem are quoted in my translation but with page references to the original text (this edition).

51. Alexandrine meter is a line of twelve syllables with a caesura after the sixth and with major stresses on the sixth and final syllables, used predominantly in sixteenth- to eighteenth-century French poetry and drama.

52. See the following works by Ernst Josef Krzywon: " 'Ich bin Empfindung und Gesang.' Schlesiens deutsche Sappho Anna Louisa Karsch (1722–1791)," in *Kontinuität und Wandel: Schlesien zwischen Österreich und Preußen*, ed. Peter Baumgart and Ulrich Schmilewski (Sigmaringen, Germany: Jan Thorbecke, 1990), pp. 335–48; and "Tradition und Wandel: Die Karschin in Schlesien (1722–1761)," in *Anna Louisa Karsch (1722–1791): Von schlesischer Kunst und Berliner "Natur." Ergebnisse des Symposions zum 200. Todestag der Dichterin*, ed. Anke Bennholdt-Thomsen and Anita Runge (Göttingen, Germany: Wallstein, 1992), pp. 12–56.

53. Plowing and threshing are accorded two lines each (Karsch, "Schlesisches Bauerngespräch," pp. 379 and 381, respectively).

54. Helene M. Kastinger-Riley, "Wölfin unter Schäfern: Die sozialkritische Lyrik der Anna Louisa Karsch," in *Die weibliche Muse: Sechs Essays über künstlerisch schaffende Frauen der Goethezeit* (Columbia, SC: Camden House, 1986), pp. 1–25, at p. 13.

55. Helene M. Kastinger-Riley, "Anna Louisa Karsch," *Dictionary of Literary Biography* 97 (1990): 139–44, at p. 142.

56. Ibid.; and Kastinger-Riley, "Wölfin," p. 14.

57. Leo Balet and E. Gerhard, *Die Verbürgerlichung der deutschen Kunst, Literatur und Musik im 18. Jahrhundert* (Strasbourg, Leipzig, and Zurich: Heitz, 1936), p. 26; and Peter Brandt with Thomas Hofmann and Reiner Zilkenat, eds., *Preußen: Zur Sozialgeschichte eines Staates. Eine Darstellung in Quellen* (Reinbek: Rowohlt, 1981), pp. 45–60.

58. Karsch, "Schlesisches Bauerngespräch," pp. 377–78.

59. "As provider of food and supplier of troops and horses, the peasant is vital to the nation's well-being and defense." Kastinger-Riley, "Anna Louisa Karsch," p. 142.

60. Karsch, "Schlesisches Bauerngespräch," p. 382.

61. Mary Leapor, letter to Bridget Freemantle, quoted by Freemantle in her review of Leapor's *Poems*, *Monthly Review* (1751), pp. 30–31.

62. Cf. the chapter on the middle-class patronage of lower-class authors in Kord, *Women Peasant Poets*, pp. 48–104.

63. Milne, *Simple Poems*, pp. 101–9; Candler, *Poetical Attempts*, pp. 53–57, at p. 53.

64. Karsch and Gleim, *"Mein Bruder in Apoll,"* vol. 1, pp. 333–34. Such stark descriptions of poverty, very often autobiographically "inspired," are relatively common in the work of lower-class women poets, often standing side by side with poems that place the theme in a more explicitly literary context. See Kord, *Women Peasant Poets*, pp. 161–93.

65. Karsch and Gleim, *"Mein Bruder in Apoll,"* vol. 1, p. 112.

66. Ibid., vol. 2, p. 230.

67. It is worth reminding ourselves here that the educational dilemma ambushed middle-class women in different ways; see note 11.

68. Anna Louisa Karsch, "Meine Zufriedenheit," in *Gedichte und Lebenszeugnisse*, ed. Alfred Anger (Stuttgart, Germany: Reclam, 1987), pp. 124–25.

69. Mary Leapor, "The Rural Maid's Reflexions, Written by a Gardener's Daughter. Inscribed to a Lady," *London Magazine, or Gentleman's Monthly Intelligencer* 16 (1747), p. 45.

70. Susanne Kord, *Little Detours: The Letters and Plays of Luise Gottsched* (Rochester, NY: Camden House, 2000).

71. See Lorely French's introduction to "Dorothea Schlegel (1764–1839)," in *Bitter Healing: German Women Writers from 1700 to 1830. An Anthology*, ed. Jeannine Blackwell and Susanne Zantop (Lincoln and London: University of Nebraska Press, 1990), pp. 335–38, specifically pp. 336–37; and the materials in *Florentin: A Novel. By Dorothea Mendelssohn Veit Schlegel*, trans., annotated, and introduced by Edwina Lawler and Ruth Richardson (Lewiston and Queenston: Edwin Mellen, 1988).

    There is good evidence that many women employed this discourse of self-subordination strategically. Many women who denigrate their work as mere legwork in forewords left other sources such as diaries, letters to other women authors, or letters to their publishers showing clearly that they did understand themselves as professional authors and that they considered their writing as work and indeed relied on this work for their livelihoods.

72. Susanne Kord, *Sich einen Namen machen: Anonymität und weibliche Autorschaft 1700–1900* (Stuttgart, Germany: Metzler, 1996); and Magdalene Heuser, " 'Ich wollte dieß und das von meinem Buche sagen, und gerieth in ein Vernünfteln.' Poetologische Reflexionen in den Romanvorreden," in *Untersuchungen zum Roman von Frauen um 1800*, ed. Helga Gallas and Magdalene Heuser (Tübingen, Germany: Max Niemeyer, 1990), pp. 52–65.

73. These questions were originally posed in Elaine Showalter, *A Literature of Their Own: British Women Novelists from Brontë to Lessing* (Princeton, NJ: Princeton University Press, 1977); and Sandra Gilbert and Susan Gubar, *The Madwoman in the Attic: The Woman Writer and the Nineteenth-Century Literary Imagination* (New Haven and London: Yale University Press, 1979).

Chapter 7

1. Mary Wollstonecraft, *A Vindication of the Rights of Woman* (1792), ed. Deidre S. Lynch (New York and London: W. W. Norton, 2009), p. 67.

2. Ibid., p. 9.

3. Ibid., p. 10.

4. Margaret Cavendish, "The Description of a New World, Called the Blazing World (1666)," in *Paper Bodies: A Margaret Cavendish Reader*, ed. Sylvia Bowerbank and Sara Mendelson (Peterborough, ON, Canada: Broadview, 2000), pp. 151–251, at p. 242.

5. On the subject of Cavendish's politics, see Catherine Gallagher, "Embracing the Absolute: The Politics of the Female Subject in Seventeenth-Century England," *Genders* 1 (1988): 24–39.

6. Alexander Pope, *The Rape of the Lock* (1712), canto 2, lines 1–4, in *Poetry and Prose of Alexander Pope*, ed. Aubrey Williams (Boston: Houghton Mifflin, 1969), pp. 78–100, at p. 84.

7. Ibid., canto 2, lines 5–8, p. 84.

8. Ibid., canto 2, lines 17–18, p. 84.

9. Ibid., canto 2, line 32, p. 84.

10. Alexander Pope, "Epistle to a Lady" (1735), lines 199–202, in Williams, *Poetry and Prose*, p. 173.

11. Ibid., lines 261–64, p. 175.

12. Wollstonecraft, *Vindication*, p. 43.

13. Amanda Vickery, "Introduction," in *Women, Privilege and Power: British Politics, 1750 to the Present*, ed. Amanda Vickery (Stanford: Stanford University Press, 2001), pp. 1–55, at p. 6.

14. Quoted in Paula McDowell, *The Women of Grub Street: Press, Politics, and Gender in the London Literary Marketplace, 1678–1730* (Oxford: Clarendon, 1998), pp. 243–44.

15. See Catherine Gallagher, *Nobody's Story: The Vanishing Acts of Women Writers in the Marketplace, 1670–1820* (Berkeley: University of California Press, 1994), p. 131.

16. Jonathan Swift, "Corinna," quoted in Delarivier Manley, *The Adventures of Rivella*, ed. Katherine Zelinsky (Peterborough, ON, Canada: Broadview, 1999), pp. 140–42, at p. 141.

17. Some readers have seen Astrea as a reference to Aphra Behn, who adopted this name. See Ros Ballaster, *Seductive Forms: Women's Amatory Fiction from 1684 to 1740* (Oxford: Clarendon, 1992), chap. 4.

18. Delarivier Manley, *The New Atalantis*, ed. Rosalind Ballaster (London: Penguin Books, 1991), p. 13.

19. Ibid., p. 138.

20. Ibid., p. 139.

21. McDowell, *Women of Grub Street*, p. 232.

22. For discussion of the keys, see Gallagher, *Nobody's Story*, pp. 125–27.

23. Ballaster, *Seductive Forms*, passim.

24. Manley, *New Atalantis*, p. 154.

25. Ibid., p. 140.

26. Vickery, "Introduction," pp. 10–11. See also Elaine Chalus, " 'To Serve My Friends': Women and Political Patronage in Eighteenth-Century England," in Vickery, *Women, Privilege and Power*, pp. 57–88.

27. Judith S. Lewis, "1784 and All That: Aristocratic Women and Electoral Politics," in Vickery, *Women, Privilege and Power*, pp. 89–122, at p. 99.

28. *History of the Westminster Election containing Every Material Occurrence from its Commencement on the First of April to the Final Close of the Poll on the 17th May, to which is prefixed A Summary Account of the Late Parliament* (London, 1784), p. 99, quoted in Lewis, "1784 and All That," p. 89.

29. Linda Colley, *Britons: Forging the Nation, 1707–1837* (New Haven: Yale University Press, 1992), p. 246.

30. Lewis, "1784 and All That," p. 109.

31. See Christopher Leslie Brown, *Moral Capital: Foundations of British Abolitionism* (Chapel Hill: University of North Carolina Press, 2006).

32. F.K. Prochaska. "Women in English Philanthropy, 1790–1830." *International Review of Social History* 19 (1974): 426–45, at p. 427.
33. Kenneth Corfield, "Elizabeth Heyrick: Radical Quaker," in *Religion in the Lives of English Women, 1760–1930*, ed. Gail Malmgreen (Bloomington: Indiana University Press, 1986), pp. 41–67, at p. 41.
34. Louis Billington and Rosamund Billington, "'A Burning Zeal for Righteousness': Women in the British Anti-slavery Movement, 1820–1860," in *Equal or Different: Women's Politics, 1800–1914*, ed. Jane Rendall (Oxford: Basil Blackwell, 1987), pp. 82–111, at p. 82.
35. Clare Midgley, *Women against Slavery: The British Campaigns, 1780–1870* (London: Routledge, 1992), p. 201.
36. Billington and Billington, "'Burning Zeal,'" p. 83.
37. Quoted in Corfield, "Elizabeth Heyrick," p. 50.
38. "A Dialogue between a Well-Wisher and a Friend to the Slaves in the British Colonies" (London: S. Bagster, 1820), p. 7.
39. Elizabeth Heyrick, "Apology for Ladies' Anti-slavery Associations" (London: J. Hatchard and Son, 1828), p. 11.
40. Elizabeth Heyrick, "Appeal to the Hearts and Consciences of British Women" (Leicester: A. Cockshaw, 1828), p. 3.
41. Association for the Universal Abolition of Slavery, "Appeal to the Christian Women of Sheffield" (Sheffield, UK: R. Leader, 1837), p. 9.
42. Quoted in Birmingham Female Society for the Relief of British Negro Slaves, *Seventh Report* (Birmingham, 1832), p. 26. Cited in Midgley, "Women and Slavery," p. 92.
43. "The Emancipation of Women," *Westminster Review* 128 (1) (1887): 165–73, quotation on p. 168. For a critique of this simple connection between the antislavery movement and the struggle for women's suffrage, see Midgley, *Women against Slavery*, pp. 203–5; and Billington and Billington, "'Burning Zeal,'" p. 109. For corresponding accounts of the relations between female antislavery activism and the beginnings of feminism in the United States, see Jean Fagan Yellin, *Women and Sisters: The Antislavery Feminist in American Culture* (New Haven: Yale University Press, 1989); and Karen Sánchez-Eppler, *Touching Liberty: Abolition, Feminism, and the Politics of the Body* (Berkeley: University of California Press, 1993).
44. Corfield, "Elizabeth Heyrick," p. 52.
45. Billington and Billington, "'Burning Zeal,'" p. 111.
46. "Highlights of Women's Earnings in 2008" (U.S. Department of Labor and U.S. Bureau of Labor Statistics, July 2009), available at: http://www.bls.gov/cps/cpswom2008.pdf (accessed November 13, 2010).
47. Virginia Woolf, *A Room of One's Own* (1929), ed. Susan Gubar and Mark Hussey (Orlando, FL: Harcourt, 2005), pp. 21–22.

Chapter 8

1. See David Johnson, *Music and Society in Lowland Scotland in the Eighteenth Century* (London: Oxford University Press, 1972).

2. William Dauney, *Ancient Scotish* [sic] *Melodies from a Manuscript of the Reign of King James VI, with an Introductory Enquiry Illustrative of the History of the Music of Scotland* (Edinburgh: Bannatyne Club, 1838), pp. 2–3.

3. Ibid., pp. 24–25.

4. Ibid., pp. 20–27.

5. The most famous of these, Charles Leslie, aka "Mussel-Mou'd Charlie," has been written about by Mary Ellen Brown, "The Street Laureate of Aberdeen: Charles Leslie, alias Musle Mou'd Charlie, 1677–1782," in *Narrative Folksong: New Directions*, ed. Carol Edwards and Kathleen Manley (Boulder, CO: Westview, 1985), pp. 362–78; and Ian A. Olson and John Morris, "Mussel-Mou'd Charlie's (Charles Leslie) 1745 Song: 'McLeod's Defeat at Inverury,'" *Aberdeen University Review* 58 (204) (2000): 317–31.

6. As early as 1642, Catherine Forbes, Lady Rothiemay, who reports that she had been bred and educated in Aberdeen, left a bequest of £1,000 Scots to support a schoolmistress to teach young women to "write and so and any other art or science whairof they can be capable." Quoted in Shona Vance, "Schooling the People," in *Aberdeen before 1800: A New History*, ed. Patricia Dennison, David Ditchburn, and Michael Lynch (East Linton: Tuckwell, 2002), pp. 309–26, at p. 319.

7. For an account of highly educated Scotswomen of Anna Gordon's time or a little earlier, see Katharine Glover's account of Andrew Fletcher of Saltoun's sisters and daughters in "The Female Mind: Scottish Enlightenment Femininity and the World of Letters," *Journal of Scottish Historical Studies* 25 (1) (2005): 1–20.

8. John Reid, "Late Eighteenth-Century Adult Education in the Sciences at Aberdeen: The Natural Philosophy Classes of Professor Patrick Copland," in *Aberdeen and the Enlightenment*, ed. Jennifer J. Carter and Joan H. Pittock (Aberdeen: Aberdeen University Press, 1987), pp. 168–79, esp. p. 170.

9. Thomas Gordon advertised for lodgers in 1740.

10. Thomas Percy's *Reliques of Ancient English Poetry* was published in 1765, and David Herd's *Ancient and Modern Scottish Songs* was first published in 1769. Anna Gordon Brown claims to have learned her ballads a good decade earlier than these.

11. "Advertisement to Part I" of Francis James Child, *The English and Scottish Popular Ballads* (1883; repr., New York: Cooper Square, 1962).

12. Robert Jamieson, *Popular Ballads and Songs from Tradition, Manuscripts, and Scarce Editions*, 2 vols. (Edinburgh: Archibald Constable, 1806).

13. Both Robert Jamieson and Sir Walter Scott were at this time collecting ballads for literary anthologies.

14. W.E.K. Anderson, ed., *The Correspondence of Thomas Percy and Robert Anderson* (New Haven: Yale University Press, 1988), pp. 42–43.

15. Scott obtained some of Anna Gordon Brown's ballads from Alexander Fraser Tytler and some from Robert Jamieson. He shared them with Matthew Lewis, who rewrote several of them, including "Clerk Colvill" (Child #42), "King Henry" (Child #32, retitled "Courteous King James"), and "Willie's Lady" (Child #6). Francis James Child notes in the headnotes to each ballad which of Anna Gordon's ballads appear in Lewis's 1801 *Tales of Wonder* or Scott's 1802–3 *Minstrelsy of the Scottish Border*.

16. For another instance of Scottish intellectuals' interest in old ballads, see Neil R. Grobman, "David Hume and the Earliest Scientific Methodology for Collecting Balladry," *Western Folklore* 34 (1) (1975): 16–31; and Leith Davis, "At 'Sang About': Scottish Song and the Challenge to British Culture," in *Scotland and the Borders of Romanticism*, ed. Leith Davis, Ian Duncan, and Janet Sorensen (Cambridge: Cambridge University Press, 2004), pp. 188–203.

17. Alexander Fraser Tytler, letter, from his estate of Woodhouselee, April 28, 1800, National Library of Scotland Acc 3639 ff.244–45.

18. Maureen McLane, *Balladeering, Minstrelsy, and the Making of British Romantic Poetry* (Cambridge: Cambridge University Press, 2008), pp. 212–13.

19. Robert Scott, *The Glenbuchat Ballads*, ed. David Buchan and James Moreira (Jackson: University Press of Mississippi in association with the Elphinstone Institute, University of Aberdeen, 2007), pp. xxii–xxiii.

20. Patrick Shuldham-Shaw and Emily B. Lyle, eds., *The Greig-Duncan Folk Song Collection*, 8 vols. (Aberdeen and Edinburgh: Aberdeen University Press and Mercat Press, 1981–2002).

21. Thomas Gordon, letter to Alexander Fraser Tytler, January 19, 1793, National Library of Scotland Acc. 3640.

22. Bertrand Bronson, *The Ballad as Song* (Berkeley and Los Angeles: University of California Press, 1969), pp. 64–78; David Buchan, *The Ballad and the Folk* (East Linton: Tuckwell, 1997), pp. 51–73; and Albert Lord, *The Singer of Tales* (Cambridge, MA: Harvard University Press, 1960).

23. The clearest exposition of this position is probably still Cecil Sharp, *English Folk-Song, Some Conclusions* (London: Simpkin, 1907).

24. See *Memoirs of Mary Saxby, a Female Vagrant* (Chelsea, n.d.) for the story of an eighteenth-century woman, the daughter of a silk weaver, who was a ballad singer in many parts of England.

25. *Corinne, ou L'Italie* was published in 1807 and translated into English in 1808—during Anna Brown's lifetime. For literary treatments of this phenomenon, see Erik Simpson, *Literary Minstrelsy, 1770–1830: Minstrels and Improvisers in British, Irish, and American Literature* (Basingstoke, UK, and New York: Palgrave Macmillan, 2008).

26. Alexander Fraser Tytler, from his estate of Woodhouselee, April 28, 1800, National Library of Scotland Acc 3639 ff. 244–45.

27. *Letters of John Ramsay of Ochtertyre, 1799–1812*, ed. Barbara L. H. Horn (Edinburgh: T. and A. Constable, 1966), p. 204.

28. Ibid. *Lugs* means "ears" in Scots. Madame Catalini is Angelica Catalini, 1780–1849.

29. Henry George Farmer, *Music Making in the Olden Days: The Story of the Aberdeen Concerts 1748–1801* (Leipzig, London, and New York: Peters Hinrichsen, 1950), p. 91. The initial rules required members to pay a crown per annum to defray the expenses of coal and candles and other necessaries.

30. Ibid., passim, and especially Appendix 2, musical inventories. For further information about the musical interests of Aberdeen in the eighteenth century, see the catalog of the *Aberdeen Musical Circulating Library: An Extensive Collection of Vocal*

and Instrumental Music, "lent out by the year, half-year, or quarter," and published by A. Brown at Homer's-Head, Aberdeen, 1798.

31. Thomas Pettitt, "Mrs. Brown's 'Lass of Roch Royal' and the Golden Age of Balladry," in *Jahrbuch für Volksliedforschung* 29 (1984): 13–31, at p. 13. Pettitt comments on the homogeneity and essential Scottishness of Mrs. Brown's repertoire and suggests the influence of her concept of "the ballad" on subsequent collectors (pp. 17–18).

32. Gordon Hall Gerould, *The Ballad of Tradition* (New York: Oxford University Press, 1957); David Buchan, *Ballad and the Folk*.

33. Robert Jamieson's copy of Robert Eden Scott's transcription, made circa 1783, is MS Laing III 473 in the Edinburgh University Library. See *The Ballad Repertoire of Anna Gordon, Mrs. Brown of Falkland*, ed. Sigrid Rieuwerts (Woodbridge, Suffolk: The Scottish Text Society, 2011), p. 3.

34. To hear it sung by me, go to PennSound, https://jacket2.org/commentary/burd-ellen-performed-ruth-perry.

35. John Jamieson, *The Etymological Dictionary of the Scottish Language*, 2 vols. (Edinburgh: Printed at the University Press for W. Creech, 1808).

36. This first-person narrative stance is very unusual in a ballad.

37. Cork-heeled shoes are made for show and not for wear. They are a symbolic sign of wealth.

38. "Dark."

39. "Wade."

40. "Breast."

41. "Cold."

42. "Stone stuck in the mud."

43. *Alane* is literary Scots in this context, according to Dr. William Donaldson (in conversation). The implication is that Robert Eden Scott—or Anna Gordon—had familiarity with the conventions of written Scots because this is a Southern form and does not fit the rhyme scheme, nor would it have been conversationally used in the northeast, where *aleen* would have been the expected form.

44. "To move aside in order to make room/make a space around me near the wall."

45. "Enfold tenderly, wrap around."

46. "Churching," that is, when a woman is formally readmitted to the church community after the symbolic defilement of childbirth.

47. Sarah Tytler and J. L. Watson, *The Songstresses of Scotland* (London: Strahan, 1871).

48. Ruth Perry, " 'The Finest Ballads': Women's Oral Traditions in Eighteenth-Century Scotland," *Eighteenth-Century Life* 32 (2) (2008): 81–97.

49. For compelling evidence that balladry is a woman's tradition in Scotland, see Mary Ellen Brown, "Old Singing Women and the Canons of Scottish Balladry and Song," in *A History of Scottish Women's Writing*, ed. Douglas Gifford and Dorothy McMillan (Edinburgh: Edinburgh University Press, 1997), pp. 44–57.

BIBLIOGRAPHY

Abelove, Henry. 1989. "Some Speculations on the History of Sexual Intercourse during the Long Eighteenth Century in England." *Genders* 6: 125–30.

Aberdeen Musical Circulating Library: An Extensive Collection of Vocal and Instrumental Music. 1798. Homer's-Head, Aberdeen: A. Brown.

Amelink-Verburg, M. P., et al. 2008. "Evaluation of 280,000 Cases in Dutch Midwifery Practices: A Descriptive Study." *British Journal of Obstetrics and Gynaecology* 115 (5): 570–78.

Amussen, Susan D. 2007. *Caribbean Exchanges: Slavery and the Transformation of English Society, 1640–1700.* Chapel Hill: University of North Carolina Press.

Anderson, W.E.K., ed. 1988. *The Correspondence of Thomas Percy and Robert Anderson.* New Haven: Yale University Press.

Aquinas, Thomas. 1920. *Summa Theologica*, trans. Fathers of the English Dominican Province. London: Burns, Oates, and Washbourne.

Argis, Boucher d'. "Séparation." In *Encyclopédie, ou dictionnaire raisonné des sciences, des arts et des métiers*, ed. Denis Diderot and Jean le Rond D'Alembert, 15.60. Available through the University of Chicago and ARTFL Encyclopédie Projet, ed. Robert Morrissey, at: http://encyclopedie.uchicago.edu/ (accessed August 3, 2010).

Aristotle's Master-Piece; or, The Secrets of Generation Display'd in all the Parts thereof. 1690. London: J. How.

Armstrong, Nancy. 1987. *Desire and Domestic Fiction: A Political History of the Novel.* New York: Oxford University Press.

Ashton, T.S. 1924. *Iron and Steel in the Industrial Revolution.* Manchester: Manchester University Press.

Association for the Universal Abolition of Slavery. 1837. "Appeal to the Christian Women of Sheffield." Sheffield, UK: R. Leader.

Astell, Mary. 1706. *Reflections Upon Marriage, The third edition. To which is added a preface, in answer to some objections.* London.

Astell, Mary. [1694] 1997. *A Serious Proposal to the Ladies*. Parts 1 and 2. Ed. Patricia
    Springborg. London: Pickering and Chatto.
Balet, Leo, with E. Gerhard. 1936. *Die Verbürgerlichung der deutschen Kunst, Litera-
    tur und Musik im 18. Jahrhundert*. Strasbourg, Leipzig, and Zurich: Heitz.
Ballaster, Ros. 1992. *Seductive Forms: Women's Amatory Fiction from 1684 to 1740*.
    Oxford: Clarendon.
Barker, Emma. 2005. *Greuze and the Painting of Sentiment*. Cambridge: Cambridge
    University Press.
Barker, Hannah. 2009. "Medical Advertising and Trust in Late Georgian England."
    Urban History 36 (3): 379–98.
Barker-Benfield, G. J. 1992. *The Culture of Sensibility: Sex and Society in Eighteenth-
    Century Britain*. Chicago: University of Chicago Press.
Barr, Juliana. 2007. *Peace Came in the Form of a Woman: Indians and Spaniards in the
    Texas Borderlands*. Chapel Hill: University of North Carolina Press.
Bell, David A. 1994. *Lawyers and Citizens: The Making of a Political Elite in Old Re-
    gime France*. New York: Oxford University Press.
Bell, Eva Mary Hamilton, ed. 1930. *The Hamwood Papers of the Ladies of Llangollen
    and Caroline Hamilton*. London: MacMillan.
Bentley, Elizabeth. 1791. *Genuine Poetical Compositions on Various Subjects, by
    E. Bentley*. Norwich, UK: Crouse and Stevenson.
Berg, Maxine, and Helen Clifford, eds. 1999. *Consumers and Luxury: Consumer Cul-
    ture in Europe 1650–1850*. Manchester: Manchester University Press.
Bianchi, Giovanni. 1751. *An Historical and Physical Dissertation on the Case of Cath-
    erine Vizzani*, trans. John Cleland. London: W. Meyer.
Billington, Louis, and Rosamund Billington. 1987. "'A Burning Zeal for Righteous-
    ness': Women in the British Anti-slavery Movement, 1820–1860." In *Equal or Dif-
    ferent: Women's Politics, 1800–1914*, ed. Jane Rendall. Oxford: Basil Blackwell.
Birmingham Female Society for the Relief of British Negro Slaves. 1832. *Seventh Re-
    port*. Birmingham.
Bjarnason, Ólafur. 1980. "Epidemics in Iceland in the Eighteenth Century." *Nordisk
    Medicinhistorisk Aarsbok* 6: 76–81.
Black, Jeremy. 1991. *The English Press in the Eighteenth Century*. Aldershott: Greg
    Revivals.
Blackstone, William. 1765–69. *Commentaries on the Laws of England*. Oxford: Clar-
    endon. Available through the Avalon Project: Documents in Law, History and
    Diplomacy, Yale University, at: http://avalon.law.yale.edu/18th_century/blackstone_
    bk1ch15.asp (accessed July 25, 2010).
Bloch, Ruth H. 2003. "Changing Conceptions of Sexuality and Romance in Eighteenth-
    Century America." *William and Mary Quarterly* 60 (1): 13–42.
Boswell, James. [1791] 1979. *Life of Johnson*. Harmondsworth, UK, and New York:
    Penguin Books.
Bowers, Toni. 1999. "'A Point of Conscience': Breastfeeding and Maternal Author-
    ity in *Pamela*, Part 2." In *Inventing Maternity: Politics, Science, and Literature,
    1650–1865*, ed. Susan C. Greenfield and Carol Barash. Lexington: University Press
    of Kentucky.

Bowers, Toni. 1996. *The Politics of Motherhood: British Writing and Culture, 1680–1760*. Cambridge: Cambridge University Press.

Brandt, Peter, with Thomas Hofmann and Reiner Zilkenat, eds. 1981. *Preußen: Zur Sozialgeschichte eines Staates. Eine Darstellung in Quellen*. Reinbek: Rowohlt.

Brewer, John, and Ann Bermingham, eds. 1995. *The Consumption of Culture, 1600–1800: Image, Object, Text*. London and New York: Routledge

Brewer, John, and Roy Porter, eds. 1993. *Consumption and the World of Goods*. London: Routledge.

Brockliss, Laurence, and Colin Jones. 1997. *The Medical World of Early Modern France*. Oxford: Clarendon.

Brodie, Janet Farrell. 1994. *Contraception and Abortion in Nineteenth-Century America*. Ithaca, NY: Cornell University Press.

Bronson, Bertrand. 1969. *The Ballad as Song*. Berkeley and Los Angeles: University of California Press.

Brouwere, Vincent de. 2007. "The Comparative Study of Maternal Mortality over Time: The Role of Professionalisation of Childbirth." *Social History of Medicine* 20 (3): 541–62.

Brown, Andrew F. 1952. *On Education: John Locke, Christian Wolff, and the "Moral Weeklies."* Los Angeles: University of California Press.

Brown, Christopher Leslie. 2006. *Moral Capital: Foundations of British Abolitionism*. Chapel Hill: University of North Carolina Press.

Brown, Kathleen M. *Foul Bodies: Cleanliness in Early America*. New Haven: Yale University Press, 2009.

Brown, Kathleen M. 1996. *Good Wives, Nasty Wenches, and Anxious Patriarchs: Gender, Race, and Power in Colonial Virginia*. Chapel Hill: University of North Carolina.

Brown, Mary Ellen. 1997. "Old Singing Women and the Canons of Scottish Balladry and Song." In *A History of Scottish Women's Writing*, ed. Douglas Gifford and Dorothy McMillan. Edinburgh: Edinburgh University Press.

Brown, Mary Ellen. 1985. "The Street Laureate of Aberdeen: Charles Leslie, alias Musle Mou'd Charlie, 1677–1782." In *Narrative Folksong: New Directions*, ed. Carol Edwards and Kathleen Manley. Boulder, CO: Westview.

Bryson, Anna. 1998. *From Courtesy to Civility: Changing Codes of Conduct in Early Modern England*. Oxford: Oxford University Press.

Buchan, David. 1997. *The Ballad and the Folk*. East Linton: Tuckwell.

Buchan, William. 1790. *Domestic Medicine; or, A Treatise on the Prevention and Cure of Diseases*. 11th ed. London.

Buck-Morss, Susan. 2000. "Hegel and Haiti." *Critical Inquiry* 26 (4): 821–65.

Burnard, Trevor G. 1999. " 'The Countrie Continues Sicklie': White Mortality in Jamaica, 1655–1780." *Social History of Medicine* 12 (1): 45–72.

Burnard, Trevor G. 2004. *Mastery, Tyranny, and Desire: Thomas Thistlewood and His Slaves in the Anglo-Jamaican World*. Chapel Hill: University of North Carolina Press.

Burnette, Joyce. 2008. *Gender, Work and Wages in Industrial Revolution Britain*. Cambridge and New York: Cambridge University Press.

Bush, Barbara. 1990. *Slave Women in Caribbean Society, 1650–1838*. Bloomington: Indiana University Press.

Candler, Ann. 1803. *Poetical Attempts, by Ann Candler, a Suffolk Cottager; with a Short Narrative of Her Life*. Ipswich: John Raw.

Caretta, Vincent. 2005. *Equiano, the African: Biography of a Self-Made Man*. Athens: University of Georgia Press.

Cavendish, Margaret. [1666] 2000. *The Description of a New World, Called the Blazing World*. In *Paper Bodies: A Margaret Cavendish Reader*, ed. Sylvia Bowerbank and Sara Mendelson. Peterborough, ON, Canada: Broadview.

Chalus, Elaine. 2001. " 'To Serve My Friends': Women and Political Patronage in Eighteenth-Century England." In *Women, Privilege and Power: British Politics, 1750 to the Present*, ed. Amanda Vickery. Stanford: Stanford University Press.

Chambaud, Lewis. 1787. *Chambaud's Dictionary, French and English and English and French*. London.

Chamberland, Celeste. 2011. "Partners and Practitioners: Women and the Management of Surgical Household in London, 1570–1640." *Social History of Medicine* 24 (3): 554–69.

Chartier, Roger, Dominique Julia, and Marie-Madeleine Compère. 1976. *L'éducation en France du XVIe au XVIIIe siècle*. Paris: Société d'édition d'enseignement supérieur.

Chevalières errantes, ou les deux sosies femelles. 1789. Paris: Maradan.

Child, Francis James, ed. [1882–98] 1965. *The English and Scottish Popular Ballads*. New York: Dover.

Child, Lydia Maria. [1829] 1855. *The American Frugal Housewife*. Boston. 33rd ed., New York.

Clark, Emily. 1997. " 'By All the Conduct of Their Lives': A Laywomen's Confraternity in New Orleans, 1730–1744." *William and Mary Quarterly*, 3rd ser., 54 (4): 769–94.

Cleland, John. 1985. *Fanny Hill; or, Memoirs of a Woman of Pleasure*. Harmondsworth, UK: Penguin.

Clendinnen, Inga. 1991. "Fierce and Unnatural Cruelty: Cortes and the Conquest of Mexico." *Representations* 33: 65–100.

Cody, Lisa Forman. 2005. *Birthing the Nation: Sex, Science, and the Conception of Eighteenth-Century Britons*. Oxford: Oxford University Press.

Colley, Linda. 1992. *Britons: Forging the Nation, 1707–1837*. New Haven: Yale University Press.

Collier, Mary, and Stephen Duck. 1985. *The Thresher's Labour [Stephen Duck] (1736) and the Woman's Labour [Mary Collier] (1739)*. Introduction by Moira Ferguson. Augustan Reprint Society Publication, no. 230. Los Angeles: UCLA William Andrews Clark Memorial Library.

Condorcet, J.-A.-N. 1791. *Cinq mémoires sur l'instruction publique*. Available at: http://classiques.uqac.ca/classiques/condorcet/cinq_memoires_instruction/cinq_memoires.html.

Condorcet, J.-A.-N. [1795] 1955. *Sketch for a Historical Picture of the Progress of the Human Mind*, trans. June Barraclough. New York: Noonday Press.

Condorcet, J.-A.-N. [1789] 1968. "Notes on Voltaire." In *Oeuvres complètes de Condorcet*, ed. A. Condorcet O'Connor and M. F. Arago, 12 vols. Paris: Didot, 1847–49; Reprint, Stuttgart: F. Frommann.

Cook, Harold J. 2007. *Matters of Exchange: Commerce, Medicine, and Science in the Dutch Golden Age.* New Haven: Yale University Press.

Corfield, Kenneth. 1986. "Elizabeth Heyrick: Radical Quaker." In *Religion in the Lives of English Women, 1760–1930*, ed. Gail Malmgreen. Bloomington: Indiana University Press.

Corley, T.A.B. 2004. "Sarah Mapp." In *Oxford Dictionary of National Biography,* ed. Colin Matthew, Brian Harrison, and Lawrence Goldman. Oxford: Oxford University Press, 2004. Available at: http://www.oxforddnb.com.ezproxy.libraries.claremont.edu/view/article/56037 (accessed June 29, 2010).

Coudray, Angélique Marguerite Le Boursier du. 1759. *Abrégé de l'art des accouchements.* Paris.

Coutanceau, Marguerite Guillaumanche. 1784. *Eléments de l'art d'accoucher en faveur des sages-femmes de la généralité de Guienne.* Bordeaux.

Coutanceau, Marguerite Guillaumanche. 1800. *Instructions théoriques et pratiques à l'usage des élèves de Mme Coutanceau.* Bordeaux.

Crawford, Patricia, and Sara Mendelson. 1995. "Sexual Identities in Early Modern England: The Marriage of Two Women in 1680." *Gender and History* 7 (3): 362–77.

Cressy, David. 1997. *Birth, Marriage and Death: Ritual, Religion, and the Life-Cycle in Tudor and Stuart England.* Oxford: Oxford University Press.

Crowston, Clare Haru. 2001. *Fabricating Women: The Seamstresses of Old Regime France, 1675–1791.* Durham, NC: Duke University Press.

Cullum, Sir John. Miscellaneous Newspaper Cuttings, 1712–1785. British Library, Shelfmark1890.c.7.

La curieuse impertinente, traduite de l'anglois. 1789. London.

Daly, Mary. 1978. *Gyn/Ecology: The Metaethics of Radical Feminism.* Boston: Beacon.

Darby, Abiah. 1770. "An Exhortation In Christian Love, To All Who Frequent Horse-Racing, Cock-Fighting, Throwing At Cocks, Gaming, Plays, Dancing, Musical Entertainments, Or Any Other Vain Diversions." 3rd ed. Newcastle: I. Thompson.

Darby, Abiah. 1765. "An Expostulatory Address To all who frequent Places of Diversion and Gaming, etc." Shrewsbury: by A. Darby of Coalbrooke-dale, printed by Mr. Cotton, Salop.

Darby, Abiah. Correspondence. John Rylands Library.

Darby, Abiah. Journal. 1744–69. Friends House Library. London.

Darby, Abiah. 1763. *Useful Instruction for Children, By way of Question and Answer.* London: Luke Hinde.

Darnton, Robert. 1982. *The Literary Underground of the Old Regime.* Cambridge, MA: Harvard University Press.

Daston, Lorraine. 1989. "Presences and Absences." *Science*, new ser., 246 (4936): 1502–3.

Dauney, William. 1838. *Ancient Scotish Melodies from a Manuscript of the Reign of King James VI, with an Introductory Enquiry Illustrative of the History of the Music of Scotland.* Edinburgh: Bannatyne Club.

Davis, David Brion. 1966. *The Problem of Slavery in Western Culture.* New York: Cornell University Press.

Davis, Leith. 2004. "At 'Sang About': Scottish Song and the Challenge to British Culture." In *Scotland and the Borders of Romanticism*, ed. Leith Davis, Ian Duncan, and Janet Sorensen. Cambridge: Cambridge University Press.

Davis, Natalie Zemon. 1975. *Society and Culture in Early Modern France.* Stanford: Stanford University Press.

Davis, Natalie Zemon. 1986. "Women in the Crafts in Sixteenth-Century Lyon." In *Women and Work in Pre-Industrial Europe*, ed. Barbara A. Hanawalt. Bloomington: Indiana University Press.

Dayton, Cornelia Hughes. 1995. *Women before the Bar: Gender, Law, and Society in Connecticut, 1639–1789.* Chapel Hill: University of North Carolina Press.

DeJean, Joan. 2010. "And What about French Women Writers?" *Eighteenth Century: Theory and Interpretation* 50 (1): 21–24.

DeJean, Joan. 1991. *Tender Geographies: Women and the Origins of the Novel in France.* New York: Columbia University Press.

DeLacy, Margaret. 1989. "Puerperal Fever in Eighteenth-Century Britain." *Bulletin of the History of Medicine* 63 (4): 521–56.

Denby, David J. 1994. *Sentimental Narrative and the Social Order in France, 1760–1820.* Cambridge and New York: Cambridge University Press.

Desan, Suzanne. 2004. *The Family on Trial in Revolutionary France.* Berkeley: University of California Press.

Desan, Suzanne. 2009. "Making and Breaking Marriage: An Overview of Old Regime Marriage as a Social Practice." In *Family, Gender, and Law in Early Modern France*, ed. Suzanne Desan and Jeffrey Merrick. University Park: Pennsylvania State University Press.

"A Dialogue between a Well-Wisher and a Friend to the Slaves in the British Colonies." 1820. London: S. Bagster.

Diderot, Denis. 1972. *Diderot's Letters to Sophie Volland*, selected and trans. Peter France. London: Oxford University Press.

Diderot, Denis. 1964. "Suite de l'entretien." In *Oeuvres philosophiques.* Paris: Garnier frères.

Dixon, Laurinda S. 1995. *Perilous Chastity: Women and Illness in Pre-Enlightenment Art and Medicine.* Ithaca, NY: Cornell University Press.

Donoghue, Eddie. 2006. *Black Women/White Men: The Sexual Exploitation of Female Slaves in the Danish West Indies.* Bloomington, IN: AuthorHouse.

Du Bois, W.E.B. [1903] 2003. *The Souls of Black Folk*, ed. Farah Jasmine Griffin. New York: Barnes and Nobles Classics.

Duden, Barbara. 1977. "Das schöne Eigentum: Zur Herausbildung des bürgerlichen Frauenbildes an der Wende vom 18. zum 19. Jahrhundert." *Kursbuch* 47: 125–40.

Dugaw, Dianne. 1989. *Warrior Women and Popular Balladry, 1650–1850.* Chicago: University of Chicago Press.

Duncan, S.R., and Susan Scott. 1994. "Smallpox Epidemics in Cities in Britain." *Journal of Interdisciplinary History* 25 (2): 255–71.

Earle, Peter. 1989. *The Making of the English Middle Class: Business, Society and Family Life in London 1660–1830*. Berkeley: University of California Press.

Edelstein, Dan. 2010. *The Enlightenment: A Genealogy*. Chicago and London: University of Chicago Press.

Edgeworth, Maria. 1994. *Belinda*. Oxford: Oxford University Press.

"The Emancipation of Women." 1887. *Westminster Review* 128 (1): 165–73.

Equiano, Olaudah. 2003. *The Interesting Narrative of the Life of Olaudah Equiano*, ed. Vincent Caretta. Rev. ed. London: Penguin.

Eustace, Nicole. 2008. *Passion Is the Gale: Emotion, Power, and the Coming of the American Revolution*. Chapel Hill: University of North Carolina Press.

Faderman, Lillian. 1993. *Scotch Verdict: Miss Pirie and Miss Woods v. Dame Cumming Gordon*. New York: Columbia University Press.

Farmer, Henry George. 1950. *Music Making in the Olden Days: The Story of the Aberdeen Concerts 1748–1801*. Leipzig, London, and New York: Peters Hinrichsen.

Fauré, Christine. [1985] 1991. *Democracy without Women: Feminism and the Rise of Liberal Individualism in France*, trans. Claudia Gorbman and John Berks. Bloomington: Indiana University Press.

Fenn, Elizabeth. 2001. *Pox Americana: The Great Smallpox Epidemic of 1775–82*. New York: Hill and Wang.

Ferguson, Margaret W. 1994. "Juggling the Categories of Race, Class, and Gender: Aphra Behn's *Oroonoko*." In *Women, "Race," and Writing in the Early Modern Period*, ed. Margo Hendricks and Patricia Parker. New York: Routledge.

Ferguson, Moira. 1995. *Eighteenth-Century Women Poets: Nation, Class, and Gender*. Albany: State University of New York Press.

Fichte, Johann. 1869. *The Science of Rights*, trans. A. E. Kröger. Philadelphia: Lippincott.

Fielding, Henry. 1746. *The Female Husband; or, The Surprising History of Mrs. Mary, alias Mr. George Hamilton*. London: M. Cooper.

Filippini, Nadia Maria. 1993. "The Church, the State and Childbirth: The Midwife in Italy in the Eighteenth Century." In *The Art of Midwifery: Early Modern Midwives in Europe*, ed. Hilary Marland. London and New York: Routledge.

Findlen, Paula. 1995. "Translating the New Science: Women and the Circulation of Knowledge in Enlightenment Italy." *Configurations* 3 (2): 167–206.

Fissell, Mary E. 2004. *Vernacular Bodies: The Politics of Reproduction in Early Modern England*. Oxford: Oxford University Press.

Fleischmann, Hector. 1910. *Madame de Polignac et la Cour galante de Marie-Antoinette*. Paris: Bibliothèque des curieux.

Fletcher, Anthony. 1995. *Gender, Sex and Subordination in England 1500–1800*. New Haven: Yale University Press.

Fletcher/Tooth Collection.

Fletcher, Mary. January 27, 1795. Journal. Fletcher/Tooth Papers MAM Fl 39/5/72.

Floyer, John. 1697. *An enquiry into the right use and abuses of the Hot, Cold, and Temperate baths in England*. London: Printed for R. Clavel.

Fonte, Moderata. [1600] 1997. *The Worth of Women: Wherein Is Clearly Revealed Their Nobility and Their Superiority to Men*, ed. and trans. Virginia Cox. Chicago: University of Chicago Press.

Fort, Bernadette. 2007. "The Greuze Girl: The Invention of a Pictorial Paradigm." In *French Genre Painting in the Eighteenth Century*, ed. Philip Conisbee. Washington: National Gallery of Art; New Haven: Yale University Press.

Foucault, Michel. 1980. *The History of Sexuality*, trans. Robert Hurley. Vol. 1. New York: Random House.

Fox, Robert, and Anthony Turner, eds. 1998. *Luxury Trades and Consumerism in Ancien Régime Paris*. Aldershot, UK: Ashgate.

Fraiman, Susan. 1995. "Jane Austen and Edward Said: Gender, Culture, and Imperialism." *Critical Inquiry* 21 (4): 805–21.

Fraisse, Geneviève. 1998. *Les Femmes et leur histoire*. Paris: Gallimard.

Fraisse, Geneviève. [1989] 1994. *Reason's Muse: Sexual Difference and the Birth of Democracy*, trans. Jane Marie Todd. Chicago: University of Chicago Press.

Freemantle, Bridget. 1751. Review of Leapor's *Poems upon Several Occasions*. *Monthly Review*: 30–31.

Freemantle, Bridget. 1748. "To the Reader." In *Poems upon Several Occasions. By Mrs. Leapor of Brackley in Northamptonshire*. London: J. Roberts.

French, Lorely. 1990. Introduction to "Dorothea Schlegel (1764–1839)". In *Bitter Healing: German Women Writers from 1700 to 1830: An Anthology*, ed. Jeannine Blackwell and Susanne Zantop. Lincoln and London: University of Nebraska Press.

Frevert, Ute. 1989. *Women in German History: From Bourgeois Emancipation to Sexual Liberation*, trans. Stuart McKinnon-Evans, with Terry Bond and Barbara Norden. Oxford: Berg.

Fricheau, Catherine. 1989. "Les femmes dans la cité de l'*Atlantide*." In *Condorcet: mathématicien, économiste, philosophe, homme politique*, ed. Pierre Crépel and Christian Gilain. Paris: Minerve.

Fuchs, Rachel G. 2008. *Contested Paternity: Constructing Families in Modern France*. Baltimore: Johns Hopkins University Press.

The Fundamental Constitutions of Carolina: March 1, 1669. Available through the Avalon Project: Documents in Law, History and Diplomacy, Yale University, at: http://avalon.law.yale.edu/17th_century/nc05.asp (accessed June 18, 2010).

Gallagher, Catherine. 1988. "Embracing the Absolute: The Politics of the Female Subject in Seventeenth-Century England." *Genders* 1: 24–39.

Gallagher, Catherine. 1994. *Nobody's Story: The Vanishing Acts of Women Writers in the Marketplace, 1670–1820*. Berkeley: University of California Press.

Gardiner, Judith Kegan. 1989. "The First English Novel: Aphra Behn's *Love Letters*, the Canon, and Women's Tastes." *Tulsa Studies in Women's Literature* 8 (2): 201–22.

Gates, Henry Louis, Jr. 2003. *The Trials of Phillis Wheatley: America's First Black Poet and Her Encounters with the Founding Fathers*. New York: Basic Books.

Gay, Peter. 1966. *The Enlightenment: An Interpretation*. Vol. 1, *The Rise of Modern Paganism*. New York: Knopf.

Gay, Peter. 1977. *The Enlightenment: An Interpretation*. Vol. 2, *The Science of Freedom*. New York: Norton.

Gelbart, Nina. 1998. *The King's Midwife*. Berkeley: University of California Press.

Gélis, Jacques. 1991. *History of Childbirth: Fertility, Pregnancy and Birth in Early Modern Europe*, trans. Rosemary Morris. Boston: Northeastern University Press.

Gentilcore, David. 2005. "Charlatans, the Regulated Marketplace and the Treatment of Venereal Disease." In *Sins of the Flesh: Responding to Sexual Disease in Early Modern Europe*, ed. Kevin Sienna. Toronto: Centre for Reformation and Renaissance Studies.

Gerould, Gordon Hall. 1957. *The Ballad of Tradition*. New York: Oxford University Press.

Gilbert, Sandra, and Susan Gubar. 1979. *The Madwoman in the Attic: The Woman Writer and the Nineteenth-Century Literary Imagination*. New Haven and London: Yale University Press.

Gilroy, Paul. 1993. *The Black Atlantic: Modernity and Double Consciousness*. Cambridge, MA: Harvard University Press.

Girouard, Mark. 2000. *Life in the French Country House*. New York: Knopf.

Glover, Katharine. 2005. "The Female Mind: Scottish Enlightenment Femininity and the World of Letters." *Journal of Scottish Historical Studies* 25 (1): 1–20.

Godineau, Dominique. [1988] 1998. *The Women of Paris and Their French Revolution*, trans. Katherine Streip. Berkeley: University of California Press.

Goodman, Dena. 2009. *Becoming a Woman in the Age of Letters*. Ithaca, NY: Cornell University Press.

Goodman, Dena. 2009. "Marriage Choice and Marital Success." In *Family, Gender, and Law in Early Modern France*, ed. Suzanne Desan and Jeffrey Merrick. University Park: Pennsylvania State University Press.

Goodman, Dena, and Kathryn Norberg, eds. 2007. *Furnishing the Eighteenth Century: What Furniture Can Tell Us about the European and American Past*. New York: Routledge.

Gordon, Thomas. Letter to Alexander Fraser Tytler, January 19, 1793. National Library of Scotland, Acc. 3640.

Goring, Paul. 2005. *The Rhetoric of Sensibility in Eighteenth-Century Culture*. Cambridge: Cambridge University Press.

Gouges, Olympe de. [1791] 1979. *The Declaration of the Rights of Woman*. In *Women in Revolutionary Paris, 1789–1795: Selected Documents*, ed. and trans. Darline Gay Levy, Harriet Branson Applewhite, and Mary Durham Johnson. Urbana: University of Illinois Press.

Gowing, Laura. 2003. *Common Bodies: Women, Touch and Power in Seventeenth-Century England*. New Haven: Yale University Press.

Green, Monica. 2008. *Making Women's Medicine Masculine: The Rise of Male Authority in Pre-Modern Gynaecology*. Oxford: Oxford University Press.

Greenfield, Susan C. 1999. "Introduction." In *Inventing Maternity: Politics, Science, and Literature, 1650–1865*, ed. Susan C. Greenfield and Carol Barash. Lexington: University Press of Kentucky.

Grobman, Neil R. 1975. "David Hume and the Earliest Scientific Methodology for Collecting Balladry." *Western Folklore* 34 (1): 16–31.

Grouchy, Sophie de. [1798] 2010. *Les "Lettres sur la sympathie" (1798) de Sophie de Grouchy: philosophie morale et réforme sociale*, ed. Marc André Bernier and Deidre Dawson. Oxford: Voltaire Foundation.

Gullickson, Gay. 1986. *Spinners and Weavers of Auffay: Rural Industry and the Sexual Division of Labor in a French Village, 1750–1850*. Cambridge: Cambridge University Press.

Gutwirth, Madelyn. 2004. "Suzanne Necker's Legacy: Breastfeeding as Metonym in Germaine de Staël's *Delphine.*" *Eighteenth-Century Life* 28 (2): 17–40.

Gutwirth, Madelyn. 1992. *The Twilight of the Goddesses: Women and Representation in the French Revolutionary Era.* New Brunswick, NJ: Rutgers University Press.

Habermas, Jürgen. [1962] 1989. *The Structural Transformation of the Public Sphere: An Inquiry into a Category of Bourgeois Society,* trans. Thomas Burger with Frederick Lawrence. Cambridge, MA: MIT Press.

Hafter, Daryl. 2007. *Women at Work in Preindustrial France.* University Park: Pennsylvania State University Press.

Hair, P.E.H. 1971. "Deaths from Violence in Britain: A Tentative Secular Survey." *Population Studies* 25 (1): 5–24.

Halsband, Robert, ed. 1965–67. *The Complete Letters of Lady Mary Wortley Montagu.* 3 vols. Oxford: Clarendon Press.

Hamilton, Alexander. 1792. *A Treatise on the Management of Female Complaints.* Edinburgh.

Hamilton, Edith. 1998. *Mythology.* Boston and London: Little, Brown.

Haraway, Donna. 1992. "Ecce Homo, Ain't (Ar'n't) I a Woman, and Inappropriate(d) Others: The Human in a Post-Humanist Landscape." In *Feminists Theorize the Political,* ed. Judith Butler and Joan W. Scott. New York and London: Routledge.

Hardwick, Julie. 2009. *Family Business: Litigation and the Political Economics of Daily Life in Early Modern France.* Oxford and New York: Oxford University Press.

Harkness, Deborah. 2007. *The Jewel House: Elizabethan London and the Scientific Revolution.* New Haven: Yale University Press.

Hausen, Karin. 1976. "Die Polarisierung der 'Geschlechtscharaktere'—Eine Spiegelung der Dissoziation von Erwerbs- und Familienleben." In *Sozialgeschichte der Familie in der Neuzeit Europas,* ed. Werner Conze. Stuttgart, Germany: Ernst Klett.

Hausmann, Elisabeth, ed. 1933. *Die Karschin: Friedrichs des Großen Volksdichterin. Ein Leben in Briefen.* Frankfurt/M.: Societäts-Verlag.

Hedley, Olwen. 1975. *Queen Charlotte.* London: John Murray.

Helman, Mimi. 1999. "Furniture, Sociability, and the Work of Leisure in Eighteenth-Century France." *Eighteenth-Century Studies* 32 (4): 415–45.

Helvétius, Claude Adrien. 1773. *De l'Homme, de ses facultés intellectuelles et de son éducation.* London: La Société Typographique.

Hempton, David. 2005. *Methodism: Empire of the Spirit.* New Haven and London: Yale University Press.

Henderson, Metta Lou. 2002. *American Women Pharmacists: Contributions to the Profession.* Binghamton, NY: Haworth.

Herd, David, ed. 1769. *Ancient and Modern Scottish Songs, Heroic Ballads, Etc.* Edinburgh.

Hesse, Carla. 2001. *The Other Enlightenment: How French Women Became Modern.* Princeton, NJ: Princeton University Press.

Heuer, Jennifer Ngaire. 2005. *The Family and the Nation: Gender and Citizenship in Revolutionary France, 1789–1830.* Ithaca, NY: Cornell University Press.

Heuser, Magdalene. 1990. " 'Ich wollte dieß und das von meinem Buche sagen, und gerieth in ein Vernünfteln.' Poetologische Reflexionen in den Romanvorreden." In

Untersuchungen zum Roman von Frauen um 1800, ed. Helga Gallas and Magdalene Heuser. Tübingen, Germany: Max Niemeyer.

Heyden-Rynsch, Verena von der. 1993. *Salons européens. Les beaux moments d'une culture feminine disparue*, trans. Gilberte Lambrichs. Paris: Gallimard.

Heyrick, Elizabeth. 1828. "Apology for Ladies' Anti-slavery Associations." London: J. Hatchard and Son.

Heyrick, Elizabeth. 1828. "Appeal to the Hearts and Consciences of British Women." Leicester: A. Cockshaw.

Hic Mulier; or, The man-woman: being a medicine to cure the coltish disease of the staggers in the masculine-feminines of our times. Exprest in a briefe declamation. 1620. London: Printed for I. Trundle.

Hill, Bridget, ed. 1984. *Eighteenth-Century Women: An Anthology*. London: George Allen & Unwin.

Hill, Bridget. 1994. *Women, Work and Sexual Politics in Eighteenth-Century England*. London: UCL Press.

Hillman, James. 1972. *The Myth of Analysis*. Evanston, IL: Northwestern University Press.

History of the Westminster Election containing Every Material Occurrence from its Commencement on the First of April to the Final Close of the Poll on the 17th May, to which is prefixed A Summary Account of the Late Parliament. London, 1784.

Hoffer, Peter C., and N.E.H. Hull. 1984. *Murdering Mothers: Infanticide in England and New England, 1558–1803*. New York: New York University Press.

Holbach, Paul-Henri Thiry, Baron d'. 1776. *La Morale universelle, ou les devoirs de l'homme fondés sur sa nature*. 3 vols. Amsterdam: Marc Michel Rey.

Holmes, Jack D. L. 1969. "Medical Practice in New Orleans: Colonial Period." *Alabama Journal of Medical Sciences* 6 (4): 433–41.

Hoolihan, Christopher. 1985. "Thomas Young, M.D. (1726?–1783) and Obstetrical Education at Edinburgh." *Journal of the History of Medicine and Allied Sciences* 40: 327–45.

Huet, Marie-Hélène. 1993. *Monstrous Imagination*. Cambridge, MA: Harvard University Press.

Hufton, Olwen. 1998. *The Prospect before Her: A History of Women in Western Europe, 1500–1800*. New York: Vintage.

Hufton, Olwen. 1975. "Women and the Family Economy in Eighteenth-Century France." *French Historical Studies* 9 (1): 1–22.

Hufton, Olwen. 1992. *Women and the Limits of Citizenship in the French Revolution*. Toronto: University of Toronto Press.

Hufton, Olwen. 1981. "Women, Work, and Marriage in Eighteenth-Century France." In *Marriage and Society: Studies in the Social History of Marriage*, ed. R. B. Outhwaite. New York: St. Martin's.

Hume, David. 1751. *An Enquiry Concerning the Principles of Morals*. London: A. Miller.

Hunt, Lynn. 1992. *The Family Romance of the French Revolution*. Berkeley: University of California Press.

Hunt, Margaret. 1996. *The Middling Sort: Commerce, Gender, and the Family in England, 1680–1780.* Berkeley: University of California Press.

Hunt, Margaret. 1999. "The Sapphic Strain: English Lesbians in the Long Eighteenth Century." In *Singlewomen in the European Past 1250–1800*, ed. Judith M. Bennett and Amy M. Froide. Philadelphia: University of Pennsylvania Press.

Hunt, Margaret. 2010. *Women in Eighteenth-Century Europe.* London: Longman.

Les imitateurs de Charles IX. 1789. Chantilly.

Israel, Jonathan. 2001. *Radical Enlightenment: Philosophy and the Making of Modernity 1650–1750.* Oxford and New York: Oxford University Press.

Iwanisziw, Susan B., ed. 2004. *Troping Oroonoko from Behn to Bandele.* Burlington, VT: Ashgate.

Jacob, Margaret. 1991. *Living the Enlightenment: Freemasonry and Politics in Eighteenth-Century Europe.* New York: Oxford University Press.

Jamieson, John. 1808. *The Etymological Dictionary of the Scottish Language.* 2 vols. Edinburgh: Printed at the University Press for W. Creech.

Jamieson, Robert. 1806. *Popular Ballads and Songs from Tradition, Manuscripts, and Scarce Editions.* 2 vols. Edinburgh: Archibald Constable.

Janeway, Elizabeth. 1971. *Man's World, Woman's Place: A Study in Social Mythology.* New York: William Morrow.

Jannetta, Ann Bouman. 1987. *Epidemics and Mortality in Early Modern Japan.* Princeton, NJ: Princeton University Press.

Jaucourt, Louis, chevalier de. [1756] 2005. "Family," trans. J. E. Blanton. In *The Encyclopedia of Diderot & d'Alembert Collaborative Translation Project.* Ann Arbor: Scholarly Publishing Office of the University of Michigan Library. Available at: http://hdl.handle.net/2027/spo.did2222.0000.444 (accessed August 3, 2010). Originally published as "Famille," in *Encyclopédie ou Dictionnaire raisonné des sciences, des arts et des métiers*, 6:390–91. Paris.

Jaucourt, Louis, chevalier de. [1765]. "Mariage (Droit naturel)." In *Encyclopédie, ou dictionnaire raisonné des sciences, des arts et des métiers*, ed. Denis Diderot and Jean le Rond D'Alembert, 10:104–6. Available through the University of Chicago and ARTFL Encyclopédie Projet, ed. Robert Morrissey, at: http://encyclopedie.uchicago.edu/ (accessed August 3, 2010).

Jaucourt, Louis, chevalier de. [1756] 2005. "Wife," trans. Naomi Andrews. In *The Encyclopedia of Diderot & d'Alembert Collaborative Translation Project.* Ann Arbor: Scholarly Publishing Office of the University of Michigan Library. Available at: http://hdl.handle.net/2027/spo.did2222.0000.444 (accessed August 3, 2010). Originally published as "Femme," in *Encyclopédie ou Dictionnaire raisonné des sciences, des arts et des métiers*, 6:471–72. Paris.

Jenkins, James. [1776] 1984. *The Records and Recollections of James Jenkins*, ed. J. William Frost. New York and Toronto: Edwin Mellen.

Johnson, David. 1972. *Music and Society in Lowland Scotland in the Eighteenth Century.* London: Oxford University Press.

Jones, Colin. 1996. "The Great Chain of Buying: Medical Advertisement, the Bourgeois Public Sphere, and the Origins of the French Reution." *American Historical Review* 101 (1): 13–40.

Juster, Susan. 1994. *Disorderly Women: Sexual Politics and Evangelicalism in Revolutionary New England*. Ithaca, NY: Cornell University Press.

Kant, Immanuel. [1784] 1996. "An Answer to the Question: What Is Enlightenment?" Trans. James Schmidt. In *What Is Enlightenment? Eighteenth-Century Answers and Twentieth-Century Questions*, ed. James Schmidt. Berkeley: University of California Press.

Kant, Immanuel. [1764] 1960. *Observations on the Feeling of the Beautiful and Sublime*, trans. John T. Goldthwait. Berkeley: University of California Press.

Kaplan, Marion A. 1991. *The Making of the Jewish Middle Class: Women, Family and Identity in Imperial Germany*. New York and Oxford: Oxford University Press.

Karsch, Anna Louisa. [1764] 1996. *Auserlesene Gedichte*, ed. Barbara Becker-Cantarino. Karben: Petra Wald.

Karsch, Anna Louisa. [1792] 1996. *Gedichte. Nach der Dichterin Tode herausgegeben von ihrer Tochter, Caroline Luise von Klencke*, ed. Barbara Becker-Cantarino. Karben: Petra Wald.

Karsch, Anna Louisa. 1987. *Gedichte und Lebenszeugnisse*, ed. Alfred Anger. Stuttgart, Germany: Reclam.

Karsch, Anna Louisa, and Johann Wilhelm Ludwig Gleim. 1996. *"Mein Bruder in Apoll": Briefwechsel zwischen Anna Louisa Karsch und Johann Wilhelm Ludwig Gleim*. 2 vols. (vol. 1, ed. Regina Nörtemann; vol. 2, ed. Ute Pott). Göttingen, Germany: Wallstein.

Kastinger-Riley, Helene M. 1990. "Anna Louisa Karsch." *Dictionary of Literary Biography* 97: 139–44.

Kastinger-Riley, Helene M. 1986. "Wölfin unter Schäfern: Die sozialkritische Lyrik der Anna Louisa Karsch." In *Die weibliche Muse: Sechs Essays über künstlerisch schaffende Frauen der Goethezeit*. Columbia, SC: Camden House.

Kates, Gary. 1985. *The Cercle Social, the Girondins, and the French Revolution*. Princeton, NJ: Princeton University Press.

Kelly, Gary, ed. 1999. *Bluestocking Feminism: Writings of the Bluestocking Circle, 1738–1785*. London: Pickering & Chatto.

King, Steven, and Alan Weaver. 2000. "Lives in Many Hands: The Medical Landscape in Lancashire, 1700–1820." *Medical History* 45 (2): 173–200.

King, Helen. 1998. *Hippocrates' Woman: Reading the Female Body in Ancient Greece*. London: Routledge.

Kintzler, Catherine. 1984. *Condorcet: L'Instruction publique et la naissance du citoyen*. Paris: Le Sycomore.

Klepp, Susan E. 2009. *Revolutionary Conceptions: Women, Fertility, and Family Limitation in America, 1760–1820*. Chapel Hill: University of North Carolina Press.

Konszacki, Janina M., and Kurt Alterman. 2002. "Regina Salomea Pilsztynowa, Ophthalmologist in Eighteenth-Century Poland." *Survey of Ophthalmology* 47 (2): 189–95.

Kord, Susanne. 2000. *Little Detours: The Letters and Plays of Luise Gottsched*. Rochester, NY: Camden House.

Kord, Susanne. 1996. *Sich einen Namen machen: Anonymität und weibliche Autorschaft 1700–1900*. Stuttgart, Germany: Metzler.

Kord, Susanne. 2003. *Women Peasant Poets in Eighteenth-Century England, Scotland, and Germany: Milkmaids on Parnassus*. Rochester, NY: Camden House.

Krzywon, Ernst Josef. 1990. "'Ich bin Empfindung und Gesang.' Schlesiens deutsche Sappho Anna Louisa Karsch (1722–1791)." In *Kontinuität und Wandel: Schlesien zwischen Österreich und Preußen*, ed. Peter Baumgart and Ulrich Schmilewski. Sigmaringen, Germany: Jan Thorbecke.

Krzywon, Ernst Josef. 1992. "Tradition und Wandel: Die Karschin in Schlesien (1722–1761)." In *Anna Louisa Karsch (1722–1791): Von schlesischer Kunst und Berliner "Natur." Ergebnisse des Symposions zum 200. Todestag der Dichterin*, ed. Anke Bennholdt-Thomsen and Anita Runge. Göttingen, Germany: Wallstein.

Laborde, Alice M. 1984. *Diderot et Madame de Puisieux*. Saratoga, CA: Anma Libri.

Labouchere, Rachel. 1988. *Abiah Darby, 1716–1793, of Coalbrookdale, Wife of Abraham Darby II*. York, UK: William Sessions.

Landes, Joan B. 2009. "The History of Feminism: Marie-Jean-Antoine-Nicolas de Caritat, Marquis de Condorcet." In *The Stanford Encyclopedia of Philosophy*, ed. Edward N. Zalta. Spring ed. Stanford: Metaphysics Lab at Stanford University. Available at: http://plato.stanford.edu/archives/spr2009/entries/histfem-condorcet/.

Landes, Joan B. 1996. "The Performance of Citizenship: Democracy, Gender, and Difference in the French Revolution." In *Democracy and Difference: Contesting the Boundaries of the Political*, ed. Seyla Benhabib. Princeton, NJ: Princeton University Press.

Landes, Joan B. 1998. "The Public and the Private Sphere: A Feminist Reconsideration." In *Feminism, the Public and the Private*, ed. Joan B. Landes. Oxford: Oxford University Press.

Landes, Joan B. 2001. *Visualizing the Nation: Gender, Representation, and Revolution in Eighteenth-Century France*. Ithaca, NY: Cornell University Press.

Landes, Joan B. 1988. *Women and the Public Sphere in the Age of the French Revolution*. Ithaca, NY: Cornell University Press.

Landry, Donna. 1990. *The Muses of Resistance: Laboring-Class Women's Poetry in Britain, 1739–1796*. Cambridge: Cambridge University Press.

Landry, Donna. 1987. "The Resignation of Mary Collier: Some Problems in Feminist Literary History." In *The New Eighteenth Century: Theory, Politics, English Literature*, ed. Felicity Nussbaum and Laura Brown. New York and London: Methuen.

Lanser, Susan S. 2010. "Mapping Sapphic Modernity." In *Comparatively Queer: Crossing Time, Crossing Cultures*, ed. Jarrod Hayes, Margaret Higonnet, and William Spurlin. London: Palgrave Macmillan.

Lanser, Susan S. 2001. "Sapphic Picaresque, Sexual Difference and the Challenges of Homo-Adventuring." *Textual Practice* 15 (2): 251–68.

Lanser, Susan S. 1999. "Singular Politics: The Rise of the British Nation and the Production of the 'Old Maid.'" In *Singlewomen in the European Past 1250–1800*, ed. Judith M. Bennett and Amy M. Froide. Philadelphia: University of Pennsylvania Press.

Laqueur, Thomas. 1990. *Making Sex: Body and Gender from the Greeks to Freud*. Cambridge, MA: Harvard University Press.

Larson, Rebecca. 1999. *Daughters of Light: Quaker Women Preaching and Prophesying in the Colonies and Abroad, 1700–1775*. New York: Knopf.

Lawrence, Anna M. 2011. *One Family under God: Love, Belonging, and Authority in Early Transatlantic Methodism*. Philadelphia: University of Pennsylvania Press.

Leadbeater, Mary. 1823. *Memoirs and Letters of Richard and Elizabeth Shackleton*. 2nd ed. London: printed for Harvey and Darton, Grace-church Street.

Leapor, Mary. 1748. *Poems upon Several Occasions. By Mrs. Leapor of Brackley in Northamptonshire*. London: J. Roberts.

Leapor, Mary. 1747. "The Rural Maid's Reflexions, Written by a Gardener's Daughter. Inscribed to a Lady." *London Magazine, or Gentleman's Monthly Intelligencer* 16: 45.

Le Doeuff, Michele. 2003. *The Sex of Knowing*, trans. Kathryn Hamer and Lorraine Code. New York and London: Routledge.

Leong, Elaine. 2008. "Making Medicines in the Early Modern Household." *Bulletin of the History of Medicine* 82 (1): 145–68.

Lerner, Gerda. 1993. *The Creation of Patriarchy*. New York and Oxford: Oxford University Press.

Letter from Abraham Darby II. Friends House Library, London. MSS Port 38 No. 2.

Letters of John Ramsay of Ochtertyre, 1799–1812. 1966. Ed. Barbara L. H. Horn. Edinburgh: T. and A. Constable.

Levy, Darline Gay, Harriet B. Applewhite, and Mary Durham Johnson, eds. and trans. 1979. *Women in Revolutionary Paris, 1789–1795: Selected Documents*. Urbana: University of Illinois Press.

Lewis, Jan. 1987. "The Republican Wife: Virtue and Seduction in the Early Republic." *William and Mary Quarterly* 44 (4): 689–721.

Lewis, Judith Schneid. 1986. *In the Family Way: Childbearing in the British Aristocracy, 1760–1860*. New Brunswick, NJ: Rutgers University Press.

Lewis, Judith S. 2001. "1784 and All That: Aristocratic Women and Electoral Politics." In *Women, Privilege and Power: British Politics, 1750 to the Present*, ed. Amanda Vickery. Stanford: Stanford University Press.

Lindemann, Mary. 1996. *Health and Healing in Eighteenth-Century Germany*. Baltimore: Johns Hopkins University Press.

Lindman, Janet Moore. 2008. *Bodies of Belief: Baptist Community in Early America*. Philadelphia: University of Pennsylvania Press.

Little, Ann M. 2007. *Abraham in Arms: War and Gender in Colonial New England*. Philadelphia: University of Pennsylvania Press.

Liu, Tessie. 1994. *The Weaver's Knot: The Contradictions of Class Struggle and Family Solidarity in Western France, 1750–1914*. Ithaca, NY: Cornell University Press.

Locke, John. [1689] 1960. *Two Treatises of Government*, ed. Peter Laslett. London: Cambridge University Press.

Locklin, Nancy. 2007. *Women's Work and Identity in Eighteenth-Century Brittany*. Aldershot, UK, and Burlington, VT: Ashgate.

Lord, Albert. 1960. *The Singer of Tales*. Cambridge, MA: Harvard University Press.

Lord, Alexandra. 1999. "The Great 'Arcana of the Deity': Menstruation and Menstrual Disorders in Eighteenth-Century British Medical Thought." *Bulletin of the History of Medicine* 73 (1): 38–63.

"Lord John and Burd Ellen." MS Laing III 473. Edinburgh University Library.

Lougee, Carolyn. 1993. Review of *La naissance de l'intime*. *American Historical Review* 98 (1): 175–76.

Lyna, Dries, and Ilja Van Damme. 2009. "A Strategy of Seduction? The Role of Commercial Advertisements in the Eighteenth-Century Retailing Business of Antwerp." *Business History* 51 (1): 100–21.

Macaulay, Catherine. 1788–90. "On the Idea of a Sexual Difference in the Human Character." In *The Aberdeen Magazine, Literary Chronicle, and Review*, vol. 3. Aberdeen: J. Chalmers.

Mack, Phyllis. 2008. *Heart Religion in the British Enlightenment: Gender and Emotion in Early Methodism*. Cambridge and New York: Cambridge University Press.

Mack, Phyllis. 2003. "Religion, Feminism, and the Problem of Agency: Reflections on Eighteenth-Century Quakerism." *Signs: Journal of Women in Culture and Society* 29 (1): 149–77.

Mack, Phyllis. 1992. *Visionary Women: Ecstatic Prophecy in Seventeenth-Century England*. Berkeley: University of California Press.

Macpherson, C.B. 1962. *The Political Theory of Possessive Individualism: Hobbes to Locke*. Oxford: Clarendon.

Manley, Delarivier. [1714] 1999. *The Adventures of Rivella*, ed. Katherine Zelinsky. Peterborough, ON, Canada: Broadview.

Manley, Delarivier. [1709] 1991. *The New Atalantis*, ed. Rosalind Ballaster. London: Penguin Books.

"A Map of the Various Paths of Life." May 30, 1794. Tract Box LL2/25. Friends House Library. London: W. Darton & J. Harvey.

Marland, Hilary. 1993. "The '*burgerlijke*' Midwife: The *stadsvroedvrouw* of Eighteenth-Century Holland." In *The Art of Midwifery: Early Modern Midwives in Europe*, ed. Hilary Marland. London and New York: Routledge.

Martens, Wolfgang. 1971. *Die Botschaft der Tugend: Die Aufklärung im Spiegel der deutschen Moralischen Wochenschriften*. Stuttgart, Germany: Metzler.

Martinez, María Elena. 2008. *Geneaological Fictions: Limpieza de Sangre, Religion, and Gender in Colonial Mexico*. Stanford: Stanford University Press.

Martinez-Alier, Verena. 1974. *Marriage, Class, and Colour in Nineteenth-Century Cuba: A Study of Racial Attitudes and Sexual Values in a Slave Society*. London: Cambridge University Press.

Mason, Julian D., Jr., ed. 1989. *The Poems of Phillis Wheatley*. Rev. ed. Chapel Hill: University of North Carolina Press.

May, Gita. 1970. *Madame Roland and the Age of Revolution*. New York: Columbia University Press.

[Maynwaring, Arthur]. 1708. "A New Ballad." London.

Maza, Sarah. 1993. *Private Lives and Public Affairs: The "Causes Célèbres" of Prerevolutionary France*. Berkeley: University of California Press.

McDowell, Paula. 1998. *The Women of Grub Street: Press, Politics, and Gender in the London Literary Marketplace, 1678–1730*. Oxford and New York: Clarendon.

McKendrick, Neil, John Brewer, and J.H. Plumb. 1982. *The Birth of a Consumer Society: The Commercialization of Eighteenth-Century England*. Bloomington: Indiana University Press.

McKeon, Michael. 2005. *The Secret History of Domesticity: Public, Private, and the Division of Knowledge*. Baltimore: Johns Hopkins University Press.

McLane, Maureen. 2008. *Balladeering, Minstrelsy, and the Making of British Romantic Poetry*. Cambridge: Cambridge University Press.

McLean, Iain, and Fiona Hewitt, eds. and trans. 1994. *Condorcet: Foundations of Social Choice and Political Theory*. Aldershot, UK, and Brookfield, VT: Edward Elgar.

McTavish, Liann. 2005. *Childbirth and the Display of Authority in Early Modern France*. London: Ashgate.

Memoirs of Mary Saxby, a Female Vagrant. n.d. Chelsea.

Mercer, A. J. 1985. "Smallpox and Epidemiological-Demographic Change in Europe: The Role of Vaccination." *Population Studies* 39: 287–307.

Mercier, Louis-Sébastien. 1782–88. *Tableau de Paris*. 12 vols. Amsterdam.

Merrick, Jeffrey. 1990. "Sexual Politics and Public Order in Late Eighteenth-Century France: The Mémoires secrets and the *Correspondance secrète*." *Journal of the History of Sexuality* 1 (1): 68–84.

Meurdrac, Marie. 1666. *La Chymie charitable et facile, en faveur des dames*. Paris.

Meyer, Sibylle. 1983. "Die mühsame Arbeit des demonstrativen Müßiggangs: Über die häuslichen Pflichten der Beamtenfrauen im Kaiserreich." In *Frauen suchen ihre Geschichte: Historische Studien zum 19. und 20. Jahrhundert*, ed. Karin Hausen. Munich: Beck.

Michaelson, Patricia Howell. 1993. "Religious Bases of Eighteenth-Century Feminism: Mary Wollstonecraft and the Quakers." *Women's Studies* 22 (3): 281–95.

Midgley, Clare. 1992. *Women against Slavery: The British Campaigns, 1780–1870*. London: Routledge.

Miller, Christopher L. 2008. *The French Atlantic Triangle: Literature and the Culture of the Slave Trade*. Durham, NC: Duke University Press.

Milne, Christian. 1805. *Simple Poems on Simple Subjects. By Christian Milne, Wife of a Journeyman Ship-Carpenter, in Footdee, Aberdeen*. Aberdeen: J. Chalmers.

Montagu, Elizabeth, to Sarah Robinson [Scott]. September 18, 1750. Huntington Library, Montagu MSS MO 5719.

Montagu, Lady Mary Wortley. 1965–67. *The Complete Letters of Lady Mary Wortley Montagu*. 3 vols. Edited by Robert Halsband. Oxford: Clarendon.

Montaigne, Michel de. [1588] 1965. "On Some Verses of Vergil." In *The Complete Essays of Montaigne*, trans. Donald Frame. Stanford: Stanford University Press.

Moore, Henry. 1824. *The Life of Mrs. Mary Fletcher, Consort and Relict of the Rev. John Fletcher, Vicar of Madeley, Salop*. 6th ed. London: J. Kershaw.

Moore, Lisa. 1997. *Dangerous Intimacies: Toward a Sapphic History of the British Novel*. Durham, NC: Duke University Press.

Moran, Mary Catherine. 2005. "Between the Savage and the Civil: Dr. John Gregory's Natural History of Femininity." In *Women, Gender, and Enlightenment*, ed. Sarah Knott and Barbara Taylor. New York: Palgrave.

Morgan, Jennifer L. 2004. *Laboring Women: Reproduction and Gender in New World Slavery*. Philadelphia: University of Pennsylvania Press.

Moscucci, Ornella. 1990. *The Science of Woman: Gynaecology and Gender in England, 1800–1929*. Cambridge: Cambridge University Press.

Murphy-Lawless, Jo. 1998. *Reading Birth and Death: A History of Obstetric Thinking*. Bloomington: Indiana University Press.

Musgrave, Elizabeth C. 1993. "Women in the Male World of Work: The Building Industries of Eighteenth-Century Brittany." *French History* 7 (1): 30–52.

Muthu, Sankar. 2003. *Enlightenment against Empire*. Princeton, NJ: Princeton University Press.

Newman, Edwina. 2009. "Abiah Darby and the Tradition of Quaker Women's Prophetic Writings in the Mid-Eighteenth Century." Unpublished paper.

Nihell, Elizabeth. 1760. *A Treatise on the Art of Midwifery*. London.

Nugent, Thomas. 1781. *The New Pocket Dictionary of the French and English Languages*. 3rd ed. London.

Nussbaum, Felicity A. 1995. *Torrid Zones: Maternity, Sexuality, and Empire in Eighteenth-Century English Narratives*. Baltimore: Johns Hopkins University Press.

O'Cinneide, Muireann. 2008. *Aristocratic Women and the Literary Nation, 1832–1867*. Basingstoke, UK: Palgrave Macmillan.

Olson, Ian A., and John Morris. 2000. "Mussel-Mou'd Charlie's (Charles Leslie) 1745 Song: 'McLeod's Defeat at Inverury.'" *Aberdeen University Review* 58 (204): 317–31.

Outram, Dorinda. 2005. *The Enlightenment*. 2nd ed. Cambridge: Cambridge University Press.

Pardailhé-Galabrun, Annik. [1988] 1991. *The Birth of Intimacy: Privacy and Domestic Life in Early Modern Paris*, trans. Jocelyn Phelps. Philadelphia: University of Pennsylvania Press. Originally published as *La naissance de l'intime: 3000 foyers parisiens, XVIIe–XVIIIe siècles*. Paris: Presses Universitaires de France.

Parsons, James. 1741. *A Mechanical and Critical Enquiry into the Nature of Hermaphrodites*. London: J. Walthoe.

Pateman, Carole. 1988. *The Sexual Contract*. Stanford: Stanford University Press.

Pekacz, Jolanta T. 1999. *Conservative Tradition in Pre-Revolutionary France: Parisian Salon Women*. New York: Peter Lang.

Percy, Thomas, ed. 1765. *Reliques of Ancient English Poetry*. London: Robert and James Dodsley.

Perry, Ruth. 1994. "Austen and Empire: A Thinking Woman's Guide to British Imperialism." *Persuasions* 16: 95–106.

Perry, Ruth. 1991. "Colonizing the Breast: Sexuality and Maternity in Eighteenth-Century England." *Journal of the History of Sexuality* 2 (2): 204–34.

Perry, Ruth. 2008. "'The Finest Ballads': Women's Oral Traditions in Eighteenth-Century Scotland." *Eighteenth-Century Life* 32 (2): 81–97.

Perry, Ruth. 2004. *Novel Relations: The Transformation of Kinship in English Literature and Culture 1748–1818*. Cambridge and New York: Cambridge University Press.

Pettitt, Thomas. 1984. "Mrs. Brown's 'Lass of Roch Royal' and the Golden Age of Balladry." *Jahrbuch für Volksliedforschung* 29: 13–31.

[Pidansat de Mairobert, Mathieu-François]. 1778. *Confessions d'une jeune fille*. In *Espion Anglois*. London.

Pollak, Ellen. 2003. *Incest and the English Novel, 1684–1814*. Baltimore: Johns Hopkins University Press.

Porter, Roy. 2000. *The Creation of the Modern World: The Untold Story of the British Enlightenment*. New York: W. W. Norton.

Pott, Percival. 1769. *Some Few General Remarks on Fractures and Dislocations*. London.

Poulain de La Barre, François. 1677. *The Woman as Good as the Man; or, The Equallity of Both Sexes. Written Originally in French, and Translated into English by A.L.* London: N. Brooks.

Prévost, l'abbé, ed. 1755. *Manuel lexique ou dictionnaire portatif des mots françois dont la signification n'est pas familière à tout le monde*. Paris: Chez Didot.

Prochaska, F. K. 1980. *Women and Philanthropy in Nineteenth-Century England*. Oxford: Oxford University Press.

Prochaska, F. K. 1974. "Women in English Philanthropy, 1790–1830." *International Review of Social History* 19: 426–45.

Puff, Helmut. 2003. *Sodomy in Reformation Germany and Switzerland 1400–1600*. Chicago: University of Chicago Press.

Rack, Henry D. [1989] 1992. *Reasonable Enthusiast: John Wesley and the Rise of Methodism*. Nashville, TN: Abingdon.

Raffald, Elizabeth. 1769. *The Experienced English Housekeeper, For the Use and Ease of Ladies, Cooks, etc.* 2nd ed. Manchester.

Raistrick, Arthur. 1950. *Quakers in Science and Industry: Being an Account of the Quaker Contributions to Science and Industry during the 17th and 18th Centuries*. London: Bannisdale.

Ramazzini, Bernardino. 1705. *A Treatise of the Diseases of Tradesmen, Shewing the Various Influence of Particular Trades upon the State of Health*. London.

Ramsey, Matthew. 1988. *Professional and Popular Medicine in France, 1770–1830: The Social World of Medical Practice*. Cambridge: Cambridge University Press.

Reichardt, Rolf, and Deborah Louise Cohen. 1998. "Light against Darkness: The Visual Representations of a Central Enlightenment Concept." *Representations* 61: 95–148.

Reid, John. 1987. "Late Eighteenth-Century Adult Education in the Sciences at Aberdeen: The Natural Philosophy Classes of Professor Patrick Copland." In *Aberdeen and the Enlightenment*, ed. Jennifer J. Carter and Joan H. Pittock. Aberdeen: Aberdeen University Press.

A Relation of the Life of Christina Queen of Sweden: With Her Resignation of the Crown, Voyage to Bruxels, and Journey to Rome. 1656. London: Henry Fletcher.

Review of *Malvern Hills: A Poem*, by Joseph Cottle. *Monthly Review; or Literary Journal*, new ser., 28 (1799): 21–25.

Riccoboni, Marie-Jeanne. 1759. *Lettres de Milady Juliette Catesby à Milady Henriette Campley, son amie*. Amsterdam [i.e. Paris].

Richardson, Samuel. 1985. *Clarissa; or, The History of a Young Lady*. Harmondsworth, UK: Penguin.

Richardson, Samuel. 1986. *The History of Sir Charles Grandison*. Oxford: Oxford University Press.

Richter, Simon. 2006. *Missing the Breast: Gender, Fantasy, and the Body in the German Enlightenment*. Seattle: University of Washington Press.

Rieuwerts, Sigrid, ed. 2011. *The Ballad Repertoire of Anna Gordon, Mrs. Brown of Falkland*. Woodbridge, Suffolk: The Scottish Text Society.

Riley, Denise. 1988. *"Am I That Name?" Feminism and the Category of "Women" in History* Minneapolis: University of Minnesota Press.

Riquetti, Honoré Gabriel, Comte de Mirabeau. 1783. *Erotika Biblion*. Rome.

Riskin, Jessica. 2002. *Science in the Age of Sensibility: The Sentimental Empiricists of the French Enlightenment.* Chicago: University of Chicago Press.

Rizzo, Tracey. 2004. *A Certain Emancipation of Women: Gender, Citizenship, and the "Causes Célèbres" of Eighteenth-Century France.* Selinsgrove, PA: Susquehanna University Press.

Roche, Daniel. 1987. *The People of Paris: An Essay in Popular Culture in the Eighteenth Century,* trans. Marie Evans with Gwynne Lewis. Berkeley: University of California Press.

Rogers, James. Autobiography, Diaries Box. John Rylands Library.

Roper, Lyndal. 1994. *Oedipus and the Devil: Witchcraft, Religion, and Sexuality in Early Modern Europe.* London: Routledge.

Rothschild, Emma. 2001. *Economic Sentiments: Adam Smith, Condorcet, and the Enlightenment.* Cambridge, MA: Harvard University Press.

Rousseau, Jean-Jacques. [1762] 1979. *Émile; or, On Education,* trans. Allan Bloom. New York: Basic Books.

Rousseau, Jean-Jacques. 1997. *Julie, or the New Heloise: Letters of Two Lovers Who Live in a Small Town at the Foot of the Alps,* trans. Philip Stewart and Jean Vaché. Hanover, NH: University Press of New England.

Rousseau, Jean-Jacques. [1771–73] 1780–89. *Lettres sur la botanique élémentaires à Madame de L[essart].* Neuchâtel; Paris: Poincot.

Rousseau, Jean-Jacques. [1762] 1913. *The Social Contract,* trans. G.D.H. Cole. London and Toronto: J. M. Dent and Sons; New York, E. P. Dutton and Co.

Said, Edward. 1993. *Culture and Imperialism.* New York: Knopf.

Sánchez-Eppler, Karen. 1993. *Touching Liberty: Abolition, Feminism, and the Politics of the Body.* Berkeley: University of California Press.

The Sappho-an: An Heroic Poem, of Three Cantos. 1749. London: Cha. Brasier.

Sargentson, Carolyn. 1996. *Merchants and Luxury Markets: The Marchands Merciers of Eighteenth-Century Paris.* London and Malibu: Victoria and Albert Museum in conjunction with the J. Paul Getty Museum.

Sayers, Dorothy L. 1971. *Are Women Human?* Grand Rapids, MI: Eerdmans.

Schiebinger, Londa. 1989. *The Mind Has No Sex? Women in the Origins of Modern Science.* Cambridge, MA: Harvard University Press.

Schiebinger, Londa. 1991. *The Mind Has No Sex? Women in the Origins of Modern Science.* Cambridge, MA: Harvard University Press.

Schiebinger, Londa. 2004. *Plants and Empire: Colonial Bioprospecting in the Atlantic World.* Cambridge, MA: Harvard University Press.

Schiebinger, Londa. 1986. "Skeletons in the Closet: The First Illustrations of the Female Skeleton in Eighteenth-Century Anatomy." *Representations* 14: 42–82.

Schiller, Friedrich. 1827. "The Song of the Bell." In *The Song of the Bell. Translated from the German of Frederick von Schiller. With the Original,* trans. Samuel Taylor Coleridge. London: Treuttel and Würtz.

Schiller, Friedrich. 1966. "Über Anmut und Würde." In *Werke in drei Bänden,* ed. Gerhard Fricke and Herbert Göpfert, vol. 2. Munich: Carl Hanser.

Schlegel, Dorothea. 1988. *Florentin: A Novel. By Dorothea Mendelssohn Veit Schlegel*, trans., annotated, and introduced by Edwina Lawler and Ruth Richardson. Lewiston and Queenston: Edwin Mellen.

Schloss, Rebecca Hartkopf. 2009. *Sweet Liberty: The Final Days of Slavery in Martinique*. Philadelphia: University of Pennsylvania Press.

Schott, Robin May. 1997. "The Gender of Enlightenment." In *Feminist Interpretations of Immanuel Kant*, ed. Robin May Schott. University Park: Pennsylvania State University.

Schwarz, Kathryn. 2000. *Tough Love: Amazon Encounters in the English Renaissance*. Durham, NC: Duke University Press.

Scott, Joan Wallach. 1996. *Only Paradoxes to Offer: French Feminists and the Rights of Man*. Cambridge, MA: Harvard University Press.

Scott, Katie. 1995. *The Rococo Interior: Decoration and Social Spaces in Early Eighteenth-Century Paris*. New Haven: Yale University Press.

Scott, Robert. 2007. *The Glenbuchat Ballads*, ed. David Buchan and James Moreira. Jackson: University Press of Mississippi in association with the Elphinstone Institute, University of Aberdeen.

Sebastiani, Sylvia. 2005. " 'Race,' Women, and Progress in the Scottish Enlightenment." In *Women, Gender, and Enlightenment*, ed. Sarah Knott and Barbara Taylor. New York: Palgrave.

Seed, Patricia. 1988. *To Love, Honor, and Obey in Colonial Mexico: Conflicts over Marriage Choice, 1574–1821*. Stanford: Stanford University Press.

Shammas, Carole. 2002. *A History of Household Government in America*. Charlottesville: University of Virginia Press.

Sharp, Cecil. 1907. *English Folk-Song, Some Conclusions*. London: Simpkin.

Sharp, Jane. 1671. *The Midwives Book. Or the whole Art of Midwifry Discovered*. London: Simon Miller.

Sheridan, Frances. 1761. *Memoirs of Miss Sidney Bidulph: Extracted from Her Own Journal*. London: R. and J. Dodsley.

Sheriff, Mary D. 2004. *Moved by Love: Inspired Artists and Deviant Women in Eighteenth-Century France*. Chicago: University of Chicago Press.

Showalter, Elaine. 1977. *A Literature of Their Own: British Women Novelists from Brontë to Lessing*. Princeton, NJ: Princeton University Press.

Shteir, Ann B. 1996. *Cultivating Women, Cultivating Science: Flora's Daughters in England, 1760–1860*. Baltimore: Johns Hopkins University Press.

Shuldham-Shaw, Patrick, and Emily B. Lyle, eds. 1981–2002. *The Greig-Duncan Folk Song Collection*. 8 vols. Aberdeen and Edinburgh: Aberdeen University Press and Mercat Press.

Simonton, Deborah. 1998. *A History of European Women's Work, 1700 to the Present*. London and New York: Routledge.

Simpson, Erik. 2008. *Literary Minstrelsy, 1770–1830: Minstrels and Improvisers in British, Irish, and American Literature*. Basingstoke, UK, and New York: Palgrave Macmillan.

Sistrunk, Albertha. 1982. "The Influence of Alexander Pope on the Writing Style of Phillis Wheatley." In *Critical Essays on Phillis Wheatley*, ed. William H. Robinson. Boston: G.K. Hall.

Smellie, William. 1752–64. *A Treatise on the Theory and Practice of Midwifery*. 3 vols. London.

Smith, Eliza. 1727. *The Compleat Housewife; or, Accomplished Gentlewoman's Companion*. London.

Smith, Lisa. 2006. "The Relative Duties of Man: Domestic Medicine in England and France, ca. 1685–1740." *Journal of Family History* 31 (3): 237–56.

Sonnet, Martine. 1993. "A Daughter to Educate." In *A History of Women in the West*, vol. 3, ed. Natalie Zemon Davis and Arlette Farge. Cambridge, MA, and London: Belknap Press of Harvard University Press.

Spence, Elizabeth. 1833. "Letters from the Northern Highlands." In *Sketches of Obscure Poets, with Specimens of Their Writings*. London: Cochrane & McCrone.

Stanhope, Philip Dormer. [1774] 1892. *The Letters of Philip Dormer Stanhope, Earl of Chesterfield, with the Characters*, ed. John Bradshaw. New York: Scribner. Available at: http://www.archive.org/stream/cu31924103071613/cu31924103071613_djvu.txt. Accessed June 18, 2010.

Starr, Paul. 1982. *The Social Transformation of American Medicine: The Rise of a Sovereign Profession and the Making of a Vast Industry*. New York: Basic Books.

Steinberg, Sylvie. 2001. *La Confusion des sexes: le travestissesment de la Renaissance à la Révolution*. Paris: Fayard.

Stephen, Margaret. 1795. *Domestic Midwife; or, The Best Means of Preventing Danger in Child-Birth Considered*. London.

Stewart, Joan Hinde. 1993. *Gynographs: French Novels by Women of the Late Eighteenth Century*. Lincoln: University of Nebraska Press.

Stone, Sarah. 1737. *A Complete Practice of Midwifery*. London.

Strachey, William. 1953. *The Historie of Travell into Virginia Britania (1612)*, ed. Louis B. Wright and Virginia Freund. London: Hakluyt Society.

Sulzer, Johann Georg. 1773. "Entwickelung des Begriffs vom Genie." In *Vermischte philosophische Schriften. 2 Theile in 1 Band* [2 vols. in 1]. Leipzig: Weidmanns Erben & Reich.

Sulzer, Johann Georg. 1995. "General Theory of the Fine Arts (1771–74): Selected Articles," trans. and ed. Thomas Christensen. In *Aesthetics and the Art of Musical Composition in the German Enlightenment: Selected Writings of Johann Georg Sulzer and Heinrich Christoph Koch*, ed. Nancy Kovaleff Baker and Thomas Christensen. Cambridge: Cambridge University Press.

Sulzer, Johann Georg. 1996. "Vorrede." In *Auserlesene Gedichte*, by Anna Louisa Karsch, ed. Barbara Becker-Cantarino. Karben: Petra Wald.

Sussman, Charlotte. 2000. *Consuming Anxieties: Consumer Protest, Gender and British Slavery, 1713–1833*. Stanford: Stanford University Press.

Sussman, George D. 1977. "Parisian Infants and Norman Wet Nurses in the Early Nineteenth Century: A Statistical Study." *Journal of Interdisciplinary History* 7 (4): 637–53.

Swift, Jonathan. "Corinna." In *The Adventures of Rivella*, by Delarivier Manley, ed. Katherine Zelinsky. Peterborough, ON, Canada: Broadview.

Taft, Zachariah. 1828. *Biographical Sketches of the Lives and Public Ministry of Various Holy Women*. 2 vols. Leeds: H. Cullingworth.

Taylor, Barbara. 2005. "Feminists versus Gallants: Manners and Morals in Enlightenment Britain." In *Women, Gender, and Enlightenment*, ed. Sarah Knott and Barbara Taylor. New York: Palgrave.

Thackrah, C. Turner. 1831. *The Effects of the Principle Trades, Arts, and Professions.* 2nd ed. London and Philadelphia.

Tilly, Louise A., and Joan W. Scott. 1978. *Women, Work, and Family.* New York: Holt, Rinehart and Winston.

Tissot, Samuel. 1761. *Avis au people sur la santé.* Paris.

Todd, Janet. 2000. *Mary Wollstonecraft: A Revolutionary Life.* New York: Columbia University Press.

Todd, Janet. 1989. *The Sign of Angelica: Women, Writing and Fiction, 1660–1800.* New York: Columbia University Press.

Torquemada, Antonio de. 1570. *Jardin de flores curiosas, enque se tratan alginas materias de humanidad, philosophia, theologia y geographia.* Salamanca: Juan Baptista de Teranova.

Traer, James F. 1980. *Marriage and Family in Eighteenth-Century France.* Ithaca, NY: Cornell University Press.

Troost, Linda V., ed. 2001. *Eighteenth-Century Women: Studies in Their Lives, Work and Culture.* New York: AMS Press.

Trouille, Mary. 2009. *Wife-Abuse in Eighteenth-Century France.* Oxford: Voltaire Foundation.

Tryon, Thomas. 1685. *The Good Housewife made a doctor, or Health's choice and sure found friend.* London: Printed and sold by Andrew Sowle, in the Holloway-Lane, near Shoreditch.

Tryon, Thomas. 1682. *A Treatise of cleanness in meats and drinks of the preparation of food, the excellency of good airs and the benefits of clean sweet beds; also of the generation of bugs and their cure.* London: Printed for the author and sold by L. Curtis.

Truant, Cynthia. 1995. "Parisian Guildswomen and the (Sexual) Politics of Privilege: Defending Their Patrimonies in Print." In *Going Public: Women and Publishing in Early Modern France*, ed. Elizabeth Goldsmith and Dena Goodman. Ithaca, NY: Cornell University Press.

Trye, Mary. 1675. *Medicatrix, or the Woman-Physician.* London.

Turner, Cheryl. 1992. *Living by the Pen: Women Writers in the Eighteenth Century.* London: Routledge.

Tytler, Alexander Fraser. Letter from his estate of Woodhouselee. April 28, 1800. National Library of Scotland Acc 3639.

Tytler, Sarah, and J. L. Watson. 1871. *The Songstresses of Scotland.* London: Strahan.

Uglow, Jennifer S., and Frances Hinton, eds. 1982. *The International Dictionary of Women's Biography.* New York: Continuum.

Ulrich, Laurel Thatcher. 1980. *Good Wives: Image and Reality in the Lives of Women in Northern New England, 1650–1750.* New York: Knopf.

Ulrich, Laurel Thatcher. 1990. *A Midwife's Tale: The Life of Martha Ballard, Based on Her Diary, 1785–1812.* New York: Knopf.

U.S. Department of Labor and U.S. Bureau of Labor Statistics. July 2009. "Highlights of Women's Earnings in 2008." Available at: http://www.bls.gov/cps/cpswom2008.pdf.

Valentine, David. 2004. "The Categories Themselves." *GLQ: A Journal of Lesbian and Gay Studies* 10 (2): 215–20.

Vance, Shona. 2002. "Schooling the People." In *Aberdeen before 1800: A New History*, ed. Patricia Dennison, David Ditchburn, and Michael Lynch. East Linton: Tuckwell.

Verjus, Anne. 2002. *Le cens de la famille: Les femmes et le vote, 1789–1848*. Paris: Belin.

Vickery, Amanda. 1998. *The Gentleman's Daughter: Women's Lives in Georgian England*. New Haven: Yale University Press.

Vickery, Amanda. 2001. "Introduction." In *Women, Privilege and Power: British Politics, 1750 to the Present*, ed. Amanda Vickery. Stanford: Stanford University Press.

Vila, Anne C. 1998. *Enlightenment and Pathology: Sensibility in the Literature and Medicine of Eighteenth-Century France*. Baltimore: Johns Hopkins University Press.

Vincent-Buffault, Anne. [1986] 1991. *The History of Tears: Sensibility and Sentimentality in France*. London: Macmillan.

Voltaire. 1877–1885. "Divorce." In *Oeuvres complètes*, ed. Louis Moland, vol. 18. 52 vols. Paris: Garnier Frères.

Voltaire. [1734] 1980. *Letters on England*, trans. Leonard Tancock. London: Penguin.

Voltaire. 1771. *Questions sur l'Encyclopédie*. Geneva.

Wahrman, Dror. *The Making of the Modern Self: Identity and Culture in Eighteenth-Century England*. New Haven: Yale University Press.

Wallace, William, ed. 1898. *Robert Burns and Mrs. Dunlop: Correspondence Now Published in Full for the First Time*. 2 vols. New York: Dodd, Mead.

Walvin, James. 1997. *The Quakers: Money and Morals*. London: John Murray.

Wanley, Nathaniel. 1673. *The Wonders of the Little World: or, A General History of Man in Six Books*. London: T. Bassett.

Warner, William B. 1998. *Licensing Entertainment: The Elevation of Novel Reading in Britain, 1684–1750*. Berkeley: University of California Press.

Watt, Ian. 1957. *The Rise of the Novel: Studies in Defoe, Richardson and Fielding*. Berkeley: University of California Press.

Weaver, Karol K. 2006. *Medical Revolutionaries: The Enslaved Healers of Eighteenth-Century Saint Domingue*. Urbana and Chicago: University of Illinois Press.

Webster, A. L. 1843. *The Improved Housewife*. Hartford. 21st ed., Boston, 1858.

Wiesner, Merry E. 1998. "Spinning Out Capital: Women's Work in Preindustrial Europe, 1350–1750." In *Becoming Visible: Women in European History*, ed. Renate Bridenthal, Susan Mosher Stuard, and Merry E. Wiesner. 3rd ed. Boston and New York: Houghton Mifflin.

Wilde, Oscar. n.d. "The Model Millionaire." Available at: http://www.wilde-online.info/the-model-millionaire.html (accessed June 1, 2009).

Williams, Aubrey, ed. 1969. *Poetry and Prose of Alexander Pope*. Boston: Houghton Mifflin.

Wilson, Adrian. 1995. *The Making of Man-Midwifery: Childbirth in England, 1660–1770*. Cambridge, MA: Harvard University Press.

Wollstonecraft, Mary. 1789. Review of Equiano. *Analytical Review*, May.

Wollstonecraft, Mary. [1792] 2009. *A Vindication of the Rights of Woman*, ed. Deidre S. Lynch. New York and London: W. W. Norton.

Woolf, Virginia. [1929] 2005. *A Room of One's Own*, ed. Susan Gubar and Mark Hussey. Orlando, FL: Harcourt.

Wrigley, E. A. 1987. *People, Cities, and Wealth: The Transformation of Traditional Society.* Oxford and New York: Blackwell.

Wrigley, E. A., R. S. Davies, J. E. Oeppen, and R. S. Schofield. 1997. *English Population History from Reconstitution.* Cambridge: Cambridge University Press.

Yellin, Jean Fagan. 1989. *Women and Sisters: The Antislavery Feminist in American Culture.* New Haven: Yale University Press.

Zinsser, Judith P. 2006. *La Dame d'Esprit: A Biography of the Marquise du Châtelet.* New York: Viking.

Zinsser, Judith P. 2009. "Volume Editor's Introduction." In *Selected Philosophical and Scientific Writings: Emilie Du Chatelet*, ed. Judith P. Zinsser, trans. Isabelle Bour and Judith P. Zinsser. Chicago: University of Chicago Press.

Ziskin, Rochelle. 1999. *The Place Vendôme: Architecture and Social Mobility in Eighteenth-Century Paris.* Cambridge: Cambridge University Press.

CONTRIBUTORS

Kathleen M. Brown is Professor of History at the University of Pennsylvania. She is the author of *Good Wives, Nasty Wenches, and Anxious Patriarchs: Gender, Race and Power in Colonial Virginia* (1996) and *Foul Bodies: Cleanliness in Early America* (2009). She is currently writing a history of changing transatlantic understandings of what it means to be human that focuses on the campaign to abolish slavery.

Lisa Forman Cody is in the history department of Claremont McKenna College. She is the author of *Birthing the Nation: Sex, Science, and the Conception of Eighteenth-Century Britons* (2005), which won several honors, including the Berkshire Conference of Women Best First Book Prize. She has published several articles on gender, politics, disease, and medicine and is currently writing a multivolume project based on several thousand marital disputes in the eighteenth-century Atlantic world.

Susanne Kord is Professor of German, Comparative Literature, and Film Studies at University College London. She has published books and articles on a wide range of subjects, from eighteenth-century women's literature to Hollywood movies. Her two most recent book publications are *Contemporary Hollywood Masculinities: Gender, Genre, and Politics* (co-authored with E. Krimmer, 2011) and *Murderesses in German Writing, 1720–1860: Heroines of Horror* (2009). She is currently working on a book on evil children in Hollywood horror films.

Joan B. Landes is Walter L. and Helen Ferree Professor of Early Modern History and Women's Studies at Penn State University. Her books include *Women* *and the Public Sphere in the Age of the French Revolution; Visualizing the Nation: Gender, Representation and Revolution in Eighteenth-Century France; Feminism: The Public and the Private*; and the coedited *Monstrous Bodies/Political Monstrosities in Early Modern Europe*. Her recent articles discuss designs for artificial life in eighteenth-century automata and anatomical figures.

Susan S. Lanser is Professor of English, Comparative Literature, and Women's and Gender Studies at Brandeis University. She has published widely in the fields of eighteenth-century European culture and literature, women's writing, narrative theory, and the history of gender and sexuality. Her books include *Fictions of Authority: Women Writers and Narrative Voice; Helen Maria Williams, "Letters Written in France"*; and the forthcoming *The Sexuality of History: Sapphic Subjects and the Making of Modernity 1565–1830*.

Phyllis Mack teaches history and women's studies at Rutgers University. Her books include *Calvinist Preaching and Iconoclasm in the Netherlands* (1978), *Visionary Women: Ecstatic Prophecy in 17th Century England* (1992), and *Heart Religion in the British Enlightenment* (2008).

Ruth Perry is the Ann Fetter Friedlaender Professor of Humanities at the Massachusetts Institute of Technology, where she teaches literary subjects as well as "The Folk Music of the British Isles and North America." The author of many books and articles on eighteenth-century English literature and culture and feminist literary criticism, she has written on canonical figures such as Pope, Sterne, Richardson, Austen, and Hawthorne as well as contemporary women writers such as Grace Paley and Mary Gordon. Her most recent books are *Novel Relations: The Transformation of Kinship in English Literature and Culture 1748–1818* (2004) and a modern edition of Charlotte Lennox's 1758 novel *Henrietta* (2008). Her current project, a biography of Anna Gordon Brown, will also examine the place of balladry and folk music in the Scottish enlightenment.

Ellen Pollak, Professor Emerita of English at Michigan State University, specializes in the fields of feminist theory and eighteenth-century literature and culture. She is the author of *Incest and the English Novel, 1684–1814* (2003); *The Poetics of Sexual Myth: Gender and Ideology in the Verse of Swift and Pope* (1985); and essays on Behn, Defoe, Haywood, Manley, Swift, and Dorothy Parker, among others. Her current project addresses the problem of nothingness in the novels of Jane Austen.

Charlotte Sussman is Associate Professor of English at Duke University. She is the author of *Consuming Anxieties: Consumer Protest, Gender and British Slavery, 1713–1833* (2000) and *Eighteenth-Century English Literature* (2012) and has coedited, with Jillian Heydt-Stevenson, *Recognizing the Romantic Novel: New Histories of British Fiction, 1780–1830* (2011). She is at work on a project tentatively entitled *Imagining the Population: British Literature in an Age of Mass Migration* and has recently published articles on Felicia Hemans and Charles Maturin.

INDEX

Abelove, Henry, 46, 55
Aberdeen, Scotland, 188, 189
    Aberdeen Musical Society, 195, 198
    Aberdeen Philosophical Society, 198
Aberdeen Journal, 189
abolition *see* slavery
abortifacients/abortion, 101, 110–11,
    115, 119
Academie des dames, 62
adultery, 55, 56, 127
advertising, 102, 114–16
African-American literary tradition,
    19–24
African-Caribbean midwives, 101,
    109–11
Alembert, Jean le Rond d', 136
"amatory fiction," 175
Anderson, Dr. Robert, 188, 191–2,
    195
Anglican Church, 89
Anne, Queen of Great Britain and
    Ireland, 25, 173
Aquinas, Thomas, 49
Aristotle, 47
Aristotle's Masterpiece, 48, 49
Arne, Thomas, 15, 198
Arnould, Sophie, 66
Astell, Mary, 5, 7, 8, 9, 14, 15, 22

on doctrine of female intellectual
    inferiority, 24
Reflections Upon Marriage, 5
Serious Proposal to the Ladies, 12
on women's learning, 13
Austen, Jane, 26, 206
    Mansfield Park, 17

Bach, J.C., 198
Bacon, Francis, 3, 121
Baillie, Lady Grisell, 206
ballads, 187, 190–208
ballad singers, 189, 206, 208, 243
Ballaster, Ros, 175
Barnard, Lady Anne, 206
Barsanti, Francesco, 198
Bauernklage (German baroque), 159
Beattie, Dr. James, 188, 198
Beaumarchais, Pierre de, 135
Beccaria, Marquis de, 135
Behn, Aphra, 10, 18, 26, 27
    *Love-Letters between a Nobleman and
        his Sister*, 25
    Oroonoko, 17–18
Bentley, Elizabeth, 148
Bianchi, Giovanni
    *Breva Storia della vita di Catterina
        Vizzani*, 58